DAVID KEEBLE

Industrial location and planning in the United Kingdom

METHUEN

First published in 1976 by Methuen & Co Ltd
11 New Fetter Lane, London EC4P 4EE
© 1976 David Keeble
Printed in Great Britain at the *Benham Press* by
William Clowes & Sons Ltd, London, Colchester and Beccles

ISBN 0 416 80060 2 hardback
ISBN 0 416 80070 X paperback

To Valerie

Contents

Preface

The fascination of studying factories, their activities, location and development, is not easy to explain to the uninitiated. Perhaps in my own case, a childhood in the industrial centres of Luton and Southampton has something to do with it. Intellectual curiosity, however, was first aroused by powerful Caesarian teaching on Britain's changing industrial geography during undergraduate days at Cambridge. The investigatory appeal of student and doctoral surveys of manufacturing firms in Southampton and north-west London provided further stimulus; and the field's obvious policy and planning relevance has played its part.

Possibly for similar reasons, many other British geographers and economists have, like myself, been drawn to study United Kingdom industrial location in recent years. The breadth and depth of consequent research, some of it as yet unpublished, provides much of the necessary underpinning of this book. My debt to others in the academic community is only too obvious from its bibliography. But the book also presents much original personal research, based on unpublished and sometimes unique official statistics generously provided by such individuals as Mr R. S. Howard and Miss H. Gaskell of the Department of Industry, Mr J. M. Lowell and Mr A. Hives of the Department of Employment, Mr P. Walls and others in the department of the Environment, and Professor Michael Chisholm, then at Bristol but now of the Cambridge University Department of Geography. Within the latter department, Dr A. D. Cliff, Mr R. L. Martin and Mr J. Lewis provided invaluable computer programming assistance, Mrs P. Morgan and Mr M. Young most expertly designed and drew the many maps, and Mr F. Whitham cheerfully and speedily xeroxed innumerable successive copies of the typescript. Most helpful comments on part or all of the work were provided by Mr P. M. Townroe, Mr A. A. L. Caesar and Mr P. J. McDermott. Valuable assistance from my department and college, St Catharine's, included a sabbatical term without which the book would never have been started, let alone finished. The Social Science Research Council also kindly supported some earlier research referred to in chapter 9.

Some writers liken book-writing to giving birth. In this case, the more apt metaphor is mountain-climbing, hard going all the way up, but a widening view too. Whether the vista from the top is particularly inspiring is for others to judge. But the climb would probably never even have been attempted without the help of two particular people. One is Gus Caesar, Fellow and Senior Tutor of St Catharine's, mentor, colleague and friend, who really must take a lot of the blame for pointing me in the direction of this particular peak. The other is my wife, without whose constant encouragement and practical help the book would never have been finished, and to whom it is dedicated.

1 Approaches to industrial location analysis

Since the late 1950s, striking changes have been taking place in the location of manufacturing activity in the United Kingdom. This book describes and attempts to explain these changes, to evaluate the effects of different influences such as government industrial location policy, and to investigate the different components of change, in the form of different individual manufacturing industries and different change processes such as firm migration or *in situ* expansion. It is concerned with manufacturing industry *only* for at least two reasons. First, adequate treatment of this complex sector of economic activity by itself necessitates detailed and lengthy analysis. Second, manufacturing industry is still arguably more important for regional policy and planning than is, for example, service activity (see section 8.2), although currently increasing research on the latter is to be welcomed.

This book thus brings together evidence from many recent studies of the location of manufacturing industry in the United Kingdom, as well as presenting original statistical analyses based on unpublished data. In focusing upon manufacturing location *dynamics*, upon growth, decline and spatial shifts in manufacturing activity between different areas over time, it shares a common approach with much recent industrial geographical work (Collins and Walker 1975, 1). At the same time, its concern with policy and planning issues, such as the evaluation of the impact of government location policy, growth centre and industrial complex programming, and the implications of policy-induced manufacturing shifts for national industrial efficiency and output, is in accord with Leszczycki's plea, in his 1972 Presidential address to the International Geographical Union, for studies of the spatial structure of national economies to be 'of practical value and serve territorial planning' purposes (Leszczycki 1972, 5). In this connection, it is interesting to note Leszczycki's identification of such studies as arguably the second most important geographical research area for the 1970s, after man-environment interaction.

1.1. Classical and behavioural location theory

Ideally, investigation of the recent locational dynamics of manufacturing industry in the United Kingdom would seem best approached in terms of some sort of theoretical framework. Industrial location theory has however developed over the last two decades in two contrasting directions. One has been concerned with refining *classical distance-minimization* theory, whether of the least-cost Weberian school or the locational-interdependence/market area school (Smith 1971, 137). Thus Smith (1971, 177–273) has attempted to integrate these two distance-minimization, partial equilibrium approaches in terms of space cost and revenue surfaces. Smith's work has in turn stimulated further studies of such concepts as the spatial margins to profitability in particular industries and countries (Taylor 1970, McDermott 1973). Another example is the Webber/Stafford approach (Webber 1972, Stafford 1972) which accepts classical industrial location theory as a starting point, but then explores the impact upon optimal locational choice of the many uncertainties inherent in locational decision-making, notably with respect to the actions of rival firms. Much of the interest of these two workers thus centres on game theory and closely allied gaming simulation models.

The alternative and more recent *behavioural* approach to industrial location theory focuses on the geography, growth and behaviour of the firm, not as an optimizing rationally-economic decision-making unit, but as one characterized by conflicting goals, limited levels of knowledge and control of its environment, irrationality of perception and behaviour, and so on. Its methodology and terminology, which is often derived from systems theory, is well illustrated by the essays in Hamilton's recent book (1974), all of which accept as a fundamental starting point 'the domination of the location issue by the *industrial organisation, firm or corporation*: its goals, growth, size, age, production profile, organisation and behaviour' (Hamilton 1974, 13). This approach appears to be particularly influenced by the rise of giant multi-plant and indeed multi-national corporations, and the implications of their behaviour for industrial location change.

Without question, both the classical and behavioural schools have yielded valuable insights into real-world manufacturing location patterns and changes. This is probably rather more true of the behavioural school, with its greater reliance on actual firm surveys for hypothesis testing, than of more abstract 'desk-bound' classical theory where, as Smith (1971, 275) acknowledges, 'very little progress has yet been made in ... direct application ... to real-world situations'. The main reason for this, in Smith's view (1971, 276), is that classical theorists have been 'more concerned with the construction of elegant theories of locational equilibrium, or with the fusion of location theory and production theory, than with providing a guide for empirical enquiry'. But additional factors are the very considerable data demands of classical theory testing, its basic preoccupation with *static* patterns rather than changes over time, and its stress upon the impact of transport costs on materials and products on manufacturing location. As later discussion shows, the latter influence would seem to be of minor and diminishing importance today, at least at the United Kingdom geographical scale. Moreover, of course, classical theory's normative economic basis, concerned as it is with long-run optimization of locational economic benefits, largely ignores variations in actual firm behaviour consequent upon environmental and other uncertainties, information availability, and varied goals and forms of company organization (Hamilton 1974, 4–5). For all these reasons, a recent study of the specific topic of manufacturing migration within developed countries such as Britain concluded that 'as far as the movement of firms is concerned, traditional theories need to be replaced by a behavioural theory of movement' (Keeble 1974a, 7).

Unfortunately, however, the behavioural approach also suffers from major defects as a framework for evaluating national-scale manufacturing location change. Thus, for example, it is even more data-demanding than classical theory. Significantly, all the survey-based studies in Hamilton's 1974 volume are forced to confine their attention to only a relatively few firms, the largest sample, that of Townroe (1974), being of approximately 200 concerns. The latter survey's relatively large scale probably explains why it was able to ask only 'a limited number of questions about post-move stability and change' (Townroe 1974, 292); while, conversely, the fact that 'the conduct and detailed analysis of lengthy, relatively unstructured interviews is immensely time-consuming' explains why Stafford's contribution was based on investigation of only six firms (Stafford 1974, 169). A sample of between twenty and 100 firms appears to be about average. The problem this raises, of course, in addition to considerable logistical difficulties of data acquisition, concerns the arguable validity of *generalizing* from small-sample findings to all manufacturing firms. The latter is clearly an essential requirement both for a general theory and comprehensive national-scale evaluation of actual manufacturing location change.

Another major problem with behavioural theory is that the more firms are treated as individuals, rather than in the aggregate, and the more detailed the information gathered about them, the more difficult it appears to be to identify behavioural regularities which might form the basis of a general location theory. This is illustrated, for example, by Townroe's 1972 study of fifty-nine mobile companies, which attempted to consider 'in some detail the procedures of locational decision making' (Townroe 1972, 261). Observations for each firm of sixty-four separate variables measuring different characteristics of the firm and its locational search behaviour were therefore subjected to statistical testing (via chi square tests) and grouping (via principal components analysis), in a search for behavioural regularities. As Townroe (1972, 267) readily admits, specifically in relation to the latter, 'the results were disappointing', since 'the patterns of behaviour which have emerged are not strong and distinct'. Rather, the results reveal 'a great diversity of experience' and attest 'the complexity and heterogeneity of the industrial location decision making process in the fifty-nine surveyed companies'.

A third and last major problem is that, perhaps as a result of these difficulties, no well-defined single holistic behavioural location theory has as yet emerged from the welter of recent behavioural industrial location studies. Such initial attempts as Pred's behavioural matrix approach were, in that author's own words, largely 'only a verbal formalisation of the fairly obvious' (Pred 1967, 121). Most of the recent conceptual models proposed are not much more than classificatory descriptions of the sequences through which firms may (or may not) pass in making some sort of locational decision.

1.2. Empirical industrial location analysis

These various deficiencies thus unfortunately rule out adoption of any formal theoretical framework for this study. On the other hand, insights derived from classical and behavioural theory are of course incorporated in subsequent discussion, with regard for example to the adoption and diffusion of manufacturing innovations (section 4.1.2), and the birth, growth and migration of individual manufacturing firms (chapter 6). The dominant approach, however, is empirical, involving in particular the testing of specific hypotheses about manufacturing location change by statistical analysis. The hypotheses selected for investigation are drawn both from theoretical and empirical studies, and are centred around the broad conceptual 'centre-periphery' and 'periphery-centre' models elaborated in chapter 4.

This study is therefore located, methodologically, squarely in the longstanding tradition of empirical geographical inquiry. Its main aims are positive, not normative, in attempting to account for real-world patterns and changes rather than propound some ideal or optimal locational arrangement. It is a problem-oriented study, as much concerned with government policy implications and impacts as with academic investigation. On the other hand, it does perhaps break some slight new methodological ground, in two ways. First, it attempts deliberate fusion of what has elsewhere (Keeble 1971a, 40–2) been termed micro-level and macro-level empirical industrial location analysis. In particular, the latter is generally designed deliberately to test findings and hypotheses suggested by the former. Micro-level analysis may be defined as investigation of industrial location change by direct data acquisition, usually by questionnaire interviews, from samples of manufacturing firms. As noted earlier, this survey approach, while sometimes necessitated by the absence of original data from any other source, 'also reflects the implicit or explicit view that the most logical method of explaining' locational change 'is to ask the decision-makers actually involved' (Keeble 1971a, 40). However, micro-level analysis undoubtedly suffers from a number of defects. One is the possibility of biased samples, strictly random sampling methods rarely being used for logistical reasons. Another is the problem of *post-facto* rationalization, which leads firms to ascribe locational decisions to factors which in reality have become important only subsequent to the decision. The cloaking of supposedly 'irrational' or personal locational motives by reference to conventional, but in reality less important, economic factors is another example. A further problem may be actual inaccuracy in the data provided, especially where this relates to past periods and is based on the interviewee's memory. Lastly, individual firms may well not be explicitly aware of environmental advantages or disadvantages which are in fact contributing to their *in situ* growth or decline relative to other areas, particularly if they have had no experience of operating elsewhere. Since the latter is true of the majority of manufacturing firms in most areas, individual 'one-off' micro-level surveys of such 'adoptive' firms (see below) in a particular area may not yield particularly meaningful results.

These problems indicate the need for an alternative but complementary approach to empirical investigation of industrial location change. Macro-level analysis represents just such an approach. This usually involves the use of aggregate published or unpublished statistics, selected as measuring possible influences upon and rates of spatial manufacturing change, in some form of hypothesis-testing statistical analysis or model. Descriptive statistical manipulation of aggregate statistics may also be included here. Clearly, one major problem with this approach is the inferential leap from observed spatial association to possible causal influence. Nonetheless, the macro-level approach has been used fairly widely to investigate industrial location change in Britain in recent years, both by geographers (Keeble 1971a, 1972b; Chisholm and Oeppen 1973; Sant 1975a) and economists (Moore and Rhodes 1976). But in the present study, perhaps unlike some others, its use has been largely confined to testing hypotheses explicitly derived from micro-level findings. In this way, both types of analysis, with their particular defects, can provide interlocking testimony on the importance or otherwise of particular locational forces, with a resultant increased likelihood of valid results.

The other minor methodological contribution is through the use of entropy index and multiple regression analyses of industrial location patterns. While neither of these approaches is strikingly new, it is nonetheless true that no previous study has utilized the disaggregated entropy index formula adopted here to measure the changing spatial concentration or dispersion of industry at the national scale in Britain; while it can also be argued that no previous national-scale industrial location study in Britain has utilized multiple regression analysis with full regard to the technical problems involved. Thus for example even Sant's stimulating recent multiple regression manufacturing movement study (Sant 1975a) appears totally to ignore the potential problem of residual spatial autocorrelation.

Of course, the use of such techniques as regression analysis does imply a particular conceptual view of manufacturing location change. In particular, it assumes that such change is spatially structured and guided by identifiable forces, which produce a non-random arrangement of manufacturing growth or decline. In this respect, therefore, the approach of the present study differs somewhat from that of workers such as Lever (1974b, 184) who has argued, admittedly at the narrower urban-region scale, that 'shifts in the distribution of manufacturing ... are difficult both to describe and to explain because of the large number of variables involved'; and that 'industrial location and relocation are probability processes and, consequently, stochastic rather than deterministic models should be used in describing them' (Lever 1972a, 22). Stochastic models, notably Markov-chain models, may indeed be of practical value for describing and forecasting short-run changes in manufacturing location patterns, as argued by Lever and Collins (1975). But they would seem to lack any great *explanatory* power, other than of a general 'random-process' kind. They also ignore the mass of evidence, as for example in this book, indicating that whereas *individual* location decisions may well incorporate a large random element (Keeble 1974a, 21), deterministic-type forces can indeed be identified as influencing manufacturing location dynamics in the aggregate. This important scale difference between the individual and the aggregate has been noted by Haggett (1965, 25–6), who concurs with Bronowski (1960, 93) that 'a society moves under material pressure like a stream of gas; and *on the average*, its individuals obey the pressure ... (although) at any instance, any *individual* may, like an atom of gas, be moving across or against the stream' (my italics). Of course at one extreme some individuals, in this case manufacturing firms, may consciously recognize and deliberately conform to the structural forces operating upon the space economy. Such firms have been termed 'adaptive' by Alchian (1950) and Tiebout (1957), in that they rationally *adapt* themselves to these environmental forces, and 'make well thought out locational decisions based on relevant information' (Pred 1967, 22). At the other extreme, however, there will be firms which do not possess the ability or information to perceive the nature and direction of these forces, and hence 'react to their environment in relative ignorance, with the lucky ones being *adopted* by the system' (Pred 1967, 22). Such 'adoptive' firms may thus initially spring up randomly in a variety of locations; but only those fortunate enough to have chosen a suitable location in terms of the underlying structural forces will survive and/or grow. This simple adaptive/adoptive dichotomy of course relates to two polar extremes, most firms probably being located somewhere along a continuum in between. But however firms may be classified, the underlying conceptual approach of the adaptive/adoptive viewpoint, which has attracted considerable attention from behavioural industrial location analysts (Smith 1971, 273; Townroe 1974, 305; Walker 1975), is that longer-run firm location, survival and growth is shaped by structural environmental forces which hence produce non-random spatial patterns of manufacturing change. This viewpoint is fully supported by, and forms the conceptual background to, the analyses presented in this book.

The focus of this study is then explanatory analysis of recent and current manufacturing location change in the United Kingdom, largely at inter-regional and inter-subregional scales. Chapter 2 describes the patterns of change, measured in particular by hitherto unpublished employment and floor-space data, both cartographically and statistically. Chapter 3 then looks at the question of inherited manufacturing structure as a control on change, while chapter 4 sets out the key centre-periphery and periphery-centre models, discussing *inter alia* such broad issues as the influence of market accessibility, innovation diffusion, labour availability, quality and cost, agglomeration economies, transport improvements, entrepreneurial and institutional factors, and government regional policy. Chapter 5 presents some of the main original explanatory findings of the study, based on multiple regression analysis. Chapters 6 and 7 are concerned with different components of aggregate spatial change, the former looking at the relative contributions of manufacturing firm births, deaths, expansion and contraction and, in particular, physical migration, the latter investigating recent locational change in four key manufacturing industries, iron and steel, clothing, motor vehicles and electronic engineering. In both cases, much of the analysis is based on hitherto unpublished statistics. The last two substantive chapters, 8 and 9, consider respectively government regional industrial location policy, its justification, historical development and impact upon the peripheral assisted areas, and the effect and effectiveness of regional planning with regard to manufacturing location at the within-region scale in the most prosperous region of Britain, South East England, together with adjacent East Anglia. The concluding chapter looks briefly at two potential future issues for manufacturing location in Britain, the impact of EEC membership and of North Sea oil and gas, before re-emphasizing some of the key findings of the book.

2 Manufacturing location in the United Kingdom: recent trends

2.1. The locational pattern in the early 1960s

Figure 2.1 maps the distribution of United Kingdom manufacturing employment in 1959, in terms of the sixty-two subregions used until recently for official statistical purposes. This subregional framework recognizes as separate entities all the major industrial conurbations, such as Greater London, Manchester and Birmingham. The year chosen is the earliest for which subregional data are available.[1] It is also roughly representative of what seems likely to become recognized as a watershed period in the country's industrial location history, the early 1960s. In essence, the map summarizes the locational pattern evolved during fifty years of above-average industrial expansion in the South-East and Midlands, and relative industrial decline in south Wales, Northern England and Scotland. Its most striking single feature is of course the remarkable concentration of manufacturing employment in the country's dominant twentieth-century growth centre, Greater London. In 1959, the capital's 1,570,000 manufacturing employees represented over 18 per cent of the United Kingdom total. London's nearest rival, the West Midlands conurbation, accounted for less than half this number (720,000). The other most important industrial subregions were Greater Manchester (600,000), the Outer Metropolitan Area around London (560,000), west Yorkshire (470,000) and Clydeside (460,000). Together, these six relatively concentrated areas contained no less than 51 per cent of the United Kingdom's manufacturing industry, measured by employment. At the same time, the map reveals that the nine least-industrialized subregions, chiefly located in Wales and Scotland, each provided less than 10,000 manufacturing jobs, while a further eight more widely-scattered subregions provided only 10–30,000. The marked spatial clustering of manufacturing activity in the United Kingdom in 1959 is well brought out by these statistics.

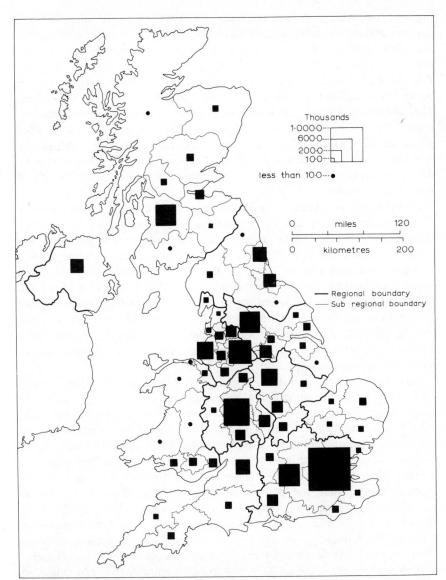

2.1 Subregional manufacturing employment in the United Kingdom, 1959
Source: unpublished Department of Employment statistics

An equally illuminating grouping for descriptive purposes is that into the three categories of central, peripheral and intermediate subregions. Centrality is here defined in terms of proximity to the London–Birmingham axis, noted as the latter conurbations have been for twentieth-century industrial growth and prosperity. Central subregions are therefore all those located in South East

England, the West and East Midlands, and East Anglia, together with the northern and central subregions of South West England. Peripheral subregions are similarly defined in terms of relative isolation from the traditional development axis, and include all those in Scotland, Northern Ireland, Northern England and Wales, together with the western and southern subregions of South West England and Merseyside and Furness in North-West England. They are thus also closely coincident with the government-designated Development Areas in force since 1966 (see fig. 8.2b). The remaining subregions, all of which are in Yorkshire and Humberside, and North West England, are intermediate in location between the central and peripheral categories, and are indeed now virtually all designated for government assistance under the title of Intermediate Areas.

In 1959, no less than 4.6 million workers, or 54 per cent of national manufacturing employment, were clustered in the twenty-two central subregions. This striking tribute to the success of these areas in attracting new twentieth-century industries such as motor vehicles, electronics and plastics may be contrasted with the share of the twenty-six peripheral subregions, whose manufacturing firms employed only 2.05 million workers, or 24 per cent of the national total. The industries of the fourteen intermediate subregions provided the remaining 1.92 million jobs (22 per cent). These statistics clearly hint at the relative twentieth-century decline of industry in the two latter categories of subregions, many of which were the industrial boom areas of nineteenth-century Britain.

Other indices of the scale and distribution of industry are much less satisfactory than the employment data discussed above, notably in terms of geographical coverage. Estimates of the 1964 total stock of industrial floorspace in each subregion of England and Wales,[2] and of total regional net output of manufacturing industry in the United Kingdom 1958–71,[3] are however mapped in figure 2.2. The latter are also given in table 2.1. The former provide a better, though still very crude,[4] index of the distribution of fixed capital in manufacturing, while the net output data measure the actual value of manufacturing production in each region. The 1964 floorspace map (fig. 2.2a), though broadly similar to figure 2.1, differs from it in certain important respects. Most notably, Greater London, though still the leading industrial centre, is much less dominant in terms of factory stock than of manufacturing employment. In 1964, the capital's 26.4 million square metres (284 million sq. ft) of industrial floorspace represented only 13 per cent of the England and Wales total, compared with its share of no less than 21 per cent of England and Wales' 1959 manufacturing employment. Indeed, Greater Manchester, its nearest rival in floorspace terms, contained 23.8 million square metres (256 million sq. ft), a total quite close to London's. These statistics thus point to a very intensive use of factory space, relative to labour force, in the capital, perhaps as an undesirable consequence of IDC controls. Conversely, certain

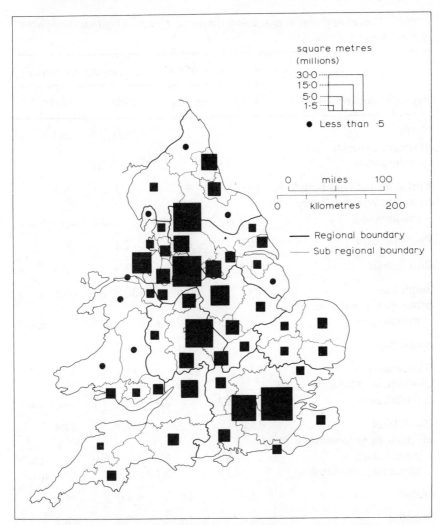

square metres
(millions)
30·0
15·0
5·0
1·5

● Less than ·5

0   miles   100

0   kilometres   200

—— Regional boundary
—— Sub regional boundary

2.2a Subregional manufacturing floorspace in England and Wales, 1964
Source: unpublished Department of Environment statistics

other subregions such as Manchester, west and south Yorkshire, and south
Lancashire record higher floorspace totals than would be expected from their
employment, suggesting perhaps the existence of underused textile or clothing
mill floorspace. However, it is still nonetheless true that the five leading subregions in floorspace terms accounted for exactly 50 per cent of England and
Wales' total factory stock, again indicating a marked spatial clustering of
manufacturing industry at the national scale, at least in the early 1960s.

Table 2.1 *Regional and conurbation shares of United Kingdom manufacturing net output, 1958–71*

Region or conurbation	Percentage of UK manufacturing net output			
	1958	*1963*	*1968*	*1971*
North	5.7	5.2	5.0	5.3
of which, Tyneside				
conurbation	1.9	1.6	1.5	n.a.
Yorkshire and Humberside	10.0	9.5	8.8	8.6
of which, West Yorkshire				
conurbation	4.6	4.4	3.8	n.a.
East Midlands	6.4	6.3	7.1	6.5
East Anglia	1.6	1.9	2.3	2.5
South East	29.2	30.6	30.3	30.6
of which, Greater London				
conurbation	18.1	17.6	13.7	n.a.
South West	4.3	4.4	4.7	4.8
West Midlands	13.2	13.4	13.4	12.7
of which, W. Midlands				
conurbation	8.4	8.1	7.1	n.a.
North West	15.8	15.3	14.7	14.4
of which, S. E. Lancashire				
conurbation	6.9	6.5	6.0	n.a.
Merseyside conurbation	3.2	3.1	2.7	n.a.
Wales	3.9	4.0	4.0	4.1
Scotland	8.4	7.8	7.9	8.5
Northern Ireland	1.5	1.6	1.8	2.0

Sources: Central Statistical Office, *Abstract of Regional Statistics*, no. 9, 1973, table 45; no. 10, 1974, table 57

n.a. = not available

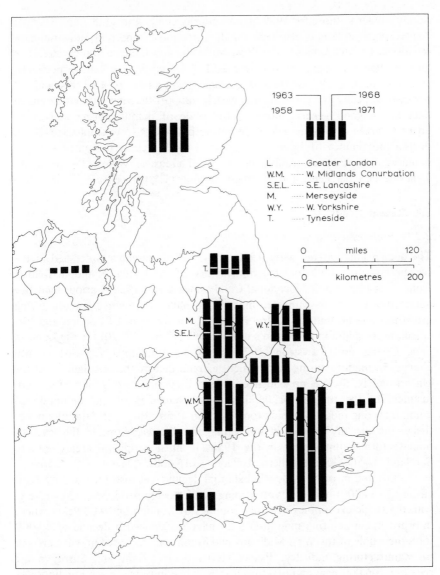

2.2b Regional manufacturing net output in the United Kingdom, 1958–71
Sources: as table 2.1

Regional and conurbation net output data for 1958 provide of course only a broad picture of the location of industry in the United Kingdom. Figure 2.2b brings out the dominance of the South East (29.2 per cent) compared with its nearest rival, the North West (15.8 per cent). Incidentally, these values are closely similar to those for 1959 manufacturing employment (28.7 and 15.9 per cent respectively), as is also true for the three most important industrial conurbations, Greater London, the West Midlands and Greater Manchester. The latter's 1958 net output shares were 18.1, 8.4, and 6.9 per cent respectively, compared with 1959 manufacturing employment shares of 18.3, 8.4 and 7.1 per cent respectively. These figures clearly support the view that employment data are a good general index of the scale of manufacturing activity in different areas of Britain. The 1958 net output data also re-emphasize the industrial dominance of London, in contrast to the relatively limited scale of manufacturing in such traditional industrial areas as Wales (3.9 per cent), Tyneside (1.9 per cent) and Northern Ireland (1.5 per cent).

2.2. Recent trends

2.2.1. Employment trends in the 1950s

The suggestion that the early 1960s may well represent a watershed in the twentieth-century industrial location history of the United Kingdom follows from an examination of locational trends since about 1959. Various evidence agrees that the 1950s witnessed massive absolute and relative manufacturing growth in and around the central industrial conurbations of London and Birmingham. In addition to Martin's calculations (1966, 217–20) for the London area, Coates and Rawstron (1971, 52–3) have mapped 1951–61 county changes in manufacturing employment as recorded by the population census. Unfortunately, there is no evidence in their discussion of this map of any adjustment of the figures for the important change in official definition of 'manufacturing industry' which took place in 1958.[5] But their data may nonetheless be broadly correct in indicating absolute *decreases* in the level of manufacturing employment in the 1950s in most peripheral areas, notably Scotland (−56,000), Northern Ireland (−15,000), Devon and Cornwall (−11,000) and most of Wales. Substantial decline was also recorded by Lancashire (−64,000) and the West Riding of Yorkshire (−13,000). Conversely, with the single exception of the old counties of London and Middlesex where outward manufacturing migration may have occasioned a decline of 49,000 jobs, the whole of the West Midlands and South East recorded massive growth of manufacturing industry. Essex, Hertfordshire, Kent and Surrey alone received 206,000 new manufacturing jobs, while industry in the remainder of the South East generated approximately another 107,000. In the West Midlands the two counties of Warwickshire and Staffordshire, comprising the West Midlands conurbation plus adjacent industrial towns such as Coventry, increased their employed manufacturing workforce by some 55,000. Although these raw figures must be treated with caution because of the classification change problem mentioned above, they substantiate beyond reasonable doubt the predominance of central area concentration and peripheral area decline as the key trends in the location of manufacturing industry in the United Kingdom up till about 1960.

2.2.2. *Employment trends in the 1960s*

Since the early 1960s, however, a dramatic reversal of these trends has become apparent. During the 1960s, and especially the later 1960s, concentration has been replaced by increasing spatial *dispersion* of manufacturing industry, both to relatively unindustrialized subregions and to the peripheral areas. Figure 2.3 maps the absolute change in aggregate manufacturing employment in each subregion for 1959–66 and 1966–71.[6] Extension of the latter period to a more recent date than 1971 is unfortunately ruled out by a major change in the method of collecting employment data in 1972, while subdivision of the whole 1959–71 period around the pivotal date of 1966 reflects three considerations. One is the different trend in the United Kingdom level of manufacturing employment during the two subperiods, with growth by 400,000 jobs 1959–66, but decline after this from 8.97 million to only 8.39 million by 1971. The post-1971 Employment Census records further decline since then (table 2.2). The choice of 1966 is also logical in that it permits direct comparison of aggregate subregional employment changes 1966–71 with trends in the movement of existing manufacturing firms as recorded by the Department of Industry for this same period (see section 6.6.5). Lastly, 1966 is not an unreasonable choice as a date marking significant changes in the relative strength and employment impact of government industrial location policy. True, Moore and Rhodes (1973, 89) identify 1963 as the turning point in government policy during the 1960s. But a later date perhaps allows more fully for the known lengthy time-lags between policy change and manufacturing location impact. Unpublished Department of Industry statistics reveal, for example, that no less than 52 per cent of all factory floorspace subject to Industrial Development Certificate control (see section 8.6) which was constructed in Britain in 1970 had been granted IDC approval two or more years earlier; 12 per cent actually involved IDC approvals five or more years earlier. Moreover, these figures do not allow for the additional time-lag in *employment* growth involved in building up the workforce to the anticipated level once the factory has been completed. On these various counts, 1966 appears a reasonable choice for subdividing the 1959–71 period.

Figure 2.3a bears witness to the growth of manufacturing employment nationally, 1959–66, in the frequency of solid black symbols. Indeed, only ten of the country's sixty-two subregions recorded absolute decline during this period. However, what is striking about this small sample of declining subregions is that four of them (London, Manchester, west Yorkshire and Clydeside) were amongst those identified earlier as the leading industrial subregions in 1959; and the country's biggest industrial centre, Greater London, recorded the greatest individual decline (−120,000 manufacturing jobs).[7] At

Table 2.2 *The changing regional distribution of manufacturing employment, 1971–75*

	1971		1973		1975	
	A	B	A	B	A	B
North	448	5.6	450	5.8	n.a.	
Yorkshire and Humberside	779	9.7	768	9.8	n.a.	
East Midlands	595	7.4	591	7.6	n.a.	
East Ánglia	190	2.4	200	2.6	198	2.6
South East	2,206	27.4	2,069	26.4	1,940	25.9
South West	407	5.1	409	5.2	400	5.3
West Midlands	1,104	13.7	1,074	13.7	1,021	13.6
North West	1,163	14.5	1,116	14.3	n.a.	
Wales	324	4.0	329	4.2	317	4.2
Scotland	669	8.3	657	8.4	637	8.5
Northern Ireland	170	2.1	164	2.1	154	2.1
United Kingdom	8,056		7,828		7,492	

Source: Central Statistical Office, *Abstract of Regional Statistics,* no. 10, 1974, table 41; Department of Employment Gazette, vol. 84, no. 8, 1976. The 1975 South East and South West figures have been adjusted by the author to ensure comparability with the earlier data

A = number of manufacturing employees in thousands   B = % share of UK total
n.a. not available

the same time, the map suggests that virtually all the country's least-industrialized subregions recorded expansion of manufacturing employment, including such traditionally unlikely industrial areas as the Scottish Highlands, rural Northumberland, central Wales and Cornwall. As these four examples also indicate, a further major trend discernible in figure 2.3a is the greatly-improved manufacturing growth performance of the peripheral areas, compared with their showing in the 1950s. Every single subregion of Wales, for example, experienced net growth in industrial employment, in striking contrast to the situation suggested by Coates and Rawstron's analysis for the previous decade.

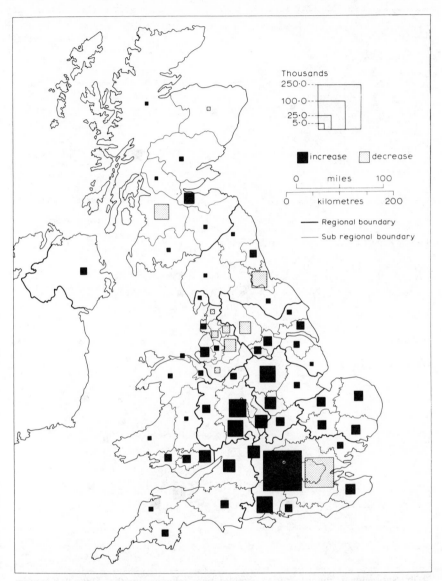

2.3a Subregional manufacturing employment change in the United Kingdom, 1959–66
Source: unpublished Department of Employment statistics

On the other hand, it is also clear from the 1959–66 map that in absolute terms the bulk of manufacturing growth was still concentrated in the favoured central subregions of Britain, with the important exception of London. Indeed,

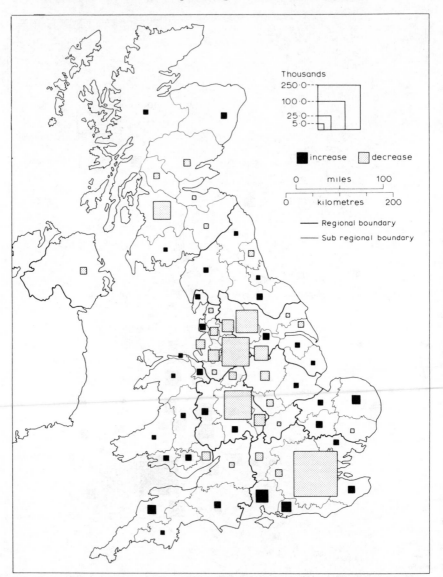

2.3b Subregional manufacturing employment change in the United Kingdom, 1966–71

Source unpublished Department of Employment statistics

industry in the Outer Metropolitan Area of the South East, by far the most important industrial growth zone of the period, expanded its employed workforce by 190,000 jobs. Substantial absolute growth was also recorded by the West Midlands conurbation and its surrounding central subregion, and by the

Nottingham–Derby area. The precise balance between central and peripheral area growth, in terms of any overall trend to greater concentration or dispersion, cannot therefore easily be assessed by visual reference to figure 2.3a, and demands quantitative analysis.

The second map, figure 2.3b, poses far fewer problems of interpretation. The spatial pattern of manufacturing employment change in the United Kingdom between 1966 and 1971 was dominated by the dramatic decline of each of the country's five greatest industrial conurbations, London (−250,000 manufacturing employees), the West Midlands (−100,000), Manchester (−90,000), west Yorkshire (−60,000) and Clydeside (−40,000). Even more striking, with the exception of those in Scotland and Northern Ireland, nearly all the declining subregions were clustered along and around the so-called London–Lancashire 'axial belt', the traditional twentieth-century focus and progenitor of industrial growth in Britain (Taylor 1938; Baker and Gilbert 1944). Even the Outer Metropolitan Area of the South East recorded net manufacturing employment decline, although its earlier considerable growth and London's continuing massive decline had substantially narrowed the size difference between these two subregions by 1971. Indeed, by 1975, the OMA and Outer South East together provided employment for 1.10 million manufacturing workers, compared with only 836,000 in Greater London.

In direct contrast to their counterparts in this central decline zone, however, virtually all peripheral subregions, with the exception of those in Scotland and Northern Ireland, recorded net manufacturing employment growth. Indeed, growing peripheral subregions encircle the central decline zone in an almost continuous ring of industrial expansion, from outer Kent, Sussex and Hampshire, to the South West peninsula, Wales, the Fylde and Furness of Lancashire, most of northern England, east Yorkshire, Lincolnshire, East Anglia and Essex. The striking spatial regularity of this pattern suggests the operation of powerful centrifugal locational forces, a thesis which will be examined in chapters 4 and 5. An important corollary of this peripheral manufacturing growth is a marked emphasis upon hitherto non-industrialized, rural areas. Even in Scotland, otherwise a significant anomaly to the trends identified above, the three subregions which recorded net growth were amongst the most peripheral and rural, relative to Scotland's central industrial core region.

Although subregional employment data are unfortunately not available for the period since 1971, the regional figures in table 2.2 suggest that the locational trends noted above for the later 1960s are still operating powerfully. Thus the South East's share of United Kingdom manufacturing employment declined still further and very substantially between 1971 and 1975, from 27.4 to 25.9 per cent. The North West's share fell, 1971–3, from 14.5 to 14.3 per cent, while that of the West Midlands remained static. Regions broadly peripheral to the London–Birmingham axis, such as the North, East Anglia, the

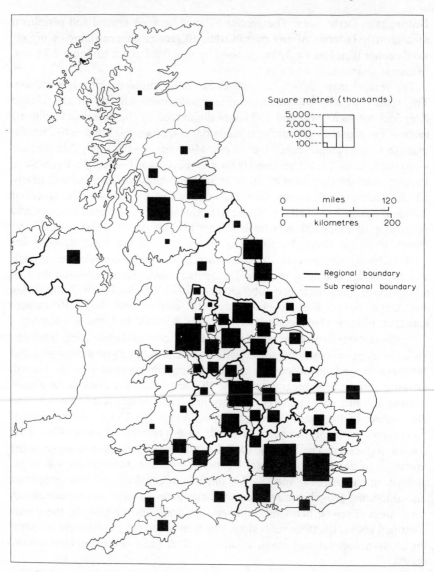

2.4a Gross increase in subregional manufacturing floorspace, 1960–71, in the United Kingdom (Department of Industry records)
Source: unpublished Department of Industry statistics

South West and Wales, continued to expand their manufacturing activity steadily relative to the rest of the country. Significantly, in view of recent developments in government regional industrial location policy (see section 8.6), this group of expanding peripheral regions has been joined since 1971 by

Scotland, and perhaps also Yorkshire and Humberside. Northern Ireland's achievement in at least maintaining its share of national manufacturing employment is perhaps noteworthy, in the light of recent events in the province.

2.2.3. Other locational indices: floorspace, net output and capital investment

As already noted, other indices of changes in the location of industry in the United Kingdom are less satisfactory than employment. However, figure 2.4 maps data on floorspace changes during the 1960s and early 1970s from two different sources. Figure 2.4a relates to gross new factory floorspace actually completed in each subregion between 1960 and 1971 inclusive, and is derived from Department of Industry unpublished IDC records. The problem with these figures is that they therefore make no allowance for possible reductions in factory space, and ignore factory space constructed in units smaller than 465 square metres (5,000 square feet), the threshold size for IDC control during much of the period.[8] Figure 2.4b is derived from the wholly different source already used for figure 2.2a. These Department of Environment figures have the very great merit of being figures of *net* change, since reductions as well as increases in industrial floorspace are recorded for each year. They can also be related to a special 1967 floorspace stock census, permitting calculation of *rates* of change over the whole 1964–72 period (see section 5.2.). However, estimates for years after 1969, although included in the map, are still only provisional and may include some minor errors. As with figure 2.2a, coverage is for England and Wales only.

The two maps present certain similarities. In both, the leading subregion is the Outer Metropolitan Area, while (if Scotland and Northern Ireland are excluded) six of the next nine subregions ranked by volume of floorspace growth are common to both maps (West Midlands central, Merseyside, West Midlands conurbation, industrial North East north, Nottingham–Derby, and South West northern). However, in view of the apparently common index used, it is the differences between the maps which are most striking. For not only are three of the top ten (indeed, of the top six) subregions on the DI floorspace map (Manchester, London and west Yorkshire) missing from the DoE map's top ten, but the latter map in fact ranks these as the three *bottom* subregions in the whole of England and Wales, each recording substantial net *decline* of industrial floorspace between 1964 and 1972. The DoE map also suggests net decline in three other, all North Western, subregions (Lancaster, north-east Lancashire and mid Lancashire). The industrial problems of these northwestern Intermediate Areas are thus strikingly revealed by both floorspace and employment statistics (fig. 2.3).

This comparison of the two floorspace maps clearly suggests that reductions in industrial floorspace have been so significant in many subregions during the later 1960s as to render the DI gross floorspace growth statistic a misleading

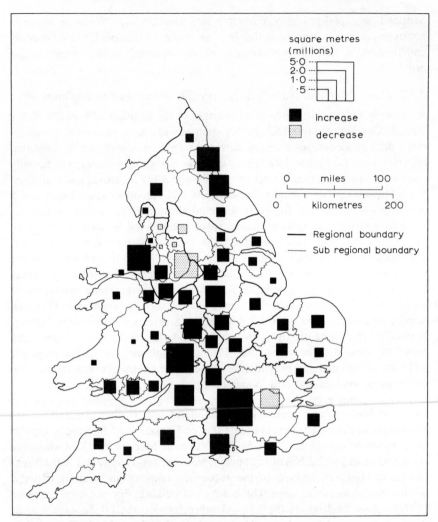

2.4b Net increase in subregional manufacturing floorspace, 1964–72, in England and Wales (Department of Environment records)
Source: unpublished Department of Environment statistics

index of locational shifts in manufacturing activity. However, the DoE map indicates that the relationship between subregional floorspace and manufacturing employment changes is a very complex one, involving for example considerable time-lags between the onset of decline in employment and eventual reduction in factory space. London, for instance, which has suffered a massive decline in manufacturing employment ever since 1961, has recorded net industrial floorspace decline only since 1969. Other complexities stem from the fact that floorspace growth can of course be stimulated by, or at least associated with, employment decline, with firms deliberately substituting capital, in the form of new plant and factory buildings, for labour.[9] Thus it is worth noting that the subregion receiving by far the greatest volume of floorspace growth, 1964–72, the Outer Metropolitan Area, in fact recorded a small *decline* in manufacturing employment in 1966–71 (fig. 2.3b). The same is true of six of the nine other leading subregions in floorspace growth terms. In the extreme case of the West Midlands conurbation, the subregion ranking fourth in volume of floorspace growth, 1964–72, manufacturing employment actually declined between 1966 and 1971 by over 100,000 workers. These differences suggest that while employment is probably the best general measure of shifts in industrial location patterns, particularly in terms of its sensitivity and rapidity of adjustment to the changing balance of locational forces, explanatory analysis using the rather different floorspace index may also be of some subsequent interest.

Two other indices of the changing distribution of industry in Britain in the 1960s are unfortunately available only or largely on a regional basis. The first are the manufacturing net output figures already mapped in figure 2.2b and listed in table 2.1. The picture revealed by these figures generally corroborates closely that given by the employment data, although there are a few anomalies. Thus the South East, in line with its employment position, increased its share of United Kingdom net output 1958–63 but has remained at a plateau since instead of declining as might have been expected. While this might be due to an inaccurate 1971 estimate based, unlike earlier figures, only on a sample of firms, it could also reflect an unusually high rate of capital-labour substitution in the South East outside London. This hypothesis is supported by the floorspace change data discussed above. However, the three other major industrial regions recorded trends in line with their manufacturing employment performance, the North West and Yorkshire declining steadily throughout the 1960s, the West Midlands increasing its share until the mid-1960s, since when there appears to have been a dramatic decline. The three regions immediately peripheral to the 'axial belt', East Anglia, the South West and Wales, all increased their net output shares steadily over the period, as did Northern Ireland. Scotland and the North recorded declining shares until the mid-1960s; but this trend appears significantly to have been reversed since 1968, in line with recent manufacturing employment trends.

The conurbation data, unfortunately available only for the decade 1958–68, further and strikingly corroborate the 1960s dispersal trend indicated by employment. All six conurbations recorded a substantial and steady decline in their manufacturing net output shares over this period, the most dramatic case being that of London. Its share, after falling only moderately in the period 1958–63, plummeted downwards between 1963 and 1968 by no less than 4 per cent, a decline of quite remarkable magnitude over this very short period. The fact that London's manufacturing employment share did not fall quite so rapidly as this (only to 14.9 per cent by 1968, compared with a net output share of 13.7 per cent) suggests that decline may have affected London's more capital-intensive industries to an even greater degree than its more labour-intensive ones. In turn, this raises interesting questions as to the possible impact upon London of the marked increase in assisted-area manufacturing investment incentives after 1963, which some commentators have argued were particularly attractive to capital-intensive industry (see section 8.8.1).

The second regional index is the total value of capital investment in manufacturing industry, 1966–9, at constant 1963 prices, for the regions of Great Britain. Table 2.3 is derived from Clark's original calculations (Clark 1976), based on unpublished Department of Industry investment grant and other government data. The figures, which are more reliable than any previously published, cover investment both in manufacturing plant and

Table 2.3 *Regional capital investment in manufacturing industry, 1966–9*

	Manufacturing investment 1966–69*		Manufacturing employment 1966		Investment per employee
	£ mill.	% GB	'000	% GB	£
North	503	9.9	457	5.2	1,101
Wales	329	6.5	323	3.7	1,019
Scotland	563	11.1	731	8.3	770
East Anglia	130	2.6	186	2.1	699
East Midlands	404	7.8	617	7.0	655
North West	809	16.0	1,344	15.3	602
South West	219	4.3	400	4.6	548
West Midlands	585	11.6	1,243	14.1	471
Yorkshire and Humberside	408	8.1	884	10.1	462
South East	1,114	22.0	2,603	29.6	428
Great Britain	5,064		8,788		576

Source: Clark (1976), and Department of Employment statistics

* The figures are for investment at constant 1963 prices

machinery and in new factory buildings, the former being by far the most important component. The two most remarkable conclusions to be drawn from Clark's figures are that the three regions recording the highest manufacturing investment levels per employee, 1966–9, were Britain's three peripheral and classic industrial problem regions, the North, Wales and Scotland; while the region with the lowest investment/employee level was Britain's erstwhile dominant industrial growth region, the South East. The West Midlands also recorded an investment/employee level substantially below the national average. Of course, variations in regional industrial structures must partly explain these differences in investment performance, the high figure for Wales, for example, reflecting in part the importance in the principality of such capital investment intensive industries as iron and steel, and oil-refining. The same probably applies in North West England, where investment levels per head were probably boosted by the region's capital-intensive chemicals industry. But the scale of the differences is so great that other factors, and notably government industrial location policy operating in the later 1960s through regionally discriminatory investment grants (see sections 8.6.3 and 8.8.1), must be involved in this remarkable inversion of the traditional centre-periphery pattern of industrial investment.

2.3. Entropy index analysis of subregional manufacturing employment change

It was noted earlier that conflicting subregional manufacturing employment changes during the early 1960s rendered it difficult to assess whether the overall picture of spatial industrial change was best categorized as dispersion or continuing concentration. Detailed, and illuminating, quantitative assessment of this point is however possible using the entropy index developed by Theil (1967, 95) from information theory as a measure of spatial inequality. When applied to the distribution of a phenomenon such as manufacturing employment between a set of areas such as the subregions of the United Kingdom at a particular point in time, this index provides a measure of the degree of dispersion or concentration at that particular time of the phenomenon over the areas. Its minimum inequality value of zero is given by the situation in which each area possesses an exactly identical share of the phenomenon, while its maximum inequality value, occurring when the phenomenon is concentrated in just one of the areas, is given by log N, when N is the number of areas. In this case, with sixty-two subregions, the maximum possible value is 4.1271 (the natural logarithm of 62). As Martin (1972) has demonstrated, this index can be used to compare the level of spatial inequality in the distribution of employment at different points in time, providing that exactly the same set of spatial units is used at each date. Moreover, the index possesses various advantages over other, more traditional, approaches to measuring spatial concentration or dispersion (Martin 1972, Chisholm and

Oeppen 1973, 34–6), particularly when as in this analysis it is calculated by the following formula:

$$I(y) = \sum_{i=1}^{N} y_i \log \frac{y_i}{1/N} = \sum_{r=1}^{R} Y_r \log \frac{Y_r}{N_r/N} + \sum_{r=1}^{R} Y_r \left[\sum_{i \in r} \frac{y_i}{Y_r} \log \frac{y_i/Y_r}{1/N_r} \right]$$

where:

$I(y)$ is the overall United Kingdom entropy index of spatial inequality

y_i is the share of the ith subregion of all United Kingdom manufacturing employment,

Y_r is the sum of the shares of all subregions in region r,

N_r is the number of subregions in region r,

N is the total number of subregions in the United Kingdom (62),

and R is the total number of regions in the United Kingdom (11).

The significance of this particular formula for calculating the entropy index is that it is designed to distinguish separately the contributions to the overall $I(y)$ value of 'between-region' inequality and 'within-region' inequality. The former is given by the first term in the main equation, the latter by the second term. The first term thus simply measures the degree of difference in the *regional* shares (Y_r) of United Kingdom manufacturing employment, while the second term measures the degree of difference in *subregional* shares within each region, weighting this value by the region's overall share of United Kingdom employment (Y_r). This distinction between within-region and between-region inequality is very useful, in that it is of course perfectly possible, if not likely, for different trends to occur at the different scales. Coates and Rawstron's data, for example, suggest that in the 1950s, increasing relative concentration of industry at the between-region scale was accompanied by increasing relative dispersion of industry at the within-region scale, at least in the case of regions such as the South East. This form of entropy index analysis has thus proved most useful in several recent studies of changing industrial location patterns (Martin 1972, Semple 1973, Garrison and Paulson 1973).

The $I(y)$ index and the respective contributions to it of between-region and within-region spatial inequality were thus calculated for the subregional distribution of United Kingdom manufacturing employment in 1959, 1966 and 1971.[10] The results, measured in natural logarithms, are given in table 2.4, and graphically in figure 2.5. The most important finding is that the total index declined significantly between both 1959 and 1966, and 1966 and 1971, indicating a powerful trend throughout the 1960s towards increasing relative dispersion of manufacturing industry. The 1971 index was thus over 16 per cent lower than that for 1959. Examination of the original data reveals that the lower 1971 index owes much to the marked relative, and indeed absolute, decline of Britain's six biggest industrial subregions (see section 2.1 above), whose share of total United Kingdom manufacturing employment was by 1971 down to only 46 per cent (from 51 per cent in 1959).

Table 2.4 *Entropy indices of subregional manufacturing employment distribution, 1959–71*

	1959	1966	1971
Within-region	0.6076	0.5525	0.4949
Between-region	0.2024	0.2027	0.1842
Total index	0.8100	0.7553	0.6791
Total as % of maximum possible inequality	19.6	18.3	16.5

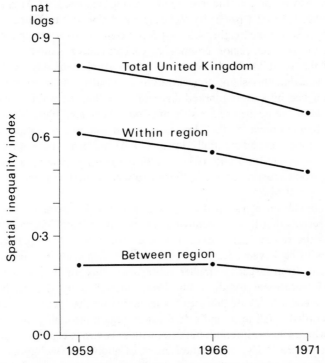

2.5 Entropy indices of United Kingdom subregional manufacturing employment distribution, 1959–71
Source: unpublished Department of Employment statistics

A second conclusion, however, is that the annual rate of decline of the total index was over twice as fast (−2.02 per cent) during the later subperiod as during the earlier one (−0.96 per cent. The reasons for this were twofold. First, while the between-region inequality index declined significantly (−1.83 per cent per annum) between 1966 and 1971, indicating decreasing differences in regional shares of manufacturing employment, it actually *increased* slightly (+0.02 per cent per annum) during the earlier 1959–66 subperiod, indicating increased regional *concentration* of manufacturing industry. Examination of actual regional shares in 1959 and 1966 reveals that this slight concentration trend was a direct reflection of continuing relative manufacturing growth in the South East (28.7 to 29.0 per cent of UK total manufacturing employment) and West Midlands (13.3 to 13.9 per cent), regions which ranked one and three in terms of 1959 employment shares, together with the continuing relative decline of the North (5.5 to 5.1 per cent), which ranked seven.

However, the substantial relative decline of the country's second largest industrial region, the North West (15.9 to 15.0 per cent, 1959–66), together with relative growth in three of the least industrialized regions, East Anglia (ranked eleven, 1959: 1.7 to 2.1 per cent), Wales (ranked nine: 3.3 to 3.6 per cent) and the South West (ranked eight: 4.3 to 4.5 per cent), did very nearly offset the effect on the between-region component of cumulative growth in the South East and the West Midlands. Moreover, the spatial inequality analysis also demonstrates that this slight concentration trend at the between-region scale was outweighed by a more marked dispersion trend at the within-region scale, affecting both the central regions of the South East and West Midlands and those of the periphery. At the same time, the annual rate of within-region inequality decline was substantially lower (−1.30 per cent) between 1959 and 1966 than between 1966 and 1971 (−2.09 per cent), providing a second and more important reason for the different subperiod performance of the total $I(y)$ value noted above.

A last conclusion concerns this striking within-region dispersion trend. For table 2.4 reveals that it is the behaviour of the within-region component which dominates the results, accounting as it does for nearly three-quarters of the total index in each year. Relative within-region dispersion of manufacturing employment, from larger to smaller subregions, thus stands out as the dominant single locational trend of the 1960s identified by this analysis. The remarkable consistency of this trend is indicated by the fact that every single region recorded a fall in its individual within-region inequality index not only over the whole 1959–71 period, but also, with only two exceptions, during each subperiod. Interestingly, the highest rates of individual within-region index decline measured over the whole period were recorded by the central regions of the South East (−1.9 per cent per annum) and the West Midlands (−1.6 per cent), together with Yorkshire and Humberside and East Anglia (both −1.6 per cent). These rates bear witness to the rapidity of the spatial shift of industry from the traditionally dominant industrial cores of these regions to surrounding, less industrialized subregions. In contrast, the peripheral regions of the North (−0.9 per cent), Scotland (−1.0 per cent) and Wales (−1.2 per cent) recorded lower rates of within-region component decline, suggesting a somewhat greater ability on the part of their main industrial centres to maintain their manufacturing pre-eminence with respect to the rest of the region. Alternatively, this could reflect subregion boundaries for these main centres which are more loosely drawn than in the South East and Midlands, and therefore include new towns and satellite industrial growth areas with the older declining core. But overall, the consistent and rapid decline of within-region inequality in each region during the 1960s suggests that very powerful locational forces are now at work bringing about increasing dispersion of manufacturing activity in all regions of the United Kingdom.

NOTES

1 I am greatly indebted to Professor Michael Chisholm for these data, aggregated by him and Mr J. Oeppen from Department of Employment local area figures: see Chisholm and Oeppen 1973, 38–9.

2 I am greatly indebted to Mr P. Walls, Mr J. Kellett and Mr W. D. McPherson for provision of these data, which are collected by the Department of the Environment from Inland Revenue rating records. No comparable figures exist for Scotland or Northern Ireland.

3 Net output is defined as the total current value of manufacturing sales, less the cost of materials.

4 In practice, the value of manufacturing plant and machinery is on average three times greater than that of the factory in which it is housed. See Clark 1976, table 7.4.

5 This redefinition resulted in the reclassification of no less than 600,000 manufacturing workers to non-manufacturing industries.

6 I am greatly indebted to Mr J. M. Lowell of the Department of Employment for the unpublished ERII employment data used here. Although recently severely criticized (Allen and Yuill 1976) ERII data is better for manufacturing than for services (Keeble and Hauser 1971, 239) and is more reliable if used, as generally in this study, in aggregate form. At least one of Allen and Yuill's criticisms, that relating to sampling errors, is also probably too extreme.

7 This in fact masks manufacturing employment growth in London to 1961, the peak year ever for GLC area manufacturing employment (1.61 million), with a reversal into rapid decline after this (Mortlock 1972, 17).

8 These data, for which I am indebted to Mr E. T. Steer of the Department of Industry, have been laboriously adjusted to allow for substantially different interpretations in different regions at different times of the type of industrial floorspace covered by the controls.

9 For a striking *inverse* correlation between changes in employment and

floorspace by industry within Greater London 1961–6, see figure 3.14 in Greater London Council (1969).

10 I am greatly indebted to Mr J. Lewis and Mr R. L. Martin of the Cambridge University Department of Geography for computing assistance.

3 The impact of industrial structure

3.1. Introduction

The fascinating recent and current shifts in the spatial distribution of United Kingdom manufacturing industry described in the previous chapter clearly demand some attempt at explanation. This and the next two chapters therefore examine possible alternative explanations, utilizing both the results of micro-level surveys of manufacturing firms and, more particularly, macro-level statistical analysis of different hypotheses (chapter 5). This aggregate level approach is complemented by chapters 6 and 7, the former of which looks at the components of change in different areas in terms of the birth and growth, decline and death, and physical movement between areas of individual manufacturing firms. The latter examines spatial shifts in four particular, important, but very different manufacturing industries.

A search of the voluminous theoretical and empirical literature on manufacturing location dynamics reveals numerous hypothesized influences which have been or might be adduced to explain locational trends in the United Kingdom at the subregional scale considered here. However, it is possible to categorize these influences in terms of two alternative conceptual models. The first of these relates to those centripetal forces which encourage cumulative manufacturing growth in the main industrial core regions of a country at the expense of more isolated peripheral areas – the *centre-periphery model*. The second concerns centrifugal forces which act to disperse manufacturing growth away from the main industrial centres to less-industrialized and peripheral areas – the *periphery-centre model*. But before discussing these alternative spatial models and the locational forces associated with them, it is necessary to consider the impact of industrial structure upon aggregate manufacturing change in different areas.

3.2. The significance of industrial structure

Many recent studies of industrial location dynamics have noted that a fundamental influence upon changing levels of manufacturing activity in different areas are spatial variations in existing industrial structure. This reflects the obvious fact that, at the national level, different industries grow or decline at different rates because of changes in demand and/or technological innovation. In turn, therefore, areas in which particular industries are concentrated might be expected to experience aggregate industrial growth or decline in proportion to their degree of specialization and the national-level trends in the particular industries involved. Thus, for example, the high income elasticity of demand[1] for television sets and washing machines in Britain in recent years means that areas specializing in the manufacture of these products are likely to have enjoyed above-average growth in aggregate manufacturing activity, all else being equal. Conversely, areas specializing in the manufacture of iron and steel are likely to have suffered static or declining manufacturing output or employment, since demand for steel has been relatively static while dramatic technological innovations have been reducing labour requirements (see section 7.2.2). Extreme examples of nationally growing and declining industries are given in table 3.1.

Table 3.1 *Employment change rates in the ten nationally fastest-growing and declining manufacturing industries, 1959–68*

Growing industries	Manufacturing employment 1959 '000	% change in manufacturing employment 1959–68	Declining industries	Manufacturing employment 1959 '000	% change in manufacturing employment 1959–68
Arms, other engineering	218	+113	Linoleum, leather cloth	18	−27
Plastic moulding, fabricating	55	+92	Perambulators, hand trucks	8	−29
Synthetic resins, plastics materials	23	+74	Rope, twine and net	13	−30
Contractors' plant, quarrying machinery	25	+60	Hats, caps millinery	16	−37
Engineers' small tools, gauges	44	+59	Motor and pedal cycles, 3-wheeled vehicles	37	−38
Shop and office fitting	24	+59	Spinning, doubling of fibres	136	−38
Radio and other electronic apparatus	213	+58	Weaving of cotton, linen fibres, etc.	124	−40
Telegraph and telephone apparatus	57	+58	Marine engineering	76	−49
Abrasives, other building materials	93	+39	Railway carriages, wagons, trams	78	−59
Bacon-curing, meat and fish products	64	+38	Locomotives, railway track equipment	72	−61

Source: Chisholm and Oeppen 1973, table 44

3.3. Shift-and-share analysis: the technique

Assessment of the impact on manufacturing change of local differences in industrial structure can take several forms. The simplest approach is to classify manufacturing industries by national performance into different categories of, for example, 'fast-growing', 'slow-growing' and 'declining' industries, and then compute the proportionate share of each category in each area studied. More sophisticated is the application of 'shift-and-share' analysis, a technique whose recent development has stimulated a vast literature.[2] Basically, shift-and-share analysis involves disaggregating an area's net change in industrial employment, output or some other index, over a given period, into three components. The first, *regional share* (or national growth[3]), component is the amount by which the area's total manufacturing employment (or whatever) would have changed if it had changed at precisely the same rate (e.g. +5 per cent) as did manufacturing in the nation as a whole. The second is the *proportionality shift* (or structural, or compositional) component. This measures the impact of industrial structure, and can be thought of as the extra amount by which manufacturing employment in the area has changed as a result of the area's specialization in particular industries which are growing or declining at particular rates at the national level. Specialization in relatively declining industries would yield a negative proportionality shift, specialization in relatively growing industries would yield a positive one.

The third, *differential shift* (or regional, or competitive) component is what is left over of actual net change after calculation of the regional share and proportionality shift components. This residual may be thought of as the extra amount of manufacturing change in the area resulting from above- or below-average growth or decline of particular industries in the area, compared with their performance at the national level. If, for example, industries are on the whole growing faster in an area than they are nationally, the area will have a positive differential shift. If they are growing less rapidly, or declining faster, the area's differential shift will be negative. The sum of the proportionality and differential shifts (the total, or comparative, shift) represents the net gain or loss to the area of manufacturing activity over and above its 'fair share' on the basis of the aggregate national trend.

The value of shift-and-share analysis as a technique for identifying the relative roles of industrial structure on the one hand, and area-specific locational influences on the other, in an area's overall manufacturing performance has admittedly been questioned by some commentators. For example, criticism has been levied (Townroe 1969, Buck 1970) at studies drawing conclusions on the basis of industrial disaggregation only to the broad Standard Industrial Classification Order level. Townroe shows that in the West Midlands conurbation case, reworking of manufacturing employment change data for 1961–6 using the much more detailed Minimum List Heading industrial breakdown increases the proportionality (or structural) shift substantially relative to the residual differential shift. Minimum List Heading data, relating to much more homogeneous industrial categories than the broad Order groups, would thus seem a better basis for shift-and-share analyses. Another criticism (Mackay 1968) questions shift-and-share's implicit assumption of independence of behaviour of different industries within the same area, on the grounds that input-output linkages and other multiplier relationships may well transmit growth or decline in a particular key industry to other local industries, against national trends in these industries. As with the industrial disaggregation criticism, this could presumably lead to an under-statement of the 'real' impact of industrial structure and an inflation of the residual differential effect.

These criticisms may have validity in particular cases. However, it should be noted that input-output relationships are in fact to some extent built in to shift-and-share analysis, through national-level linkages which result in a common trend of national decline or growth in particular pairs of industries. Shift-and-share can only be criticized for ignoring special relationships peculiar to particular regions, over and above average national-scale links (Randall 1973, 16). Moreover, it can be argued that in the manufacturing case, Mackay's independency criticism is probably of little significance even at the regional scale. The reason for this is the remarkably low general level of within-region manufacturing input-output linkages in Britain recorded by recent empirical studies. Thus Lever's recent and detailed analysis (Lever 1974c, 318–19) of linkages in six selected manufacturing industries (glass products, engineers' small tools, paint, electrical switchgear, paper packaging, and light clothing) in west central Scotland found that no less than four-fifths of all inputs by value in 1970 were purchased from firms in other regions of Britain or from abroad, only one-fifth being provided by suppliers from the whole of Scotland! The industrial disaggregation criticism is, however, a more pertinent one, although Stilwell (1969, 166) argues that while Order-level analyses should be treated with caution, their conclusions are generally broadly correct. In short, most commentators conclude, with certain reservations, that shift-and-share analysis is of some value in identifying the impact of variations in industrial structure upon the spatial pattern of aggregate manufacturing change.

3.4. The structural versus locational controversy

In the British context, the utility of shift-and-share analysis has perhaps been enhanced by its obvious relevance to a very important controversy over the causes of regional variations in manufacturing growth since the first world war. This controversy has involved what may be termed the structural and the locational schools of thought (Keeble 1969b, 853; McCrone 1969, 169). Put simply, the structural school argues that the sluggish industrial growth of such peripheral regions as Scotland, Northern England and Wales, at least until the 1960s, was due basically to earlier nineteenth-century over-specialization in industries for whose products demand has been relatively static or declining during this century. A key factor in this demand decline has been the loss of former export markets to which the scale of these industries was in large part geared (Caesar 1964, 231). In the manufacturing sector, such industries would include iron and steel, shipbuilding and textiles. This type of peripheral industrial structure is illustrated, for example, by the Tyneside conurbation (Keeble 1972a, 109–10), where in 1961 shipbuilding and mechanical engineering alone accounted for 41 per cent of manufacturing activity measured by employment. In turn, however, this over-specialization at the periphery partly reflected the geological accident that many British coalfields happened to be located on or near the coast; and coal was the motive power and magnet for industrial expansion during the later nineteenth century. The structural school would thus regard the peripheral distribution of the industrially-lagging regions as largely or entirely fortuitous (Norcliffe 1970, 5.5–5.8).

The locational school, on the other hand, while acknowledging the short-term importance of its historical legacy, argues that the basic reason for the periphery's relatively sluggish industrial growth since the first world war lies in its inability to attract modern growth industries spontaneously. The latter, traditionally epitomized by the motor-vehicle and electronic-engineering industries amongst others, have preferred to locate and grow in the more centrally-situated South East and Midlands of England. The main reason for this preference, and the corollary of spatial discrimination against the peripheral regions, is seen by the locational school as the need of these modern industries for rapid access to customers and suppliers. The very fact of peripheral location and distance from the country's main markets is thus viewed as the fundamental underlying explanation for sluggish peripheral industrial growth.

This controversy is not just of academic importance; for implicit in it are major opposing conclusions for government industrial location policy. Thus while acknowledging the psychological handicap of an historical legacy of slag-heaps, back-to-back slums and derelict mills in attracting new industry, the structural viewpoint suggests that there is no inherent locational reason why new growth-industry plants, once attracted by government pressures and incentives, should not operate in the long run every bit as efficiently in peripheral as in central locations. The locational viewpoint, on the other hand, implies that there are sound economic reasons for the traditional reluctance of newer industries to move to the periphery, in the shape of increased long-term costs of manufacturing or marketing and decreased long-run efficiency and vitality. Acceptance of the locational argument thus leads to the further conclusion that the steering of industry to peripheral assisted areas will result in a high-cost, low-growth and economically undesirable national industrial location pattern.

3.5. Shift-and-share analysis: previous findings

The relevance of shift-and-share analysis to this controversy lies of course in the fact that it would seem to provide a technique for distinguishing in any particular instance of manufacturing change the relative contributions of precisely the two influences in question – structure and location. Has traditionally below-average peripheral, and above-average central, industrial growth been due wholly or largely to structure? Or can additional, presumably locational, influences be detected? These questions have prompted many recent United Kingdom shift-and-share studies. Three of the most important are by Thirlwall (1967), Stilwell (1968, 1969) and Brown (1972).

Thirlwall's study was concerned with regional changes in total employees (i.e. employed *and* unemployed workers, taken together) between 1948 and 1963. Over this period, he found that virtually all the central, or as he terms them the 'overemployed', regions increased their employee totals faster than did the United Kingdom as a whole.[4] Exactly the opposite was true of the 'underemployed' regions (Scotland, Northern Ireland, Wales, the North and the North West). These findings are of course in full accord with the descriptive analysis of manufacturing employment trends already presented in section 2.2.1. Even more interesting, Thirlwall's shift-and-share analysis, conducted at the SIC Order level, suggested that in three of the five main central regions (East and South, South West and North Midlands) it was a favourable differential shift which was the more important component in change. The impact of industrial structure, though generally positive, was here of secondary significance. However London and the West Midlands, where above-average growth was largely or entirely due to a favourable industrial structure, were important exceptions to this. The peripheral regions fell into two categories with respect to proportionality and differential shifts. In Wales and the North, sluggish employee growth was almost wholly due to an unfavourable initial industrial structure: but in the three other peripheral regions, marked negative differential shifts were even more important than poor structure as a component in only limited expansion of total employees. Moreover, analyses for four subperiods revealed no consistent tendency over time towards any improvement in the periphery's differential shift performance. Indeed, that of the Northern region deteriorated steadily from 1948 to 1963. Thirlwall's findings thus provide qualified support for the locational argument, at least in terms of empirically observed trends during the 1950s, when government regional policy measures were relatively insignificant (see chapter 8).

Stilwell's Order-level analysis, dealing only with employed workers, not total employees, tends to corroborate Thirlwall's conclusions for the overlapping but somewhat later 1959–67 period. Again, Stilwell found that the central regions all recorded above-average, the peripheral regions all below-average, employment growth. And again, a favourable differential shift played an important role in the former's expansion. However, in the South East, massive absolute employment growth was entirely due to a very favourable initial industrial structure, the differential shift being slightly negative. The four peripheral regions studied[5] again fall into two groups, a large negative differential shift being chiefly responsible for only sluggish employment growth in Scotland and the North West, in addition to an unfavourable structural effect. In Wales and the North, sluggish growth was due entirely to the latter.

The third study was carried out at the National Institute of Economic and Social Research as part of its major research project on regional economic change in the United Kingdom (Brown 1972, 131–46). This study is particularly interesting for at least three reasons. First, it adopts a more complex variant of shift-and-share analysis which permits construction of analysis of variance models to which significance testing may be applied. Second, it includes analysis of regional total employment change for the period 1921–61 at the Order level. Third, it alone of the three national-scale studies discussed here examines trends for less than total employment, singling out for analysis the non-service industries (agriculture, mining and manufacturing) as a single entity.

The 1921–61 analysis presents findings (Brown 1972, 134) which are in substantial and perhaps surprising accord with the Thirlwall and Stilwell studies for postwar years. They also, of course, therefore provide some support for the locational interpretation of regional economic change in the United Kingdom. Thus above-average employment growth in two of the three main central regions (the West and North Midlands) over this forty-year period is shown to be due almost entirely to a marked and positive differential growth component. In the South East, massive growth was in contrast primarily a reflection of an initially very favourable industrial structure; but even here there was a measurable (though not statistically significant) positive differential shift as well. These results seem to point to the existence of additional locational advantages for employment growth in these regions, over and above any inherited structural factors. Conversely, the results for the five main peripheral regions (Scotland, Wales, Northern Ireland, the North West and Northern England) indicate statistically significant *negative* shifts for both the structural and differential components in every case except the North, which recorded a slight positive differential value. In Wales, Northern Ireland and the North the dominant effect, as suggested by Thirlwall and Stilwell, was exerted by the unfavourable industrial mix; in the other two regions, the problem was one of a marked negative differential shift. These findings, given the long period examined and the close similiarity with those of Thirlwall and Stilwell, are of great interest and importance.

The NIESR analysis of non-service employment changes is necessarily restricted to the 1950s and earlier 1960s, and excludes Northern Ireland. It is however conducted at the detailed MLH level. For the period 1953–9, results are somewhat similar (Brown 1972, 139) to those for total employees during the 1950s arrived at by Thirlwall, despite the exclusion of the important service employment element. Interestingly, the chief differences from the latter's findings tend to provide even stronger support for locational-type explanations of the spatial distribution of manufacturing growth. Thus the South East is shown to have experienced a marked and statistically significant positive differential shift as well as one reflecting a very favourable industrial structure; while Wales, characterized by Thirlwall chiefly in terms of a negative structural effect, is accorded the biggest negative differential shift of any region. However, the results for the subsequent 1961–6 period tell a rather different story. True, the North, Wales and Scotland on the one hand, and the South East and West Midlands on the other, are still characterized by marked and statistically significant negative and positive structural shifts respectively. But in the South East a previous markedly positive differential shift has been transformed into a substantial *negative* differential value, surpassed only, and slightly, by that for the West Midlands. Conversely, Wales' previously large negative differential shift is now equally substantially *positive*. This remarkable reversal of fortune suggests of course an apparently marked transformation in the balance of locational influences on manufacturing change, with respect to at least two classic central and peripheral regions. But as Brown (1972, 140) points out, this transformation should not be regarded as the product of any 'natural' spatial forces, being almost certainly a product of intensified regional policy (see chapter 8).

3.6. Regional manufacturing shifts, 1965–9

As noted above, nearly all national-level shift-and-share analyses unfortunately relate to total economic activity, not just manufacturing. So too do most local or regional studies, such as that by Cameron (1971) of 1961–6 employment change in the Clydeside conurbation (see section 8.5). The latter, which is a particularly detailed and objective appraisal, does present some analysis of the manufacturing sector, and is relevant to the earlier discussion in concluding (Cameron 1971, 331) that 'whilst structure is the major explanation of Clydeside's relatively poor economic performance there are also other elements which have caused this relative weakness'. Interestingly, exactly the same conclusion is reached by Randall (1973) using data for the longer 1959–68 period.

However, as an illustration of the application of shift-and-share analysis purely to the manufacturing sector, and in order to throw light on variations in proportionality and differential shifts as components in regional manufacturing changes since the mid-1960s, table 3.2 records the results of an Order-level analysis for manufacturing industry only for the period 1965–9. This is the most recent four-year period for which regional employment data – comparable

Table 3.2 *Shift-and-share analysis of regional manufacturing employment change in the United Kingdom, 1965–9*

Region	A Actual manufacturing employment change		B Regional share		C Total shift		D Proportionality shift		E Differential shift	
	'000	%	'000	%	'000	%	'000	%	'000	%
North	+7.0	(+1.6)	−5.6	(−1.2)	+12.6	(+2.8)	−3.3	(−0.7)	+15.9	(+3.5)
Yorkshire and Humberside	−24.0	(−2.7)	−11.0	(−1.2)	−13.0	(−1.5)	−14.4	(−1.6)	+1.4	(+0.1)
East Midlands	+16.0	(+2.6)	−7.6	(−1.2)	+23.6	(+3.8)	−7.8	(−1.3)	+31.4	(+5.1)
East Anglia	+26.0	(+14.4)	−2.2	(−1.2)	+28.2	(+15.6)	+2.6	(+1.4)	+25.6	(+14.2)
South East	−95.0	(−3.6)	−32.3	(−1.2)	−62.7	(−2.4)	+39.5	(+1.5)	−102.2	(−3.9)
South West	+15.0	(+3.8)	−4.9	(−1.2)	+19.9	(+5.0)	+2.1	(+0.5)	+17.8	(+4.5)
Wales	+20.0	(+6.3)	−3.9	(−1.2)	+23.9	(+7.5)	−4.0	(−1.3)	+27.9	(+8.8)
West Midlands	−33.0	(−2.6)	−15.3	(−1.2)	−17.7	(−1.4)	−2.4	(−0.2)	−15.3	(−1.2)
North West	−45.0	(−3.3)	−16.8	(−1.2)	−28.2	(−2.1)	−3.4	(−0.3)	−24.8	(−1.8)
Scotland	+2.0	(+0.3)	−9.1	(−1.2)	+11.1	(+1.5)	−4.7	(−0.6)	+15.8	(+2.1)
Northern Ireland	0.0	(0.0)	−2.3	(−1.2)	+2.3	(+1.2)	−4.2	(−2.3)	+6.5	(+3.5)
United Kingdom	−111.0	(−1.2)	−111.0	(−1.2)	0		0		0	

in terms of regional definition, industrial classification and collection methods – are available.[6] It can be argued that four years is the minimum period for which shift-and-share analyses should be conducted, given observed instability in results for very short time-periods (Randall 1973, 3). Although unfortunately somewhat dated, this period at least falls within the post-1966 decade of active regional policy (see chapter 8): 1965–9 shift-and-share findings on the relative significance of structural as opposed to other, possibly policy-induced, changes could therefore arguably still be of some current relevance.

Column A of table 3.2 list the actual volume and rate of manufacturing employment change recorded by each region of the United Kingdom between 1965 and 1969. In the country as a whole, the period was one of declining manufacturing employment (see section 2.2.2). However, no less than seven of the eleven regions expanded or at least maintained their manufacturing employment levels, the most rapid and substantial expansion being recorded by East Anglia and Wales. The fact that four of these regions (Wales, Northern England, Scotland and Northern Ireland) were classic peripheral regions is noteworthy. So too is the fact that the South East and West Midlands both recorded a very substantial decline, the former at a percentage *rate,* as well as volume, greater than any other region.

Column B records the regional share (or national growth) component of change in each region. Simply on aggregate national trends, each region should have recorded a manufacturing employment decline of 1.2 per cent over the period. The difference between this regional share value and actual manufacturing employment change (column A) is the total shift recorded in column C. This measures the degree to which each region gained or lost manufacturing employment over the period, relative to all other regions and allowing for national aggregate trends. It will be noted that the sum of all regional total shifts is zero. By definition, positive shifts in certain regions towards a bigger share of the national manufacturing cake are cancelled out by reductions in the share of less fortunate regions.

Columns D and E then divide this total shift into the proportionality and differential shifts. The former is calculated as follows. For each industrial Order (fourteen in this case) in turn, the national rate of change of total manufacturing employment is subtracted from the national rate of change of manufacturing employment in that industrial Order. In the present case, 1969 total manufacturing employment divided by 1965 total manufacturing employment yields a value of 0.9877. In contrast, the same calculation for the first industrial Order only (Order III: food, drink and tobacco) gives a figure of 1.0083. The latter minus the former is +0.0206, which when multiplied by each region's 1965 Order III manufacturing employment in turn yields the contribution of this Order to each region's total proportionality shift. An alternative example of a negative contribution is that of Order X, textiles, where an Order change rate at the national level of 0.9195 yields a proportionality shift parameter of −0.0682 (0.9195−0.9877). This procedure is thus repeated for each Order in each region, and the fourteen values for each region summed to give the total regional proportionality shift. The differential shift is most easily calculated as the residual left when the proportionality shift has been subtracted from the total shift.

The substantive conclusions which can be drawn from columns D and E must of course be carefully qualified by the fact that the analysis is based on broad industrial Orders rather than more meaningful and homogeneous Minimum List Headings. This means that in some regions some part of the apparent differential shift is possibly a product of a particular structural specialization *within* certain Orders. This said, however, the two columns suggest that there was a striking difference in the components of regional manufacturing change between the four classic peripheral regions, Wales, Scotland, Northern England and Northern Ireland, and the two traditional industrial growth regions of the South East and West Midlands. The four former regions all recorded negative proportionality shifts, indicating industrial structures biased towards nationally-declining industries. In Wales, the problem was a specialization in metal manufacturing, in Scotland in textiles, shipbuilding and metal manufacturing. The last two industries were the chief cause of Northern England's negative proportionality shift, with textiles in Northern Ireland.

However, and again in each case, these negative proportionality shifts were in fact offset by substantial positive differential shifts, resulting in positive overall total shifts. The most remarkable case was Wales, which recorded a positive differential manufacturing shift second only in percentage rate and absolute volume to those of East Anglia and the East Midlands respectively. But even in Northern England and Northern Ireland, above-average growth of particular industries resulted in a fairly considerable relative gain, clearly pointing at some additional influence operating to boost manufacturing employment levels in most industries in these regions relative to the rest of the country. The contrast with Thirlwall and Brown's findings of substantial *negative* differential shifts for all employment in several of these peripheral regions before the 1960s is very striking.

The results for the South East and the West Midlands are very different. In both, the total shift is substantially negative. But this is basically a product, not of an unfavourable industrial structure, but of a negative differential shift which in the South East was greater in volume and rate than any other region. Indeed, it could well be that the South East's already massive negative differential understates its actual dimension, since the South East's large positive Order-level proportionality shift, a feature revealed by every single postwar shift-and-share analysis of the region, is generally regarded as understating the region's specialization in faster-growing industries *within* particular Orders (notably engineering and electrical goods, by far the chief contributor to the

South East's large positive proportionality shift). Again, this would seem to be clear evidence of a very powerful force or forces operating to divert potential indigenous manufacturing expansion from these core regions to other areas. The West Midlands' small but negative proportionality shift perhaps bears out fears in the region that a reliance upon traditionally virile but now declining industries such as vehicles is a potentially serious threat to the region's manufacturing prosperity.

The most interesting performances amongst the remaining regions were recorded by East Anglia, the South West and the East Midlands. In each case, a large positive total shift appears almost wholly attributable to a large positive differential shift. While East Anglia may specialize *within* manufacturing Orders upon relatively fast-growing industries (see section 5.3.1), rapid growth in these three regions is thus generally due to non-structural forces. In this connection, their common and close proximity to the South East and West Midlands, a locational attribute which they share with Wales, by far the most rapidly growing peripheral region, is noteworthy.

The two remaining regions, the North West and Yorkshire and Humberside, both recorded negative total shifts, in line with shift-and-share analyses of total employment since 1945. In the latter area this reflected an unfavourable industrial structure, dominated by textiles and metal manufacturing. In the North West, a negative differential shift was chiefly to blame. Admittedly, the NIESR study (Brown 1972, 136–8) concluded that much of the North West's differential shift in the early 1960s actually reflected structural considerations, because of hidden specialization in less-favourable industries at the within-Order level, notably in textiles (see also section 5.3.1). But this has now apparently changed, with a more recent and detailed MLH study (North West Joint Planning Team 1974, 150) concluding that 'the principal cause of the region's poor employment record (over the period 1959–1969) is no longer the structural factor . . . rather, it emerges that the growth of employment has been retarded to a large extent by the performance (i.e. the differential shift) factor'. This finding thus fully corroborates the results for manufacturing alone given in Table 3.2.

3.7. Industrial structure: conclusions

Various conclusions may be drawn from this discussion of the significance of industrial structure for spatial variations in aggregate manufacturing change. In the context of the structural/locational controversy outlined in section 3.4, shift-and-share analyses of regional employment changes up to about 1960 provide considerable empirical support for locational explanations of sluggish and rapid manufacturing growth in peripheral and central regions respectively. These studies of course identify structural factors as playing a considerable part in these differences, particularly when analysis at Minimum List Heading levels is possible. But they broadly agree that additional, regionally specific forces have been operative. The conclusions of the NIESR study for the forty-year period ending in 1961 are particularly significant in this respect.

Since then, and especially since the mid-1960s, however, there has been a dramatic centre-periphery reversal in differential manufacturing shift performance. While proportionality shifts have on the whole continued to favour the centre and constrain the periphery, the opposite now applies with regard to the differential shift component. True, certain regions immediately adjacent to the traditional core regions are recording substantial differential gains, clearly implying some sort of distance-constrained spatial manufacturing diffusion process from the traditional manufacturing centres. But as the 1965–9 manufacturing analysis strikingly reveals, considerable differential gains are now also being achieved by all the classic peripheral regions, most of which have never before during probably the entire twentieth-century recorded differential manufacturing growth. The obvious spatial coincidence of these regions with government-assisted Development Areas suggests a very probable explanation for this reversal.

In view of the emphasis on industrial structure in preceding sections, the last main conclusion which needs stressing might appear somewhat strange. Despite the above findings, it can be argued that *in the long term*, structural factors provide no explanation whatever for spatial manufacturing shifts. The point of this argument is simply that structural analyses by their very nature beg what can be regarded as *the* fundamental question: why *does* a particular area possess a particularly favourable or unfavourable industrial structure in the first place? This basic inadequacy of structurally-focused studies as an approach to long-term explanation of industrial location patterns and trends does not appear properly to have been recognized in the literature. The fairly obvious reason for this is that most shift-and-share analyses, for example, deal only with relatively short time periods, usually of a decade or so: and in the short-run, existing structure, which must be taken as 'given', is clearly an important control on aggregate change. True, several writers have stressed, as does Cameron (1971, 326), that shift-and-share analysis is only 'a standardization technique and not a theory of growth'. But there is little explicit recognition of the more fundamental and clearly long-term question posed above.

The answer to this question would seem logically to involve a choice between alternative explanations. The first is that structure is in fact itself largely the product of locational forces, which in the long term bring about different mixes of industry in different areas. This approach is of course the essence of the locational school's viewpoint, which argues that central, nodal locations afford significant relative advantages to most of the newer manufacturing industries which have sprung up in twentieth-century Britain. At the same time, relative remoteness together with the fossilised character of manufacturing in the periphery acts as a barrier to the ingress of these newer types of enterprise. Proponents of this view accept that chance factors can affect manufacturing location at the local, site-level, scale. But at broader sub-regional and regional scales, identifiable locational controls and forces are viewed as of key importance in shaping industrial structure. As Caesar (1964, 232) argues, 'the location of the Morris car plant in Oxford is frequently quoted as purely fortuitous. It was, but equally fortuitous was the fact that Oxford lies in the southern part of the English Midlands. Had William Morris's original shop been located in some relatively remote part of the country, it is almost certain that any car plant developed from it would have been located in a more central position.' The striking general correlation, discussed in section 5.3.1, between favourable subregional manufacturing structures and location in the South East or West Midlands, is in full accord with this sort of argument.

The second, alternative explanation is that structure and location are un-connected, the former being entirely randomly-determined. Thus Norcliffe (1970, 5.5) argues that 'except at the intra-urban scale, spatial variations in in-dustrial composition are *not* a function of the position of an area within a structured space economy'. Instead, industrial composition may be regarded as 'determined by a random growth process', or chance factors, unrelated systematically to location. As evidence for this Norcliffe cites the 'fortuitous location', of Britain's coalfields in peripheral positions, and his own study of South West England which could detect no spatial regularity whatever in the distribution of proportionality shift values for manufacturing employment change, 1956-64, for 178 areas within the region. However, the latter of course relates to a level of spatial disaggregation at which, as already pointed out, locational protagonists accept the likelihood of chance factors being involved; while Norcliffe's point on the relationship between nineteenth-century in-dustries and Britain's coalfields ignores the undoubted spatial preference of newer twentieth-century industries for centrally-located areas evident in figure 5.3. Indeed, it is obvious that any statistical test for randomness of spatial pattern applied to figure 5.3, such as calculation of the Cliff-Ord spatial autocorrelation statistic, would yield a highly significant non-random value.

At the national level, therefore, the evidence appears to accord with the first explanation, relating long-term structural differences to location. This is not to say that random factors may not sometimes be involved in particular cases, notably where manufacturing activity is only developed on a limited scale. But the evidence suggests that spatial regularities in structure do exist on broad spatial scales, hinting at the underlying and long-term dominance of locational factors. At the same time it must be stressed that the relationship between loca-tion and manufacturing structure appears to be weakening substantially at the present time. This, in effect, is one of the main findings, both of the NIESR in-vestigation (Brown 1972, 147–51) into changes in regional total employment structure, 1953–66, and of the interesting study by Chisholm and Oeppen (1973, 42–73). The latter's analysis of changes in subregional manufacturing structures at the Minimum List Heading level in Britain between 1959 and 1968 concluded that 'there have been strong forces at work leading to convergence in the level of employment specialisation' within the manufacturing sector. In particular, those subregions with the highest specialization levels in 1959 recorded the most rapid shifts towards greater industrial diversification, and hence greater manufacturing similarity to the average national pattern. Moreover, these general conclusions are supported by evidence for particular regions such as the North West, where the North West Joint Planning Team (1974, 150) found from shift-and-share analysis that 'over the period used in our analysis (1959–1969), the structural factor was of diminishing importance (i.e. the region's industrial structure has been coming closer to the national average) while the performance factor was of increasing importance'. This widespread structural convergence process is clearly in part linked with the spatial diffusion, often through physical migration, of manufacturing growth industry discussed in section 6.6. But its effect must be to weaken the hitherto marked traditional twentieth-century relationship between location and manufacturing structure noted earlier.

NOTES

1 Income elasticity of demand refers to the relationship between changes in the level of demand for a good or service and changes in per capita income levels. Products with high income elasticities of demand are those for which rising (or falling) incomes generate a more than proportional increase (or decrease) in demand. A low income elasticity of demand means that income changes have little effect on demand levels. See Chisholm 1970a, 154–8.

2 See, for example, Stilwell 1968, 1969 and 1970; Steed 1967; Smith 1969; Bishop and Simpson 1972; and Randall 1973.

3 Different authorities use different terms for the same component. The discussion here follows Stilwell's nomenclature (Stilwell 1969).

4 The exception was Yorkshire, whose inclusion in the 'overemployed' regions is somewhat arguable.

5 Stilwell's study does not include Northern Ireland.

6 The employment statistics were derived from the Abstract of Regional Statistics, volumes 2 and 6. Major changes in the Standard Industrial Classification in 1969, in the method of employment data collection in 1971, and in official regional boundaries in 1974, rule out analysis of a more recent period.

4 Centre and periphery: alternative models

4.1. The centre-periphery model

The significance of the discussion in chapter 3 for subsequent analysis lies in the conclusion that, particularly in the long run, the basic explanation for national-scale spatial shifts in manufacturing industry should be sought in identifiable locational forces, rather than in random processes or even industrial structure. As noted earlier, most of the wide range of forces discussed in the industrial location literature can be classified into two basic groups, the first of which comprises forces promoting the cumulative and relative manufacturing growth of the dominant, centrally-located, and most prosperous industrial regions of a country. These forces are thus the driving mechanisms of the *centre-periphery model* of manufacturing location dynamics. In Britain, this conceptual model has been applied, implicitly or explicitly, to explain the cumulative twentieth-century growth of manufacturing in the South East and Midlands, and the relative industrial decline of Wales, Northern England, Scotland and Northern Ireland. Amongst the variety of forces put forward as mechanisms for this model, six are perhaps of key importance – market accessibility, innovation leadership, the quality of transport facilities, agglomeration economies, labour supply advantages, and entrepreneurial and institutional factors. Each will be considered in turn.

4.1.1. Market accessibility

Probably the most important single mechanism of the centre-periphery model is the hypothesized powerful attraction of modern manufacturing industry to those areas of a country which are most accessible to regional, national and international markets. The locational pull of the market has of course long been recognized as an important factor in normative industrial location theory. For example, as Hamilton (1967, 372) has pointed out, Weber's classic cost-minimization theory (Weber 1929) in fact recognizes more market-oriented than material-oriented industrial location types, contrary to traditional impressions; while the alternative locational interdependence/market area approach (Hotelling 1929; Lösch 1954) assumed that regional market oligopolistic control was *the* basis for a theory of manufacturing location.

More significantly, perhaps, much empirical evidence also stresses the importance of market accessibility to modern manufacturing industry. Thus for example Smith (1954, 49), reviewing a number of studies of locational decisions by manufacturing firms in the United States, concluded that 'the market emerges as the locational consideration of first importance, regardless of the area studied'. A similar view is expressed by Manners (1972, 2): 'proximity to large or specialised consumer markets ... has emerged as one of the most decisive (location) factors for manufacturing industry' in Britain. This judgment echoes that of numerous earlier commentators[1]. Indeed, it even receives support from industrial location surveys in areas relatively isolated from Britain's major market regions. Thus Loasby's study of industrial movement from Birmingham (Loasby 1961, 309) found that half of all those Birmingham firms which had moved as far away as south Wales expressed dissatisfaction with their new location, and that 'the biggest single cause of complaint seems to have been the inferiority of South Wales as a distributing centre, partly because it is in one corner of the national market, whereas Birmingham is near the centre, and partly because of poor transport facilities'. Similarly, Begg's investigation of existing manufacturing firms in the Tayside region of Scotland discovered (1972, 50) that the locational disadvantage most frequently reported by such firms (70 per cent of his sample) was remoteness, notably from customers and clients, 89 per cent of which were located outside Tayside.

Empirical studies such as these therefore provide considerable support for a centre-periphery model which relates national-scale spatial variations in manufacturing growth to variations in market accessibility. The exact nature of the advantage conferred by maximum market proximity is however more debatable. The traditional and most obvious approach has been to cite assumed transfer cost savings on shipments of finished products to customers. Certainly, such savings may be considerable in particular cases, where products are especially bulky, fragile, perishable or where a plant's scale of output is very large. Thus the Chrysler motor vehicle company, which operates car assembly plants (fig. 7.4a) at both Coventry and Linwood (central Scotland), pointed out in evidence to the Trade and Industry subcommittee of the House of Commons Expenditure Committee in 1972 that '85 per cent of all our domestic sales of cars produced at Linwood are sold to dealers situated within 150 miles of Coventry, whereas only 15 per cent are to dealers within 150 miles of Linwood. As our delivery charges are priced competitively we suffer a cost penalty on the majority of vehicles shipped from Linwood. This has amounted to approximately £2.2 million since 1963, with a recurring annual cost of £400 thousand.' Additional overland cost penalties with regard to shipments to Liverpool and London for export were claimed to have amounted to '£550 thousand with a recurring cost of £100 thousand per annum'. Another example is the furniture industry, the transport of whose bulky products is relatively costly. Indeed, the cost of transport, almost exclusively on finished products, as a percentage of the value of net output for the broader timber and furniture Order (XIV) in 1963 (Chisholm 1971, 231) was the third highest (6.6 per cent) of all industries in the United Kingdom. Not surprisingly, furniture manufacturing is traditionally heavily concentrated in South East England (54 per cent of 1959 UK employment, compared with the region's 29 per cent share of all UK manufacturing employment).

It should be noted with regard to both these examples that most British manufacturers themselves absorb the cost of transporting their finished products within Britain, via the so-called c.i.f. (cost, insurance, freight) pricing system (Smith 1971, 66), and hence charge a uniform delivered price to customers wherever these are situated. This practice, all else being equal, must encourage location of producers (though not consumers: see Chisholm 1970a, 180) at points central to the market served, as in the case of the furniture industry cited above. Moreover, as Edwards and Townsend (1958, 147) argue, and the Chrysler figures suggest, 'the emphasis commonly placed by manufacturers on the advantage of being near to their main markets' might be justified even when transport costs on finished products are only 'a small percentage of turnover', since this 'may be a large amount when converted into £.s.d. and may equally well be expressed as a large percentage of profits' (see also Chisholm 1971, 217–18). Edwards and Townsend also point out that distance from markets may impose extra costs over and above actual transport charges, because of the need for 'larger stocks ... throughout the distribution network', and because 'supply depots have to be set up'. The same kind of conclusion is drawn by Begg (1972, 51) from his Tayside survey: 'long distances between manufacturer and market increase the chances that goods will be subject to costly, time-consuming double handling at transference points and centres of distribution', and this in turn 'may significantly increase the volume of expensive working capital which the manufacturer must find at any one time'.

This all said, however, other evidence reviewed later in section 8.5 suggests that for many firms in a country as small as Britain, the finished product transport cost argument is not particularly convincing as a justification for market proximity. Yet the need for such proximity is still cited with great conviction by many British firms. Thus for example the 1966–7 London Employment Survey revealed that 'access to buyers of product or services' was rated as 'important' to the firm in its present location and 'essential' to its remaining in London by a larger proportion (56 per cent) of the very considerable number of London manufacturing firms investigated than was any other location factor (Hoare 1975, 44–5). The reason for this apparent paradox would seem to lie not so much in crude transport cost differences as in a real but unquantifiable requirement for maximum customer contact and information linkage if the firm is to compete successfully with its rivals for orders and sales. Close and frequent customer contact is undoubtedly seen by many firms, especially smaller firms, as absolutely essential if sales, and hence production and growth, are to be maintained or increased. The importance to the firm of a high intensity of face-to-face contacts has perhaps been underrated by location analysts in the past, because of its subjective nature and measurement difficulties. But most would probably now agree that, as Brown (1969, 778) concludes from a review of postwar industrial location studies in Britain, 'managerial communications with clients, suppliers, sub-contractors, colleagues and various professional services loom large' in location decisions.

When viewed from this particular perspective of sales maximization through close customer contact, the disadvantages of market *in*accessibility may be substantial. Thus the Tayside survey (Begg 1972, 50) pinpointed 'remoteness from the point of view of making personal contacts with customers and suppliers' as one of the three main components in the region's inaccessibility handicap syndrome: while Cameron and Reid's survey (1966, 26–7) of firms which investigated but then rejected a Scottish location found not only that 'the most frequently quoted disadvantage of locating in Scotland was the distance from the main market', but also that one of the major reasons for this was that 'several companies felt that to be too distant from their main customer was likely to affect company *revenue*', by making it more difficult 'to maintain sales at a given level'.

Close market proximity thus permits a frequency and intensity of customer contacts which may be of great significance in winning orders, and is thus highly valued by many manufacturing firms. In one sense, this is likely to be particularly true for smaller firms, which are less able than larger firms to afford to split production and marketing/decision-making functions between two separate units, only the latter of which needs to be market-located (Keeble 1971a, 35–7). However, it has also recently been argued (Norcliffe 1970, 2.7–2.25) that market accessibility is becoming increasingly important in Britain because of the increasing average size of factories. As Chisholm (1970a, 61) shows, large plants are accounting for an ever increasing proportion of total manufacturing employment and, to an even greater degree, output in Britain. In 1935, plants employing 500 or more workers accounted for only 35.4 per cent of total manufacturing employment in Britain. By 1963, this proportion had risen to no less than 51.1 per cent. Lower per unit costs through economies of scale internal to the plant in many industries provides the logic for this trend.

In spatial terms, however, as Norcliffe stresses, this means in effect the concentration of production at one or a few locations serving perhaps the whole national market, in place of a previous pattern of smaller factories, probably dispersed throughout the country in relation to particular regional markets. Norcliffe thus sees the non-spatial trend towards increasing dominance of manufacturing activity by large plants as leading, under free-market conditions, to an increasing spatial emphasis on central locations with maximum access to the whole national market. This argument is moreover supported by empirical evidence such as that provided by Watts' study (1972, 271–2) of the recent spatial impact of increasing plant size and small unit closure in the south Wales brewing industry. Numerous small brewery closures in peripheral areas reflect the general policy adopted by national brewing firms of concentrating investment in large centrally-located plants, such as Whitbread's at Luton, and Watney Mann's at Isleworth, Mortlake and Manchester (Riley 1973, 153–4). Resultant economies of scale in production more than offset additional transport costs to customers.

Applied to Britain, the market accessibility hypothesis clearly implies the concentration of manufacturing growth in the central regions, which are highly favoured as market locations both by the geography of demand and by the spatial configuration of the country's key transport facilities. Thus the South East and Midlands not only contain the bulk of the United Kingdom's population (46 per cent in 1973), but enjoy above-average personal incomes and hence purchasing power per head. In 1971/2, income per head in the South East was £718, compared with a United Kingdom average of £624 and a value in Northern Ireland, the lowest recorded for any region, of only £440. Final demand for manufactured consumer goods is thus concentrated around the London–Birmingham axis. But so too is demand for intermediate or semi-finished goods, a very important aspect of modern manufacturing production. In 1963, no less than 40 per cent of total United Kingdom manufacturing output was sold to other manufacturing firms (Buck and Lowe 1972, 255); and these firms are also concentrated in the South East and Midlands, regions which accounted for 50 per cent of United Kingdom manufacturing net output by value in 1971 (see table 2.1). Moreover, location in these regions provides maximum possible access not just to their own dominant regional markets, but also to wider national and international markets, via the unrivalled communication links and terminal facilities concentrated here (section 4.1.3).

One way of measuring spatial variations in market accessibility is via the concept of 'market potential' (Harris 1954; Olsson 1965). The latter measures the intensity of possible interaction between firms in an area and customers as they are distributed throughout the country. It is usually calculated by a formula such as

$$V_0 = \sum_{i=1}^{k} \frac{P_i}{d_i}$$

where Vo is the potential of area o, P_i is a measure of market demand for area i, and d_i is a measure of distance or cost of movement between area o and area i. Summing for all k areas in a country yields the potential value for o, expressed in arbitrary units. It should be noted that although a measure of movement cost may be used in the calculation, the resultant index is not measuring the total transport cost of serving the whole national market in direct proportion to each area's demands. As Harris (1954, 328) points out, the latter is given by $\sum_{i=1}^{k} P_i d_i$. Rather, market potential assumes a fall-off with distance in the volume of sales proportionate to demand, because of increasing distance costs, an assumption which empirical evidence on marketing patterns for particular firms tends to suggest is more realistic than that implied by the total transport cost calculation. Although not without its critics (Houston 1969), market potential does seem to provide a useful index of spatial variation in market accessibility (Smith 1971, 301–4).

Figure 4.1 maps market or, as they term it, economic potential values for 1960 calculated by Clark and Peters (Clark 1966) from personal income totals by county of Great Britain. Their calculation is particularly interesting in that it incorporates actual freight rates instead of simple distance (Keeble and Hauser 1971, 250) and allows for exports. The latter were included by allocating a notional income value (£3.35 million) to the nearest major seaport, such as London, Southampton or Liverpool. Unfortunately, minor errors in the original calculations mean that some of the peripheral values plotted in figure 4.1 are slightly inaccurate, being inflated by between 5 and 10 per cent.

The pattern is dominated by the ridge of high market potential or accessibility running from London towards Birmingham, with a lower broader extension taking in Manchester and Liverpool. Potential values fall in all directions from this, to minima of less than 55 per cent of the maximum London value in Cornwall, and northern Scotland. West Wales also records very low values. Scotland's general market inaccessibility is clearly apparent. The striking inverse correlation between this pattern and that of 1966 subregional unemployment rates (fig. 4.4b) is worth noting in passing; the actual product-moment correlation coefficient between these two variables, measured over sixty-two subregions, is −0.670.

4.1.2. Innovation leadership

A second hypothesis which may be incorporated in the centre-periphery model of manufacturing growth concerns the adoption and diffusion of innovations. This hypothesis stems from geographical research, notably in Sweden and North America, on the spatial spread of new ideas and techniques within countries, and has only very recently been put forward as an explanation for twentieth-century cumulative central manufacturing growth in Britain

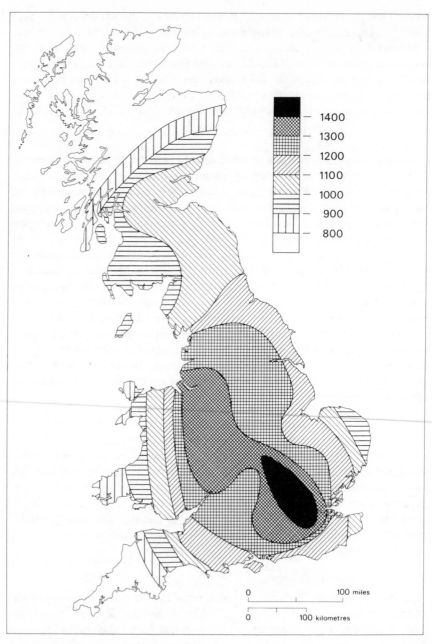

4.1 Market potential in Britain, 1960
Source: Clark 1966

(Norcliffe 1970, 2.36–41; Keeble 1972a, 111–13). Basically, it suggests that many technological and other innovations affecting manufacturing production are first adopted and tested in the central region of a country's space economy, and particularly in its largest metropolis, such as London. These 'entrepreneurial' innovations then spread to other areas, towns and cities according to the two principles of 'hierarchical' and 'neighbourhood' diffusion (Robson 1973, 137). The former means that they then tend to appear at the next lower level of urban centre in the hierarchy – Birmingham, Manchester, for example – then at the next lower level, and so on. The latter means that there also occurs, simultaneously, a more localized spread to much smaller towns and areas immediately adjacent to the initial innovating metropolis.

The explanation for this postulated innovation leadership, with all its implications for manufacturing growth, lies in the crucial advantages enjoyed by entrepreneurs in the dominant metropolis of a central region in terms of *information-maximization* and *risk-minimization*. First, there is no doubt that the availability of information of all kinds even in developed economies such as Britain is spatially biased towards these urban centres, which act as nodal points in national and international information networks and permit maximum intensity of interaction between individuals and hence local transmission of new ideas. Thus, as Lloyd and Dicken (1972, 143) point out, in economies such as Britain 'the volume and range of information is directly related to the hierarchical status of an urban centre'. Or, from the peripheral region viewpoint, 'the persistent problem of slow rates of industrial growth and change in the Development Areas (of Britain) could be as much the result of poor access to specialist information and knowledge as to problems of physical inaccessibility for the transport of goods' (Goddard 1974, 107). This view is strongly endorsed by Pred (1974, 127–30). All else being equal, therefore, invention and innovation are significantly more probable in the 'information-rich', centrally-located metropolis of a given country, such as London.

Second, and of equal importance, these centres are also the least-risk locations for the testing and promotion of entrepreneurial innovations. After all, innovations are by definition new, perhaps completely untried, ideas, techniques or products. To adopt them involves the entrepreneur in much greater financial risks than does the implementation of more traditional ideas or technology. These risks are however reduced if the innovation is first introduced and tested in the country's 'safest' market – its largest urban centre with its surrounding region. In an area such as the London city region, the size and average wealth of the market, people or firms which can be reached by the innovation are greater than anywhere else (see section 4.1.1), while its more cosmopolitan and progressive character increases the likelihood of innovation acceptance. For these two reasons, therefore, of information-maximization and risk-minimization, 'the large urban area would seem to have a great advantage in the critical functions of invention, innovation, promotion and rationalisation of the new' (Thompson 1968, 53). Only at a later stage, when the innovation has become more standardized and accepted, is diffusion to smaller urban centres and peripheral regions feasible.

This hypothesis of central urban area innovation leadership offers an intuitively-appealing explanation for the above-average twentieth-century industrial growth of regions such as South East England. In a modern competitive world, the firm or area which first succeeds in launching a new product, or utilizing a new technology, tends to cream the profits. Subsequent imitators are generally forced to accept much lower rates of return. In Berry's memorable phrase, 'biggest means first, earliest means most'. Thus the high profits and growth rates characteristic of the industrial pioneer may in part explain the remarkable twentieth-century industrial vitality of the regions surrounding London and to a lesser extent Birmingham. In contrast, much lower rates and later-stage adoption of innovations in the peripheral regions may help to explain their 'less efficient, and sometimes outmoded, industrial equipment, lower levels of output, and frequently lower levels of profitability' (Norcliffe 1970, 2.41). Of course, as Pred (1974, 109) has recently stressed, 'the diffusion of manufacturing innovations in well-developed economies is not a catch-all for the spatial manifestation of development'. Many other factors are at work, influencing spatial patterns of manufacturing growth. But specific evidence supporting this hypothesis (reviewed in Keeble 1972a, 111–13) suggests that it is applicable to the British case, and helps to explain twentieth-century industrial concentration in London and the South East.

4.1.3. The quality of transport facilities

Closely interrelated with both the preceding hypotheses as a key factor in the centre-periphery model of manufacturing growth is the impact of the spatial configuration of the national transport network. It is of course true that the pattern of roads, railways, air and sea ports within a country is not in one sense an autonomous, independent, variable, but largely reflects the demand for transport arising from the country's existing spatial distribution of people and economic activity. It is also true that good communications with more central regions are regarded by many as vital for successful industrial growth in the peripheral areas (see section 4.2.4). But it can nonetheless be argued that the configuration and improvement of transport links in Britain tends to increase still further the relative advantages of central as opposed to peripheral regions as a location for new manufacturing industry, all else being equal.

One reason for this is that the central regions, with greater populations and economic activity, usually sustain a denser within-region transport network. For example, in 1973 the South East contained 0.32 kilometres (0.81 miles) of principal and trunk roads per thousand square kilometres (thousand acres), compared with only 0.19 (0.49) and 0.13 (0.34) in Wales and Scotland

Table 4.1 *Car ownership per head of resident population, 1965–73*

	Cars per head, relative to UK average	
Region	1965	1973
North	0.80	0.76
Yorkshire and Humberside	0.90	0.81
East Midlands	1.10	1.09
East Anglia	1.31	1.34
South East	1.10	1.11
South West	1.24	1.31
West Midlands	1.06	1.05
North West	0.83	0.88
Wales	0.98	0.99
Scotland	0.76	0.74
Northern Ireland	0.90	0.84

Source: Abstract of Regional Statistics, 1969 and 1974

respectively.[2] A similar centre-periphery pattern characterizes rail networks, train and bus services, and private car ownership (table 4.1). Indeed, regional differentials in car ownership, which largely reflect income variations,[3] have increased in recent years, despite a vast increase in car registrations nationally (from 8.9 to 13.5 million, 1965–73).

The significance of this denser within-region transport access for regional manufacturing growth lies chiefly in its possible enhancement of manufacturing innovation rates through more frequent face-to-face contacts. As Norcliffe (1970, 2.30) points out explicitly in relation to car ownership patterns in Britain, 'high vehicle ownership rates are part and parcel of a mobile society where ideas circulate rapidly: these are conditions which engender entrepreneurship and innovativeness'. A denser central region transport network must also aid intra-regional industrial linkages, a form of agglomeration economy considered in the next section.

A second and even more important argument focuses on the impact of transport improvements at the between-region scale. This argument is summed up in Manners' claim (1962, 122) that 'the constant improvement of communications within an economy has a powerful centralizing effect upon economic activities'. Empirical observation of the fact that new major transport facilities tend disproportionately to be located, for a crucial and substantial initial period at least, to serve the major central prosperous regions of Britain is only too easy to document. Figure 4.2, for example, depicts the current and planned motorway network of the United Kingdom. Not only was the very first fullscale motorway (the M1) in Britain constructed to link the two leading traditional central manufacturing conurbations of London and Birmingham,

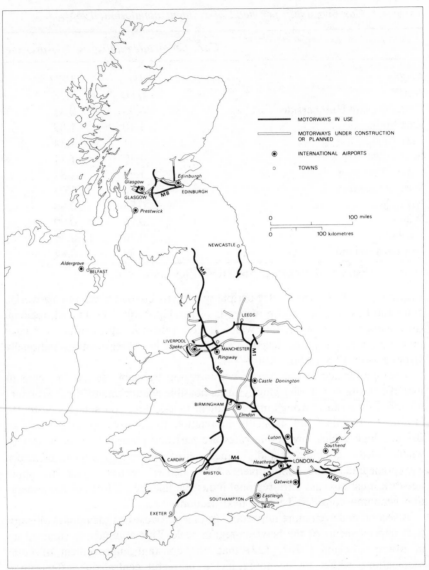

4.2 Motorways and international airports, 1975
Source: Secretary of State for the Environment (1975), *Roads in England
1974–75*, HMSO London, 84 pp.

but the pattern revealed in figure 4.2 is one centred on a four-sided figure linking London, Bristol, Manchester and Leeds, with Birmingham situated at its
heart. The classic peripheral regions are served only by individual extended
links.

Norcliffe (1970, 2.30–31) has actually quantified the resultant spatial variation in accessibility by motorway within England and Wales, based on motorway plans at the end of the 1960s, in terms of Konig's *associated number* accessibility index. The latter is calculated by

$$N^{A_i} = \sum_{j=1}^{n} d_{ij}$$

where the lefthand term relates to the accessibility (A) of node i in network N, and the righthand term is the sum of the shortest distances (d) from i to all other defined nodes (j). Thus the smaller the index, the greater a node's accessibility. On the basis of this very simple measure, Norcliffe shows that the extreme periphery in England and Wales (Cornwall, west Wales and Northumberland) records motorway network accessibility indices of more than 25,760 kilometres (16,000 miles) compared with values of less than 12,880 kilometres (8,000 miles) in the central high-accessibility zone focused on Birmingham and Nottingham. A similar finding by March (1969) is that the central 'backbone' of England between London and Manchester, which contains only about one-third of the land area of England and Wales, will have no less than two-thirds of the total connectivity of the existing or planned motorway and trunk road network, as measured by Kansky's alternative β-value connectivity index.

Disproportionate concentration of rail improvements in the centre, together with declining services in the periphery, are again easy to document. Railway closures in the 1960s following the 1963 Beeching report on the reshaping of British Railways were markedly concentrated in peripheral areas (Caesar 1964, 238). Indeed, as Norcliffe shows (1970, 2.28), areas of England and Wales suffering closure of over 30 per cent of their rail mileage comprised most of the South West, Wales and Northern England east of the Pennines. Cornwall and south-west Wales lost over half of their rail network. Only South East and North West England retained 80 per cent or more of their existing lines. The chief improvements in rail services in the last decade or so have been electrification schemes and the introduction of so-called freightliner services linking special freight terminals in the main industrial centres and certain container ports such as Tilbury, Felixstowe, and Parkeston Quay (Harwich). The latter, which offer a fast delivery service in special liner trains, have had some effect in halting the decline in rail transport's share of United Kingdom freight movement (17.5 per cent in 1974, measured in ton-miles). In 1973, Freightliners Ltd operated 175 different daily services and carried nearly 650,000 containers. But in spatial terms these services were initially at least largely geared to the needs of the existing dominant industrial centres, such as London (three terminals), Birmingham and Manchester (two each). While parts of the periphery have subsequently been connected to the network, large areas

– the South West, central Wales, much of Northern England and Scotland – are still remote from a freightliner terminal. The geography of recent rail electrification schemes is even more strikingly oriented to central areas. Outstanding here is the London-Birmingham-Manchester-Liverpool link, completed in 1967 at a cost of £160 million. This has recently (1974) been extended north to Scotland. But other shorter central area schemes have also been completed or are in progress, notably the £15 million London-Bournemouth project and the £35 million London-Royston scheme (Keeble 1972a, 99–100).

Similar trends characterize seaport and airport development. Since the 1960s, container ports such as Tilbury, Southampton, Felixstowe, Liverpool and Glasgow, have come increasingly to dominate overseas shipments of manufactured goods. A single container berth can handle up to ten times more cargo per day than a traditional berth. However, most of these container facilities, including the two biggest, four-berth, ports of Tilbury and Liverpool, are of course located to serve the central industrial regions (Tanner and Williams 1967, 8–9). So too are the country's major international airports. For the relatively unplanned growth of air transport facilities in the United Kingdom since 1945 has in practice been heavily focused upon South East England (fig. 4.2), with vast expansion of Heathrow, Gatwick and Luton airports. In 1973, these handled no less than 29.7 million passengers, or 67 per cent of the total for all British civilian airports. Heathrow alone, which handled 21 million passengers, now totally dominates international air passenger services to and from Britain, while its air freight shipments render it in value terms Britain's third most important port. Moreover, despite major controversy over the location of new South East international airport facilities, variously proposed for Stansted (Essex), Cublington (Buckinghamshire) and Maplin (Essex), the economic case for such development somewhere in the region appears overwhelming. A notable fact here is that British Airports Authority surveys show that approximately 80 per cent of all international passengers using London's present airports are bound for, or have come from, locations in the South East.

All this empirical evidence suggests the operation of very powerful economic forces favouring central regions in terms of transport improvements. These forces may however be summarized in two words – cost and demand. Motorways, electrified rail links, container and air ports, are all extremely expensive facilities. For example, the 23-kilometre (14-mile) M11 extension around western Cambridge, due for construction by 1979, will cost £1 million per kilometre (£1.5 million per mile) at 1972 prices (Keeble 1974b, 9); electrification between London and Manchester cost over £800 thousand per kilometre (£1.3 million per mile) in 1967. As an inevitable consequence, they are only justified economically where substantial existing demand indicates that they will be utilized fully. However, almost by definition, the greatest demand is concentrated in the densely-populated central regions. So these regions are the first if not the only beneficiaries of major transport investments, linking them still more closely with each other and with the global economy. In turn, these transport improvements enhance the relative potential of these regions for manufacturing growth, by increasing still further their relative accessibility to national and international markets and suppliers,[4] and enhancing possibilities of innovation, especially by the import of new ideas from abroad. This sequence is of course a classic illustration of Myrdal's 'circular and cumulative causation' mechanism at work in a regional development context (Myrdal 1957, 26–34; Keeble 1967, 258). Central region relative advantages in terms of the quality and density of transport facilities are thus an important component of the centre-periphery model.

4.1.4. Agglomeration economies

One of the most long-standing explanations for the concentration of manufacturing growth in large urban areas and their surrounding regions is that such areas offer firms significant external economies of scale in production. Such agglomeration economies may be *general*, in that they are available to a wide variety of industries and firms simply through location in such an area, or *specific* to a particular industry, in that they arise only where there is a considerable clustering of firms in that industry or associated industries (Hall 1969, 60). These two categories have also been termed economies of *urbanization* and *localization* respectively (Townroe 1970, 18), although their undoubted availability today on geographic scales wider than simply urban and local suggests that the former terms are to be preferred. Broadly defined, agglomeration economies are thus cost savings to a firm accruing because of the scale of industry in a particular conurbation or region, and the resultant ability of the firm to share some of its external expenses with others.

The existence and scale of such cost savings is a matter of some debate. As Chisholm (1970a, 71) points out, the short answer to such questions as 'what is the minimum size and population density of a region and the level of development that will confer external economies, how great are these, and at what point do diseconomies begin to outweigh the advantages of further development?' is 'that we do not know'. However, the considerable qualitative evidence for the existence of significant agglomeration economies for manufacturing in the large central regions of the South East and West Midlands (Keeble 1972a, 115–16) has recently been supplemented by important new quantitative evidence, arising from the NIESR study mentioned earlier (Brown 1972, 151–8). In this study, which looked at individual manufacturing industries (MLH level) as well as all manufacturing activity, hypothesized regional agglomeration economies in Britain were measured by the proportion of national employment in the industry concerned in each region. This measure was then included as one independent variable in multiple regression analyses of regional variations in 1954 manufacturing net output per head. The most important finding of these analyses was that, for manufacturing as a whole, net output per head was positively and significantly related to regional employment shares, in accord with the agglomeration economy hypothesis. In addition, positive relationships with the latter measure were recorded for a number of individual industries, such as metal manufacture, engineering, precision instruments, food, drink and tobacco, leather and fur, clothing, and timber and furniture, although only in the last three cases did the relationship achieve the 5 per cent significance level. That more of these industries did not record significant coefficients almost certainly arises, as Brown (1972, 155) confesses, because 'the equations are not formulated in the best way for bringing out the benefits of an industrial complex; high productivity in a particular engineering trade is more likely to be associated with an agglomeration of engineering or other metalworking trades in general than with a large representation of the trade itself in particular'. His basic conclusion, then, in view of this and other imperfections of the analysis, is that 'it is striking that some evidence for economies of aggregation should emerge' (Brown 1972, 156). This is an important finding, substantiating much earlier qualitative work.

The nature of the general manufacturing agglomeration economies which have been recognized in central regions is extremely varied. One example arises from the relatively dense concentration of factory premises in these regions. In 1969, the South East and West Midlands contained no less than 33,600 and 13,600 factories respectively, compared with only 3,200 and 3,700 respectively in Wales and the North. Because of this huge stock of premises, central region entrepreneurs wishing to set up in business for the first time, or firms needing to expand, can usually find premises reasonably close to their homes or former factories more readily than their counterparts in smaller industrial zones; and establishment or movement costs may be reduced accordingly. Even more important, however, is ready access to the great range of specialist ancillary services which have sprung up in the South East and Midlands during the twentieth century to serve manufacturing industry. These include material stockholders, firms engaged in packaging and despatching manufactured exports, road haulage specialists, industrial development and market research consultants, machinery service and repair firms, specialist banking, insurance and financial concerns, industrial advertising and printing firms, and so on. The disproportionate concentration of such activities in the central regions because of the scale of industrial activity there undoubtedly in turn affords external economies to central region industry. So too does the relative concentration of more general higher-order facilities, for similar cost/demand reasons as with transport improvements (section 4.1.3). Examples are universities, polytechnics and technical colleges, exhibition centres such as the new national centre at Elmdon, Birmingham, commercial computer installations, Post Office telecommunication facilities, and innovations and improvements in electricity, gas and fuel supply services. Although often included as agglomeration economies, benefits through readier access to particular types of labour, especially skilled labour, are sufficiently important to be discussed separately in the next section.

Specific agglomeration economies primarily reflect the existence of what is called *industrial linkage*. Industrial linkage is most simply defined as occurring when one manufacturing firm purchases inputs of goods or services from, or sells outputs to, another manufacturing firm. Although early definitions of linkage confined the term specifically to localized flows between firms in the same concentrated and specialized industrial area, linkages can and do occur over considerable distances, and the term is not usually now restricted in this way (Keeble 1969a, 163–4). The most characteristic and important type of industrial linkage is where the sales and purchases involve semi-finished goods or components. The classic example here is the motor vehicle industry, where assembly of a single vehicle, such as British Leyland's Triumph Herald, involves the buying-in of components from as many as 150 other manufacturing firms. Indeed, British Leyland as a whole were making use of no less than 4,000 different manufacturing suppliers in the early 1960s (Turner 1964, 49).

The logic of inter-firm linkages of this kind stems from the economies attainable per unit of output through *specialization*. Given sufficient demand, a firm specializing in the production of a single component, part or process can often achieve a lower cost and higher quality of product than larger vertically-integrated concerns producing a range of individual parts, each on a smaller scale. Of course, successful specialization and associated industrial linkage depends upon minimization of *total* costs, including both production *and* transport of the parts to the customer. All else being equal, therefore, industrial linkage economies are likely to be greatest where distance between supplier and customer is least. Linkage also offers a useful and frequently-employed method of coping with unexpected extra orders, without expensive and time-consuming expansion of the firm's own plant and machinery, through the putting-out of subcontract work to other firms. As with linkage generally, the need for close supervision, dovetailing of production schedules and frequent interchange of information usually results in the choice as subcontractor of a firm which is reasonably accessible to the firm putting out the work. Spatial biases in knowledge of potential subcontractors also work to this end. In turn, subcontracting may offer potential entrepreneurs a foothold in a particular industry from which they may later be able to develop into major end-product manufacturers in their own right.

Empirical investigation of the extent and importance of industrial linkage as an explanation for above-average central region manufacturing growth in Britain has generally taken one of two forms. First, many studies have adopted a micro-level approach, gathering original data on linkage relationships from samples of firms in particular central industrial areas. The earliest such studies (Wise 1951, Beesley 1955, Martin 1961, Hall 1962) investigated the remarkable and often sharply-demarcated 'swarms' of small firms in particular industries which may still be found in inner London – clothing, furniture and precision engineering – and Birmingham – metalworking, jewellery, guns. Their findings on these 'industrial quarters', as they are commonly called, may broadly be summed up by Martin's conclusion (1961, 4) on the inner north-east London case: 'the existence of these quarters at the present time depends on a high degree of specialisation by product and a system where linkages between different firms and activities are strongly developed'.

However, although a fascinating phenomenon, these inner-city quarters are undoubtedly a legacy of nineteenth-century industrial development, and are not generally characterized by twentieth-century growth industries. Linkage patterns in the latter, which have tended to locate in the suburbs and settlements surrounding London and Birmingham, have only recently been investigated in detail (Keeble 1969a, Taylor 1973). The present author's study of industry in suburban north-west London, a major centre of such modern industries as electrical and mechanical engineering and vehicles, examined the local linkage patterns of 153 manufacturing firms operating in this area in 1963. Three main conclusions were drawn from the results. First, taking the area's industry as a whole, *local* linkage relationships were not as developed or significant as in the quarters of inner London. But, and secondly, they did appear to be of importance in the growth of the three key industries mentioned above, particularly through the role of smaller *subcontract* and *engineering service* firms. The latter term refers to firms specializing in particular engineering processes, notably metal-finishing via heat treatment, electroplating etc., and in tool-, jig- and pattern-making. Detailed examination of the activities of these firms led to the conclusion that because of specialization and low unit production costs, 'the existence of a locally dense undergrowth of small "service" (and subcontracting) firms thus represents a most valuable external economy for many larger north west London (engineering) concerns' (Keeble 1969a, 175). Thirdly, the study also however drew attention to the even greater importance of linkages in these industries 'within a wider spatial matrix than north west London', notably that 'defined broadly by South East England and the Midlands'. In other words, the specific external economies associated with linkage in these modern industries can be enjoyed by firms throughout the central regions, and not just those located in particularly concentrated industrial zones such as outer London.

Taylor's recent study (1973) in part confirms these results for the iron-foundry industry of the West Midlands, though with important qualifications. Taylor develops a statistical market interaction model to predict flows of West Midland ironfoundry products on the basis of transport costs and nationwide variations in demand. Comparison of these predictions with actual flows recorded by 103 ironfoundry plants suggested that the latter are far more localized than might be expected. Taylor (1973, 393) interprets this as meaning that 'the benefits offered by the immediately local industrial environment cause West Midlands ironfounders to deal twice as much as would be expected with the local area', these benefits being some form of external economy. He also concludes, as in the north-west London study, that 'the system of local linkage and local integration . . . appears to extend beyond the narrow confines of the conurbation to embrace adjacent areas'. His qualification centres on his finding that local flows are least in that type of ironfoundry production – for the automobile industry – which has grown fastest in the West Midlands in recent years. He therefore argues that local external economies do not seem to explain this above-average growth, unless such economies are regarded as 'behavioural, yielding "psychic" rather than monetary benefits' (Taylor 1973, 399).

A second approach to investigating the extent and importance of industrial linkage in modern industries is the use of macro-level manipulation of aggregate published statistics on linkage and location. The most interesting recent study here is that by Lever (1972b). Lever's approach was to compare the degree of spatial association of pairs of manufacturing industries, defined in terms of sixty-one industrial groups, with the level of each pair's functional, input-output relationships as revealed by national data on inter-industry purchases and sales. The former was measured by correlation coefficients derived from 1966 employment in each industry in each of the sixty-two United Kingdom subregions, the latter by 1963 United Kingdom Census of Production input-output data. In particular, Lever specifically distinguished between the newer expanding and the older declining industries.

His chief finding was that there was indeed a significant relationship between functional linkage and spatial association. For example, purely by chance, one would expect to find that forty-three of the top 10 per cent (183) of pairs of industries in terms of level of spatial association were also significantly related by industrial linkage. In fact, no less than seventy-nine pairs were thus significantly related. However, he also discovered that there were important differences in this respect between newer and older industries. Not only was there 'a general tendency for the expanding industries to be more closely associated spatially than the older declining industries' (Lever, 1972b, 380), but functional linkages seemed to be more important as an explanation for the spatial association of the former than the latter. Thus only 'forty-five per cent of the spatially associated pairs of older industries are functionally linked whereas 62 per cent of the spatially-associated pairs of new industries are' (Lever, 1972b, 381). Of key importance in this difference was a web of functional linkages between different but spatially-associated metalworking industries, including mechanical and electrical engineering, and motor vehicles.

These findings again support the contention that industrial linkages between firms and industries located in the central regions of Britain are highly developed, yield specific external economies of agglomeration, and are one factor in above-average twentieth-century manufacturing growth.

4.1.5. Labour supply advantages

The nature of centre-periphery differentials with regard to labour supply factors is complex. While the labour force available in central regions possesses certain characteristics, considered here, which encourage manufacturing growth in these regions rather than the periphery, other labour factors are key components of the alternative periphery-centre model (see section 4.2.1). Central region labour advantages may be summarized under the headings of *quality* and *skills*.

Many observers have argued that the quality of the workforce available in South East England and the Midlands, in terms of productivity, attitude to work, reliability and general efficiency, is greater than that of labour in the peripheral regions. Indeed, on a more theoretical basis, Myrdal's seminal inter-regional economic growth model (1957, 27) postulates selective migration from periphery to centre of the more enterprising and higher quality workers of the former as one of the key mechanisms explaining cumulative industrial growth in the latter (Keeble 1967, 259). Labour quality is extremely difficult to measure objectively; but two types of evidence provide some support for this argument. The first are official statistics on such measurable labour quality indices as rates of absence from work and general educational attainment. Table 4.2 shows that in 1971 three of the four regions recording the lowest rates of absence from work were central regions, namely the East Midlands, the South East and East Anglia (the fourth was Scotland). Conversely, three of the four regions recording the highest rates of absenteeism were peripheral regions, namely Wales, the North West and the North (the fourth was the West Midlands). While the explanation for this pattern is undoubtedly complex, and may be linked for example with the type of industry in different regions, these figures do lend general support to the hypothesis that there is a favourable attitude to work in the central regions.

Table 4.2 also presents statistics on full-time students as a percentage of regional population. The South East records by far the highest values, although the West Midlands is again a major anomaly. All the peripheral regions record percentages lower than the national average, the Welsh figure being particularly low. While the very high South East figure is of course partly a reflection of the concentration of institutions of higher education in the region, to which students come from other areas, this concentration also reflects the much higher proportion of the South East's own young people who elect for full-time higher education compared with other regions (Keeble 1968b, 69). The important point, however, is that many of the students who are trained in

Table 4.2 *Selected labour quality indicators, by region of Great Britain*

	Absences from work, 1971 %*	Full-time students, 1972 %**	
		male	female
North	18.7	3.46	2.12
Yorkshire and Humberside	17.5	3.08	2.65
East Midlands	14.4	4.02	3.09
East Anglia	15.8	3.73	3.28
Greater London	15.6	5.91	4.49
Rest of South East	16.4		
South West	17.4	5.21	3.22
West Midlands	19.9	1.15	3.33
North West	20.0	3.87	2.95
Wales	20.4	2.31	2.31
Scotland	15.8	3.55	3.27
Great Britain	17.4	4.89	3.76

* Percentage of all persons working in each region absent in reference week, for reasons of illness, holiday, strike, etc., or personal considerations
** Students aged 18–20 on full-time courses in the region, as a percentage of extimated total resident population aged 18–20
Sources: Central Statistical Office, 1974, *Social Trends*, table 47; 1974, *Abstract of Regional Statistics*, table 37

the South East move into the region's labour force on completing their studies. In terms of educational attainment, then, these figures imply that the South East's workforce is more highly educated than is the case with other regions.

The second type of evidence on regional variations in labour quality is that provided by surveys of manufacturing firms which have moved production, by complete transfer or branch factory establishment, from the central to the peripheral regions. The significance of this evidence is of course that these particular firms are in a position accurately to compare their direct experience of the labour force in the two types of location. Two studies are of especial interest in this context. The first is the massive ILAG survey of all mobile manufacturing firms which established factories in new locations of the United Kingdom[5] between 1964 and 1967 inclusive, and were still operating in 1969, when the survey was carried out (Department of Trade and Industry 1973, 633). Among the many questions asked by this survey was the following: 'how do you think labour costs per unit of output compare with those at your first location now?' This question clearly is concerned with general labour productivity. Admittedly, Luttrell's much earlier study (1962) of factory movement to the assisted areas in the late 1940s did reveal that labour productivity in such new plants was initially low because of the problems of movement and labour training, but rose to levels comparable with those in the old location after a few years. Some might therefore argue that the relatively short time between the date of the ILAG survey and movement for some of the firms included could have resulted in answers unrepresentative of the eventual longterm labour productivity situation. Against this, however, is the fact that the comparison here is between moves to the Development Areas, and those to more central locations. There is no reason to think that this time-lag operates differentially for the two types of move.[6]

The answers to this question revealed a striking difference in experience between firms in these two movement destination categories. For all cases, the percentage of respondents replying 'higher', 'the same' and 'lower' were 32, 32 and 36 respectively. However, for moves to those peripheral regions for which figures are given, the percentages were: South West, 39, 26, 35; North West Development Area, 50, 17, 33; Northern England, 29, 27, 44; Scotland, 40, 27, 33; Development Areas as a whole, 44, 25, 31. Thus in four of these five destinations, per unit labour costs were judged to be higher than in the previous location by a proportion of respondents significantly greater than the national average. The North West and overall Development Area cases are particularly striking. Moreover, exactly the opposite experience was reported by moves, generally intra-regional moves, to destinations in central regions. For the three regions distinguished, the figures are: East Anglia, 18, 41, 41; East and West Midlands, 26, 33, 41; South East, 25, 41, 34. The first two of these thus recorded significantly fewer and more respondents in the 'higher' and 'lower' cost categories respectively than the national average, while the former though not the latter was also true of the South East.

The other mobile firm study throwing light on labour quality differentials is Green's most interesting analysis of eighty-two manufacturing firms which moved from the South East and West Midlands to Development Area locations in England and Wales between 1967 and 1970 (Green 1974, 273–82). Of these the bulk (sixty-eight) were from the South East, while the Development Area destinations most represented were the South West (thirty-one moves), the North East (twenty-one moves) and south Wales (twenty moves). The novelty of Green's analysis lies in his use of a sophisticated scaling technique, which he applied to judgments by each firm, recorded on a seven-point graded scale from 'favourable' to 'unfavourable', on fifteen different attributes of both its old and new locations. The technique allowed him to telescope the eighty-two replies to a single quantitative value for each attribute, this being accurately positioned relative to a zero indicating the 'neither favourable nor unfavourable' situation. The distance of the value from this zero in either direction thus measured the degree of 'favourableness' or 'unfavourableness' attached to each attribute in each location.

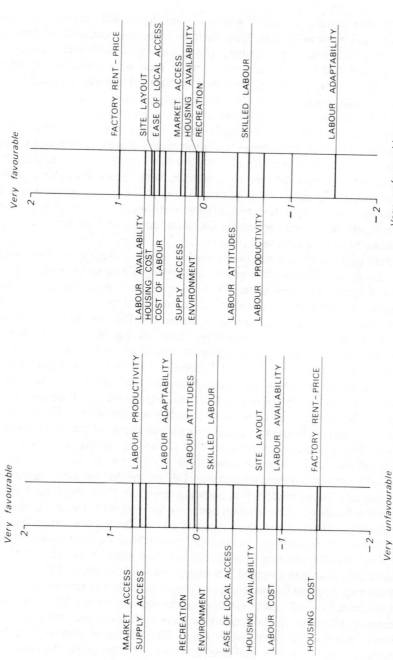

FORMER LOCATION

NEW LOCATION

4.3 Locational evaluation of central and peripheral manufacturing areas: Green's survey results
Source: Green, 1974

Green's results, recorded graphically in figure 4.3, reveal fascinating differences in the evaluation, from direct and personal experience, of firms' old and new locations. In the former, six attributes were on average regarded as being favourable; and no less than three of these were characteristics of the labourforce – its productivity (ranked second), adaptability (ranked fourth) and attitude (ranked sixth). Not surprisingly in view of earlier comments, market access was accorded the most favourable rating of any attribute, with supply access (industrial linkage?) third. In the new Development Area locations, however, the judgement of firms on the above three labour attributes was completely reversed. Of only four attributes rated as unfavourable, three were precisely these labour characteristics, with labour adaptability in particular recording an 'unfavourableness' rating as low as any attribute in either location. This independent and striking confirmation of the ILAG survey results provides strong support for the labour quality and productivity component of the centre-periphery model.

Skill differentials are however probably almost as important. The centre's success in attracting modern growth industries, its innovatory leadership, and its dominance of national decision-making in many different spheres, have resulted in turn in a concentration here of at least three types of skill of great importance for continuing manufacturing growth. The first is production skills in modern, science-based industries such as electronics and electrical engineering. The early concentration of innovation and development in the electronics industry in South East England, for example, now means that this area possesses an above-average concentration of skilled and semi-skilled workers in this rapidly-developing (see table 3.1) and highly labour-intensive industry. One simple way of measuring such a concentration is by its *location quotient*. This is obtained by calculating the percentage of the national total of a particular group of workers found in a given area, and the percentage of the national total of *all* workers found there. The former is then divided by the latter. A location quotient greater than 1.00 means that the area's labourforce is unusually biased towards that particular group. In 1971, the South East and West Midlands recorded location quotients for workers in Order IX, electrical engineering including electronics, against a Great Britain base, of no less than 1.22 and 1.38 respectively. In contrast, two of Britain's three main peripheral regions recorded location quotients of less than unity (Wales 0.86; Scotland 0.66), only Northern England recording a value above this (1.12).[7] As far as South East England is concerned, an even more marked concentration is found in the science-based instrument engineering industry (Order VIII), the region recording a location quotient of no less than 1.57, compared with only 0.76 in Wales and 0.45 in Northern England. The anomalies here are the West Midlands, with only 0.38, and Scotland, with 1.26. But taking the central and peripheral regions together, the differential is clear.

A second, and very important, type of skill which is unusually represented amongst the centre's workforce is that possessed by research scientists and technologists. This bias reflects the remarkable concentration of industrial and government research laboratories in the South East and, to a lesser extent, the West Midlands. As Buswell and Lewis (1970) demonstrate, these two regions contained in 1968 no less than 48.6 and 8.9 per cent respectively of all industrial research institutions in the United Kingdom, both public and private. Wales, the North, Scotland and Northern Ireland contained *between them* only 14.8 per cent. For private industrial research laboratories, by far the most important single component, the differential was even greater, the central and peripheral regions specified above containing 67.6 and 14.0 per cent respectively. The centre's remarkable concentration can itself be explained by its attractiveness in terms of information linkages, national and international accessibility, residential environment and its dominance as a location for Britain's most research-oriented modern growth industries. But in turn, of course, the concentration of research skills here must result in a higher entrepreneurial innovation rate than in the peripheral areas, with all the implications this has for manufacturing growth. While more is sometimes made of the relationship than is warranted by its actual scale, it is true that 'spin-off' of entrepreneurial innovations emanating from individuals associated with Cambridge University, one of the world's leading scientific research centres, has resulted in some industrial growth in and around Cambridge itself (Cameron 1965; Lewis 1974, 327–32). Examples include the establishment in 1881 of Cambridge Scientific Instruments Ltd, which manufactures medical and scientific research equipment, and more recently of such small firms as Techne Ltd of Duxford (chemical research equipment), Torvac Ltd of Histon (vacuum equipment) and Metals Research Ltd of Melbourn (metallurgical research equipment).

A third category of skill which is unusually concentrated in the centre is that of managerial expertise. The relative concentration of administrators and managers here is clearly indicated by 1971 location quotients for this category of workers (Order XXIV of the Occupational Classification) of 1.27 and 1.05 respectively for the South East and West Midlands. In contrast, location quotients for the North, Wales and Scotland were all below unity (0.87, 0.92 and 0.96 respectively). Moreover, as Westaway (1974, 66–7) has shown, recent years have witnessed a marked trend towards an *increasing* concentration of such workers in the central regions, particularly South East England, relative to the periphery. This clear spatial differential, which applies just as much to industrial and commercial managers as to administrators in government and public services, must again have significant implications for the spatial pattern of manufacturing efficiency, productivity and growth.

4.1.6. Entrepreneurial and institutional factors

The last component of the centre-periphery model distinguished here is the entrepreneurial and institutional differential. Though extremely difficult to quantify, it seems arguable that the central regions enjoy advantages for growth because of the relative concentration of entrepreneurial talent and ability here, and because the institutional environment is more conducive to innovation, risk-taking and new enterprise than it is in the peripheral regions. A concentration of potential entrepreneurs – the individuals who bear the responsibility and financial risks of establishing and directing new firms – is strongly suggested by the concentration, already demonstrated, of professional, managerial and skilled manufacturing workers, from whose ranks entrepreneurs are most usually drawn. It is also implied by the bias in population migration to the South East in favour of younger, and therefore possibly more enterprising, individuals. As Brown (1972, 259) points out in discussing the 1961–6 period, while inter-regional migration in the United Kingdom is generally heavily biased towards younger people of working age, there are some significant regional variations on top of this. In particular, 'the South East is a great magnet for the young . . . with those aged 15 to 24 about 20 per cent more numerous among its incomers than they are among inter-regional movers generally'. The role of the Civil Service and the major industrial and commercial corporations, with their London-oriented university and school-leaver recruitment policies, may well be significant here. Looking at the *net* balance by age of in- and out-migration, Brown (1972, 260) also concludes that 'the net losses of the North and South . . . were proportionately higher in men of working age than in women, children and retired men'. In contrast, 'the South East was a net gainer of men of working age from the rest of the country'. These findings, which are in close accord with the selective migration hypothesis of Myrdal's inter-regional economic growth model (section 4.1.5), also provide general support for the hypothesis of centre-periphery differentials in potential entrepreneurship.

Differentials in institutional environment may also be put forward, however, as a component of the centre-periphery model. Workers in other countries, such as Perroux (1955, 102) and Chinitz (1961), have drawn attention to the considerable institutional barriers to new enterprise in areas such as the Ruhr and Pittsburgh resulting from over-specialization in monolithic nineteenth-century industries such as iron and steel. This contrasts with the situation in more highly-diversified industrial cities such as New York and London (Keeble 1972a, 108–11). Manners (1972, 44) argues that this also explains sluggish industrial growth in Britain's peripheral regions, in that 'with the industrial revolution, these regions attracted and prospered with a group of industries which by and large were oligopolistic in structure, and in which entrepreneurial decisions were concentrated in relatively few hands. Their societies, as a consequence, were denied a widespread tradition of enterprise', while in addition, they 'did not develop institutions and traditions which made capital readily available to the small man anxious to pioneer a new enterprise'. This verdict echoes that of Steed and Thomas (1971, 358) on the reasons for Northern Ireland's inadequate postwar rate of industrial development, one of which has been the 'sad dearth of new entrepreneurs of local origin. The paucity of such people was certainly a function of the region's cultural and industrial heritage, particularly its narrow range and type of industries as well as their organisation'. This institutional environment differential also extends to the cost of capital for new industrial development. In 1972, a survey by *The Times* reported that the commercial interest rate on loan finance for industrial development in South East England was only $7\frac{3}{4}$ per cent, compared with a figure of over 9 per cent for what were presumably regarded as higher-risk projects in peripheral regions such as the North and Wales. In various ways, therefore, there seems little doubt that an unfavourable institutional environment and limited entrepreneurial opportunities have been an important factor retarding manufacturing growth in the periphery of the United Kingdom.

4.2. The periphery-centre model

Despite the dominance of cumulative central concentration as the chief industrial location trend of the first half of the twentieth century in Britain, recent studies have begun to draw attention to the existence of centrifugal forces promoting, at long last, the converse trend of relative industrial decentralization to the periphery. The *periphery-centre model*, as it may be termed, thus postulates a shift in the spatial balance of industrial growth from the centre to the periphery as a consequence both of free-market forces and of government intervention. The most important mechanisms of this model may be considered under the headings of labour supply advantages, agglomeration diseconomies, physical resource access, and government regional policy.

4.2.1. Labour supply advantages

That labour supply advantages should somewhat paradoxically figure in both the centre-periphery and periphery-centre models has already been noted (section 4.1.5). The key to this paradox is however Green's diagram (fig. 4.3). As this shows, peripheral area disadvantages of labour productivity, adaptability and attitudes are apparently coincident with peripheral area advantages in terms of labour *availability* and *cost*. The former was ranked second in overall relative 'favourableness' of all Development Area locational attributes by the firms investigated, the latter sixth (out of eleven 'favourable' attributes). Moreover, these two labour variables were also, and conversely, rated as highly *unfavourable* with regard to firms' previous locations, only two other attributes being regarded with stronger disfavour. It would thus appear that greater labour availability and lower wage costs represent an important stimulus to peripheral area manufacturing growth *vis-à-vis* the central regions.

This view is fully endorsed by other evidence. Greater labour availability in the peripheral areas has been suggested, for example, by official unemployment and activity rate statistics ever since the 1920s. As a simple illustration, figure 4.4 plots unemployment rates and totals for the subregions of the United Kingdom in June 1966. The remarkable centre-periphery pattern of the rate map has already been noted (section 4.1.1). While central subregions such as the West Midlands conurbation, Greater London and the Outer Metropolitan Area recorded unemployment rates as low as 0.46, 0.62 and 0.62 per cent respectively, Tyneside, Clydeside, the south Wales valleys and Northern Ireland were experiencing rates of 2.19, 2.61, 3.50 and 6.11 per cent respectively. In absolute terms, these last four peripheral areas between them contained 80,000 registered unemployed workers, while the Development Area subregions as a whole accounted for 148,000 or 52 per cent of the United Kingdom total. London's apparently substantial pool of unemployed workers is chiefly a reflection of its exceptionally large total workforce, and is somewhat misleading as a guide to labour availability there.

Moreover, these crude unemployment figures make no allowance for workers, especially female workers, who never bother to sign on as unemployed because they know there is little or no prospect of local employment. In 1961, male activity rates, measured as the percentage of total males of working age who are either at work *or* registered as unemployed, varied only very slightly between regions (Brown 1972, 206). However, *female* activity rates ranged from 42 per cent in both the London and South East and West Midland regions, to only 31 per cent in the North and South West and 28 per cent in Wales (Brown 1972, 208). As a result, Brown (1972, 213) estimates on the basis of 1966 figures that

> raising the age-specific activity rates to those of the region where they are highest (the South East for the two younger age-groups, the North West and the West Midlands for the two older ones respectively) would increase female employment in the United Kingdom by some 884,000. This is about 3.4 per cent of the total economically active population (of both sexes), and more than twice the registered unemployment at the census date. The levelling-up we have postulated would raise the active populations of the regions by proportions varying from a negligible one in the South East to 8.9 per cent in the North, 9.0 per cent in East Anglia, 9.9 in the South West, 10.2 in Northern Ireland and 12.8 in Wales.

On this basis, Brown estimates the inactive potential female labour reserve of the four main peripheral regions plus the South West as no less than 595,000 workers (in 1966), or 67 per cent of the United Kingdom figure. The periphery-centre differential in potential labour availability is strikingly illustrated by these calculations.

Official statistics also support the hypothesis of periphery-centre differentials in wage costs. For example, in April 1973, average gross weekly earnings for full-time manual men aged twenty-one and over were £39.30 and £40.30 in the South East and West Midlands respectively, but only £38.70, £37.90 and £37.10 in Wales, the North and Scotland respectively.[8] Female earnings ranged from a South East maximum of £20.90 per week to a Welsh minimum of £18.80. Moreover, adjustment for differences in regional industrial structure, as carried out by Brown (1972, 60) for 1961 male manual earnings per employee, does not fundamentally alter this pattern. 'Levels within industries in the South East and the Midlands are significantly above the national average, those in Scotland and the South West significantly below. There are to some extent generally high-earnings and low-earnings regions.' Admittedly, the regional variations are not nearly as great as those for labour availability. But they are sufficient to suggest some relative encouragement of manufacturing growth, especially perhaps of labour-intensive industries, in peripheral rather than central regions.

Micro-level evidence from firm surveys both on the fact, and significance for growth, of greater labour availability in the periphery is overwhelming. The fact of the differential is neatly illustrated by the ILAG survey (Department of Trade and Industry 1973, 617), which revealed that a much higher proportion of peripheral area moves reported an 'easier' labour situation in their new as compared with their old location, than was the case with moves to central areas. Thus the relevant percentages for moves to Wales, Scotland and the North were 63, 57 and 59 respectively, while those for moves to the Midlands and South East were only 41 and 50 respectively. The significance for growth of this differential lies in its great importance as a factor encouraging the physical migration of existing manufacturing firms from the centre to the periphery. This component of manufacturing change is considered in detail in chapter 6. But it must be noted here that every single survey of such movement since 1945 has pinpointed greater availability of labour as one of the key influences, and often the single most dominant one, on locational choice (Keeble 1971a, 43; 1974a, 31). Moreover, this micro-level finding has been directly substantiated by macro-level regression model analysis of spatial variations in peripheral-area manufacturing migration flows (Keeble 1972b). The ILAG survey's findings on reasons given by firms for selection of their new location may be used as an illustration. At a general nationwide level, and of no less than 632 firms replying, 'a far higher proportion ... regarded availability of labour as the outstanding single influence on their choice than so regarded any other factor' (Department of Trade and Industry 1973, 574). Moreover, peripheral assisted-area movers reported this factor as a major influence on their locational decision far more frequently (80 per cent of cases) than did firms moving, for example, to new locations in the West Midlands or South East (59 and 63 per cent respectively). This very high assisted-area response rate was surpassed only, and marginally, by the frequency of a positive response on the availability of government financial inducements (see section 4.2.4).

Survey evidence on the impact of favourable labour cost differentials on peripheral manufacturing growth is much less impressive. True, the ILAG survey revealed (Department of Trade and Industry 1973, 629) that firms which had moved to Wales and Northern England reported a more favourable wage-cost situation than did those moving to sites in central regions. Percentage replies of 'higher', 'the same' and 'lower', in answer to a request for a comparison of rates of pay in the new and old locations, by firms in the former two regions were 5, 63, 32 and 3, 68, 29 respectively. In slight contrast, the pattern of replies by movers to the South East and Midlands was 11, 63, 26 and 17, 61, 22 respectively. But these differences are very small, and are in any case offset by the fact that in Scotland and Merseyside 17 and 23 per cent respectively of movers reported *higher* rates of pay than formerly! Moreover, only a tiny handful of ILAG firms volunteered the factor of low wage costs as an influence on their locational choice. Admittedly, the survey did not ask a specific question on this point, and a higher response rate might have been expected if it had (Department of Trade and Industry 1973, 591). In addition, there is evidence for the impact of low wage costs on the movement to the periphery of firms in certain labour-intensive industries such as electronics (Keeble 1968a, 16) and electrical engineering (Cameron and Clark 1966, 96), whose cost structures and profit margins are peculiarly susceptible to wage costs. But for manufacturing in general, the ILAG and most previous surveys (Keeble 1968a, 31; Cameron and Clark 1966, 94) do suggest that this factor is not of great significance as an element in the periphery-centre model.

4.2.2. Agglomeration diseconomies

That beyond a certain concentration level agglomeration economies may give way to agglomeration *dis*economies has been recognized for many years (Weber 1929). Evidence for the impact of such diseconomies in the British case is however relatively recent. Their existence is most apparent with regard to the two central industrial conurbations of Greater London and the West Midlands, rather than surrounding settlements; while to a lesser extent they also appear to characterize certain older industrial conurbations of the intermediate and peripheral areas, such as Manchester, west Yorkshire, Clydeside and Tyneside. But in general it can be argued that regional-scale diseconomies of agglomeration in the South East and Midlands do exist as an influence promoting relative peripheral manufacturing expansion. In one sense, of course, the labour shortages and higher labour costs already discussed are very important examples of such agglomeration diseconomies. However, the diseconomies which will be considered here stem from two factors – the very high cost of land and premises, and to a much lesser extent at the between-region scale, the relative congestion and age of buildings. These affect the cost and efficiency of manufacturing both directly and indirectly through their impact on the labour situation already discussed.

Of direct significance is the considerable current centre-periphery differential in factory and industrial land costs. This reflects variations in demand, government controls on factory construction, and the inelastic supply of land in major conurbations such as London. In 1973, average rents per square metre per annum for new industrial units advertised by Richard Ellis Ltd, one of the country's largest private property and development consultants, ranged from over £10.80 (£1.00 per sq. ft per annum) in Greater London and over £7.50 (70p) throughout the rest of the South East, to less than £6.50 (60p) in the South West, Wales and the North, and less than £5.40 (50p) in Scotland, Cumberland and south west Wales (Wray, Markham and Watts 1974, 162). In selected parts of London and surrounding areas such as Watford, rents were as high as £21.60 per square metre (£2.00 per sq. ft). Not surprisingly, therefore, no less than 88 per cent of those ILAG survey firms which selected a new location in a Development Area reported paying lower rents than would have obtained for similar premises in their previous location. Factory purchase costs exhibit a similar marked gradient, with 93 per cent of firms with an origin in South East England reporting lower costs in their new location (Department of Trade and Industry 1973, 652), most of which must have been in peripheral areas. While cheap assisted-area government factories play an important role in this differential, the Ellis figures confirm that it also applies to privately-built premises.

Moreover, it can be argued that this factory/land cost gradient may well be becoming more important as a locational consideration for modern industry, for at least two reasons. One is the steady increase in factory space requirements per employee in many types of modern industry. Thus between 1960 and 1969, the area of new factory floorspace actually constructed in Great Britain rose from only 60 square metres (647 sq. ft) per employee involved to no less than 70 square metres (751 sq. ft), an increase of 16 per cent. In the South East and West Midlands, regions which have undoubtedly been in the forefront of trends towards increasing mechanization, capital/labour substitution and hence a rising floorspace/employee ratio, the figure increased very substantially indeed, from 46 to 140 square metres (498 to 1,511 sq. ft) per employee, and 75 to 190 square metres (808 to 2,040 sq. ft) per employee, respectively.[9]

The other reason is that the land/factory cost differential is now so considerable as to encourage centrally-located manufacturing firms to sell their existing site, often for residential or commercial redevelopment, for a very considerable sum, which can then be used to purchase an entirely modern factory and machinery in a peripheral area while still leaving surplus capital for other purposes (Keeble 1968a, 33). This trend could also have been accentuated in recent years by the national trend towards multi-plant firms, and increased government company taxation and hence low profit levels from which to finance new investment. Multi-plant firms are of course uniquely able directly to compare operating costs and benefits in different locations, and to appreciate the potential capital locked up in a London or South East factory site (Keeble 1971a, 33). At the same time, it has been argued that the imposition of corporation tax in the mid-1960s coupled with relatively sluggish home demand for manufactured goods since then has reduced the profitability of many manufacturing companies, thus perhaps enforcing reappraisal of alternative sources of capital for new investment such as that represented by an existing highly valuable factory site.

Unfortunately, very recent surveys of manufacturing location decisions are not available by which to test whether the land/factory cost differential is now of greater importance than formerly. A hint, though no more than this, is provided by Green's survey (fig. 4.3) of 1967–70 Development Area moves, where the lowest and highest favourability rating respectively of any attribute in the former and new location situations was recorded by the rent or price of factories, a fairly striking contrast. However, for the postwar period before the mid-1960s, industrial migration studies suggest that this consideration was of only limited significance in manufacturing location change. For instance, the present author's survey of industrial movement from north-west London (Keeble 1968a, 31–3) found that only ten of the forty-four cases of movement to peripheral regions studied mentioned cheapness of factory premises as a reason for their locational choice; and none of these regarded it as the most important factor. Cameron and Clark (1966), the ILAG survey (Department of Trade and Industry 1973, 591) and Morley and Townroe's study of moves to the North (1974, 21) appear to rate factory cost differentials even lower than this. This agglomeration diseconomy factor is perhaps therefore best viewed as only a minor component of the periphery-centre model, though its importance may possibly be growing.

Direct agglomeration diseconomies through acute building congestion, which prevents factory extension and accentuates space shortages experienced by expanding firms, are confined to the older industrial conurbations of London and Birmingham, together with the major industrial cities of both the intermediate and peripheral areas. So too is the impact of a high proportion of older, often multi-storeyed, premises which require expensive maintenance and are ill-designed for modern flowline production methods. These two related diseconomies thus tend to influence periphery-centre dispersal at the within-region, rather than between-region scale (Keeble 1974a, 25). While of great importance in explaining locational trends at the former scale, and the substantial absolute industrial decline of London and Birmingham, they do not therefore fit neatly into the national-scale periphery-centre model except in so far as they encourage existing industry in these central conurbations to look for a new location and therefore render them susceptible to influences promoting choice of a peripheral area.

The most important *indirect* impact of agglomeration diseconomies in central regions operates through exceptionally high housing and travel costs (Brown 1972, 79) for workers and industrial decision-makers. Thus in the last quarter of 1974, the average price of new houses for which mortgages were provided by the Nationwide Building Society was no less than £14,153 and £13,176 respectively in the Society's London and South Eastern and Southern regions, compared with only £8,732 and £8,297 in the North East and Northern Ireland.[10] New houses in London were thus 71 per cent more expensive than in Northern Ireland, partly as a result of higher land costs (28 per cent and 15 per cent respectively of the average house price). Green's survey (fig. 4.3) of industrialists involved in moves from South East England (and to a lesser extent the West Midlands) not surprisingly reveals a very high unfavourable rating for the housing cost attribute in the former location, together with a reasonably high favourable rating in the new Development Area location.

High housing costs in South East England of course reflect exceptional twentieth-century population growth, high regional incomes and a relatively fixed supply of housing land, especially in and around London. Their significance for industrial location, however, is that they encourage migration of workers and industrialists to other regions, where houses are cheaper. Thus Hall (1975) concludes that Greater London's massive net emigration in 1966–71 of 475,000 people was dominated by a loss of younger couples 'driven out of London by housing problems – above all, high prices'. Migration losses from London, and indeed from the South East as a whole, which recorded the biggest net loss by migration in 1966–71 of any British region (46,630), must obviously exacerbate the region's already acute labour shortage, all else being equal. In this connection, it is interesting to note that no less than 30 per cent of the Hatfield Polytechnic's 1970–72 survey of 438 Hertfordshire industrial firms reported shortages of workers' housing as a noteworthy problem, in relation to significant labour recruitment difficulties (Wray, Markham and Watts 1974, 135).

High travel costs incurred by workers in the South East probably also contribute to these difficulties, by increasing wage demands and costs relative to other regions (Brown 1972, 157). Thus in 1972–3, South East households spent on average £6.11 per week on transportation, compared with only £4.77 in Wales, £4.63 in Scotland and £3.83 in Northern England.[11] Related time and energy costs of enforced longer distance South East commuting, especially to London (Brown 1972, 79–80), also encourage migration by workers and their families to towns and regions where much shorter journeys to work are possible. In these ways, agglomeration diseconomies in South East England act to intensify labour shortages and increase wage costs, thereby indirectly enhancing peripheral labour advantages for manufacturing growth.

4.2.3. Natural resource access

Nineteenth-century industrial growth in Britain's peripheral areas was a direct reflection of their access to two key natural resources, coal and deep water for overseas shipments and trade. While the former has long ceased to be of great significance for the location of industry, the latter has assumed new importance in recent years. The reason for this is the remarkable increase in the scale of imported raw materials of all kinds for industry since the second world war. Most striking here is the growth of crude petroleum imports, which have expanded from only 28 million tons in 1957 to 115 million tons in 1973. But considerable increases have also taken place in the import of high-quality iron ore, alumina and other metallic minerals. Moreover, these increases have been accompanied by a remarkable growth in average size of ocean bulk carriers, prompted by the substantial economies of scale which accompany such growth. In 1951, the largest crude oil tankers in world fleets were only 32,000 tons deadweight. By 1963 the figure had reached 132,000 tons, and by 1972, with the launching of the massive Globtik Tokyo, it was no less than 477,000 tons.

Increasing material inputs and shipping size have thrown into dramatic relief the hitherto dormant advantages of certain peripheral areas in terms of deepwater access to ocean-going carriers. At the same time, however, the considerable cost-minimization advantages of a 'break-of-bulk' site for manufacturing or processing these materials (Smith 1971, 80) has strongly encouraged the establishment and growth of such activities at these deepwater tranship-ment points. Admittedly, some growth of dependent manufacturing activity, such as oil-refining, has taken place at a few central waterside locations, notably lower Thameside and Southampton Water (and to a lesser extent Severnside). Until 1973 Thameside was the largest single centre of oil-refining in Britain (Keeble 1972a, 137): its 1974 refining capacity was 595,000 barrels per day. The Esso refinery at Fawley on Southampton Water is in fact still the largest single installation in the country (398,000 barrels per day capacity, 1974). But in general, it is the peripheral regions which have had most to offer in this respect, because of the existence of natural deep-water anchorages and sheltered harbours. Moreover, this advantage has been enhanced, at least in the Scottish and Northern England case, by the discovery and landing of oil from the northern North Sea.

Thus by 1974 the peripheral regions accounted for no less than 58 per cent (1.75 million b/d) of total United Kingdom oil-refining capacity, with major in-stallations at Milford Haven in Pembrokeshire, Britain's largest refining centre (four refineries: 672,000 b/d capacity, 1974), and on Merseyside (414,000 b/d, 1974), notably at Shell's huge Stanlow refinery. Indeed, 1974 witnessed

Milford Haven's rise to leadership amongst Britain's ports generally, measured by volume of goods handled (60 million tonnes), London probably for the first time this century being relegated into second place (46 million tonnes); and virtually all Milford Haven's tonnage was oil. Smaller peripheral oil-refining centres were Teesside (235,000 b/d), Llandarcy in south Wales (183,000 b/d), and Grangemouth in Scotland (196,000 b/d). Virtually all recent major expansion has been in these peripheral locations. If Humberside, with its recently-expanded capacity (292,000 b/d, 1974) is included, the periphery's share of the United Kingdom total rises to 67 per cent. Moreover, as Chapman (1973) shows, with the exception of Fawley all the growth of petro-chemical manufacturing, which is usually very closely associated spatially with oil-refining, has occurred around oil refineries in the peripheral regions, notably at Llandarcy/Baglan Bay, at Stanlow (which is also linked by pipeline to the Carrington petro-chemical works near Manchester), at Grangemouth, and at Wilton on Teesside. The availability of oil from the North Sea must maintain this pattern in the future, perhaps to the greater benefit of the latter rather than former two petro-chemical complexes.

A further very interesting illustration is that of the recent major expansion of Britain's previously tiny aluminium-smelting industry. The then Labour government decided in the mid-1960s that development of a substantial British smelting industry was desirable to reduce foreign currency payments on imported aluminium, and in view of probable future growth in demand. After negotiations with different private companies, three large-scale smelters were sanctioned, all in peripheral area locations – Holyhead, Lynemouth (Northumberland) and Invergordon (Scotland). These have now been constructed at a total cost of over £140 million. There is no doubt that a major reason for the choice of peripheral areas was the availability of substantial assisted-area investment grants from the government, grants which must have totalled over £50 million. But of importance too was access to deep-water harbours which could handle bulk alumina carriers from as far away as Australia and Jamaica, and the availability of peripheral area coal, hydro-electricity and nuclear power as the basic energy sources for smelting. Natural resources, notably deep-water access, must therefore be accorded some role in the periphery-centre model, although their impact has of course been chiefly felt by material-oriented capital-intensive industries. The effect of this component of the model upon manufacturing employment is therefore probably relatively slight.

4.2.4. Government regional policy

The importance of this component of the periphery-centre model can hardly be overstressed. However, since it is considered in detail in chapter 8 only four points will be made here. First, because United Kingdom regional policy has been heavily conditioned by considerations of unemployment relief (Keeble

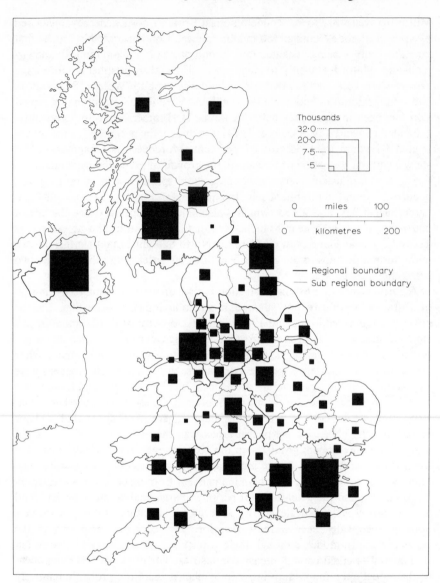

4.4a Subregional unemployment totals in the United Kingdom, June 1966
Source: unpublished Department of Employment statistics

1974b, 15–17), its spatial expression has for many years been cast in the same periphery-centre framework as that which so strikingly characterizes the pattern of unemployment rates (see fig. 4.4b). As a generalization, it may thus be argued that the Board of Trade/Department of Industry has constrained industrial expansion most markedly along the London–Birmingham axis, control

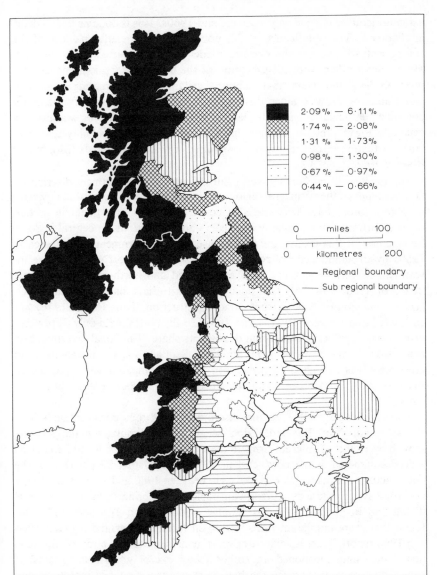

4.4b Subregional percentage unemployment rates in the United Kingdom, June 1966
Source: unpublished Department of Employment statistics

levels in practice declining with distance in all directions from this until replaced by increasing encouragement with attainment of the assisted areas (see figs 8.1 and 8.2).

Second, and with the possible exception of the 1945–50 period, regional policy has been most powerful as an influence on periphery-centre differentials in manufacturing change only since the mid-1960s. This is documented in detail in chapter 8. The significance of this point is that the relative balance of the components of the periphery-centre model has thus shifted since the mid-1960s. Before then, with the exception of the late 1940s, regional policy was probably less important than labour availability in promoting peripheral manufacturing growth. Since then regional policy has become of crucial importance, particularly since the later 1960s and earlier 1970s witnessed a generally lower pressure of national demand and hence probably an easier labour situation in central regions compared with earlier periods (Moore and Rhodes 1976, tabe A2).

The third point concerns government infrastructure investment discrimination in favour of the peripheral regions. It has already been noted that powerful economic forces have encouraged a concentration of investment in certain types of infrastructure, notably high-cost communications, in central regions. Recognition of this fact by the then Conservative government led in the early 1960s to an announced policy of discriminatory transport infrastructure investment in peripheral areas such as Scotland and north-east England (e.g. Board of Trade 1963, 6). This policy appears to have had some real effect, notably on motorway and trunk road construction. Thus Clark (1976) has calculated that between 1963–4 and 1969–70 the North, with only $5\frac{1}{2}$ per cent of national population, more than doubled its share of national investment on new roads, from 6 to 14 per cent. Similarly, Scotland's share of national road investment was as high as 13 per cent in 1963–4, compared with a population share of only $7\frac{1}{2}$ per cent, and remained above 11 per cent at least until 1969–70.

The significance of this regional discrimination in road construction is that, at least in north-east England, it does seem to have stimulated manufacturing growth by attracting migrant firms to the area. Thus a British Road Federation survey conducted in the north-east in 1970 claimed that 82 per cent of the manufacturing firms which had moved in between 1960 and 1970 regarded the new road system there as 'a significant factor . . . in bringing them to the area' (Estall and Buchanan 1973, 39). Similarly, Morley and Townroe (1974, 20) found that more immigrant firms settling in Northern England between 1966 and 1968 reported 'accessibility/transport' considerations as a reason for location choice than mentioned any other factor except government grants. It would thus seem that, given the bait of substantial financial incentives and grants, a deliberate policy of motorway investment to link the peripheral and central regions does encourage industrial expansion in the former.

The last point is to note, briefly, the very considerable evidence affirming the substantial direct impact of recent government policy upon the spatial pattern of manufacturing growth in Britain. Moore and Rhodes' studies (1973, 1974 and 1976), discussed in detail in chapter 8, are of key importance here. But this is also clear from the numerous surveys of migrant central region firms which have established new factories in the peripheral areas since 1945 (Keeble 1971a, 44). Thus the present author (Keeble 1968a) found that government controls had been of great importance in stimulating industrial movement from north-west London between 1945 and 1964, both directly and through their impact on factory availability and cost, while government inducements were mentioned more frequently as a factor in the locational choice of the forty-four peripheral area factories studied than any other consideration except labour availability. This finding is particularly interesting since it relates to moves occurring before the marked increase in assisted-area incentives which took place after 1963. More recent surveys, notably the ILAG study, reveal that current incentives are now of crucial importance. Thus '47 per cent of all new plants were opened in what were, at the time the firms made their respective decisions, assisted areas. Of these cases 81 per cent said that the availability of inducements was a major factor determining their choice and a further 14 per cent said it was a minor one' (Department of Trade and Industry 1973, 578). This major factor response rate was higher than that associated with any other assisted-area location factor, although labour availability was mentioned nearly as often.

4.3. Environment, amenity and residential space preferences

The centre-periphery and periphery-centre models represent useful conceptual devices for ordering virtually all the varied forces influencing the national spatial pattern of manufacturing industry. But there is at least one important exception to this. As will be shown in section 5.3.6, the geography of residential amenity in Britain does not appear to conform to any neat centre-periphery arrangement. Yet various evidence suggests that this factor may be becoming a powerful influence upon manufacturing location in developed countries. Increasing affluence and living standards, shorter working hours, longer holidays, all appear to be increasing the premium placed by workers and entrepreneurs on access to an attractive local or subregional residential environment. Put another way, consumption of local living space, attractive countryside, coastal scenery, a pleasant climate, or the environment afforded by a distinctive historic town, would all seem to possess a high-income elasticity of demand. In the 1930s, this factor was seen as enhancing the attractions of the London area to entrepreneurs (and their wives!). In the 1960s, with a much wider spread of higher incomes, it is undoubtedly a key component in the substantial population decline by net out-migration of all Britain's large industrial conurbations.

The significance of this factor for industrial location lies of course partly in the importance placed on labour availability by most manufacturing firms in Britain (see section 4.2.1). And as Chisholm (1970a, 129) points out, increasing geographical mobility means that labour availability is progressively a matter of where labour is willing to go, rather than of where it already is.

'Traditionally, willingness to migrate has been largely conditioned by the job opportunities available; but rising standards of living in an era of full employment confer increasing scope for choice based on personal preferences of area, kind of society and access to open country or urban amenities'. The remarkable net migration gains, 1966–71, of the attractive rural regions of East Anglia and South West England (73,680 and 116,350 people respectively: see Hall 1975), by far the leading regions of the United Kingdom in this respect, provide some evidence supporting this view. Residential space preferences, as they are sometimes termed, may thus be a migration determinant of growing importance, particularly for skilled and hence more highly-paid workers. As a result, and particularly 'in those industries where rapid technological development is taking place, firms are beginning to find it necessary to consider locations for plants where it will be possible to recruit and keep staff' of this type (Chisholm 1964, 12).

These space preferences however also of course apply to the entrepreneurs, managers and industrialists who make the crucial location decisions. What Eversley (1965) refers to as 'irrational, psychological and especially social' factors, or others have termed 'psychic income' (Richardson 1969, 94), may play a very important part in decision-making about the location of new manufacturing plants, especially when the decision-maker is likely to be directly affected in terms of his own residential environment by his factory location choice. While particularly true of small firms, run by individual entrepreneurs or family companies (Keeble 1974a, 7), it is possible that this sort of consideration affects very many location decisions (Hall 1970). Thus Green (1974, 190) found that even with relatively long-distance moves to the Development Areas, detailed economic evaluation of alternative locations was rare. 'Fifty-two firms (of a sample of 82) admitted that they had made no attempt at analysis at all. Personal impressions of the areas must then be all important at this stage of the search process. The image which the areas give is probably the most important factor.'

The problem here, of course, is that it is very difficult adequately to measure this type of socio-psychological factor, particularly in a micro-level firm survey situation. In such questionnaire surveys, *post-facto* rationalization is likely to lead to a cloaking of just this sort of personal motive by reference to more 'acceptable' economic factors which, while perfectly valid, were in reality less important in swaying the decision than the question of residential amenity for the industrialist and his family (Keeble 1971a, 41). That this does affect decisions more frequently than such surveys reveal is suggested, for example, by the study of industrial migration from north-west London reported in Keeble (1968a). For while 20 per cent (nine) of the forty-six firms studied and moving to the South East or East Anglia reported residential amenity as a factor in location choice, at least another five proved subsequently also to have been so influenced, although initially unwilling to confess this. Similarly,

Spooner (1972, 207–8) found that while admittedly more (30 per cent) of his immigrant postwar Devon and Cornwall firms reported perceived residential attractiveness to key workers and managers as the dominant reason for location selection than so reported any other factor, nonetheless 'many were reluctant to admit that their decisions had been influenced by such apparently un-businesslike motives', so that even this striking survey finding may be an underestimation. The dominance of the environmental factor in the Cornwall case is also suggested by Green's study (1974, 283), where it was ranked by firms settling in the area as more favourable than any other attribute of their new location. This is in considerable contrast to its very low ranking by firms in such other Development Area locations studied by Green as south Wales and north-east England. East Anglia is undoubtedly another region benefiting from this 'psychic income' factor, the attractions of a 'pleasant environment' being reported as a locational influence by respondents to Lemon's survey (1975, 20) of eighty-eight firms settling in East Anglian market towns between 1945 and 1969 more frequently (sixteen firms) than any other factor except availability of premises (forty-five firms) and of labour (thirty-four firms).

Residential space preferences appear therefore to be of considerable and probably underrated significance for recent manufacturing growth, at least in certain areas and situations. A quantitative measure of their possible impact is therefore included in the ensuing statistical analysis.

4.4. Intra-regional planning: new and expanded towns

A less important exception than residential space preferences to the grouping of locational forces represented by the centre-periphery and periphery-centre models concerns the intra-regional impact of government new and expanded town policies. These policies do not form part of the above models since they have traditionally operated almost solely at the within-region scale, being concerned with the redistribution of population and industry from congested conurbations to better-designed smaller communities in surrounding areas of the same regions (Manners 1972, 25–35; see also chapter 9). Moreover, their impact has been largely confined, at least until recently, to particular regions such as the South East and East Anglia. On the other hand, given the subregional framework adopted for this study, it seems clear that such policies cannot be ignored as a possible influence on the spatial pattern of recent manufacturing change in certain cases. For example, the rapid growth of the eight new and two expanded towns in the Outer Metropolitan Area which received immigrant London industry between 1959 and 1966 resulted in a net increase of no less than 51,000 manufacturing jobs,[12] or 27 per cent of total net manufacturing employment growth (190,000 jobs) in the OMA during this period. Again, the planned movement of manufacturing firms to East Anglia's seven main expanded towns during this period resulted in the creation of 11,000 manufacturing jobs, or 29 per cent of the total net manufacturing employment growth of East Anglia as a whole. In one sense, of course, it could well be true that the manufacturing growth of these planned communities partly reflects their possible locational advantages in terms of market access, or attractive residential environment, so that separate identification of the role of planned expansion is not needed. However, there is considerable evidence, which the above figures support, that new or expanded town status and machinery has resulted in even greater industrial expansion in areas such as the OMA and East Anglia than might otherwise have been expected. Important factors here are the unique opportunity such towns have afforded of relocating a firm's total workforce in specially-provided housing (Keeble 1968a, 44), the much greater possibility of IDC approval, and the impact of official publicity directing firms' attention to these centres. For these reasons, some attention to the impact of intra-regional news and expanded town development would seem desirable in the context of the multivariate statistical analysis, results of which are presented in the next chapter.

NOTES

1 See, for example, Taylor 1938, 39; Political and Economic Planning 1939, 71; and Caesar 1964, 232.
2 Central Statistical Office (1974), *Abstract of regional statistics,* 10, table 66.
3 High rates in the relatively low-income regions of East Anglia and the South West are an exception, being an enforced response to lack of public transport and a dispersed population pattern. See Sleeman (1969) and East Anglia Regional Strategy Team (1974, 69).
4 The exact spatial relationship between particular transport facilities and manufacturing growth varies with the facility and geographic scale involved. For example, Hoare (1974, 94) has recently demonstrated that a major international airport such as Heathrow exerts a *negative* impact upon manufacturing growth in its immediate vicinity (within 16 kilometres, or 10 miles), but a positive one at the wider regional scale, as postulated by Keeble, 1968c.
5 This survey, named after the interdepartmental Inquiry into Location Attitudes Group, investigated all moves between the fifty DTI subregions defined in Howard, 1968. It achieved 80 per cent (632 firms) and 69 per cent (543 firms) response rates respectively for questionnaire return and interview. Some 64 per cent of the moves originated in the South East and West and East Midlands, while 50 per cent selected new locations in the peripheral regions.
6 Moreover, Morley and Townroe's study (1974, 21) of manufacturing moves to Northern England showed that for most such firms, the decline in

unit labour costs had occurred within two years of commencing production, and virtually all ILAG firms had been operating for more than this length of time.

7 Population Census Summary Tables 1971.

8 Central Statistical Office (1974), *Abstract of Regional Statistics*, 10, table 86.

9 DTI unpublished records, adjusted by the present author. Unlike the national figures, the 1969 regional values may well be inflated by firms deliberately understating the expected employment, for IDC control reasons.

10 Nationwide Building Society (1975), *Occasional Bulletin*, 125.

11 Central Statistical Office (1974), *Abstract of Regional Statistics*, 10, table 91.

12 Data from *Town and Country Planning*, vol. 28, 23 and vol. 35, 39. 'Expanded towns' are those which have signed formal agreements under the 1952 Town Development Act with an exporting conurbation such as London for receipt of population and/or industry.

5 Regression analysis and manufacturing location change

The discussion in preceding chapters has already in effect yielded certain major conclusions. Of key importance, for example, is the considerable evidence pointing to the operation of the centre-periphery model as the basic determinant of manufacturing location trends in the United Kingdom both during the interwar years and, more recently, during the 1950s. The locational trends documented briefly in chapter 2, the independent shift-and-share analyses discussed in chapter 3, and the range and depth of evidence assembled in chapter 4 all support this major conclusion. However, more recent trends clearly cannot simply be categorized as cumulative central growth and peripheral decline. As already noted, the pattern revealed in figure 2.3a appears to contain elements of both these trends; that of figure 2.3b, while exhibiting a striking spatial regularity, suggests a complete reversal in the earlier centre-periphery balance of manufacturing employment change. Qualitative assessment of the likely forces behind the pattern of floorspace change revealed in figure 2.4b is also by no means easy.

5.1. Multiple regression analysis: procedure and problems

For this reason, the data used to compile the three maps were incorporated as dependent variables in a series of multiple regression analyses with a variety of independent variables selected as measuring the subregional incidence of different forces discussed in chapter 4. Linear regression analysis using ordinary least squares procedures is a very widely used and powerful parametric statistical technique which permits estimation of the direction and strength of the relationship between two variables, measured over a set of units (in this case subregions), one of these variables being viewed as dependent upon, or influenced by, the other. In the multiple regression case, several independent variables are included together, their impact upon the dependent variable being estimated jointly. The usual form of such a regression model is given by the equation

$$Y = a + b_1 X_1 + b_2 X_2 + \cdots + b_n X_n + e$$

where Y is the dependent variable, X_i is the i'th independent variable, $i = 1$, $2, \ldots n$, b_1 is its associated regression coefficient specifying the amount of change in Y for a unit change in X_1 and e is an error term. The sign of a particular regression coefficient indicates whether or not the relationship is a positive or negative one, while the analysis also yields a coefficient of multiple determination (R^2), which measures the amount of variation in the dependent variable which is statistically explained by the independent variables.

Multiple regression analysis has been very widely used in geographic research, largely because of its obvious apparent suitability for testing the spatial impact of one phenomenon upon another. In the industrial location sphere, early studies were largely confined to North America, as illustrated by the work of Fuchs (1959), McCarty and others (Smith 1971, 397–405). An interesting recent study is that by Wheat (1973). Recent applications in relation to manufacturing location in the United Kingdom include studies of manufacturing movement at national and regional scales (Keeble 1972b, 1972c; Townsend and Gault 1972; Sant 1975a) and of intra-regional manufacturing location change (Keeble and Hauser 1971, 1972). Such studies do seem to have yielded useful insights and identified logical relationships. However, it is important to recognize the existence and estimate the effect of certain technical problems with regression models, which follow from the fairly rigorous assumptions on which they are based (Poole and O'Farrell 1971; Keeble and Hauser 1972, 12). The failure to do this of many earlier studies may render their conclusions somewhat suspect.

5.1.1. Linearity, collinearity and spatial autocorrelation

One of the basic assumptions of standard regression analysis is that the relationship between the dependent and independent variables is linear. Clearly, fitting of a straight 'best-fit' regression line to a scatter of points on a graph of Y against X, when the relationship between the two variables is in reality curvilinear (e.g. a straight line only on semi-logarithmic graph paper), will result in a very inaccurate estimation of this relationship. A second major assumption in the multiple regression case is that the X_1s, or independent variables, are independent of each other. If, on the contrary, a particular pair of such variables in a multiple regression equation is highly intercorrelated, the sampling error of the regression coefficients is large, resulting in their imprecise estimation. Where so-called stepwise procedures are employed (see section 5.1.2), the presence of such *collinear* variables may also result in the uncertain specification of the model, and the inclusion of illogical relationships, often reflected by a meaningless reversal of the postulated negative or positive sign of the particular regression coefficient (Keeble and Hauser 1972, 13; Hauser 1974, 151–2). A pairwise correlation coefficient of more than 0.80 is usually taken as evidence of serious collinearity, although estimation of the presence of *multi*collinearity, or a high correlation with a *combination* of other variables, is more difficult (Hauser 1974, 152).

A third problem arises from the basic regression assumption that the error terms, or in practice the residuals unexplained by the regression equation, are independent of one another. It is also assumed that they are identically normally distributed, but significance tests are relatively robust to violations of this particular point. In the spatial case, where observations are for areas, the independency assumption is however violated if mapping of the residuals reveals a significant pattern, with marked clustering of positive or negative residuals in different areas. Such mapping has been advocated by statistical geographers for many years as a basis for generation of further casual hypotheses which would improve the overall explanation. But only recently has work by Cliff and Ord (1972) and Hepple (1974) revealed the extent of the distortion and inefficiency of estimation in the regression model itself which follows from spatial interdependence in the error terms. Cliff and Ord's contribution here is particularly important in that they were the first to develop a method of estimating the *degree* of spatial autocorrelation in regression residuals, by computation of their I statistic together with its first two moments. It is thus now possible to calculate whether or not the residuals are significantly spatially autocorrelated, in any particular case. The absence of such significant autocorrelation affords important further evidence of the general validity of a regression equation, all else being equal.

It should be noted that there are other important assumptions of the regression model, such as those of homoscedacity, lack of measurement error in the independent variables, and so on, which are generally difficult to test for and usually perforce assumed met. In addition, as Martin (1974) and Hepple (Unwin and Hepple 1975, 220–21) both emphasize, the presence of spatial autocorrelation in the independent or regressor variables themselves also causes problems, since although in the theoretical regression model the independency assumption applies only to the random error terms and not to the regressor variables (Hepple 1974, 111), calculated residuals in real-world applications *are* dependent on the regressor variables as well as on the true errors (Johnston 1972, 247–9). So spatial autocorrelation in the regressors themselves is technically a problem for empirical regression analysis. Against this, however, it can be argued that it is extremely difficult to imagine situations in which spatial autocorrelation in the regressor variables does not pass through into the residuals, *given* that the regression model has made no attempt to model this autocorrelation. In view of this, it is assumed here that the crucial problem posed by spatial autocorrelation in regression analysis relates to its presence in the residuals, rather than in the regressor variables themselves, a conclusion which is implicitly supported by the literature cited above.

5.1.2. Stepwise regression and autocorrelation estimation

In this study, multiple regression was used as a search procedure to identify those particular independent variables which seem most strongly to be related to the observed dependent variable of subregional manufacturing employment or floorspace change. It is for just such a situation that so-called 'stepwise' regression procedures have been developed. The most common of these is a 'forward' procedure, which begins as in this study by identifying the independent variable which exhibits the strongest relationship with Y, measured by its correlation coefficient. The procedure then 'adds variables on the basis of their partial correlations . . . with the dependent variable, such that at each stage the variable with the highest partial correlation coefficient is added to the equation. The procedure continues until no further variables which are significantly non-zero can be added' (Hauser 1974, 150). The basic aim in this sort of hypothesis-testing, exploratory situation is thus to maximise R^2, the overall statistical fit, while including in the regression equation only those variables which really are significantly related to Y.

The various specific problems which arise in stepwise regression are discussed in Hauser (1974). Many of these are associated with the presence of collinearity in the independent variables. However, in none of the analyses presented in this chapter did collinearity prove to be a problem of great significance. Not only were there no cases in any of the independent variable correlation coefficient matrices of pairwise correlations reaching the 0.80 level, but with only two exceptions, pairwise correlations between variables, both of which were selected for inclusion in the best-fit equation, did not rise above approximately the 0.50 level. In only one case, that of percentage floorspace change, did inclusion of a particular independent variable appear to be a response to collinearity. In this case, the procedure selected both assisted-area status and 1966 unemployment rate, the latter, selected later, being accorded a somewhat meaningless negative relationship with the dependent variable. In fact, inspection of the independent variable correlation matrix revealed that these two variables were more highly correlated (0.770) than any other pair included for investigation in any of the analyses discussed in this chapter. It was therefore decided to apply 'zero restriction' (Keeble and Hauser 1972, 13) and drop the latter variable from the equation. In general, then, the absence of significant levels of collinearity in the independent variables encourages confidence in the validity of the regression results, all else being equal.

The assumption of linearity of relationships between dependent and independent variables was also investigated, by normalization of those variables, the distribution of which was notably skewed. In practice, normalization was thus confined to percentage rate values, and to totals of manufacturing employment or floorspace stock, and involved transformation of the raw data into natural logarithms, sometimes with the addition of a constant to eliminate negative values. In four of the seven main analyses presented in this chapter, this procedure resulted in higher R^2 values for the overall equation. Moreover, in three of these four cases, the particular independent variables selected by both types of analysis were identical, the only difference being the somewhat higher coefficient of determination in the normalized case. The equations relating to these four normalized variable data sets have thus been selected for discussion here, since these particular results do suggest the presence of non-linear relationships which are not adequately measured by linear regression of the raw data.

An important further problem in stepwise regression is the choice of a cut-off level beyond which the strength of the relationships between the dependent variable and particular remaining independent variables is so low that the procedure stops. In practice, the particular computer programme used[1] adopted a very low cut-off level, to permit estimation of all possible equations, from steps 1 to n. The 'best-fit' equation was then selected by testing the significance of the individual regression coefficients in each successive equation, and accepting that equation in which all the selected independent variables recorded t-values greater than 1.67, indicating a 0.10 significance level. Adoption of a relatively low level such as this is advocated by Hauser (1974, 155) with respect to stepwise procedures, on the grounds that 'a rigorous concern with Type 1 errors ... and high significance levels is out of place in exploratory studies, since the chance is increased of rejecting differences which actually do exist'. In fact, however, as inspection of later tables shows, the great majority of independent variables selected for 'best-fit' equations also yielded t-values greater than 2.00, or an 0.05 significance level.

Though not part of the stepwise regression procedure, a final and most important stage of the analysis was calculation of the Cliff-Ord I statistic for the residuals from each 'best-fit' equation. This statistic was then expressed in z score form, and a 0.05 probability level, indicated by a z value of 1.96, selected as the basis for accepting or rejecting the hypothesis of a significant level of spatial autocorrelation of regression residuals. As Cliff and Ord (1973, 87) point out, one important possible byproduct of such a procedure may be the identification of additional causal regressor variables, following the discovery of a significant level of residual spatial autocorrelation. In the present analysis, identification of an unacceptably high spatial autocorrelation level in only one case, percentage employment change 1959–66, did lead via residual mapping to incorporation of a measure of a further variable, the impact of new and expanded town manufacturing growth (section 5.5.1). The regression residuals from the equation which allowed for this further influence recorded a z score below the 0.05 significance level.

5.2. The dependent variables

Three of the dependent variables examined in the subsequent analysis relate to absolute net changes in subregional manufacturing activity, expressed in two cases in terms of numbers of employees (1959–66 and 1966–71 respectively) and in the third in terms of area of industrial floorspace (1964–72). These data sets are mapped in figures 2.3a, 2.3b and 2.4b, and have already been discussed in detail. So too has the map of 1959 subregional manufacturing employment totals (fig. 2.1), which was also included as a dependent variable for reasons explained later. The three other dependent variables have not however yet been mapped or discussed. All of these relate to percentage *rates* of change, of manufacturing employment for the two subperiods noted above, and of floorspace for the period 1964–72. No published study has previously utilized or statistically analysed the last dependent variable.

The manufacturing employment rate of change maps (figs. 5.1a and 5.1b) amplify the picture already presented in chapter 2. In terms of percentage rate, the 1959–66 map reveals the striking growth performance of the South East and East Anglia (with the exception of Greater London), and of Wales. In these and other cases, such as the outlying subregions of North-East England, the most rapid industrial development appears to be occurring in environmentally attractive but traditionally rural areas within 80 to 160 kilometres (50 to 100 miles) of major conurbations such as London and Birmingham. However, taking the central and peripheral regions as a whole, the map acknowledges the continuing dominance in manufacturing employment growth rate terms of the former compared with the latter. As table 5.1 indicates, the group of twenty-two central subregions defined in section 2.1 accounted for no less than twelve of the twenty fastest-growing subregions during this period, but included only two of the twenty slowest-growing or declining subregions. Conversely, the group of twenty-six peripheral subregions defined in section 2.1 accounted for only seven of the fastest-growing, but no less than ten of the slowest-growing or declining, subregions. Table 5.1 also pinpoints the even poorer manufacturing growth performance of the intermediate regions of North-West England and Yorkshire and Humberside noted earlier (section 2.2.3).

The 1966–71 map, however, presents a rather different picture, as with the absolute change map (fig. 2.3b; see section 2.2.2). While the trend to rapid industrialization of traditionally rural areas is equally and strikingly apparent as during the earlier period, exemplified by the inclusion of Cambridgeshire, Kent, Cornwall, mid-Wales, rural southern North-East England, and the Highlands and Islands of Scotland in the group of ten fastest-growing subregions, the previously almost-continuous zone of significantly above-average employment

Table 5.1 Subregional rates of manufacturing employment growth and decline, 1959–66 and 1966–71

	1959–66			1966–71		
	Centre*	Periphery*	Intermediate*	Centre*	Periphery*	Intermediate*
Fastest-growing subregions (20)	12	7	1	8	11	1
Moderately growing subregions (22)	8	9	5	8	9	5
Slowest-growing, or fastest declining, subregions (20)	2	10	8	6	6	8

* For definition of the regional categories, see section 2.1

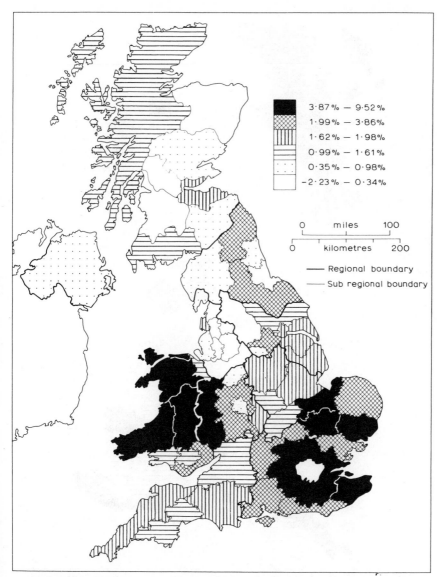

5.1a Subregional annual average percentage manufacturing employment change in the
United Kingdom, 1959–66
Source: unpublished Department of Employment statistics

growth in the South East and East Anglia has largely broken down. The basic
difference is thus a significant decline in the performance of central subregions, and a significant improvement in that of the periphery. As table 5.1
shows, the centre's share of the country's twenty fastest-growing subregions

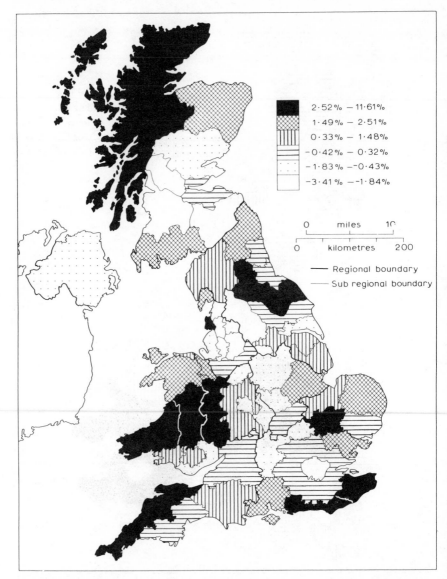

5.1b Subregional average annual percentage manufacturing employment change in the United Kingdom, 1966–71
Source: unpublished Department of Employment statistics

fell during the 1966–71 period to only eight, while the periphery's increased to eleven. Equally striking was the periphery's decreased share (down to six) and the centre's increased share (up to six) of the group of fastest-declining sub-regions. The intermediate areas recorded an exactly similar relative share of

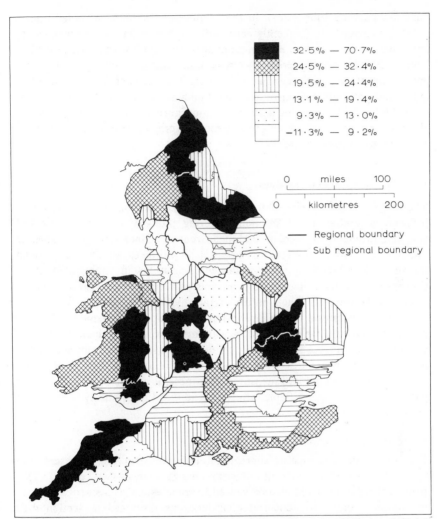

32·5% — 70·7%
24·5% — 32·4%
19·5% — 24·4%
13·1% — 19·4%
9·3% — 13·0%
−11·3% — 9·2%

0   miles   100

0   kilometres   200

—— Regional boundary
—— Sub regional boundary

5.2 Subregional percentage manufacturing floorspace change in England and Wales, 1964–72
Source: unpublished Department of Environment statistics

each of the three subregional growth categories as in the 1959–66 period. In a sense, then, the periphery's 1966–71 gains were all at the expense of the centre, and the centre's losses were all to the periphery.

The last remaining dependent variable is mapped in figure 5.2. Although unfortunately confined to subregions of England and Wales, this floorspace map reveals interesting similarities with that of employment change 1966–71, with a comparable emphasis on manufacturing growth in traditionally rural areas and in the peripheral areas (the latter including ten of England and Wales' eighteen fastest-expanding subregions). In this connection, it should be noted that the DoE floorspace data frequently necessarily exclude estimates for such capital-intensive plants as oil refineries, shipyards and steel works, because of the great difficulty of deriving meaningful internal factory floorspace measurements for such complex structures. The substantial recent peripheral oil-refinery and aluminium-smelter development noted in section 4.2.3 is thus probably excluded from the data mapped in figure 5.2, leading to a certain understatement of the periphery's recent above-average performance in attracting new manufacturing capacity.

5.3. The independent variables

The range and complexity of forces hypothesized in chapter 4 as likely to be influencing spatial trends in manufacturing industry in Britain pose considerable problems of selection and measurement of independent variables for multiple regression analysis. Clearly, such variables should each ideally measure, unambiguously and accurately, variations in subregional attractiveness to manufacturing industry in terms of a single hypothesized locational influence. However, of their nature certain hypotheses, such as for example that relating to central region innovation leadership, are extremely difficult to quantify. And even where precise measurement would seem logically feasible, as with the labour cost hypothesis, the absence of accurate subregional data poses insoluble difficulties. In the event, therefore, only six basic independent variables were selected and measured. But these, it can be argued, do encompass all the major quantifiable influences examined qualitatively in chapters 3 and 4.

5.3.1. Industrial structure

The first of these is existing subregional industrial structure, an essential explanatory factor for short-run industrial change analysis (see section 3.7). A structural measure might also be viewed to some extent as a surrogate for the institutional and entrepreneurial considerations discussed in section 4.1.6. Previous multiple regression analyses have identified, as expected, significant positive relationships between structure and manufacturing location change (Keeble and Hauser 1972, 23).

In the present study, structural measurement was made possible by the availability of detailed unpublished Department of Employment Minimum List Heading employment statistics.[2] These listed for each subregion its 1959 employment in each of 108 separate manufacturing industries, while the Chisholm and Oeppen study (1973, table 4.1) for which they were compiled gives national (Great Britain) percentage rates of employment change in each of these industries for 1959–68. It was thus possible to group these industries into three categories on the basis of these national percentage rates. The first, comprising thirty-five industries, was made up of all those which expanded their employment nationally by 10 per cent or more over the period. They therefore included all the industries, for example, listed in the left-hand column of table 3.1. The second category, comprising thirty-one industries, included all those recording an employment *decline* of 10 per cent or more over the period, examples being the industries listed in the right-hand column of table 3.1. The third, residual, category of forty-two industries thus comprised those in which employment remained relatively static.

The industrial structure index was then constructed by calculating the percentage of total 1959 manufacturing employment in each subregion in each of the first and second categories of growing and declining industries, respectively, and simply subtracting the latter percentage from the former.[3] This yielded an index whose theoretical range is from +100.0 per cent (all manufacturing employment concentrated in the growth category) to −100.0 per cent (all manufacturing employment concentrated in the decline category). The logic of this rests of course on the assumption that the third group of industries can be ignored as a significant influence on subregional manufacturing employment change, the crucial impact being that of the subregion's fastest-growing or -declining industries, and the relative proportion of each.

While obviously somewhat crude, this index possesses the great merits of being based on a very detailed industrial disaggregation, and of being both easy to calculate and to comprehend. The calculated values are mapped in figure 5.3. No previous study has presented detailed evidence at this subregional level on the nation-wide spatial incidence of favourable or unfavourable manufacturing structures. The first point worth noting is the wide range of actual index values, from +68.2 per cent in South Lindsey to −57.7 per cent in Furness. This in itself suggests that the index may be a useful discriminator between favourable and unfavourable structures.

Secondly, however, figure 5.3 strikingly illustrates the spatial centre-periphery pattern of such structures within the United Kingdom. Thus all but one of the West Midland and East Anglian subregions, and all but two of the South Eastern ones, fall in the top two categories of subregions with the most favourable manufacturing structures (+18.2 per cent and over). The only significant anomalies here are certain East Midlands subregions and South Hampshire/Dorset, with its declining shipbuilding and repairing industry. Interestingly, the central zone of highly favourable manufacturing structures appears to extend north-eastwards to include the Eastern Lowlands of the East Midlands and South Lindsey, technically in the Yorkshire and Humberside region. On the other hand, of the peripheral subregions defined in section 2.1, only six fall in the top two industrial structure categories (only one, south-west Scotland, in the very top category), while eight are located in the bottom two categories of subregions with the most unfavourable structures. The most striking concentration of such unfavourable structures is however to be found

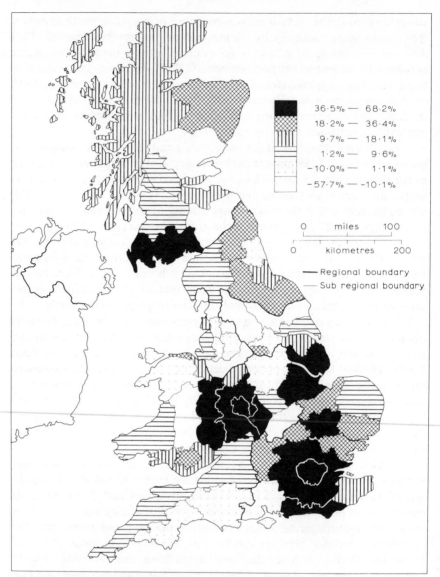

36·5% — 68·2%
18·2% — 36·4%
9·7% — 18·1%
1·2% — 9·6%
−10·0% — 1·1%
−57·7% — −10·1%

0   miles   100
0   kilometres   200

—— Regional boundary
—— Sub regional boundary

5.3 Industrial structure indices, 1959, by United Kingdom subregion
Source: unpublished Department of Employment statistics

in the 'intermediate' subregions of the North West and Yorkshire and Humberside, no less than nine (64 per cent) of which record indices placing them in the
two bottom categories shown on the map. The role of the declining textile and,
to a lesser extent, clothing industries in this concentration is substantial. On
this basis, it could be argued that the industrial problems of these intermediate

subregions are in fact more serious and deeprooted than those of many peripheral areas, which by 1959 possessed rather more favourable manufacturing structures. In general, however, figure 5.3 provides striking evidence of a centre-periphery pattern of industrial structure within the United Kingdom, and strongly supports the argument put forward in section 3.7 concerning the non-random nature of such distributions. It is perhaps also interesting to note the relatively high indices recorded in 1959 by a number of traditionally rural subregions located reasonably close to major industrial conurbations, examples being subregions in and to the north of East Anglia, the 'rural west' of the West Midlands, and the southern and northern 'rural north-east' of Northern England. This pattern strongly suggests the operation of a spatial manufacturing diffusion mechanism, given the established and very significant association of manufacturing migration with expanding industries and firms (Keeble 1971a, 26–9).

5.3.2. Market accessibility

The most widely-used index of market accessibility, itself the key component of the centre-periphery model, is of course market potential. The nature and spatial pattern of this index have already been considered (section 4.1.1, fig. 4.1). Inclusion of market potential as an independent variable in the multiple regression analysis therefore simply involved superimposition of a framework map of subregional boundaries over Clark's 1960 market potential map, and the reading off for each subregion of an average potential value relative to the whole area of the subregion. Values were expressed as a percentage of central London, and hence ranged from 99 for Greater London to 52 for the Highlands and Islands of Scotland. Since Clark's study unfortunately did not include Northern Ireland, the latter was somewhat arbitrarily allocated the same value as that for the Scottish Highlands. Market potential could also be taken as a measure of relative access to and quality of major transport facilities (section 4.1.3), given the pattern revealed in figure 4.1, and perhaps, though to a much lesser degree, of innovation leaders' ip. It could probably also be argued however that the latter, almost unquantifiable, consideration is equally associated with the industrial structure index just discussed.

5.3.3. Agglomeration and scale of manufacturing activity

This study adopts the simplest and most obvious measure of possible manufacturing agglomeration economies and diseconomies in different subregions, namely the existing scale of manufacturing activity (total employment or floorspace as appropriate) in the subregion at the beginning of the relevant period (see, for example, figs 2.1 and 2.2a). A positive relationship between this variable and manufacturing growth would thus be viewed as suggesting the operation of agglomeration economies through increasing size of industrial area, while a negative relationship would suggest agglomeration diseconomies reducing growth or initiating decline in the largest centres. The association of this simple measure with agglomeration economies and diseconomies follows previous studies and is reasonably logical. But at least one major problem must be stressed. This is the *de facto* correlation between strength of government IDC controls and the two largest industrial subregions, London and Birmingham. Least-squares regression is noted for being heavily influenced by individual large observations. Subsequent significant *negative* relationships between industrial size and manufacturing change could therefore also partly reflect the negative impact of government regional policy, through IDC controls in London and Birmingham. More stringent local planning constraints in these and other conurbations could also be involved. In addition, the variable makes little or no allowance for the existence of wider regional-level economies, as suggested by section 4.1.4.

5.3.4. Labour availability

The key importance of labour availability as a component of the periphery-centre model rendered essential inclusion of some measure of this locational influence. Following earlier studies, measurement involved calculation from unpublished Department of Employment local area statistics of subregional unemployment totals and percentage rates for 1959 and 1966 (see, for example, fig. 4.4). Unemployment was defined so as to include juveniles, but exclude workers only temporarily stopped. The choice of this somewhat crude index of labour availability reflects both the availability of data at the subregional scale, and the fact that unemployment figures seem to be the data source most widely used by firms themselves in estimating local labour supply situations. Thus for example Green (1974, 190) found that for most of his sample of Development-Area migrant firms which carried out any statistical investigation of possible new locations, 'analysis consisted simply of comparison of figures provided by the various regional agencies on variables such as unemployment and available skilled labour along with distances between the regions and the present location'. Unemployment rates are probably also useful as a very rough guide to relative wage costs. On the other hand, it is also true that Brown's calculations (section 4.2.1) draw attention to female activity rates as a potentially key source of under-used labour. Moreover, in cases such as London, a large absolute total of unemployed workers is a misleading guide to available labour (see section 4.2.1); while conversely a high percentage rate in a small subregion may denote only a small absolute total of available unemployed workers. Thus in 1959, north-west Wales, with the third highest unemployment rate in the country (5.29 per cent), actually contained only 3,002 unemployed workers; whereas Merseyside, with a lower rate (4.06 per cent), had nearly ten times as many people registered as unemployed (29,235). These particular technical problems would, however, of course also apply to an index of activity rates or totals. It should be noted that the unemployment rate index was used for regression analyses of rates of manufacturing change, the absolute total unemployed index being used for the absolute total manufacturing change studies.

5.3.5. Regional policy and assisted-area status

Interval or ratio scale measurement of subregional variations in this important variable proved to be impossible. Moore and Rhodes (1976) have been able so to quantify changes in the strength of regional policy nationally over time for inclusion in multiple regression analyses, by measures such as official IDC refusals in the South East and Midlands as a percentage of all refusals and approvals in these regions per annum, or annual changes in the discounted present value of regionally-differentiated investment incentives per £100 of capital expenditure. But all of their measures are either not applicable to the spatial variation situation or, as with the former of the two variables described above, are available only on a broad regional, not subregional, basis. Inclusion of this influence therefore necessarily involved measurement on a presence-absence basis, in dummy variable form, a value of 1 being assigned to subregions enjoying assisted-area status for most if not all of the period in question (1959–66, 1966–71 or 1964–72), a value of 0 being assigned to non-assisted subregions. The scattered pattern of Development Districts (fig 8.2a) during the early 1960s did pose a few difficulties in relating them to current subregions. But in general, assignment was automatic.

While the only feasible method, this dummy variable approach is obviously somewhat crude. Its chief demerit is that it fails to measure subregional variations in the intensity of regional policy controls within the set of non-assisted areas, and to a much lesser extent, of regional policy incentives within the assisted areas. For example, in the latter case, dummy variable measurement does not allow for the designation of Special Development Areas in 1967, or of Intermediate Areas in 1970 (chapter 8). In fact, however, until 1971, Special Development Areas were confined almost entirely to certain coalmining areas and hence affected only a very few subregions (McCallum 1973, 278); while the Intermediate Areas came too late and were designated on too limited a scale to have any real effect on manufacturing change during the periods studied here. More significant, almost certainly, is the variable intensity of Board of Trade/Department of Industry controls within the non-assisted areas. There is considerable evidence, not least the Department's own statements (Department of Trade and Industry 1971), that certain subregions, such as those in what were subsequently to become Intermediate Areas, in northern and eastern East Anglia, and in outer Kent, have been treated relatively leniently with regard to the granting of IDC's because of local unemployment and other economic problems. The Department has also undoubtedly co-operated in new and expanded town industrial expansion in the South East and West Midlands. Conversely, the Department's policy towards industrial growth in London and Birmingham has generally been one of relatively stringent control, an attitude probably extended in recent years to areas such as the OMA. These spatial policy variations, which are very difficult to quantify, must be borne in mind when interpreting the results of the regression analyses. So also must the fact, already noted (section 5.1.2), of a fairly strong correlation between assisted-area status and high unemployment rates ($r = 0.673$ for all sixty-two subregions, 1966 values), indicating that the former variable is also in fact a rough index of labour availability.

5.3.6. Residential space preferences

Inclusion of a measure of this variable was made possible by Gould and White's study (1968) of the residential desirability perception maps of school-leavers from twenty-three different locations within Britain. This study was the first to attempt quantitatively to measure spatial variations in residential space preferences in this country, the latter postulated on the basis of an absolutely free locational choice, other things being equal. As a result, Gould and White were able, from county scores produced by a principal components analysis of the average maps associated with each of the twenty-three groups, to derive a general or national map of residential desirability (fig. 5.4). The values on this general map represent percentages between the highest (100) and lowest (0) county preference scores. The most striking features of the pattern are the zone of very high scores along the south coast from Kent to Cornwall, the relatively low values recorded by the London and West Midland conurbations, the two northward 'prongs' of higher preference extending into East Anglia and Hereford/Shropshire, the Lake District high value dome, and the very low preference recorded by the central valley of Scotland, excluding Edinburgh. As with the market potential map, inclusion of this residential space preference measure in the regression analysis was effected simply by reading off average subregional values from a subregional boundary map superimposed upon the Gould and White national preference map.[4] The present study is thus the first ever to incorporate a quantitative measure of this hitherto intangible influence in a regression analysis of manufacturing change in Britain.

One possible criticism of this approach might of course be that school-leavers differ from industrialists in their perception of spatial variations in residential amenity in Britain. However, Gould and White (1968, 163) explicitly disagree, asserting that in cases such as this 'where there is considerable agreement about the desirability or undesirability of areas for residential purposes, the overall perception surfaces may throw important light on . . . the location of "footloose" industries'. More important still, recent direct surveys of perception and decision-making by British industrialists, such as those by Spooner, Green and Lemon discussed in section 4.3, clearly support the view that their images of areas as residential locations generally conform to the pattern mapped in figure 5.4. On the other hand, it is probably true that some

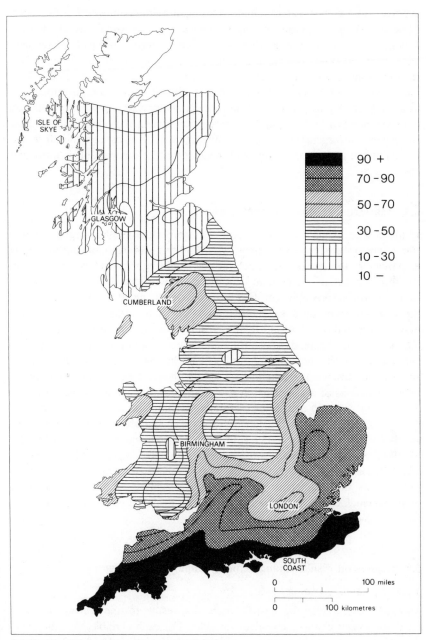

5.4 Residential space preferences in Britain
Source: Gould and White 1968

average subregional values cloak significant within-subregion differences; while others are probably inaccurate because of the smallness of the sub-regions involved, compared with the counties in terms of which preferences were collected. Thus the value assigned to the large doughnut-shaped OMA represents an attempt at averaging preference scores ranging from under 50 to approaching 90 per cent of the maximum; while in Lancashire, included only as a single county in Gould and White's original analysis, individual values had to be allocated from the generalized perception surface to no less than six small subregions. Overgeneralization and averaging of values are therefore un-avoidable but unfortunate defects of measurement of this variable in particular cases.

5.4. Regression results: the 1959 pattern

In the absence of data on locational trends before the 1960s, a regression was run in which the dependent variable was 1959 total subregional manufacturing employment. In a sense, this static variable might be regarded as a measure of the total impact of differential centre-periphery forces during the twentieth century. Not surprisingly, the first and only independent variable selected by the stepwise procedure as significantly related to 1959 employment was market potential ($r = 0.452$).[5] In simple descriptive terms, British manufactur-ing industry has become concentrated in market locations during the twentieth century. However, the most interesting point here is the comparison with the performance of market potential as a hypothesized explanatory variable in later regressions of absolute *changes* in manufacturing employment during the 1960s. Not only did neither of these identify potential as significant, but the simple correlation coefficient between the latter and absolute change declined from the value for total 1959 employment given above, to only 0.114 for 1959–66 change, and to a *negative* relationship, −0.343, for 1966–71 change. These three coefficients thus appear strikingly to illustrate a steep recent decline in the influence of market accessibility upon manufacturing employment location in Britain, which other evidence (sections 3.5 and 3.6, for example) also suggests.

5.5. Regression results: manufacturing employment change

5.5.1. Percentage change

Tables 5.2 and 5.3 list the 'best-fit' regression results for the four manufactur-ing employment change dependent variables. For each variable, the tables give the independent variables selected as being significantly related to Y, together with their regression coefficients (b) and the standard error and calculated t-value of each of these coefficients. Also given are the regression equation con-

Table 5.2 *Regression results: manufacturing employment, 1959–66*

Percentage change equation (log *Y*)

	b	*SE*$_b$	*t-value*
Manufacturing employment, 1959 (log)	−0.13214	0.02396	5.52
Residential space preference	0.00530	0.00156	3.40
Industrial structure	0.00370	0.00135	2.74

Constant = 1.93245   *SE*est = 0.2613 R^2 = 0.492   *z* = 2.04

Absolute change equation

	b	*SE*$_b$	*t-value*
Unemployed workers, 1959	−0.00077	0.00039	1.97

Constant + 11.66756 *SE*est = 29.9312 R^2 = 0.060   *z* = −0.64

stant, the standard error of the overall regression estimate, the coefficient of multiple determination (R^2), and the *z* score of the spatial autocorrelation *I* statistic as calculated for the regression residuals.

Of these results, those for percentage change are both most interesting and most consistent. The 1959–66 equation explains approximately 50 per cent of the statistical variation in *Y*, a not unreasonable level given the fairly large number of observations (sixty-two), in terms of only three variables – a marked negative relationship with 1959 manufacturing employment, and a significant positive relationship with both residential space preferences and the industrial structure index. Each of these results is entirely consistent with the postulated relationships considered earlier. The negative scale of manufacturing activity relationship suggests the existence of agglomeration diseconomies in the major industrial centres, and the attraction of industry to relatively unindustrialized areas. Government IDC controls may however also be involved here, as noted in 5.3.3.

The industrial structure relationship is exactly that postulated and expected, indicating the importance for short-run analysis of manufacturing change of national-level demand trends and local structure. However, in many ways the most fascinating of the three relationships is that with the residential space preference index, whose associated regression coefficient yielded the second most significant *t*-value in the equation. The inclusion of this variable provides striking and novel quantitative evidence of what has hitherto been almost entirely a matter of qualitative and subjective evaluation, namely the importance for modern manufacturing location change of the residential attractiveness of different areas. Despite its defects, the index used is shown to be significantly related to percentage manufacturing change in an equation *which has already allowed* for the shift of manufacturing industry from the large, congested, and environmentally less attractive conurbations to less industrialized areas, via inclusion of the negative total manufacturing employment relationship.

Admittedly, this result demands qualification in one important respect. The regression residuals are slightly, but nonetheless by definition significantly, spatially autocorrelated, with a z score greater than 1.96. Examination of the mapped residuals, however, revealed that the major reason for this was a clustering of high positive residuals in the South East and East Anglia, with the exception of London. This immediately suggested the impact of a variable discussed earlier, but not yet incorporated in the analysis – the planned migration of industry to these regions' new and expanded towns. This process was in many ways at its peak during the 1959–66 period (see section 4.4). To allow for its impact, therefore, subregional figures for the 1959–66 expansion of manufacturing employment in such towns throughout the United Kingdom were calculated from detailed statistics published annually in the journal *Town and Country Planning*. These estimates were then subtracted, for each subregion involved, from overall manufacturing employment change, and a new percentage change value calculated which excluded growth in new and expanded towns. The best-fit regression, equation with this new dependent variable again selected exactly the same three independent variables as in the first analysis,[6] while recording only a very slightly lower R^2 value (0.480). However in this case, the z score of the regression residual statistic was only 1.32, well below the level indicating significant spatial autocorrelation. This result indicates both the localized but substantial impact in the early 1960s of the new and expanded town programme, and, more important, the general consistency and validity of the variables selected by the main regression equation.

The latter conclusion is still further strengthened by the 1966–71 percentage employment change results. As table 5.3 shows, the regression analysis of this quite separate data set again selected the same three variables as also significantly related to manufacturing change in this later period. Existing manufacturing employment and residential space preference again yielded the two highest t-values, indicating the continuing and powerful impact, even under the very different national-level employment circumstances obtaining between 1966 and 1971, of the forces redistributing industry from congested urban centres to attractive and relatively unindustrialized areas. However, equally interesting is the selection in this later analysis of the assisted-area status variable. This is exactly the result which might be expected on the basis of the marked increase in regional policy incentives since the mid-1960s referred to in section 4.2.4, and provides powerful additional support, for the first time at the detailed subregional level, for recent regional-scale identification of the considerable impact of these incentives on the spatial pattern of manufacturing

Table 5.3 *Regression results: manufacturing employment, 1966–71*

Percentage change equation (log *Y*)

	b	*SE_b*	*t-value*
Manufacturing employment, 1966 (log)	−0.25056	0.04428	5.66
Residential space preference	0.01318	0.00298	4.42
Assisted-area status	0.55827	0.14165	3.94
Industrial structure	0.00478	0.00224	2.13

Constant $= 1.48893$ $SE_{est} = 0.4316$ $R^2 = 0.598$ $z = 0.54$

Absolute change equation

	b	*SE_b*	*t-value*
Manufacturing employment, 1966	−0.15256	0.01189	12.83
Residential space preference	0.18877	0.09703	1.95
Unemployed workers, 1966	0.00071	0.00044	1.62

Constant $= 0.30241$ $SE_{est} = 16.1334$ $R^2 = 0.816$ $z = −1.60$

employment change. The overall success of the equation is indicated by a relatively high R^2 value of approximately 0.60, and a very low regression residual z score. In view of the latter, adjustment in this case for the impact of new and expanded town development was deemed unnecessary, particularly since no simple spatial trend in such development existed during the late 1960s as in the earlier years of the decade.

5.5.2. Absolute change

In contrast to the above results, the 1959–66 absolute change regression (table 5.2) was virtually entirely unsuccessful in identifying any significant influences upon the sheer quantity of manufacturing employment change in particular subregions. This illustrates the great importance of looking separately at *absolute* changes and *rates* of change in quantitative analyses of this kind. Although the absolute change variable was significantly related to total 1959 unemployment, the negative sign of the relationship is the opposite of that hypothesized and largely meaningless. The *t*-value of its coefficient is low, and the explanatory power of the equation insignificant.

However, the results of the comparable 1966–71 analysis are strikingly different. For one thing, this equation yielded the highest overall R^2 value of any of the regressions carried out in this study, the variables identified explaining 82 per cent of the statistical variation in Y. For another, two of the variables listed in table 5.3 are ones already selected by both the two percentage change analyses, namely existing manufacturing employment and residential space preferences. The almost total dominance of the former as an influence on manufacturing change, already suggested qualitatively from map evidence (section 2.2.2), is strikingly indicated both by a t-value of nearly 13, and by an individual contribution to total R^2 of no less than 0.800. Over this period, and almost certainly since for that matter, all the country's leading industrial conurbations have been declining in terms of manufacturing capacity at a remarkable rate, a phenomenon interpreted here largely though not entirely in terms of the impact of significant agglomeration diseconomies. The third variable listed in the bottom half of table 5.3 should not of course strictly have been included, since its regression coefficient t-value is just below the already modest significance level (1.67) used in these analyses. However, its inclusion, which increases R^2 by less than 1 per cent, does not in fact distort the overall result, while the positive sign of its regression coefficient does support the hypothesis of some slight relationship between labour availability, notably in the peripheral areas, and manufacturing growth. The latter is revealed more clearly by subsequent analysis of the important migration component of this absolute change variable (see section 6.6.4).

5.6. Regression results: manufacturing floorspace change

The results of the analyses of percentage and absolute manufacturing floorspace change in England and Wales, 1964–72, are given in table 5.4. It will be recalled that these dependent variables are derived from a totally different and independent source from that used for the employment variables. Yet, and quite remarkably, the percentage change analysis identified exactly the same four independent variables – existing manufacturing capacity (in this instance, of course, measured by floorspace stock), assisted-area status, industrial structure, and residential space preference – as in the chronologically comparable 1966–71 percentage manufacturing employment change regression. This striking consistency of results for two quite different indices of manufacturing activity provides strong support for the assertion that these analyses have identified the most important basic influences upon recent manufacturing location change rates in Britain. This assertion is of course further supported by the relative technical success of the equations, the percentage floorspace change analysis for example yielding a fairly high R^2 value (0.60) and a z score below the accepted significance level.

It is interesting to note that in this floorspace case, the assisted-area status variable is selected as second only to manufacturing capacity in terms of t-value significance. This contrasts with its lower ranking in these terms, below residential space preference, in the employment case (table 5.3). It must be

Table 5.4 *Regression results: manufacturing floorspace, 1964–72*

Percentage change equation (log *Y*)

	b	*SE*$_b$	*t-value*
Manufacturing floorspace, 1964 (log)	−5.53185	1.15649	4.78
Assisted-area status	14.28698	3.55903	4.01
Industrial structure	0.19239	0.05748	3.35
Residential space preference	0.14320	0.07653	1.87

Constant = 23.38451   *SE*est = 9.9483 R^2 = 0.609   *z*=1.81

Absolute change equation

Market potential	0.35247	0.12702	2.77
Residential space preference	0.11685	0.05249	2.23
Assisted-area status	5.39755	2.57108	2.10

Constant = −32.55615   *SE*est = 6.2257 R^2 = 0.154   *z*=0.16

remembered, of course, that the latter included Scotland and Northern Ireland, which introduces an element of non-comparability to the analyses. But perhaps the implication here is, as has also been argued frequently elsewhere, that government regional policy has had a more pronounced effect upon differential centre-periphery rates of capital investment and factory construction than upon rates of change in manufacturing employment. This is entirely consonant with the undoubted stress in government policy, except for the 1967–9 period and since 1974,[7] upon IDC floorspace controls and regionally-differentiated investment grants for new buildings, plant and machinery, rather than upon employee subsidies. Also of interest is the fact that the residential space preference index is accorded a much less significant *t*-value in the floorspace than in the employment analyses. This suggests that residential amenity considerations exert a more powerful influence upon locational trends in labour-intensive than in capital-intensive industry, a hypothesis which is intuitively logical. The fact that these details of the regression analyses do accord exactly with what might be expected on *a priori* grounds provides further support for the overall validity of the results.

The absolute floorspace change analysis is in one respect much less successful than the percentage change regression: the level of statistical explanation provided by the former equation is very low, at only 15 per cent.

However, it is nonetheless true that no significant spatial autocorrelation remains in the regression residuals, while the three independent variables selected all yield significant regression coefficient t-values above 2.00. Moreover, the sign of each variable is that expected from the postulated hypothesis. The most fascinating and statistically significant of the three is market potential, the positive sign indicating a tendency for subregions favoured in terms of market access to record above-average rates of net floorspace growth. This of course corroborates the visual impression afforded by figure 2.4b of a clustering of growth symbols along the London–Liverpool axis, albeit with net decline in the two polar conurbations of London and Manchester.

This finding has at least two interesting implications. First, it is consistent with an above-average rate of capital/labour substitution by manufacturing industry in the central belt of high market accessibility. This is suggested by comparison of the significant and *positive* relationship between absolute floorspace growth and market access (table 5.4) with the *negative* relationship between the latter and 1966–71 absolute employment change noted earlier (section 5.4). In turn, relatively increasing central area capital intensity would of course accord with Norcliffe's hypothesis (section 4.1.1) of the attraction of larger, more capital-intensive, plants to central market locations. The second implication is that at least in terms of floorspace change, the centre-periphery model with its stress on the axial belt's advantages of market access, better transport infrastructure, innovation leadership and so on, still has some validity. This may however only reflect a time-lag between trends in influencing variables and employment change, on the one hand, and eventual floorspace response on the other, as suggested in section 2.2.3. The other two variables selected for the absolute floorspace change regression are residential space preference and assisted-area status. Both are entirely meaningful choices, and provide further consistent support for the view that local residential environment and government regional policy are now of key significance in influencing the national spatial pattern of manufacturing change, in this case as measured by factory floorspace.

5.7. Regression results: conclusions

A number of important conclusions may be drawn from these national-scale, aggregate manufacturing change analyses. The general validity of these conclusions is strongly suggested by the consistency and stability of the results, notably with respect to the three different percentage change analyses, by the considerable technical success of most regressions measured in terms of fairly high R^2 values and the elimination of residual spatial autocorrelation, and by the inherent logic of virtually all the relationships identified, several of which are directly corroborated by other independent evidence. The general success

of the regression analyses indicates the utility of macro-level statistical investigation of industrial location change as one important approach to the
study of this phenomenon. *general law of general application*

The first main conclusion must be that at first sight the preceding analyses
provide very little support for the traditional centre-periphery model as either a
description or explanation of industrial location trends in Britain since 1959.
Only in the one absolute floorspace change case was market potential selected
as a significant independent variable; while the employment analyses suggest
that market access is now *negatively* associated with manufacturing employment growth (see section 5.4). Moreover, four of the six analyses also pinpointed a very marked negative relationship between manufacturing capacity,
taken in this context as an index of possible agglomeration economies, and industrial growth. The latter relationship, which in earlier studies has in part been
identified as a product of the mathematics of percentage calculations (Keeble
and Hauser 1971, 244), appears in the present study to indicate genuine diseconomies of one kind or another, since of course the largest centres in all
three percentage change analyses exhibit absolute *decline*, not just sluggish
relative growth. However, two qualifications to this broad conclusion on the
centre-periphery model are perhaps necessary. One, of course, is that unacceptably high spatial autocorrelation of residuals in the 1959–66 percentage
analysis was shown to be due to the scale of new and expanded town development in the South East and East Anglia during this period, a phenomenon
which can be viewed as reflecting the locational advantages of these regions as
set out in the centre-periphery model. The other qualification relates to the inclusion in all three percentage change analyses of a positive relationship with
the industrial structure index. This clearly indicates the importance for short-
run analysis of inherited structure. But it is also true that the subregions
recording the most favourable structures, and hence on this basis identified as
generally enjoying above-average percentage growth all else being equal, are
markedly concentrated in the central regions of South East England, the West
Midlands and East Anglia (fig. 5.3). In a sense, therefore, the consistent selection of the structural index is indicating a certain tendency towards cumulative
manufacturing expansion in these central areas, although this tendency is
balanced if not largely offset by other influences also identified by the regression analyses. These qualifications do suggest, however, that despite the
negative market accessibility relationship, the centre-periphery model may still
represent one, though no longer the major, determinant of current manufacturing location trends in Britain.

The second conclusion is that the regression analyses provide considerable
support for the alternative periphery-centre model, at least since the mid-
1960s. Most striking here is the performance of the assisted-area status
dummy variable. While neither of the 1959–66 analyses selected this as
significantly related to manufacturing change, no less than three of the four

analyses for the later 1960s and early 1970s did so. This dramatic shift is exactly what might be expected in view of the now fully documented transformation which occurred in regional policy between 1963 and 1966, from a relatively passive phase to one characterized by a very high recent level of assisted-area financial incentives to manufacturing growth (Keeble 1969b, 854; Moore and Rhodes 1973; Hart 1971, 184). This finding, the first at the detailed subregional scale, thus substantiates the fact that government regional policy is now a major influence upon manufacturing location trends in Britain, whether measured by employment *or* floorspace. Although the labour availability component of the periphery-centre model does not figure, except in one limited instance, in the regression results, it is of course true that assisted-area status is fairly closely correlated with unemployment rates (section 5.1.2). So above-average manufacturing growth in assisted areas since the mid-1960s has taken place in the context of greater local labour availability than elsewhere in Britain.

The marked negative impact of existing scale of manufacturing activity is of course also one of the main findings of the regression analyses. This impact is here interpreted in terms of substantial agglomeration diseconomies, and perhaps stringent IDC controls and planning constraints, in the largest industrial centres. In part, this too may be viewed in periphery-centre model terms, as exemplified by the fact that the five biggest subregions in both 1959 and 1966 were all non-peripheral; and that no less than eleven of the fifteen subregions with fewer than 25,000 manufacturing employees in 1959 were in the periphery, compared with only one in the centre. But as suggested in section 4.2.2, agglomeration diseconomies and governmental controls also and powerfully appear to be influencing within-region trends, encouraging a shift in the locational balance of manufacturing from central industrial conurbations to surrounding, traditionally non-industrial subregions. This marked trend towards industrial dispersal from major to minor industrial centres, which seems to be occurring at all spatial scales – national, regional and indeed subregional (see section 9.4.2) – within Britain, is one of the key findings of the present study.

The last major finding concerns the remarkably consistent selection of the residential space preference index by no less than five of the six regression analyses presented here. This variable was thus identified as significantly and positively related to manufacturing location change more frequently than any other variable included in the analyses. This is a most striking finding, and represents in many ways the first national-scale objective evidence of the real current importance for manufacturing location trends in Britain of residential environment and general subregional 'image', given the survey measurement problems noted earlier (section 4.3). Moreover, the t-values recorded in tables 5.2 and 5.3 suggest that the significance of this factor as an explanatory variable may well be increasing, at least as far as the location of manufacturing employment is concerned.

The implications of this for the future manufacturing geography of Britain, and for local and regional planning, are thus likely to be very considerable, not least in terms of the reduced relevance as an explanatory framework of both the traditional centre-periphery *and* periphery-centre models to which such considerable attention has been devoted in the literature.

NOTES

1 The 02R stepwise regression option of the BIOMED package programme, devised by the Health Sciences Computing Facility, University of California at Los Angeles. The programme was run on the Cambridge University IBM 370/165 computer. I am greatly indebted to Dr A. D. Cliff of the Cambridge University Department of Geography for assistance with this programme, and that for calculation of the Cliff-Ord I statistic.

2 I am greatly indebted to Professor Michael Chisholm for his kind provision of these data.

3 Unpublished 1959 MLH data for Northern Ireland, which was not included in Chisholm and Oeppen's study, were kindly provided by Mr A. R. Gillespie of the Cambridge University Department of Geography.

4 Gould and White's study unfortunately excluded Northern Ireland. The latter was therefore arbitrarily accorded the same value as that for Clydeside and northern Scotland (15).

5 The t-value of the associated regression coefficient was 3.94, while the spatial autocorrelation statistic z score for regression residuals was only 1.56, below the 5 per cent significance level.

6 The t-values for these variables were 5.77 (manufacturing employment), 2.77 (industrial structure) and 2.67 (residential space preference), all well above the 2.00 level.

7 The real value of REP had fallen substantially by 1970, being restored only in 1974 (see section 8.6.4).

6 The components of change

6.1. Introduction

The discussion in preceding chapters has been concerned chiefly with recent net changes in the *aggregate* level of manufacturing industry in different sub-regions of Britain. However, as section 3.1 noted, a different but complementary approach to studying locational shifts in manufacturing is via component analysis. The latter views a change in the level of manufacturing activity in a particular area during a given time period as the net product of six basic change components – the birth in the area of entirely new firms, the expansion, the contraction, the death or the emigration of the area's existing firms, and the immigration to the area of existing firms from elsewhere. These six components of change can of course be subdivided still further, or aggregated, as for example in terms of a net migration component.

Conceptually, the significance of component analysis of spatial manufacturing change lies in the possibility of quite different forces occasioning different trends in different components over the same time period. Net aggregate change may thus mask considerable differences in component performance, and the operation of different locational forces upon different components. For example, Stewart (1972, 7) reports an unpublished study which concluded that between 1961 and 1966, South East England's manufacturing workforce recorded a net decline of about 30,000. But this in fact masked a gross creation by existing, newly-born or immigrant manufacturing firms of nearly 300,000 jobs, offset however by a gross loss of well over 300,000 manufacturing jobs resulting from contraction of employment, emigration or death of existing South East firms. This very substantial gross growth component could well reflect continuing advantages of a South East location for certain types of industry or enterprise, in terms of maximum market access, external economies, and so on; while the gross losses through firm decline, death and through firm decline, death and migration might reflect the quite different impact of labour shortages and costs, or government regional policy. Conceptually, therefore, component analysis would seem to be potentially of great importance for understanding subregional manufacturing shifts.

Unfortunately, however, the available evidence about the recent relative importance of particular components in particular British subregions is limited, fragmentary and partial. The reason for this is of course the enormous difficulty of collecting and monitoring manufacturing activity data at the firm or factory level, bearing in mind, for example, the existence in the United Kingdom of no less than 92,000 separate manufacturing establishments (in 1968). Only in the case of the migration component, concerning which British statistics and research are substantially in advance of those in most other countries, is detailed evaluation of current spatial trends feasible. This is one major reason for the emphasis given to migration later in this chapter.

6.2. Births

The birth of a manufacturing firm in a particular area is here defined as involving the creation of an entirely new enterprise which did not formerly exist as a manufacturing organization in that or any other area. In very broad terms, it seems probable that most births fall into one or other of two categories. First, and much the more common, is the coming into existence of a very small firm, as a result of the initiative, enterprise and risk-taking of one or two individuals with a particular idea or skill. Such individuals were often formerly employed as managers or technicians by a larger local firm, and break away from it to set up on their own. This 'hiving-off' process is most typical of certain industries, such as engineering and metal-fabricating, and clothing, to which entry by individual entrepreneurs is relatively easy in terms of technological, financial and factory-building requirements. Thus a clothing entrepreneur in inner north-east London requires only a rented workroom some sewing machines and operatives, and some orders, to be in business (Hall 1962, 119).

However, it is almost certainly no accident that industries of this type, and births of new firms, seem traditionally to have been concentrated in the larger centrally-located industrial subregions of Britain. Although actual birth rate data are not available, much circumstantial evidence supports Hammond's claim (1964, 140) that 'small concerns ... breed and thrive in much greater numbers on the London fringe and in the West Midlands than elsewhere'. The reasons for this probably centre on the external economies and institutional environment of these areas. The former (section 4.1.4) are probably of peculiar and vital importance to new firms, in that they reduce the risks and uncertainty which inevitably threaten the viability of such new enterprises. The readier availability of premises reasonably close to the entrepreneur's home, the host of available supporting services, the variety and scale of local demand for manufactured goods, the greater possibilities for local linkage and product specialization, more rapid access to information about technological innovations or demand shifts, and even in the past cheaper loan finance for development (section 4.1.6), all help to provide an environment for so-called 'seedbed' growth of new firms which few other areas can emulate. Such growth is also encouraged by the *diversity* of manufacturing in these central subregions, which, as already stressed (section 4.1.6), is associated with an open, innovative institutional environment, a relatively high degree of crossfertilization of ideas and technology, and an increased probability of new births. The relationship between manufacturing diversity, institutional environment and high birth rates is strikingly attested by Beesley's study (1955) of the development of new engineering firms in the West Midlands conurbation during the 1920s and 1930s. Using detailed unpublished Factory Inspectorate data, Beesley showed that in those parts of the conurbation – the north-west and Birmingham areas – in which the engineering industry was most diversified and complex, there had developed 'an environment favouring experimentation with new combinations of parts to form product innovations. This opportunity to combine parts represented an incentive to form new enterprises, which were reflected in the creation of new establishments' (Beesley 1955, 47–8). The resultant high birth rate of new engineering firms in these zones was in marked contrast to the low birth rate recorded by the south-west of the conurbation, with its more specialized and hence less adaptable type of engineering activity and more rigid institutional environment.

Further evidence suggesting above-average twentieth-century manufacturing firm birth rates as a response to central region external economies and institutional environment is provided by the present author's study of manufacturing growth in outer north-west London (Keeble 1966, 161–201). Although dealing only with surviving firms, this study found that exactly 50 per cent of a stratified random sample of all north-west London manufacturing firms employing ten production operatives or more in 1962 had originally begun life in the area as completely new firms, the remainder being immigrants of one kind or another. Moreover, this relative proportion did not appear to have changed over time, 49 per cent and 51 per cent respectively of the pre-1939 and post-1939 firms included in the survey being new births. The survey revealed that nearly all such firms began in a very small way, median firm size at birth for the two sets of pre-1939 and post-1939 new concerns being only ten and six employees respectively, and that the area's external economies, notably in terms of a large supply of small, cheap, rented premises, and its diverse institutional environment resulting from a wide range of engineering activities and skills, had been of key importance in stimulating new births.

In contrast, Spooner (1974) records an apparently much lower birth rate for post-1939 factories employing more than thirty workers in 1966 in the peripheral and relatively-unindustrialized area of Devon and Cornwall. Only 26 per cent of these plants proved to have originated locally as entirely new births. Even allowing for the slightly larger size threshold, a significant difference compared with the north-west London study would seem to obtain. This is certainly accepted by Spooner (1974, 74), who stresses that 'the nature of the area itself with a lack of industrial conglomerations and external economies and "atmosphere" would suggest both a low birth rate and low survival rate of new enterprises'. Moreover, a similar finding is arrived at by Firn (1975) for the peripheral but heavily industrialized region of west-central Scotland. Explicitly stressing the region's 'low rate of formation of indigenous enterprise', Firn (1975, 397) points out that between 1958 and 1968 'only 37% of employment created in new (manufacturing) establishments came from local enterprise, against 33% from the rest of the United Kingdom, and 30% from overseas, mainly north America', the latter two categories comprising of course immigrant plants. So here as well a significant centre/periphery differential in manufacturing-firm birth rates, linked in Firn's view to basic differences in entrepreneurship, does seem to obtain.

The second, much less frequent type of new birth is the creation of a new manufacturing firm by an existing but *non-manufacturing* organization. New firms set up by older manufacturing companies, but in a rather different industry and product market, may also perhaps be included in this category, although definitional problems *vis-à-vis* migration (section 6.6) obviously arise here. While less common than 'break-away' births, planned firm creation of this kind may well however often be more important than the former, in that it usually results in larger establishments, which command greater financial resources, are the product of more careful planning and market forecasting, and are hence less vulnerable to subsequent closure. Thus North's recent survey (1974, 238–9) of larger plastics firms in South East and North West England revealed that of the twenty-five firms (one-quarter of his sample) which began as new births between 1960 and 1971, a greater number (sixteen) were set up as subsidiaries of other organizations than resulted from the classic 'hiving-off' process (nine). This finding for a very recent period also supports the view that this second type of new birth is becoming relatively more important, as increasing output and financial thresholds decrease ease of entry by small entrepreneurs to many industries. However, as North also stresses, the locational pattern of such planned births is probably often similar to that of 'hived-off' concerns, being characterized by an initial need for the external economies and linkages provided by central industrial concentrations.

The implicit assumption in much of the preceding discussion is of course that a high new firm birth rate is important for an area's industrial vitality and prosperity. In the long term this is probably true. As Beesley (1955, 49) stresses, a high birth rate

> is a form of insurance for the employment in an area in the long run. A few of the new small establishments will grow, and will be able to absorb resources falling into disuse in the area... Many new products which eventually command a wide market are first produced on a very small scale by 'breakaways' from existing industries. The more new establishments an area has, the greater are the chances for such developments to occur, and the better are its prospects for keeping in the van of industrial change.

This conclusion is fully supported by the north-west London study (Keeble 1966, 188), which found that at least twelve of the twenty-nine largest manufacturing firms in the area, each employing over 1,000 production operatives, had begun life somewhere in Greater London in exactly this way.

But at the same time, a high birth rate must be seen in proportion. For one thing, particularly when associated with industries to which entry is relatively easy, it is often matched and offset by an equally high firm death rate (Smith 1933, 173). For another, the great majority of new breakaway firms are most accurately characterized as imitators rather than innovators (Edwards and Townsend 1958, 4), their activities thus simply duplicating those of existing firms. In the north-west London survey, only four of the twenty-two post-1939 breakaway births studied gave any sign of being responsible for significant product or processing innovations. A further major point is that in the short or even medium term, the small size of such new firms, however high the local birth rate, renders unusual any major impact by the birth component upon aggregate manufacturing change in a particular area. Thus the north-west London survey revealed that even allowing for the effect of births over as long a period as twenty-five years (1939–63), a mere 7 per cent of total 1963 manufacturing employment in the 124 firms randomly sampled was provided by new post-1939 firms originating in the area. This sample excluded the area's twenty-nine largest firms, all of which were operating in the area before 1939. A similar picture arises from Spooner's study (1974) of Devon and Cornwall, where only 2.5 per cent of total 1966 employment in his sample of 189 larger factories was attributable to the establishment and growth of indigenous, post-1939 new companies. One must therefore look elsewhere for the major components in short-run manufacturing change in most areas.

6.3. In situ expansion

Without much doubt, the leading contender in this respect is the expansion (or contraction) *in situ* of existing manufacturing firms. Admittedly, some earlier commentators in this field, such as Dennison (1937, 155) tended to dismiss existing concerns in sentences like 'the expansion of plants already in existence is an important feature in development, which does not depend entirely upon the creation of new plants'. But considerable recent evidence focuses attention on the performance of existing industry. A key finding here is that of Kuklinski (1967, 17), who concludes from a European-wide survey of industrial location trends that 'probably 60–80 per cent of investment in manufacturing industry in developed countries is allocated to the expansion of existing plants and something under 40 per cent to the construction of new ones', the latter presumably including both migrant plants and new births.

This generalization is supported, at least for growing manufacturing areas or industries, by much recent British case-study evidence. Thus, for example, North's survey (1974, 221) of 100 larger English plastics firms discovered that by far the most common type of locational decision taken during the twelve years 1960–71 was to extend the existing premises (46 per cent of firms sampled) rather than, for example, to move to a new location or set up a branch factory. In terms of numbers of decisions, extensions were more than twice as frequent (seventy-eight cases) as the next most common category, branch plant establishment (thirty-eight cases). Again, the present author's explicit evaluation of the components of north-west London's postwar industrial expansion (Keeble 1966, 176) concluded that 'the dominating mechanism of growth since 1945 has not been the establishment of new firms, but the expansion of larger, existing concerns'. Thus 88 per cent of the area's total 1963 manufacturing employment was found to be in firms which had established themselves in north-west London before 1939. While between 1952 and 1962, a very slight fall in the total number of manufacturing operatives in north-west London's three key industrial boroughs of Acton, Willesden and Wembley, from 87,400 to 85,400, in fact masked a significant *growth* (+7,600) in the numbers employed in the boroughs' thirty-seven largest factories, all of which were prewar (Keeble 1966, 177–9). The role of existing firms in maintaining and expanding postwar employment levels in the area is clearly indicated by these statistics.

A third study providing evidence is that by Lewis (1971) on the process of manufacturing growth between 1945 and 1966 in Berkshire, Buckinghamshire and Oxfordshire. From Lewis' data, it may be estimated that manufacturing employment in this area probably expanded by about 90,000 workers or 75 per cent over this period. Of this 30,000, jobs may on Board of Trade evidence be attributed to *net* industrial migration, with gains of 35,000 and losses of 5,000 jobs. The gains were almost all from Greater London. Births of entirely new manufacturing firms indigenous to the area, what Lewis terms 'original' enterprise, may on the evidence of his sample survey (Lewis 1971, 127) have provided a further 13,000 jobs, or 14 per cent of total net growth. This leaves a residual expansion of perhaps 47,000 manufacturing jobs, or 53 per cent, as the major single contribution to growth, attributable to the within-area expansion of firms already operating in the three counties in 1945, and allowing for decline and closure. Lewis's study also indicates that *in situ* expansion was almost totally dominant in particular industrial centres within his study area, notably Slough and Oxford, the latter alone benefiting from an *in situ* growth in vehicle-manufacturing employment of over 10,000 jobs between 1945 and 1966 (Lewis 1971, 119). This and the previous evidence thus indicate that in growing industrial areas of a reasonable initial size, expansion by existing manufacturing firms is usually the key single component in short or medium-term manufacturing growth.

6.4. In situ contraction

Evidence on the *in situ* contraction of manufacturing firms is very limited, not least because large-scale decline, at least of employment, has only been common in Britain since the mid-1960s. *A priori,* however, it might be expected that aggregate subregional decline, as with growth, is likely to be dominated by changing activity levels in existing firms. Thus the recent massive manufacturing employment losses of Britain's main conurbations might be expected primarily to reflect *in situ* contraction, rather than complete closures or emigration.

However, this *a priori* expectation is not borne out by the available evidence. The most important and authoritative such evidence is a recent but unpublished research study by the Department of Industry.[1] This suggests that between 1966 and 1974 net manufacturing employment decline in Greater London resulted in a loss of 383,000 jobs, defined on the new Census of Employment basis. However, no less than 280,000 of these, or 73 per cent, were lost through complete factory closures, including closures resulting from transfer emigration. The residual 103,000 job loss reflects a net *in situ* contraction of 116,000, offset by a very limited growth through new births (10,000 jobs) and immigration (3,000 jobs). So net *in situ* contraction accounts for only 30 per cent of London's massive recent manufacturing decline, the bulk of this being due to closures including transfers.

Moreover, this comprehensive study is corroborated by other, more limited, evidence. Thus, for example, Martin and Seaman (1975) estimate that between 1954 and 1968, the total number of large factories (100 workers or more) in the GLC area fell by no less than 28 per cent, from 1,905 to only 1,370. In inner London (the ILEA area), the closure rate was even greater, at 44 per cent (784 down to 443), with a corresponding smaller rate of decline (17 per cent) in outer London. This massive rate of closure of large factories, over only a fourteen-year period, clearly provides indirect support for the DI research findings. So too does a detailed recent study of the port-based industrial area of Canning Town, in inner north-east London, which reveals that closures accounted for 64 per cent of the gross total of 10,500 manufacturing jobs lost between 1966 and 1972 (Canning Town Community Development Project 1975). *In situ* contraction of existing firms resulted only in 3,800 job losses, or 36 per cent of the gross total. A rather lower *net* manufacturing decline figure, of 8,800 jobs or 37 per cent, 1966–72, reflects some small-scale manufacturing job creation as a result of new births and, to a lesser extent, existing firm growth (&1,700 jobs, taken together). But overall, factory closures, not *in situ* contraction, have dominated Canning Town's recent industrial history, in accord with trends at the wider conurbation level. Whether or not Greater London, by far the most dramatic industrial decline centre of the United Kingdom, is typical in this respect of the other major industrial conurbations is a most interesting but as yet unanswered question.

6.5. Deaths

The preceding section has suggested from London evidence that complete closure, or death, of local firms or factories is of dominant importance in recent conurbation industrial decline. This can be amplified from the Department of Industry London data. Of total closure job losses, 1966–74, only 97,000 were due to transfer emigration from Greater London, 183,000, by far the largest component, being due to complete closure or death of the factory or firm involved. Again, this conclusion is supported by the Canning Town study, which clearly implies that most local closures have been deaths, not transfers, and by Seaman's earlier research (1970, 297–302) on inner south-east London. The latter found that total closures of large manufacturing plants in this area resulted in a loss of over 20,000 manufacturing jobs between 1964 and 1970, or 13 per cent of the area's total manufacturing workforce.

As the last two studies both emphasize, large-plant closures in centres such as London often reflect locational re-evaluation in the light of demand and technological changes by *multi-plant* national companies, who are in a position accurately to compare operating and marginal production costs in factories in different areas. Plant rationalization by such companies, often following merger or takeover, appears to be of considerable recent significance for manufacturing location change in Britain (Keeble 1971, 33–4; Watts 1974; North 1975). As Watts points out, British manufacturing industry is dominated by multi-plant companies: in 1963, nearly 1,000 enterprises of over 1,000 employees actually operated 11,000 plants and provided 60 per cent of United Kingdom manufacturing employment. And of the three distinct multi-plant rationalization strategies identified by Watts, two – concentration/partial disinvestment, and complete disinvestment/greenfield site – involve plant closures, the latter drastic strategy involving shut-down of all existing plants. It is interesting that Watts quotes, as an example of the former, the case of the AEI Woolwich (London) factory closure, which involved a 110-year-old factory, a highly valuable 160,000-square-metre (40-acre) site, a loss of several thousand London manufacturing jobs, and a switch of production to group plants at Coventry, in Scotland and in the North East, the latter two locations enjoying of course regional policy labour subsidies (Seaman 1970, 299). It is perhaps not therefore surprising that direct operating cost comparisons by multi-plant corporations appear normally to be to the disadvantage of the older conurbation plant. Key location factors in this particular component of change are thus the relative age, congestion and inefficient layout of premises, relatively high wage costs, and the absence of government regional policy incentives.

Complete closures are preferred to contraction for various reasons. One is probably the avoidance of trades-union protest over redundancies by the *fait accompli* of complete rather than partial shut-down. Another is the powerful scale-economy logic of operating $n-1$ plants each at full capacity, rather than n plants each at reduced capacity. A third, and very important factor, is the possibility of realizing substantial returns from the sale of the usually very valuable site occupied by older conurbation factories, compared with that of their more modern counterparts elsewhere (see section 4.2.2). Thus the 1975 closure of the long-established Rockware Group's glass factory at Greenford in outer north-west London, with a loss of 600 jobs, was apparently chiefly a reflection of the high book value – £3 million – of the 140,000-square-metre (35-acre) site. The only other Group factory considered as a candidate for closure – St Helens, Lancashire – was valued at under —1 million. The Greenford site is thought by independent observers actually to have realized some £6 million on sale.[2] Very high industrial site values are in fact singled out by the Canning Town study as the first of a list of factors explaining manufacturing closures in the area, the study quoting a figure of —505,000 per 1,000 square metres (—100,000 per acre) as the 1974 valuue of industrial land in the area.

The economic logic of large-plant closure may thus be considerable. However, the loss of such plants may of course have further effects, particularly if local linkages have been developed with smaller manufacturing concerns. In Canning Town, an example has apparently been the impact of closures in the ship-repairing industry upon small local suppliers, producing further contraction and closure. In inner south-east London many small local subcontractors have also apparently been seriously hit by the closure of certain large engineering firms, and a number have ceased operations (Seaman 1970, 302). Further local contraction and closure, in a negative cumulative causation sequence, is therefore likely. Moreover, many other non-economic problems may arise from this process. As the Canning Town study emphasizes, factory closures in that area have resulted in a rate of job loss which has been twice as fast as the accompanying decline in the resident workforce (−18 per cent, 1966–71). At the same time, selective migration of younger skilled workers from the area, partly as a response to closures, is producing an increasing proportion of older, unskilled workers in the remaining resident workforce. Between 1966 and 1973 the number of unemployed males resident in Canning Town increased by 220 per cent, compared with a rise of only 70 per cent in the South East as a whole; and redundant workers who have found new employment have often been forced to accept significantly lower wages in other activities, and/or to accept longer-distance and more expensive commuting out of the area to jobs elsewhere. The recent scale and rate of factory closures in inner city areas such as Canning Town may thus pose significant socio-economic problems for local residents and workers.

This said, however, it is necessary to emphasize that overall, multi-plant manufacturing firms are probably more often a growth element in the national, regional and subregional manufacturing system, than one associated predominantly with factory closures. Thus Rake's very interesting recent study of such firms in the East Midlands reveals (Rake 1972, 930) that although his sample of forty-three multi-plant manufacturing companies recorded some 115 disinvestment, or closure, decisions between 1945 and 1971, they were also responsible for the establishment and acquisition by takeover of even larger numbers of new branch units (148) and existing manufacturing units (189). The latter two growth elements thus involved nearly three times as many plants as those lost through disinvestment decisions; and although this relates only to plant numbers, there is no obvious reason why the balance in terms of total employment or manufacturing capacity should be significantly different. A further point is that sixteen of the closures involved transfer of production to another nearby local factory, and redundancies were not therefore necessarily a consequence.

In conclusion, then, plant deaths appear to represent the key component in London's recent massive manufacturing decline, and possibly also in that of the other United Kingdom conurbations. This in turn suggests the existence of an increasingly unfavourable manufacturing environment in these centres, particularly in their inner-city areas where closures are concentrated. It also focuses attention on the role of larger multi-plant firms which are uniquely able to quantify and compare factory operations in different areas and regions. The importance of closures in subregional industrial decline is referred to again in section 6.7.

6.6. Migration

A clear distinction between industrial migration to a new location on the one hand, and multi-plant closure and rationalization on the other, is not at all easy in particular cases. Industrial migration is however normally defined (Howard 1968, 3; Keeble 1971a, 33) as including *both* the complete relocation or transfer of a firm or factory's existing manufacturing activity from one location to another, *and* movement through the establishment in a new location of a branch unit of the firm concerned, which nonetheless maintains its manufacturing activity to some degree in its existing location.

Migration therefore excludes shifts in the locational distribution of the firm as a result of *acquisition* by financial takeover of another existing firm or plant. That the latter may well be a significant form of locational adjustment from the viewpoint of the firm is of course indicated by the findings of Rake's study noted in section 6.5, with plants acquired by takeover outnumbering new branch factories set up by his sample of East Midland multi-plant firms. But for changes in *area* manufacturing levels, takeovers are likely to be less significant than migration, both because of their almost certainly more limited impact upon employment or output, and because choice of a new location by acquisition is by definition markedly circumscribed by the existing spatial, distribution of the industry concerned. Migration trends are to this extent much less spatially constrained and hence likely to be a more sensitive indicator of significant shifts in area locational advantage within a country such as the United Kingdom. Moreover, as North (1974, 222) demonstrates for the British plastics industry, *total* migration decisions including both transfers and branches in any case undoubtedly substantially outnumber acquisition decisions in most industries. His sample of 100 firms thus recorded over twice as many migration decisions in total (seventy-two, made up of thirty-four transfers and thirty-eight branches) as acquisitions (thirty-five) during the 1960–71 period. This said, however, the locational impact of firm takeovers in Britain certainly deserves far more attention by geographers than it has hitherto received, its all-too-brief mention here largely reflecting the marked dearth of available information on this subject.

In the past, observers have often regarded manufacturing migration as here defined as a phenomenon of only limited significance, both in terms of its frequency and its impact upon local manufacturing change. This view is evident in such comments as that by Luttrell (1962, 39): 'for most firms, the question of looking for new locations at which to manufacture seldom arises', and that by Smith (1954, 49), to the effect that manufacturing movement accounts for 'but a small part of the overall change in manufacturing importance of an area'. However, these early judgements were necessarily based on only limited and fragmentary evidence, and substantial recent British migration research suggests that they underrate the frequency and significance of this component of manufacturing location change. Thus, for example, work in north-west London by the present author has revealed (Keeble 1971a, 31–2) that if migration is defined as movement to any new site not actually contiguous with that already occupied by the firm concerned, nearly 80 per cent of all 1963 north-west London manufacturing firms employing ten production operatives or more had been involved in at least one move since beginning manufacture. The whole sample in fact recorded no less than 184 moves, or 1.94 moves for each of the ninety-five firms reporting movement. Admittedly, a high proportion of these moves were over only short distances (61 per cent were of less than ten kilometres). But even longer-distance migration was more frequent than implied by comments such as Luttrell's.

Again, recent research has also revealed the great importance of manufacturing movement as a component of industrial change in a number of areas. This is considered further at the detailed subregional level in section 6.6.5. But its regional significance is indicated by cases such as Wales, in which immigrant factories 1945–65 (including firms from abroad) were providing no less than 28.7 per cent of all manufacturing employment by 1966 (Howard 1968, 9), and Devon and Cornwall, where immigrant firms 1939–67 were responsible by the latter date for at least 27.5 per cent of all manufacturing employment (Spooner 1972, 201). The significance of movement for regional manufacturing *change* is even greater, areas such as Wales and Northern England recording aggregate manufacturing employment growth 1966–71 *only* because of net manufacturing immigration (Keeble, 1976). The latter also played a major role in East Anglia and South West England, the only other two United Kingdom regions to record net manufacturing growth over this period. These facts, together with the much greater availability of reliable data and research findings, perhaps justify giving considerably more attention to this component of industrial change than to those examined in previous sections. It should be noted however that most of the following discussion is concerned implicitly or explicitly only with migration at the inter-subregional or inter-regional scales, and not with intra-urban movement, extensive though this may be (Keeble 1974a, 22–3).

6.6.1. The characteristics of migrant plants

It is now well-established that migrant firms and factories differ significantly from non-mobile manufacturing firms and plants in Britain, in terms of a considerable number of variables. Chief amongst these are rate of growth, market linkages, industrial structure, size and organizational type. Each of these characteristic differences will be considered in turn.

That mobile firms are predominantly expanding firms, forced to move by growth which brings the firm up against a local output 'ceiling' beyond which further *in situ* expansion is extremely difficult or costly (Keeble 1968a, 3), is attested by a variety of evidence. Table 6.1, for example, records actual growth-rate frequencies for two samples of mobile (forty-one firms, complete transfers only) and non-mobile (ninety-eight firms, randomly selected) firms, all formerly or then currently (1963) operating in north-west London. The former had all selected new locations at least sixteen kilometres (ten miles) away from their previous north-west London factories (Keeble 1968a, 3–4). As the table shows, approximately 50 per cent of the mobile firms recorded growth rates of ten employees per annum or more (measured since movement occurred), whereas only 20 per cent of non-mobile firms had experienced rates

Table 6.1 *Employee growth rates in mobile and non-mobile north-west London firms*

Employee growth rate per annum	Non-mobile firms		Mobile firms	
	No.	%	No.	%
20 and over	9	9	14	34
10–19.9	11	11	6	15
5–9.9	21	22	6	15
less than 5 (inc. decline)	57	58	15	36
Total sample	98	100	41	100
Sample median growth rate	3.2 emps/annum		7.8 emps/annum	

Source: unpublished survey records; see also Keeble 1968a, 4

as high as this (since inception to north-west London). A chi-square test not surprisingly reveals that the sample differences given in the table are very significant ($\chi^2 = 22.2$, significant at the 0.001 level). So too is the difference in median growth rates, that for mobile firms being more than twice as great as for non-mobile firms.

A second type of evidence is the very high proportion of mobile firms noted by recent surveys as reporting 'expansion of production' as the basic reason for movement at all. Thus migrant firm surveys of movement to the assisted areas generally (Cameron and Clark 1966), to Devon and Cornwall (Spooner 1972), and from north-west London (Keeble 1968a) all agree that approximately 85 per cent of the firms investigated in each case reported movement to be a direct consequence of growth. Moreover, these findings have since been strikingly corroborated by the authoritative ILAG enquiry, which found (Department of Trade and Industry 1973, 534) that 83 per cent of 531 mobile firms surveyed reported output expansion as a major reason for movement. No other factor was reported as frequently. This further finding would appear to substantiate beyond much doubt the author's earlier conclusion (Keeble 1971a, 29) 'that a value of approximately 85 per cent represents a kind of equilibrium level which defines the relative contributions of expanding and contracting industry in any reasonably large sample of postwar migrant British manufacturing firms'.

A third category of evidence is afforded by inter-industry variations in mobility and growth. Various studies (Howard 1968, 26–9; Keeble 1971a, 26–7) agree that at this aggregate level, too, fast-growing industries are more mobile than slow-growing industries. A particularly authoritative finding is that by Townroe (1973), whose multiple regression analyses of 1960–65 United Kingdom movement rates for thirty-eight detailed industries pinpointed percentage employment growth as a very significant positive influence in all the equations presented. More recently still, and despite declining national manufacturing employment, three of the four nationally fastest-growing (or least-declining) manufacturing industries 1962–71,[3] 'other manufacturing' (+15 per cent), 'engineering' (+3 per cent) and 'chemicals' (−1.5 per cent), still accounted for five of the six most mobile industries 1966–71 (table 6.2). So all the evidence agrees that mobile firms and industries are significantly more growth-oriented than manufacturing industry as a whole.

Differences in market linkage patterns between mobile and non-mobile firms have received much less attention in the migrant industry literature.[4] However, unique data derived from the present author's 1963 surveys of mobile and non-mobile north-west London manufacturing firms clearly indicate two important differences in this respect. One is that mobile firms serve significantly wider spatial markets within the United Kingdom than do non-mobile firms. Thus only 69 per cent of 124 randomly-selected non-mobile north-west London firms reported full nationwide market penetration, compared with 89 per cent of the sample of sixty-five transfers from this area to the rest of the country. Nationwide market linkages were here specifically defined necessarily to include delivery of goods at least to customers in Wales and Scotland, while the transfer replies relate to the market pattern when still operating in north-west London immediately before movement. As measured by the chi-square test (χ^2 = 8.22), the difference is highly significant (at the 0.01 probability level).

So too is that revealed ($\chi^2 = 6.94$) by the same surveys with respect to a second market linkage characteristic, exporting. As reported in Keeble (1968a, 35), 84 per cent of the transfer sample were engaged to a greater or lesser extent in exporting to countries outside the United Kingdom, compared with only 65 per cent of the non-mobile firms. For firms exporting one-quarter or more of their production by value, the respective proportions were 39 and 27 per cent. Mobile firms thus appear to be significantly more export-oriented, and to exhibit significantly wider spatial patterns of customer linkage within the United Kingdom than non-mobile firms. The latter characteristic is of course intuitively reasonable, in that firms heavily dependent upon local customers are likely, all else being equal, to resist pressures to move any distance from their existing location, whereas firms with a national market orientation are in this respect at least likely to be more footloose. Greater export-orientation, on the other hand, is probably more a reflection of the generally progressive, growth oriented character of mobile firms, than a reflection of any locational influence (Keeble 1968a, 35). But these differences are striking, and clearly significant in the context of regional and national economic planning.

Differences in the industrial structure of mobile industry are well

Table 6.2   *Manufacturing movements rates, 1966–71, by industry and employment*

Industry	A UK employment, June 1971, '000	B Mid-1971 employment in moves 1966–71,* '000	B as % of A
Coal and petroleum products	57.6	2.5	4.3
Other manufacturing	343.6	11.0	3.2
Electrical engineering	880.5	19.5	2.2
Clothing and footwear	472.8	10.5	2.2
Instrument engineering	157.4	3.0	1.9
Chemicals and allied industries	466.1	8.5	1.8
Textiles	612.3	9.5	1.6
All manufacturing	8,431.6	123.5	1.5
Bricks, pottery, glass, cement, etc.	324.9	4.5	1.4
Mechanical engineering	1,142.3	15.0	1.3
Paper, printing and publishing	617.8	7.5	1.2
Food, drink, tobacco	837.4	9.0	1.1
Metal goods	614.2	6.5	1.1
Metal manufacture	554.8	5.5	1.0
Vehicles	812.9	8.0	1.0
Timber and furniture	293.3	2.5	0.9
Shipbuilding and marine engineering	191.8	0.4	0.2
Leather, leather goods and fur	51.9	0.1	0.2

*Moves under 22 miles are excluded

Sources: unpublished Department of Industry movement data; Department of Employment Gazette, 81, 1, 1973, table 103

documented (Howard 1968, 25–33; Keeble 1971a, 26–8, 1975; Smith 1975). Taking the whole postwar period, five major industry groups stand out with above average movement rates relative to manufacturing as a whole, both in terms of employment created (Howard, 1968, table 8) and plant movement frequency (Keeble 1974a, table 1). These are 'other manufacturing industry', 'engineering and electrical goods', 'vehicles', 'chemicals and allied industries' and 'clothing and footwear'. Of these, engineering and electrical goods is probably the most important, since although only second to the 'other manufacturing' category in employment and plant *rate* terms, the sheer scale of engineering activity in Britain means that it is by far the leading industry in terms of total *volume* of movement. By the end of 1966, for example, 1945–65 engineering moves had generated 345,000 jobs or 40 per cent of all those created by movement during the period. This compares with its 26 per cent share of 1966 United Kingdom manufacturing employment, and the 53,000 and 106,000 jobs respectively created by 'other manufacturing' and 'vehicle' moves. Relatively immobile industries include 'shipbuilding', 'timber and furniture', 'leather and fur', 'paper, printing and publishing' and 'metal manufacture'. These conclusions are generally illustrated by the hitherto unpublished 1966–71 movement data of table 6.2, although the very low movement rate of vehicles, reflecting recent and of course continuing decline in this industry, is noteworthy.[5]

Structural differences between mobile and non-mobile firms are explicable partly by the industrial growth rate differences discussed above, but partly also by variations in the average gradient of what may be termed an industry's locational net benefit surface. Three alternative situations may be envisaged with respect to this latter concept (Keeble 1974a, 12). First, spatial variations in the net balance of locational costs and benefits within the United Kingdom may be relatively small. This is probably the case, for example, with many engineering firms, particularly those producing 'standardized' products for which design criteria, production technology and nature of demand are not changing rapidly. Movement is thus comparatively easy, *but* will occur on a substantial scale only if there is rapid growth to stimulate it.

The second situation is where net locational benefits increase significantly with distance from a particular industry's main traditional centres of activity. In this case, movement will occur even without growth. Excellent examples of above-average movement for this reason in Britain are the clothing and footwear, and textile, industries. As table 6.2 illustrates, these have recorded fairly high movement rates in recent years. Yet over the 1962–71 period they recorded faster rates of national employment *decline* (−18 and −23 per cent respectively) than any other industry except shipbuilding (−21 per cent). Movement of firms in these industries appears largely to have been a response to a markedly peaked labour cost/availability surface, with decentralization from traditional centres in which labour shortages, especially of female workers, had pushed up costs to levels significantly higher than in more rural, non-industrialized, locations. Thus the ILAG survey (Department of Trade and Industry 1973, 575) found that mobile firms in these two industries recorded by far the highest percentage response, 97 per cent for clothing and footwear, and 90 per cent for textiles, of any industry with regard to the major importance of labour availability in selecting a new location, the average response for all moves being only 72 per cent (see section 4.2.1).

The third situation which may occur is where a peaked net benefit surface involves a significant *decrease* in net benefits, or increase in net costs, with distance from traditional centres. Movement, other than locally, is thus severely inhibited. Examples here include specialized engineering industries, such as the metal-finishing and electro-plating trades (see section 4.1.4), and certain paper and printing industries, such as book-binding. Motor vehicle manufacturing may possibly also fall into this category (table 6.2), although its former rate of growth, coupled with particular intense government pressure, did generate substantial albeit reluctant movement before 1966. Inter-industry variations in growth rates and the configuration of locational net benefit surfaces thus almost certainly explain most of the differences in industrial structure between mobile and non-mobile firms.

Firms engaged in inter-subregional movement also differ from their non-mobile counterparts in being on average significantly larger, and dominated by multi-plant rather than single-plant companies. The size difference is clearly illustrated by the north-west London study, which revealed (Keeble 1968a, 21) that no less than 58 per cent of the 203 migrant factories, 1939–63, for which firm-size data were available had been established by larger north-west London firms employing 176 workers or more in the origin area. On the basis of the size structure of all north-west London manufacturing firms operating between 1956 and 1960, a contribution of only 25 per cent would have been expected. Not surprisingly, this difference between the expected and observed frequencies is very highly significant statistically ($\chi^2 = 114.1$, p 0.001), demonstrating clearly that mobile firms are distinctively large firms. Connected with this, almost certainly, is the characteristic of organizational type. Thus the ILAG survey revealed (Department of Trade and Industry 1973, 529) that only 30 per cent of the grand total of 787 mobile firms, 1964–67, investigated were single plant companies,[6] 49 per cent being multi-plant British firms, with a further 21 per cent being owned by foreign corporations. If the last category is excluded, this means that the breakdown into single and multi-plant firms is 38:62, compared with an estimated but conservative 1963 breakdown for all United Kingdom manufacturing enterprises of approximately 79:21.[7] Again, this is a very significant difference. While the explanation for this dominance of larger, multi-plant companies in manufacturing movement in Britain is probably fairly simple, being related to the greater financial resources, locational experience and national market-orientation of

The components of change   133

larger companies, its implications are perhaps less clear cut and more controversial (see section 8.8.2).

6.6.2. Temporal variations in migration

Manufacturing migration within the United Kingdom varies over time and space. Temporal variations undoubtedly follow the national economic cycle, given the established relationship between growth and movement noted above. Indeed, Moore and Rhodes (1976) have recently estimated from multiple regression analysis that a decrease of 1 per cent in the national male unemployment rate, indicating an upswing in national economic activity, generated some 10–15 additional moves per annum to the assisted areas alone during the 1960s. Similarly, Sant's interesting time-series regressions of annual movement 1945–65 identify rate of change of national manufacturing output as a significant positive influence on movement volume (Sant 1975a, 95–7). However, superimposed on this annual fluctuation appears to be a longer-term trend towards increased movement rates within the United Kingdom, as indicated by table 6.3 for the period since about 1952. Although relating, because of boundary changes, only to inter-regional movement, these data are also supported to some extent by less comparable subregional figures (Keeble 1976). True, this appears to reflect increased movement by smaller firms, so that total *employment* involved has not risen. Thus average late-1966 employment in the 1.277 1960–65 surviving interregional moves was 180 workers, compared with only 99 workers in mid-1971 for the 1,639 surviving 1966–71 moves. But increased movement nonetheless warrants some explanation.

Table 6.3 *Inter-regional manufacturing movement rates in the United Kingdom, 1945–71.*

	Average annual inter-regional manufacturing moves	Total UK manufacturing plants ('000)	Movement rate per 1000 UK plants
1945–51	142	98.6 (1948)*	1.44
1952–59	69	92.8 (1958)	0.74
1960–65	140	89.9 (1963)	1.56
1966–71	191	91.8 (1968)	2.08

*indicates estimate only
Sources: published and unpublished Department of Industry manufacturing movement statistics; Abstract of Regional Statistics, 1973

One factor is almost certainly the increasing speed and ease of road and rail communications within Britain. This of course renders it easier for mobile firms to retain close links with existing customers, suppliers and parent factories, despite movement. Thus for example, Britain's motorway network expanded from only 240 kilometres (150 miles) actually in use in 1962 to no less than 1,950 kilometres (1,200 miles) by 1975 (fig. 4.2). Moreover, as noted in section 4.2.4, there is direct survey evidence from areas such as Northern England that firms have been encouraged to move to new locations partly by accessibility improvements. It therefore seems reasonable to conclude that continuing improvement of surface transport facilities, in shrinking effective distance and decreasing distance friction, is encouraging a longer term trend towards increasing firm mobility.

In addition, however, recent years have almost certainly witnessed a significant increase in the average gradient of the locational net benefit surface for most manufacturing industry (see section 6.6.1), resulting from *both* a decrease in the net benefits enjoyed in traditional and especially central industrial conurbations *and* an increase in net benefits afforded by more peripheral and non-industrialized areas. In more traditional terminology, the former decrease reflects an intensification of 'push' factors encouraging industrial decentralization from major manufacturing centres. The nature of these forces is considered at length in the literature (Keeble 1968a, 1974a). But there is evidence that intensified labour shortages, resulting from rapid resident workforce decline, increasing problems of factory obsolescence, space shortages and cost, and growing psychological dissatisfaction on the part of industrialists and managerial staff with conurbation residential living conditions or long distance commuting, are factors behind, for example, an increase in Greater London's annual average manufacturing emigration rate from 4.0 to 4.7 mobile plants per 1,000 London factories between 1960–65 and 1966–71 (Keeble 1976).

An increase in net benefits afforded by more peripheral areas is most evident with respect to government regional policy incentives (see section 8.6.3). During the 1950s, the gross annual average value of regional policy assistance to manufacturing industry was only £5.3 million. But the 1960s witnessed this rise to £105.9 million, and 1970–71 to £270.2 million (Moore and Rhodes 1974a, 61–2). This vast increase in government grants and subsidies undoubtedly accelerated the flow of migrant industry to the assisted areas. Indeed, Moore and Rhodes (1976) have recently concluded from multiple regression analysis that regional policy was probably stimulating an additional 128 or so moves each year to the Development Areas by the late 1960s. This is over and above what would have occurred without policy as a result of normal pressures, notably of labour shortage (section 4.2.1). Sant's national-level time series analysis yields a similar result, with annual government expenditure on regional policy selected as *the* single most significant influence on annual variations in inter-area movement volumes 1945–65 (Sant 1975a, 95–7). The present author's regression analysis of employment mobility presented later (section 6.6.4) also supports this conclusion. While some of the additional, policy-induced moves may be regarded as 'diversions' of firms which would have preferred to migrate to locations closer to their origin areas, but were not allowed to do so, most are probably directly attributable to government regional policy in that they would not have migrated at all without it. This assertion is supported both by the dual population hypothesis (see 6.6.3) and empirical data. The latter for example shows that average annual movement from Greater London, Britain's leading origin area (fig. 6.1a), to surrounding subregions of South East England and East Anglia continued at virtually exactly the same level in 1966–71 (2.65 moves per 1,000 London factories per annum), despite the vast increase in assisted-area incentives, as in the earlier 1960–65 period of less powerful regional policy (2.70 moves per 1,000 London factories per annum).[8] All the evidence therefore suggests that regional policy is a major reason for the recent increase in national mobility rate. In particular, it would appear to be the single dominant explanation for the substantial rise in interregional movement 1952–71 recorded by table 6.3.

6.6.3. Spatial variations in migration and the dual population hypothesis

Earlier work on the spatial pattern of manufacturing migration within the United Kingdom suggests that most movement can be classified into two distinct spatial types. One comprises short-distance 'overspill' migration from the major industrial conurbations of Britain, notably in the South East and Midlands, to surrounding settlements. The other embraces long-distance movement, almost all of it from the central regions of the country, to the lagging peripheral areas of higher unemployment. That this spatial typology also distinguishes two groups of mobile firms which differ significantly in terms of such key characteristics as size, type of mobile establishment, and industrial structure, is the crux of the so-called dual population hypothesis, for which considerable evidence now exists (Keeble 1971a, 42–53; 1972b, 11–13; 1974a, 18–20; Sant 1975a, 40–59, 62–3). Previous work was necessarily concerned with movement before 1966. This section will therefore assess the validity of the hypothesis with regard to the 1966–71 period, for which data have not hitherto been published.

In spatial terms, the 1966–71 movement data provide just as strong support for this hypothesis as do earlier patterns. Examination of detailed origin-destination flows reveals that 33 per cent of 1966–71 movement, measured by employment created (50,000 jobs), was short-distance 'overspill' from key conurbations, while 52 per cent (79,300 jobs) involved long-distance between-region flows to the periphery. As figure 6.1b shows, of especial importance in the former category was movement to South East England outside London (28,500 jobs), to East Anglia (8,200) and to the West Midlands outside the conurbation (6,900). The most important long-distance inter-regional flows

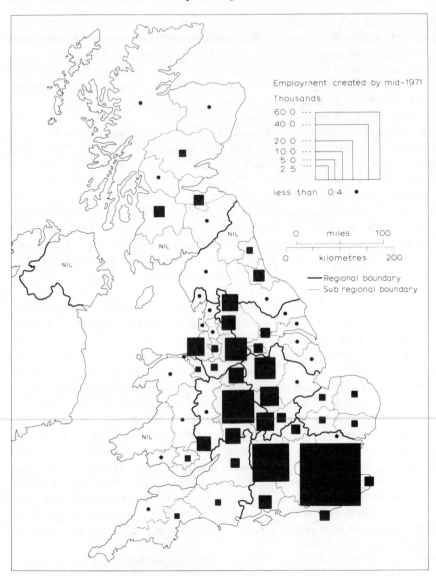

6.1a Subregional manufacturing movement within the United Kingdom, 1966–71, by area of origin and 1971 employment
Source: unpublished Department of Industry statistics

were to industrial north-east England (15,400 jobs), south Wales (13,400), Northern Ireland (10,000) and Merseyside (8,500). In terms of origins (fig. 6.1a), by far the most important area was Greater London, which alone generated moves which had created 53,000 jobs, or 35 per cent of all inter-

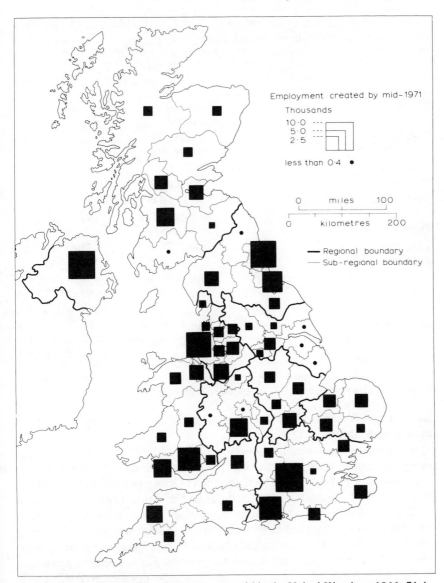

6.1b   Subregional manufacturing movement within the United Kingdom, 1966–71, by
area of destination and 1971 employment
Source: unpublished Department of Industry statistics

subregion United Kingdom mobile employment, by 1971. Of secondary but
still very substantial importance were the Outer Metropolitan Area (20,500
jobs) and the West Midlands conurbation (13,000). These three areas alone
were thus responsible for no less than 57 per cent of all United Kingdom

Table 6.4 *Average UK-origin migrant factory size, 1966–71, by mid-1971 employment, central and peripheral areas*

Central areas	No. of factories	Mean size (employees)	Peripheral areas	No. of factories	Mean size (employees)
Solent	50	124	Northern Ireland	57	175
Outer Metro-			Tyneside	58	164
politan Area	107	98	Merseyside	55	155
Central West					
Midlands	74	74	Clydeside	45	116
East Anglia	127	65	Scotland excl.		
			Clydeside	102	93
Outer South			Wales excl.		
East, excl.			south Wales	75	92
Solent	111	61			
			South Wales valleys	85	88
			Cornwall/		
All central			north Devon	51	76
'overspill'			All peripheral		
reception areas	632	75	assisted areas	676	115

Source: unpublished Department of Industry statistics.

mobile employment shown on the map. All these figures exclude emplyment in moves from abroad.

Interestingly, the overall 1966–71 central 'overspill' proportion of total movement noted above (33 per cent) is not significantly different from that calculated for earlier 1945–65 movement (31 per cent) on the basis of the different set of subregions used by the Board of Trade before 1966 (Keeble 1972b, 11). But that for long-distance peripheral destination flows is, being somewhat larger during the more recent period (52 per cent as compared with 46 per cent). So while increasing industrial mobility is evident at both the intra- and inter-regional scales, long-distance movement has nonetheless apparently grown at a substantially faster rate than either short-distance overspill or non-categorized moves. This is almost certainly a direct result of more active government regional policy.

The continuing relevance of the dual population hypothesis is also attested by differences in the size of establishments created by recent movement. As table 6.4 shows, the average migrant factory established by an existing United Kingdom firm in the peripheral assisted areas between 1966 and 1971 employed 115 workers by mid-1971. In Northern Ireland, the figure was as high as 175 workers. But even rural peripheral areas such as Cornwall and rural Wales recorded values above the much lower central overspill area mean of only seventy-five workers. The exceptions in the latter case were Solent and the rest of the OSE/East Anglia, with above and below average values respectively. The difference between average factory size in central and peripheral reception areas is however very clear, and statistically very significant ($t =$ 9.74, significant at the 0.0001 level).

Moreover, these figures omit data for plants established for the first time in the United Kingdom by foreign companies, which for objective comparison are excluded from the dual population hypothesis. In fact, however, not only are such plants heavily concentrated in the peripheral areas (fig. 6.2a), but the average size of peripheral plants established by such foreign companies was even larger, at 129 employees per factory, than the average for all United Kingdom origin mobile plants in these areas. So if new foreign factories are included, the size differential is increased still further.

Differences in type of mobile establishment are equally striking, notably in terms of the proportions of branch plants or complete transfers. Between 1945 and 1965, for example, transfers made up only 17 per cent of all moves to the peripheral areas, but 57 per cent of those to outer South East England and East Anglia (Keeble 1971a, 52). More recent DI data are unfortunately biased towards transfers in including large though indeterminable numbers of local *within*-subregion moves. But even so, 60 per cent of 1966–71 moves attributed to destinations in Northern Ireland, Northern England, Scotland and Wales were branches, compared with only 24 per cent of moves in the West Midlands, the South East and East Anglia. In terms of employment, peripheral region moves were even more heavily dominated by branches (75,500 jobs in 1971, or 66 per cent of the total created by movement). In the three central regions, employment in branches totalled 23,000, or 29 per cent of jobs created. So the striking centre-periphery difference in branch/transfer proportions noted for earlier periods still obtains.

The third measurable difference between the two samples of 1966–71 between-subregion mobile firms is in industrial structure. As table 6.5 shows, engineering firms, especially mechanical engineering firms, were more numerous than those in any other industry in both cases. In addition, roughly similar proportions of central and peripheral area movement were provided by firms in the food, drink and tobacco, chemicals, metal manufacture, electrical engineering, and other manufacturing industry groups. However, these similarities are offset by major differences, chief of which are the significantly greater proportions of mechanical engineering plants in the central area sample, and of textile and clothing/footwear plants in the peripheral area sample. These are exactly the same differences noted in earlier work for the 1945–65 period (Keeble 1972b, 12). Overall, therefore, but largely because of

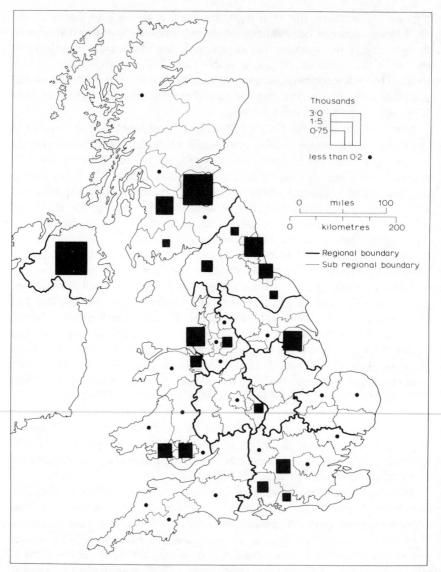

6.2a Subregional 1971 employment in new foreign manufacturing firms, 1966–71, within the United Kingdom
Source: unpublished Department of Industry statistics

these three industries, a chi-square test reveals that the two distributions are very significantly different ($\chi^2 = 67.4$, $p = > 0.001$).

It is therefore clear that the significant measurable differences in mobile firm

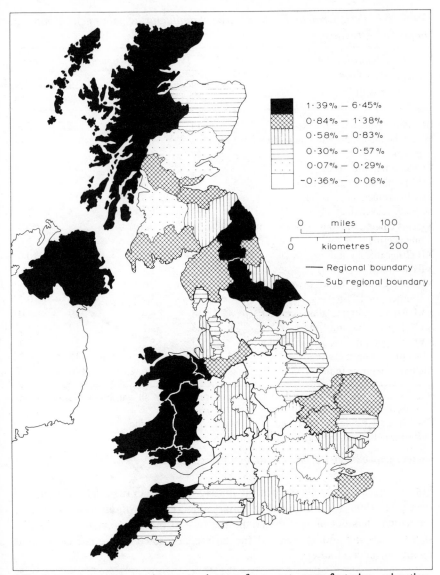

6.2b Average annual employment change from net manufacturing migration, 1966–71, as percentage of total 1966 manufacturing employment
Sources: unpublished Department of Industry and Department of Employment statistics

characteristics noted for earlier postwar movement to the two categories of reception area apply equally strongly to recent moves. This is an important finding, not only because it further substantiates the dual-population hypothesis,

Table 6.5 *Peripheral and central area manufacturing movement, 1966–71; industrial structure*

Standard Industrial Classification Order (1968 edn)	Migrant factories,* 1966–71, still operating mid-1971			
	Central areas†		Peripheral areas‡	
	No.	%	No.	%
III Food, drink and tobacco	14	5.0	28	5.8
IV/V Chemicals, coal and petroleum products	18	6.4	33	6.9
VI Metal manufacture	13	4.7	21	4.4
VII Mechanical engineering	64	22.9	57	11.9
VIII Instrument engineering	11	3.9	11	2.3
IX Electrical engineering	27	9.6	55	11.5
X/XI Vehicles, shipbuilding and marine engineering	7	2.5	24	5.0
XII Other metal goods	21	7.5	48	10.0
XIII Textiles	3	1.1	51	10.6
XIV/XV Clothing and footwear, leather, leather goods, fur	9	3.2	49	10.2
XVI Bricks, pottery, glass, cement, etc.	18	6.4	19	4.0
XVII Timber, furniture, etc.	23	8.2	17	3.5
XVIII Paper, printing and publishing	23	8.2	25	5.2
XIV Other manufacturing	29	10.4	42	8.7
All manufacturing industry	280	100.0	480	100.0

*Moves under twenty-two miles, and therefore virtually all within-subregion cases, are excluded

† South East England, East and West Midlands, East Anglia

‡ Northern Ireland, Scotland, Northern England and Wales

Source: unpublished Department of Industry statistics

but also because it suggests that the massive increase in regional policy incentives after 1966, while stimulating a marked increase in *volume* of assisted-area movement, has not altered materially the *type* of move involved. The possible significance and implications of the differences noted above are considered further in later chapters.

6.6.4. Spatial variations in migration: regression analyses

Clearly, one of the most important questions concerning manufacturing migration in the United Kingdom concerns the reasons for observed spatial variations in volume and direction of movement. In this context, the various separate influences and broad centre/periphery and periphery/centre models of manufacturing location change discussed at length in chapter 4 are of course equally and fully applicable to the special case of manufacturing migration. Indeed, much of the evidence presented there is derived from the experience of mobile firms. At the same time, the success of the multiple regression analyses outlined in chapter 5 suggests that a similar approach to location factor hypothesis testing might prove fruitful in the migration sphere.

A measure of net migration impact by subregion was therefore included in a stepwise multiple regression analysis utilizing all but one of the independent variables discussed in section 5.3. The omission was the industrial structure index which, by definition, of course pertains only to 'indigenous' manufacturing industry already existing in each subregion in 1959. Two different 1966–71 net migration indices were measured for each subregion and used as dependent variables. The first was calculated by taking mid-1971 employment created by immigrant manufacturing firms (branches, transfers and new foreign firms) between 1966 and 1971 in a particular subregion, and subtracting from this employment *lost* to the subregion by emigration of complete transfers only over the period. The degree to which this net migration employment measure underestimates actual migration impact is considered in the next section. This absolute volume of net migration index is mapped as the left-hand 'migrant industry' symbol for each subregion in figure 6.4. As that shows, it ranges from a minimum of 26,300 jobs *lost* to Greater London to a maximum of 13,000 jobs *gained* by Northern Ireland.

The second index is a rate measure, and simply expresses net migration volume as an average annual percentage rate measured against the base of total 1966 subregional manufacturing employment. This rate index is mapped in figure 6.2b. Not surprisingly, the map reveals a number of similarities with figure 5.1b. But the dominance by peripheral subregions of the very highest class of maximum employment growth rate is in this case total, all eleven of the subregions recording the fastest rates of net manufacturing immigration being peripheral assisted areas. Conversely, the central London/Bristol/West and East Midland zone of very low or negative migration employment gains stands out much more clearly in figure 6.2b than in the total growth rate map of figure 5.1b. The net migration rate map also draws attention to the high immigration rates enjoyed by a number of traditionally rural and central subregions outside the assisted peripheral areas, most notable here being the performance of East Anglia, and to a lesser extent of the belt of subregions running all along the south coast of England from Kent to Cornwall.

The results of the stepwise regression analyses of both these net migration indices are given in table 6.6. As this shows, both regressions achieved good R^2 and low residual spatial autocorrelation z score values. Indeed, the R^2 value for the percentage change equation was the second highest of all those presented either here or in chapter 5. Moreover, the relationships identified are all entirely logical and in the hypothesized direction, while all but one, market potential, yield associated t-values which are significant not just at the 0.10, but at the 0.002, level. All these considerations support the view that the analyses have identified meaningful and influential location factors affecting subregional variations in net immigration balance.

The percentage change equation is of particular interest for two reasons. The first is because it does in fact pinpoint exactly the same set of independent variables as the 1966–71 percentage total employment change analysis (table 5.3), allowing of course for the omission of the industrial structure index, *even though* the net migration analysis is based on the quite independent migration employment data collected by the Department of Industry. As with total

Table 6.6 *Regression results: employment from net manufacturing migration, 1966–71*

Percentage change equation (log Y)

	b	SEb	t value
Assisted-area status	0.96836	0.15960	6.07
Manufacturing employment, 1966 (log)	−0.29459	0.05011	5.88
Residential space preference	0.01137	0.00333	3.41

Constant $= 0.21681$ $SE_{est} = 0.4889$ $R^2 = 0.655$ $z = -0.1307$

Absolute change equation

Manufacturing employment, 1966	−0.02172	0.00301	7.22
Unemployed workers, 1966	0.00052	0.00010	5.20
Market potential	0.08008	0.04927	1.63

Constant $= -3.89502$ $SE_{est} = 3.2334$ $R^2 = 0.533$ $z = -1.6411$

change, net immigration rates are indicated as varying negatively with 1966 manufacturing employment levels, and positively with assisted-area status and the residential space preference index. The first of these of course suggests the impact of agglomeration diseconomies and government/planning controls in large urban-industrial centres, together with the apparent attractions to mobile industry of non-industrialized, traditionally rural areas. The remarkable consistency of these and the earlier results is of course further evidence for the general validity of the relationships identified. However, and secondly, the percentage migration results are of great interest because they suggest that for migrant industry these three influences must be ranked somewhat differently as an influence upon spatial variation than in the total manufacturing case.

Most notably, the migrant industry analysis pinpoints assisted-area status as the most significant individual variable, whereas for total manufacturing change it ranked bottom in t-value significance of the three variables common to both analyses. This is fully consistent with the differences in spatial pattern between the two dependent variables discussed above, and is entirely logical, given the dominant traditional emphasis in regional policy upon the attraction of mobile industry to the assisted areas, rather than the stimulation of indigenous manufacturing growth. The finding that regional policy was the single most important variable influencing the subregional pattern of migrant industry between 1966 and 1971 is a very important one, providing independent support at a very detailed geographical scale for other recent conclusions of a substantial 'policy effect' upon manufacturing employment change in both Development Areas and central regions (Moore and Rhodes 1973). But the analysis is of course also interesting in giving statistical support to the hypothesis that general environmental attractiveness is a much more important influence on industrial migration decision-making than is often acknowledged by migrant firms themselves (see section 4.3).

The absolute net migration results, like those relating to absolute total employment change 1966–71 (table 5.3), identify the existing scale of manufacturing activity in a subregion as the single most important influence upon *volume* of net migration, the relationship being a negative one. However, the most interesting aspect of this analysis is the selection of the total unemployment index. It will be recalled that this variable did not figure to any meaningful and significant degree in the earlier total manufacturing analysis (tables 5.2, 5.3 and 5.4). A highly significant positive relationship here is however again entirely logical, in view both of the established dominance of the labour availability factor as the greatest single reported influence upon mobile firm location selection in Britain (section 4.2.1), and of the success of previous multiple regression analyses of pre-1966 migration flows incorporating this same variable (Keeble 1972b). Micro- and macro-level evidence thus yield exactly the same conclusion, namely that the volume of postwar manufacturing migration to a particular destination area in the United Kingdom is to a significant degree a function of the availability of workers in that area, measured even by such a crude index as local total unemployment. The third variable included in the absolute migration change results, market potential, should of course technically have been omitted, given a t-value lower even than the 0.10 probability level. But there is perhaps just a hint here at a preference on the part of some mobile industry for new locations reasonably close to Britain's main market areas, a tendency probably more pronounced during earlier postwar years when regional policy was less active.

Interestingly, since these regressions were run and findings analysed, Sant (1975a, 148–59) has published the results of a somewhat similar multiple regression movement analysis for the sixty-one British subregions and the

1966–71 period (and indeed for three earlier periods between 1945 and 1965). Utilizing only the total number of moves rather than employment as the dependent variable investigated, his attraction model (i.e. moves by destination subregion, 1966–71) achieved a best-fit equation R^2 value of 0.60, lower than that for percentage migration rate but higher than that for the more comparable absolute change analysis (table 6.6). However, Sant's equation required the inclusion of no less than seven different independent variables, five of which were measuring in one way or another three of the key variables identified here (table 6.6): labour availability and cost, regional policy, and manufacturing employment levels and congestion. Of the other two, one distance-decay measured in Sant's analysis by a gravity model index based on the summation of distances of each subregion destination from seven major origin areas weighted by the volume of movement generated by each of these origins, is discussed in relation to further regression findings below. Sant's other significant variable measured the impact of new and expanded town development in each subregion. This is undoubtedly an influence upon manufacturing migration, as was indicated by its effect upon the 1959–66 total manufacturing employment change analysis of section 5.5.1; its inclusion in the models presented here might thus have increased the overall fit of the equations. On the other hand, as Sant (1975a, 157–8) explicitly acknowledges, part of the residual variation unexplained by his model could reflect spatial variations in behavioural image and 'psychic income'. This is of course directly tested and found to be very significant in the present migration analysis. So comparison of the two studies suggests substantial agreement on the main influences channelling recent manufacturing migration to particular areas, together with complementary identification of such further variables as distance-decay and new town impact in the Sant case, and residential space preferences in the present case.[9]

The analyses presented in table 6.6 thus throw considerable light on possible factors influencing spatial variations in migration. But as already noted in relation to Sant's study, they do omit assessment of a further important control on movement flows over space, namely the friction of *distance*.

Much micro-level firm survey evidence (Keeble 1971a, 44–5), for example, agrees that all else being equal, mobile firms tend to move the shortest possible distance consonant with achieving the locational benefits for which movement is undertaken. Distance-minimization here represents a surrogate for various important influences upon locational choice, including the ease and speed of search, the minimization of risk and uncertainty associated with distant, less-well-known, locations (Keeble 1974a, 7), the need to maintain contact with parent factories, existing suppliers and customers, and the feasibility of persuading key workers to settle in a new area. Its impact is neatly illustrated, for example, by Murie's recent survey (Murie *et al.* 1973, 241) of mobile firms 1965–9 which considered but rejected a Northern Ireland location. Their replies isolated very clearly 'the importance of geographical distance in deciding against establishing production in 'Northern Ireland', this being listed as a major reason for rejection over four times more frequently than any other factor.

The significance of distance is also strongly attested by macro-level regression analyses, such as those of 1945–65 movement to the periphery from the South East and West Midlands (Keeble 1972b) and from London to the rest of South East England and East Anglia (Keeble 1972c), as well as, of course, those by Sant (1975a, 152). In both the former studies, distance was statistically very significantly but negatively related to movement volume, allowing for variations in the availability of labour. Again, each of Sant's four national-level separate regression analyses, for different subperiods between 1945 and 1971, showed his distance-based gravity model index to be a significant, and usually very significant, control on subregional movement attraction (Sant 1975a, 152). At an even more detailed level of analysis, and distinguishing, as the dual population hypothesis suggests one should, between peripheral and central movers, the regression models presented in table 6.7 reveal that distance is also closely and negatively related to 1966–71 movement from the West Midlands region to those twenty-three peripheral subregions which enjoyed assisted-area status during this period (fig. 6.3b). Together, in fact, road distance from Birmingham and labour availability, the latter measured by 1966 unemployed workers, explain statistically nearly 60 per cent of the variation in movement flows measured by mid-1971 employment.[10] The regression coefficients of both these independent variables yield highly significant t-values (p   0.001). However, and surprisingly, distance is not apparently significantly related to the 1966–71 flow pattern of movement from the South East (fig. 6.3a), by far the main origin region in Britain (fig. 6.1a), to this set of peripheral assisted areas, although the distance variable is accorded a negative sign as expected. Instead, labour availability provides the only significant explanatory relationship, accounting by itself for 54 per cent of statistical variation in movement flows. This finding on the insignificance of distance is in direct contrast both with that for 1945–65 movements from the South East to the same areas mentioned above, and with Sant's finding for 1966–71 migration within Great Britain. One possible reason, however, may stem from the fact that in the South East case, the largest single flow in the period 1966–71 was to Northern Ireland (fig. 6.3a), the fourth furthest subregion from London. This observation, which may reflect Northern Ireland's significantly more favourable incentives (McCrone 1969, 140) to mobile industry than other Development Area regions, must have had a big impact upon the least-squares regression model results. For the rest of the United Kingdom, however, figure 6.3a at least suggests the possibility of a significant distance/movement relationship, although this has not been tested here. In general, then the 1966–71 flow regressions again powerfully substantiate the labour availability hypothesis for periphery-centre

148

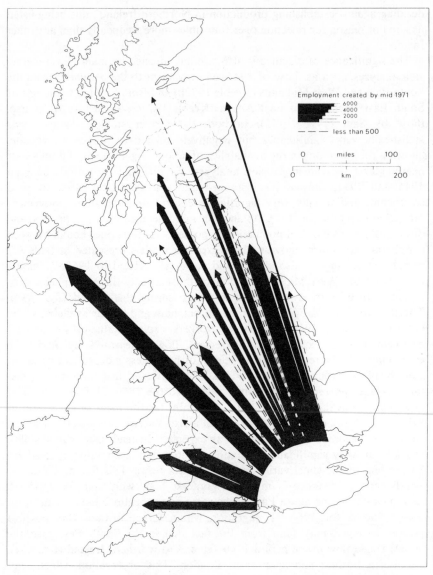

Employment created by mid 1971

6000
4000
2000
0

——— less than 500

0   miles   100

0   km   200

6.3a Manufacturing movement from South East England to the assisted areas, 1966–71
Source: unpublished Department of Industry statistics

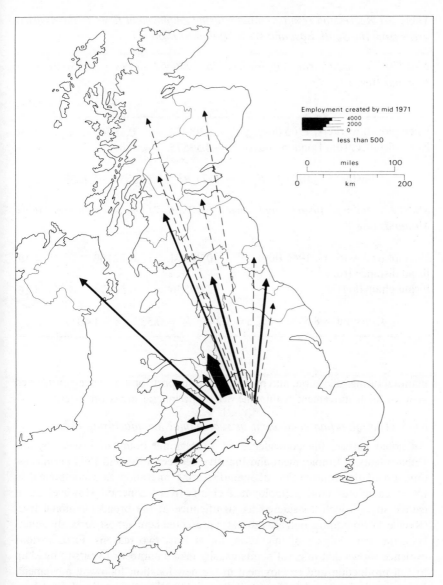

6.3b Manufacturing movement from the West Midlands to the assisted areas, 1966–71
Source: unpublished Department of Industry statistics

Table 6.7 *Regression results: manufacturing employment flows to the assisted areas from the South East and West Midlands, 1966–71*

Mid-1971 manufacturing employment in 1966–71 moves from South East England (log *Y*)

	b	*SE*ᵦ	*t*-value
Unemployed workers, 1966 (log)	0.98072	0.19760	4.19
Road distance from London (log)	−0.59575	0.69815	0.85

Constant = 2.03164 SE_{est} = 1.1171 R^2 = 0.553 z = −1.1335

Mid-1971 manufacturing employment in 1966–71 moves from the West Midlands (log *Y*)

	b	*SE*ᵦ	*t*-value
Unemployed workers, 1966 (log)	0.92804	0.22169	4.19
Road distance from Birmingham (log)	−2.09556	0.50374	4.16

Constant = 8.57886 SE_{est} = 1.2485 R^2 = 0.583 z = −1.4312

manufacturing migration, and provide some support for a distance-constrained view of such movement within the set of peripheral areas on offer.

6.6.5. The migration component in subregional manufacturing change

As noted earlier, the coincidence of subregional boundaries used by the Departments of Employment and Industry between 1966 and 1971 permits estimation of the contribution of manufacturing migration as a component in total local manufacturing employment change over this period. However, as an earlier study which considered its significance at the broader regional level (Keeble 1976) pointed out, the estimates presented here almost certainly understate the 'true' impact of migration, for at least two reasons. First, various evidence shows that migrant plants usually take a number of years to build up to full production and employment in the new location following movement. For example, work for the *Strategic Plan for the South East* (South East Joint Planning Team 1971a, 158–61) revealed that the growth of migrant firms following relocation in South East new towns typically occurred in two phases. Thus an initial 4–6 year period of very rapid expansion was followed in a majority of cases by further growth at a slower rate for at least 5 more years. Most firms actually moving between 1966 and 1971 were therefore unlikely to have reached their full employment potential by as early a date as mid 1971,

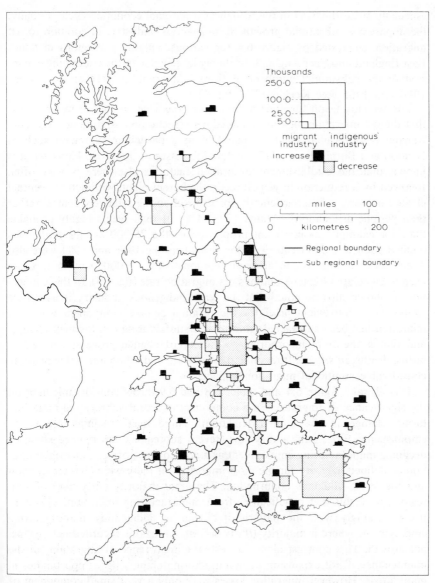

6.4 Subregional employment change in migrant and 'indigenous' manufacturing industry, 1966–71
Sources: unpublished Department of Industry and Department of Employment statistics

especially since this was in the trough of a national economic cycle. Equally, the apparently substantial growth of 'indigenous' industry, in addition to net migration, suggested by figure 6.4 for various outlying subregions in South East England and East Anglia, is probably largely due to the continuing expansion of the substantial numbers of firms immigrant to these areas between 1960 and 1965 (see Keeble 1976, fig. 4).

The second reason for underestimation of the 'true' impact of movement is that the net migration measure adopted here (section 6.6.4) assumes that only transfers, not branch plants, originating in a particular subregion such as London and Birmingham involve actual job losses to that area. However, it is known that the establishment of branch factories elsewhere is very often followed by a reduction in workforce in the parent plant, with actual eventual closure in many cases, particularly for firms choosing relatively central rather than peripheral locations (Atkins 1973, 438). It thus seems highly probable that, for example, a significant proportion of the 25,000 *branch plant* jobs created elsewhere by Greater London firms between 1966 and 1971 were also direct losses to that origin area, in addition to the 28,000 *transfer* job loss used to calculate Greater London's net migration rate (fig. 6.4). In this connection, it should also be noted that the term 'indigenous' industry is used here simply as a convenient label for the residual change component when net migration has been subtracted from total manufacturing employment change, and that it therefore incorporates a variety of change processes, including births, deaths, *in situ* contraction and expansion, and, of course, some possibly considerable additional migration impact.

This all said, figure 6.4 and tables 6.8 and 6.9 throw considerable light on the significance of migration as a component in recent subregional manufacturing change in the United Kingdom. Three main findings are worth emphasizing. First, only a very few (seven) subregions experienced static or declining manufacturing employment as a consequence of net industrial migration as defined here. By far the most important of these were Greater London and the West Midlands conurbation. The great majority (fifty-five) of subregions were thus net beneficiaries from manufacturing migration. This contrasts strikingly with the pattern of change in 'indigenous' manufacturing employment, where a majority (thirty-six) of subregions recorded net decline, not growth. This contrast alone suggests the importance of migration for the maintenance if not expansion of manufacturing employment opportunities in many areas. However, migration losses were only a very small component of overall change in the few subregions noted above where migration did lead to a net loss of jobs. In London and the West Midlands conurbation, for example, massive decline in 'indigenous' industry (−221,000 and −95,000 jobs respectively) far outweighed the net loss from manufacturing migration (−27,000 and −6,000 jobs respectively). On *a priori* grounds, therefore, migration would

Table 6.8 *Migrant and 'indigenous' industry employment change 1966–71; central and peripheral regions*

	Total sub-regions	% subregions recording net growth in total manufacturing industry	% subregions recording net growth in 'indigenous' industry	% subregions in which growth of migrant industry outweighted `change in 'indigenous' industry
		Manufacturing employment change, 1966–71		
Peripheral regions*	26	65	46	38
Central regions*	22	50	46	9
Rest of United Kingdom	14	29	21	14
All United Kingdom	62	52	40	23

*As defined in section 2.1

seem likely to provide a much better explanation of the spatial pattern of manufacturing growth than of that of manufacturing decline.

A second finding is that the *relative* importance of migration as a component in overall change was greater in the peripheral areas than in the rest of the country, despite the not insubstantial volume of movement to centrally-located subregions around London and Birmingham. As table 6.8 shows (column 4), two-fifths of all peripheral subregions recorded employment gains through migration which were larger in absolute terms than growth or decline in 'indigenous' industry. Indeed, in five of the ten subregions involved, overall manufacturing employment would have declined between 1966 and 1971 without the arrival of the migrant plants. In contrast, in 91 per cent (twenty) of the subregions defined as central, employment changes due to migration were outweighed by changes due to the growth or decline of 'indigenous' industry. In a majority (eleven) of these subregions, the more substantial impact of 'indigenous' industrial change manifested itself as a decline. Interestingly enough, these declining subregions were nearly all spatially clustered along the central London-Midlands axis. The nine central subregions in which 'indigenous' industry *expanded* more considerably than immigrant industry were in contrast all peripheral to this principal axis. The point made above about the impact of the continuing growth of earlier immigrant firms upon the 'indigenous' component in these areas should however be noted. But in general, migration was less important for manufacturing employment change in this group of twenty-two central subregions than was 'indigenous' in-

Table 6.9 *Migrant and 'indigenous' industry employment change, 1966–71: major and minor subregions*

	Manufacturing employment change, 1966–71			
	Total sub-regions	*% subregions recording net growth in total manufacturing industry*	*% subregions recording net growth in 'indigenous' industry*	*% subregions in which growth of migrant industry out-weighed change in 'indigenous' industry*
Major industrial subregions (more than 100,000 employees)	21	14	5	10
Medium subregions (40–100,000 employees)	21	52	38	24
Minor industrial subregions (less than 40,000 employees)	20	90	80	35
All United Kingdom	62	52 *	40 **	23

*difference significant at 0.005 level
**difference significant at 0.001 level

dustry, even though the difference in this respect between central and peripheral areas was not quite great enough to be statistically significant (at the 0.05 probability level) in terms of the chi-square test.

The third important set of findings concerns the marked contrast in growth performance of major and minor manufacturing subregions, defined in terms of 1966 manufacturing employment levels. As table 6.9 indicates (column 2), no less than 90 per cent of minor subregions recorded net growth of total manufacturing employment between 1966 and 1971, whereas this was true of only 14 per cent of the major industrial subregions. The set of medium-sized subregions occupied a middle position in terms of growth performance. The difference between the three sets of subregions in this respect is very significant, statistically. To some extent, this appears to reflect differences in the relative importance in growth of migrant and 'indigenous' industry. For although the difference is not quite great enough to be identified as significant by the chi-square test, table 6.9 (column 4) does show that migrant industrial

growth outweighed change in 'indigenous' industry in a much higher proportion (35 per cent) of minor subregions than of major subregions (10 per cent).
The set of medium-sized subregions again occupied an intermediate position
(24 per cent). So the relative importance of migration as a component in
manufacturing change was greatest in traditionally non-industrial, and often
rural, subregions, and least in Britain's main industrial conurbations, even
allowing for the underestimation problems noted earlier.

Interestingly, table 6.9 (column 3) also suggests that the three sets of
different-sized subregions also differ markedly in terms of the performance of
'indigenous' industry. While 80 per cent of minor subregions recorded 'indigenous' manufacturing growth, 1966–71, 95 per cent of major subregions
recorded 'indigenous' industrial decline. At face value, this suggests that the
forces operating to redistribute manufacturing industry from large to small industrial areas within most regions of Britain are effecting this redistribution as
much if not more by their impact on the level of 'indigenous' industry, through
differential rates of *in situ* growth, decline, births, deaths and so on, as by
promoting industrial movement. However, while undoubtedly true of major
subregion decline, given the scale of the latter even relative to an enlarged 'true'
migration component (see fig. 6.4), this conclusion is almost certainly less valid
for minor subregions, where earlier immigration is probably the key to
apparently relatively substantial 'indigenous' growth.

In summary, then, industrial migration appears to be a very significant component in recent manufacturing change in the two categories of minor,
traditionally unindustrialized subregions and the peripheral assisted areas. It is
however only one of several components in the manufacturing decline of the
country's leading industrial conurbations.

6.7. A component model of area industrial change

The preceding discussion of the different components of area manufacturing
change in Britain suggests a very simple four-stage conceptual model of this
process, the stages being differentiated by the rate and direction of aggregate
manufacturing change, and the nature of the dominant components. Assuming
as a starting point a relatively unindustrialized area, such as East Anglia or
rural north-east England in the 1940s or 1950s, the *growth* phase is
characterized by a relatively rapid rate of increase in manufacturing capacity,
output and employment, generated primarily by the immigration of firms from
elsewhere. An analogy here would be with the early and middle stages of
epidemic infection in an area, described as these are by the left-hand lower limb
of an S-shaped logistic curve, when proportion of susceptible population in-
fected is plotted against time from the onset of the epidemic. The *mature*
phase, paralleled perhaps by the upper right-hand limb of the logistic curve, is
where area manufacturing growth *rate* declines, eventually to zero, although

the volume of growth remains substantial at least for the first part of the phase. Such growth is now very largely generated by the net *in situ* expansion of resident firms, many of them formerly immigrant to the area, although the spawning of new births and some continuing immigration are minor components in change. The ensuing *equilibrium* stage is characterized by a relatively static – slowly growing or slowly declining – level of manufacturing activity. This apparent relative equilibrium however masks, in particular, a rising rate of emigration from the area of its most progressive and virile firms, forced out by 'ceiling' constraints on expansion. The final *decline* stage sees the onset of significant and substantial manufacturing decline, in terms of employment and output. While emigration plays an important role here, too, this stage is dominated by a high closure rate of local manufacturing firms and plants. Whether this decline phase eventually gives way to some stable 'low-level' manufacturing equilibrium, and if so at what level of employment or output, is as yet impossible to say from British empirical evidence. The onset of the decline stage can however probably be delayed by government policy and the 'artificial' attraction of new migrant industry, as exemplified by the recent experience of some of the older peripheral conurbations of Britain.

This very crude and largely descriptive model does seem to fit recent trends in most British subregions. Thus areas such as Devon and Cornwall, the Highlands of Scotland, or the eastern lowlands of the East Midlands, are currently to a greater or lesser degree in the growth phase, while maturity characterizes previously rapidly-expanding industrial subregions such as Solent, the Sussex coast and possibly the Yorkshire coalfield. The OMA and Bristol subregions are in relative equilibrium, while rapid manufacturing decline of course now characterizes most of Britain's largest conurbations, probably reflecting, as in London, high plant closure rates. The latter stage is most dramatically illustrated by inner-city areas. Of particular interest are subregions which appear to have reached the transition point between consecutive phases. Examples are the Nottingham-Derby and Bristol areas, both of which may well be about to enter the decline phase. While presented largely as a simple conceptual framework for viewing current changes in manufacturing activity levels in different parts of Britain, the model may thus have some very limited predictive value and even possible policy implications, although space precludes their analysis here.

NOTES

1 I am greatly indebted to Mr R. D. Dennis of the Department of Industry for information about this research study.
2 I am indebted to Mr P. J. McDermott of the Cambridge University Department of Geography, for this information.
3 See Treasury Information Division 1973.

4 An exception is Spooner 1974.
5 I am greatly indebted to Mr R. S. Howard and Miss H. Gaskell of the Department of Industry for these and all other unpublished movement statistics.
6 That is, immediately *prior* to movement, which includes the opening of new branch plants.
7 Derived from 1963 Census of Production data. Though very crude, the calculation is unlikely significantly to have underestimated the multi-plant firm proportion.
8 These are surviving moves, to 1966 and 1971 respectively.
9 Sant's analyses may be criticized in that he does not investigate the question of residual spatial autocorrelation: see review in the *Times Higher Education Supplement*, 6 February 1976.
10 To avoid a small number of zero observations, a constant of ten employees was added to all subregional movement values in the West Midland and South East analyses.

7 Case studies: iron and steel, clothing, motor vehicles and electronics

7.1. Introduction and entropy analysis

Earlier analysis has indicated that individual United Kingdom manufacturing industries have recorded different postwar national rates and directions of employment change (table 3.1), have exhibited different movement propensities and destination choices (tables 6.2 and 6.5), and are apparently adjusting their interregional distribution at such a rate that in ten of the country's eleven regions, the differential shift calculated in the 1965–9 shift and share analysis of chapter 3 (table 3.2) substantially outweighed the 'fair-share' proportionality shift expected on the basis of the region's initial industrial structure. It would thus seem likely that the aggregate all-manufacturing analyses of chapter 5 conceal significant differences in locational change, and in the forces producing such change, in different industries. This chapter thus singles out four major but very different industries for detailed spatial analysis.

Two of these – iron and steel, and clothing[1] – are relatively older industries, which developed in the United Kingdom on a substantial basis during the nineteenth century. Although both still employ large numbers of workers (table 7.1), they have each declined in employment in recent years.[2] Indeed, employment in the clothing industry, the more rapidly declining of the two (table 7.1), has been falling ever since the turn of the century, with a 28 per cent decline between 1907 and 1957 (Dunning and Thomas 1963, 36–7). However, in other respects these two industries are very different, iron and steel being a classic capital-intensive industry, traditionally located close to material sources, while clothing is a classic labour-intensive and traditionally more market-orientated activity. These attributes are also illustrated by table 7.1, which reveals the very significant net output value per employee difference between the two, and the difference in material input and labour cost ratios. Indeed, iron and steel records the highest material cost ratio and lowest labour cost ratio of all four

Table 7.1 Industry indices: steel, clothing, motor vehicles and electronics

	UK employment	UK employment change		Net output per employee	Material input cost ratio*	Labour cost ratio**	Mean size of establishment (employees)	% females in total workforce
	1971 '000	1959-71 '000	%	1968 £	1968	1968	1968	1974
Iron and steel	312	−18	−5.5	1,981	0.64	0.18	398	9.4
Clothing	393	−67	−14.6	1,029	0.47	0.27	52	81.0
Motor vehicles	514	130	33.8	2,105	0.58	0.21	233	12.3
Electronic engineering	350	133	61.3	1,833	0.40	0.26	166	45.4
All manufacturing	8,395	−179	−2.1	1,954	0.47	0.20	85	30.7

* Total cost of material inputs for use in production, packaging and fuel per unit value of gross output
** Total wage and salary cost per unit value of gross output

Sources: Unpublished Department of Employment statistics: Department of Industry, Business Statistics Office (1973, 1974). *Report on the Census of Production 1968*, HMSO, London; Department of Employment Gazette, 83. 7. 1975

industries studied, whereas clothing records the second lowest material cost ratio and the highest labour cost ratio.

The other two industries – motor vehicle manufacturing and electronic engineering[3] – are much newer, twentieth-century, activities whose employment and output, in contrast to steel and clothing, have grown enormously since their inception in Britain. Thus, for example, the broad vehicle industry group, centred on motor vehicle production but including also aircraft manufacturing, expanded its employment by no less than 800,000 workers, or 1090 per cent, between 1907 and 1957, while engineering and electrical goods employment, within which is included electronics, grew by over 700 per cent (Dunning and Thomas 1963, 36–7). These have thus been the United Kingdom's two fastest-growing manufacturing industries during the twentieth century, a growth which continued between 1959 and 1971 (table 7.1). The very substantial rate of increase in electronic engineering employment over this period is particularly impressive, although in absolute terms this was admittedly equalled by motor vehicles. However, it should be noted that most of the latter's 1959–71 growth occurred during the early years of the period, the later 1960s and 1970s witnessing relatively static or declining employment and output levels. Moreover, as with the two older industries, motor vehicles and electronics differ significantly in that the former is characterized by capital-intensive mass-production, whereas the latter is significantly more labour-intensive and, in part at least, manufactures highly unstandardized products. Thus motor vehicles (table 7.1) records the highest net output per employee value of all four industries, together with a high material cost and moderate labour cost ratio; whereas electronics records a net output value lower than that for all manufacturing, together with the lowest material cost and second highest labour cost ratios.

These industries' marked differences in recent growth performance clearly suggest the additional possibility of differing recent rates of locational change. For example, the relatively moderate national decline in iron and steel employment suggests that significant *locational* change is unlikely here, all else being equal. On the other hand, substantial growth, as recorded by the electronic and motor vehicle industries, suggests the possibility of significant locational shifts, given the need to establish new manufacturing capacity and the likely pressures for movement on existing firms in these industries created by growth (section 6.6.1). The electrical engineering and vehicles industries have of course already been singled out (section 6.6.1) as being in the van of postwar United Kingdom manufacturing migration, as also has the clothing industry, where overall decline has also apparently provided a stimulus to locational change. To examine the relationship between national growth performance and spatial shift, spatial entropy indices were therefore calculated for employment in each of the four industries, measured across the sixty-two United Kingdom subregions, for both 1959 and 1971, using the formula given in section 2.3. The results are given in table 7.2.

Table 7.2 *Industry entropy indices of subregional employment distribution, 1959–71*

		1959	1971	% change in index, 1959–71
Iron and steel	Between-region	0.3790	0.3783	−0.2
	Within-region	1.0624	1.0272	−3.3
	Total index	1.4414	1.4056	−2.5
Clothing	Between-region	0.3357	0.2331	−30.6
	Within-region	0.9563	0.7482	−21.8
	Total index	1.2920	0.9814	−24.8
Motor vehicles	Between-region	0.8237	0.5286	−35.8
	Within-region	0.6749	0.6522	−3.4
	Total index	1.4986	1.1808	−21.2
Electronic	Between-region	0.7844	0.7355	−6.2
engineering	Within-region	0.9674	0.7347	−24.1
	Total index	1.7517	1.4701	−16.1
All	Between-region	0.2024	0.1842	−9.0
manufacturing	Within-region	0.6076	0.4949	−18.6
	Total index	0.8100	0.6791	−16.2

As this shows, no very marked relationship emerges between employment growth performance and spatial shift. It is true that the 'non-growth' iron and steel industry did record the lowest spatial shift (column 3), while the other three industries, with their more rapidly-changing national employment levels, each recorded significantly higher rates of spatial dispersion. Within this latter group, however, rate of growth or decline is not simply related to rate of spatial shift, the fastest-growing industry, electronics, for example, recording the lowest rate of locational change of the three. Clothing, with its moderately declining employment (table 7.1), recorded the fastest spatial shift. The overall conclusion then must be one of only a weak employment growth rate/spatial shift relationship, within which other locational forces specific to particular industries are of equal or greater importance in dictating detailed inter-industry variations in spatial change. This finding is in full accord with those of the earlier Chisholm and Oeppen (1973 81, 94) dispersion/concentration analysis for the 1959–68 period.

More important, perhaps, is the fact that table 7.2 indicates that increasing spatial dispersion, noted for aggregate United Kingdom manufacturing in section 2.3, also characterizes all four of these individual industries. Indeed, every single row of table 7.2, column 3, records a declining index, indicating the predominance of dispersion for each industry *and* spatial scale. Within this overall dispersion trend, however, significant inter-industry differences exist, as also in the absolute level of spatial concentration at the beginning of the period (column 1).

In terms of the latter, the 1959 indices reveal that the most spatially concentrated industry of the four was electronics, with an index 42 per cent of the maximum possible (4.1271, indicating total concentration in a single subregion). Motor vehicles and iron and steel recorded somewhat lower concentration indices (36 and 35 per cent of the maximum, respectively), with clothing exhibiting the most dispersed pattern of all. Interestingly, the two twentieth-century industries recorded the two highest 1959 *between-region* indices, indicating that the forces promoting the spatial concentration of these rapidly-growing industries have operated powerfully at the broad inter-regional, and in practice centre-periphery, scale. However, in addition, the electronics industry also recorded a high within-region index, along with the two nineteenth-century industries, clothing and steel. This indicates of course a fairly high degree of clustering in the larger centres of particular regions, with only limited development of these industries in smaller, usually outlying, areas. On the other hand, clothing and iron and steel were fairly widely dispersed at the between-region scale, unlike the other two more modern industries.

Considerable variation also characterizes rates of change in component index values. For example, increasing spatial dispersion of the motor vehicle industry, 1959–71, is revealed (table 7.2, column 3) as almost entirely due to substantial *between-region* decentralization, with virtually no change in the within-region distribution of the industry, with its moderately high level of concentration in relatively few subregions. On the other hand, the other twentieth-century industry, electronics, owes its increased dispersion very largely to a *within-region* shift, with only a small fall in its 1959 between-region index. In the clothing case, substantial dispersion appears to be taking place at both geographical scales – and this despite a 1959 spatial pattern already the most widely dispersed of all four industries. The picture appears to be one of an industry in the very vanguard of the national shift in manufacturing location away from congested industrial conurbations to less industrialized, rural areas. Locational change in iron and steel industry employment, at whatever scale, is so small as to be virtually a 'no-change' situation.

These entropy index findings thus bear out the expectation of important inter-industry variations in locational pattern and trends. The remainder of the chapter examines the spatial distribution of each industry within the United Kingdom in turn.

7.2. Iron and steel

Iron and steel manufacturing is Britain's greatest traditional heavy industry. Basically, it consists of three distinctive activities – the smelting of pig iron in a blast furnace charged with iron ore, coking coal, limestone and some scrap; the refining of the pig iron into steel by removal of impurities, traditionally in an open-hearth furnace but increasingly today either in a large-scale vessel or converter through which is blown oxygen, or in an electric-arc furnace; and the rolling and shaping of the steel into strips, plates, girders, tubes or other pieces. While Britain's biggest integrated plants, such as the British Steel Corporation's massive £233 million Anchor complex at Scunthorpe, commissioned in 1973, carry out all three activities, many smaller steel plants are engaged in the later stages of production, often on the basis of the processing of local scrap. Thus for example the Sheerness Steel Company's £21 million 'mini-mill', opened in 1972 to supply customers in London and the South East with reinforcing bars and engineering sections, depends for its 400,000 tonnes annual steel production entirely upon scrap, refined in two electric-arc furnaces.

7.2.1. The industry to 1945

Iron and steel manufacturing was of course the foundation of Britain's nineteenth-century industrial growth. Its origins, and the reasons for its phenomenally rapid development during the last century on the coalfields of the West Midlands, south Wales, Yorkshire, Northumberland and Durham, and Lanarkshire, are well documented (Smith 1953, chapter 8; Warren 1970; Riley 1973, 85–104). Though intricate in detail and timing, with significant locational shifts between these areas during the nineteenth century, the development of the industry was throughout locationally constrained by the need for bulky, low-value raw materials, notably coking coal and iron ore, and associated high material transport costs per mile. Access to large local coal supplies was especially crucial, given a crude blast-furnace technology which in the mid-nineteenth century required no less than four tons of coal per ton of pig iron produced (Estall and Buchanan 1973, 179). Technological developments, which reduced this to under 2.5 tons by 1900, 1.7 tons by 1938, and 1.0 tons by 1973 (Riley 1973, 92), have thus played a very important part in freeing iron and steel manufacturing from the dominating requirement of a transport-cost minimizing coalfield location. One important consequence of this was the substantial expansion between 1890 and 1940 of steel production in the Jurassic iron ore-producing areas of Scunthorpe, Lincolnshire, and Corby, Northamptonshire.[4] This was also crucially dependent upon the development of the Thomas-Gilchrist process (1879) which made possible for the first time the smelting of phosphoric ores. Since the Jurassic ores are of a very low grade — only 35 per cent iron content at Corby, for example — very high ore transport costs per ton of pig iron produced necessitated orefield iron and steel production. The greater centrality of Corby in particular, compared with all other major United Kingdom iron and steel plants, with regard to the national market (Heal 1974, 26–8) was probably also a minor stimulus to the development of orefield production there.

However, an even more important trend associated in part with the decline in coal inputs relative to ore was a long-term shift in the location of the industry *away* from central, inland locations to coastal sites. This trend is illustrated, for example, by the decline of the once dominant sheet steel industry of the Black Country in the West Midlands after about 1890, as a result of the earlier exhaustion of local iron ore and coal reserves (Warren 1970, 18) and of the rapid increase in exporting relative to production for the domestic market, especially after 1900. High overland freight rates on steel sheets carried to the ports for export placed Black Country manufacturers at a substantial disadvantage relative to coastal coalfield sheet steel producers, notably in south Wales. This centre-periphery disadvantage and the shift to the coast were epitomized by the actual relocation of the large John Summers sheet plant in 1899 from Stalybridge, east of Manchester, to a large area of reclaimed marshland at Hawarden Bridge, Shotton, on the Dee estuary. Steel-making and the development of a major integrated steelworks has continued on this site to the present day (Warren 1970, 77; see fig. 7.1a).

This trend continued in the twentieth century, with the decline for example of the former important steel-producing areas of west Yorkshire and central Lancashire and the relative growth of the south Wales steel industry. Indeed, locational shifts towards the coast occurred even at the within-region scale, the 1920–39 period for example witnessing the complete cessation of iron and steel production at Dowlais and Blaenavon high in the south Wales valleys, and the opening or expansion of plants on the coastal plain at Port Talbot (the Margam works was opened in 1923), Newport, and East Moors, Cardiff (Warren 1970, 179). The only, though very spectacular, exception to this was the construction of Britain's first ever continuous steel strip mill at Ebbw Vale, announced in 1935 and completed by 1938 at a cost of over £10 million, by the firm of Richard Thomas. This was partly at least the result of government encouragement in order to provide jobs in an area of high unemployment and social distress. As an undoubted locational anomaly, the plant's long-term economic viability has been in question for many years, and the BSC plan for closure of steel-making operations there, though not of tinplate manufacture, by 1977 with a loss of 3,300 jobs was reluctantly accepted by the government in 1975.

In general, however, the reasons for coastal site selection altered appreciably after 1918, with a shift away from exporting advantages towards minimizing overland transport and break-of-bulk handling costs of imported high-grade foreign ore. The earlier massive increase in British iron and steel production which occurred between 1880 and 1920, from 10 to over 20 million tons, had been heavily geared to exporting, together of course with domestic munitions production during the first world war (Dunning and Thomas 1963, 15–20).

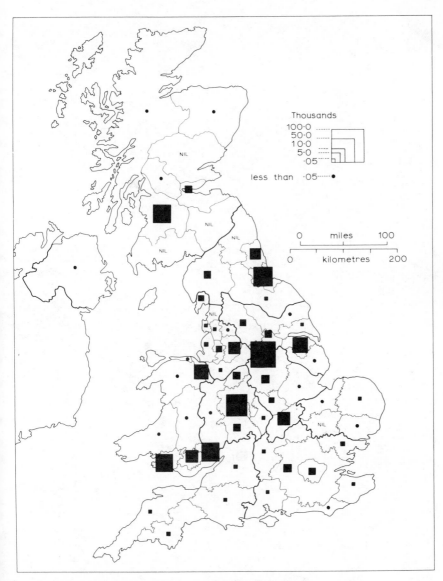

7.1a Subregional employment in iron and steel manufacturing, 1971
Source: unpublished Department of Employment statistics

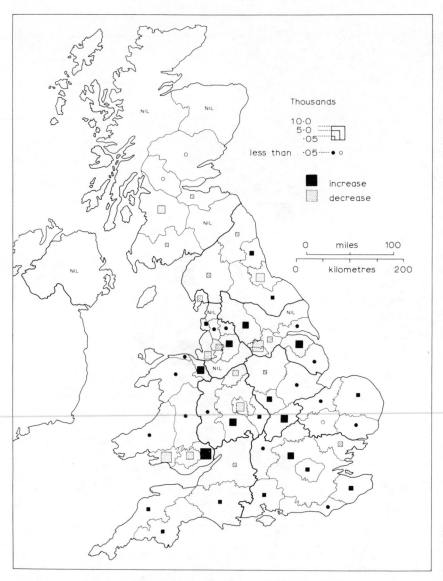

7.1b Subregional employment change in iron and steel manufacturing 1959–71
Source: unpublished Department of Employment statistics

But the radically changed international economic situation of the 1920s resulted in a 15 per cent fall in United Kingdom iron and steel exports during the 1920s, with a further colossal 60 per cent decline between 1929 and 1937 (Dunning and Thomas 1963, 29). The British steel industry thus became almost wholly dependent on domestic demand, a development perhaps epitomized by the 1936 construction of the centrally-located Corby works. However, while the coastal coal- and steel-producing regions were badly hit by this radical demand shift (Caesar 1964, 231), the longer-term advantages of such locations as steel manufacturing centres with regard to freight costs on imported iron ore remained. When recovery and indeed boom conditions ensued after 1938, with war-time demands for munitions of all kinds, it was the coastal steel-producers which benefited most.

7.2.2. Postwar developments

As with the first half of the twentieth century, shifts in the location of the British iron and steel industry since 1945 have almost all occurred through the *in situ* expansion or contraction of already existing plants, rather than either the construction of new 'greenfield' projects, or actual complete closures (Warren 1969a, 343). Indeed, only one completely new integrated 'greenfield' plant has been constructed in Britain since 1945, this being the Richard Thomas and Baldwins £150 million Llanwern strip mill near Newport, announced in 1958 and completed in 1962. However, this plant in many ways embodies each of the three key influences which have in practice shaped the industry's development and locational change since 1945, together with a fourth whose potentially substantial impact has been heavily muted for socio-political reasons. These influences are increasing scale economies in production resulting from radical technological change, increasing dependence on cheap imported iron ore and hence pressure for coastal development, government modification of economically-efficient location decisions on socio-political grounds, and proximity to domestic markets.

The first of these results chiefly from the radical shift in steel-making technology away from the traditional Bessemer open-hearth process to much lower cost basic oxygen steel-making (BOS) in massive pneumatic converters through which is blown a jet of almost pure oxygen. The resultant high-quality steel is produced in only a fraction of the time formerly required by the open-hearth method, while there are also considerable savings in fuel and labour. Thus for example, the two 300-tonne BOS converters installed at the Port Talbot works in 1970 at a cost of £20 million possess a capacity of no less than 2.8 million tonnes of steel a year, replaced a whole array of open-hearth furnaces, and require a labour force of only 500 to do a job once carried out by 2,000 men. The massive Anchor complex which has been grafted onto two of Scunthorpe's existing steelworks (Appleby-Frodingham and Redbourn) is centred on a new BOS plant whose three 300-tonne converters have an initial capacity of 4.4 million tonnes per annum. The scale of this dramatic shift in steel-making technology is well illustrated by national statistics. Between 1963 and 1973, the number of open-hearth furnaces in the United Kingdom dropped from 292 to 107, while their share of total production of steel ingots and castings fell from 76 per cent to only 32 per cent. On the other hand, the number of pneumatic furnaces, originally air-blown but now fed by pure oxygen, rose from nineteen to thirty, and their share of production from 14 per cent to 48 per cent. A small but significant production share increase was also recorded by the electric-arc furnace sector, since although the number of such furnaces fell slightly (from 405 to 391), this was more than offset by the installation of larger furnaces, such as the 200-thousand tonne units in the Sheerness mill referred to above. Their growth reflects the increased use of scrap as a material for steel-making, the marketing advantages of small electric-arc steel plants in centres such as the West Midlands (fig. 7.1a), and the increasing demand for specialist high quality and alloy steels, largely produced in the Sheffield area (Warren 1969a, 345). Though less spectacular, it should be noted that in the iron-making stage too, technological progress and economies of scale have also led to a steadily increasing average United Kingdom blast furnace size, from 60,000 to 300,000 tons capacity, 1938–70, with the largest recent furnaces being of no less than 2 million tons capacity (Estall and Buchanan 1973, 192).

These technological changes and the economies of scale which can be realized are inevitably, though far too slowly for many in the industry and outside, bringing about the closure of smaller steelworks and the concentration of the bulk of United Kingdom steel production in a relatively few major integrated plants. Indeed, the former Chairman of the British Steel Corporation is on record as stating that the ideal 1980 United Kingdom steel industry, geared to a production of 38 million tons of crude steel per annum, would be based for three-quarters of its production on only 14 300-ton BOS converters, compared with the 140 or so open-hearth and oxygen converters in use in 1973. The pig iron required could, on conservative estimates, be produced by only fourteen blast furnaces, compared with the eighty-two in production in 1967. It would also be desirable for these converters and blast furnaces to be grouped in not more than seven major integrated iron and steel complexes (Warren 1969a, 353). A hint that development towards such an ideal industry is proceeding only very slowly is however given by the entropy analysis' conclusion (table 7.2) of increased *dispersion*, 1959–71, not concentration, although it must be remembered that this relates to employment, not output.

By itself, of course, production concentration for reasons of technological development and economies of scale does not answer the key question, where? However, as Warren (1969a, 353) points out, the BOS process does operate most efficiently in terms both of capital and running costs on low-phosphorus ores. This in itself points to the use of imported ore and a 'break-of-bulk' coastal steel plant location to minimize overland ore transport costs, given the greatly reduced modern significance of coal relative to ore as a blast-furnace input noted in section 7.2.1. At the same time, however, the rapid increase in the use of large bulk ocean-going ore-carriers and the opening-up or increased exploitation during the 1960s of massive, high-grade and cheaply-mined ore deposits in Scandinavia, Canada, Liberia/Mauritania and Venezuela/Brazil,[5] have reduced substantially the cost of imported ore (of average 59 per cent *fe* content) relative to home ore (of average 27 per cent *fe* content: Heal 1974, 210) in recent years. Thus between 1957 and 1965, imported ore prices fell by 28 per cent, whereas that of home-produced ore rose by 26 per cent (Warren 1969a, 356). The opening in 1970 of the £17 million Port Talbot deep-water iron ore terminal, designed to handle 100,000 tonne bulk carriers, and in 1973 of the Immingham terminal, designed for 65,000 tonne carriers bringing ore for Scunthorpe, indicate the significance of bulk ocean-going transport in lowering imported ore costs, and the associated inevitable spatial concentration of massive ore imports at a relatively few, specially-designed, terminals. As Warren (1969a, 359) points out, 'the effect, as with technical change, is to stress the desirability of a few large agglomerations of capacity but to localise them near deepwater'. Home ore output has thus inevitably declined, mining of the Oxfordshire ore field being abandoned completely in 1967, while longer-term cessation of all domestic iron-ore mining is, according to some experts, inevitable (Heal 1974, 142). The longer-term prospects for the Corby steel-making plant must therefore be bleak. On the other hand Scunthorpe, formerly heavily geared to these home ores, has been the major single beneficiary of the British Steel Corporation's first-stage and so-called 'heritage' development strategy, following nationalization of the United Kingdom steel industry in July 1967. The massive Anchor project, dependent upon the construction of the Immingham ore terminal twenty miles away and the import of 6 million tons of foreign ore a year for blending with the Lincolnshire product, has increased Scunthorpe's steel capacity to 5.5 million tons but may well represent a satisfactory locational decision only in the medium, rather than long, term (Warren 1969a, 358; Heal 1974, 176). The other, less spectacular heritage strategy developments were the integration of production at adjacent, formerly independent works as at Rotherham, and consolidation and expansion of previously imbalanced production at others, notably Lackenby on south Teesside, but also Llanwern and Ravenscraig. The latter two plants are being substantially expanded under the heritage strategy to 3.5 and 3.1 million ingot tons per year capacity respectively.

The third major influence on locational trends is government intervention in maximum-efficiency decisions for socio-political reasons. The classic illustration of this is in fact the Llanwern plant, which arose from the 1958 judgement of Solomon made by the then Prime Minister, Mr Harold Macmillan, in adjudicating between Scottish and Welsh claims for Britain's fourth modern 1 million ton capacity strip mill.[6] Ignoring the obvious economies of scale argument for a single plant, and understandably swayed by political and social pressures, the government took the initiative in persuading the Scottish Colvilles company to build a 500,000-ton hot strip mill at Ravenscraig, Motherwell, while allowing Richard Thomas and Baldwins to go ahead with their Llanwern strip mill plan, but on a limited 500,000-ton capacity scale. The result was the creation of two relatively uneconomic plants, one of which, Llanwern, has been dogged by intractable labour relations problems and ore import difficulties.[7] The other, Ravenscraig, incurs substantial transport costs in being forced to market approximately three-quarters of its output outside Scotland (Heal 1974, 101). It might therefore be thought surprising that the British Steel Corporation's second (1972), ten-year development strategy again included both these plants among the five key centres proposed for further concentrated investment and capacity expansion during the later 1970s, building on the substantial expansion already launched there as part of the heritage plan. But this is of course a striking illustration of the force both of the economies of scale factor *given* an existing inherited location pattern of too-small but relatively modern plant, and of regional social and political pressures.

The last potential locational influence on steel-making in Britain, market proximity, is striking for its lack of measurable impact since 1945. For example, South East England consumes approximately one-quarter of Britain's total steel production (Warren 1969b, 38); yet its steel production, even including that based on the oft-quoted but tiny Ford Motor Company's Dagenham blast furnace, is negligible. While relative proximity to markets in the Midlands and South East has aided the development of such plants as Llanwern, the much more radical step of constructing a market-located deepwater 'greenfield' plant on Thameside to serve the South East along the lines of developments in other advanced countries such as the USA and Japan has been suggested by some commentators (Warren 1969a, 350, 361–4). While there are economic and possibly environmental arguments against such a project, there seems little doubt that the main reason for lack even of detailed evaluation of such a scheme is socio-political, in the shape of potentially-fierce regional objections to any major new investment outside the industry's traditional locations.

As already noted, the locational forces outlined above have in practice so far produced little, let alone radical, change in the actual locational pattern of the postwar United Kingdom steel industry. This is illustrated by figure 7.1, with plots 1971 employment and 1959–71 change in employment in the industry by standard subregion (note that the symbol scales in both maps are identical with one another and with those adopted for figures 7.2, 7.3 and 7.6). Small-scale employment growth in Scunthorpe, the south Wales coastal belt, at Shotton and, surprisingly, at Corby was more than offset by minor declines on Teesside, Sheffield/Rotherham, Lanarkshire, central Lancashire and Ebbw

Vale/west south Wales. In terms of steel output, changes between 1963 and 1973 were slightly different, in that Scotland increased its share of United Kingdom production from 9.2 to 12.2 per cent, presumably reflecting increased production at Ravenscraig, while Wales as a whole recorded a slight decline (33.9 to 31.7 per cent), relative to other areas. It nonetheless retained its dominance as the country's major steel-producing area. Yorkshire and Humberside's share increased (23.1 to 24.6 per cent), but those of the North (18.4 to 16.9 per cent) and North West (3.3 to 2.0 per cent) fell. But in general, the locational changes were relatively small, and conformed to no simple pattern, despite the radical technological and other changes affecting the industry.[8]

7.2.3. Iron and steel: the future

Without doubt, a major reason for this lack of radical locational adjustment is the fact of strong political influence upon the now nationalized United Kingdom industry, and the reluctance of governments to countenance plant closures, the inevitable corollary of such adjustment (Warren 1969b, 32), for socio-political reasons. This is nowhere better illustrated than by the recent history of BSC's ten-year development strategy, designed to restructure the industry to meet the demands of the 1980s. Even this strategy, announced in late 1972 and accepted by the then Conservative government, represented 'a triumph for compromise and caution' (Heal 1974, 177), rather than radical innovation. But it nonetheless involves a number of steel-making plant closures, notably at Shotton, West Hartlepool, Clydebridge, East Moors (Cardiff) and Ebbw Vale. The obverse of this coin is heavy concentration of the £3,000 million investment[9] envisaged over the ten-year period, firstly upon high quality alloy and special steel production in the Sheffield area based chiefly on electric arc furnaces, and secondly upon five massive hot metal integrated complexes. Chief of these by far will be Lackenby-Redcar on south Teesside, where the greatly expanded (to 5 million ingot ton capacity) existing Lackenby works will be augmented on an adjacent site by a brand new 7 million ton Redcar plant. The latter alone will cost over £900 million, at 1973 prices, and will be served by the new Redcar deepwater ore terminal, opened in 1973, and designed to handle 150,000 ton bulk carriers. A second major complex at Port Talbot, south Wales, will be expanded to a 5.75 million ton capacity. The other three investment preferences will be the Anchor works at Scunthorpe, Llanwern and Ravenscraig, to be expanded to 5, 3.65 and 3.55 million ingot ton capacity respectively (Heal 1974, 179). Together, therefore, these five complexes should eventually account for nearly 30 million tons, or around 80 per cent of the total 36.8 million ton capacity to be provided under the strategy programme. The dominant influence upon the strategy of the economies of scale factor, and the emphasis on coastal plants utilizing bulk imports of foreign high-grade iron ore, is abundantly clear.

This strategy clearly recognizes the force of regional political pressures in allocating some substantial investment to each of the main traditional peripheral steel-producing regions, Wales, Scotland and Northern England.[10] But although accepted by the then Conservative government, the proposed closures aroused such local opposition that the new 1974 Labour government promptly decided upon a further review. The interim results, announced during 1975, were decisions to continue steel-making at Shotton, East Moors and Hartlepool for periods longer than BSC had wished, to preserve the 13,500 jobs involved for a further 2–4 years, while accepting the closure of steel-making plant at Ebbw Vale. In Scotland, Clydebridge and other open-hearth plants are eventually to be closed. But a £55 million 800,000 tonne direct reduction iron-making plant is to be built at Hunterston on the Firth of Clyde, beside the new deepwater ore terminal which is due for completion in 1976. The latter will be able to handle 350,000 tonne carriers. The longterm future of Shotton, the biggest single steel plant closure envisaged, remains undecided. Political and social pressures, in an industry dominated by government control, are thus 'already tarnishing the bright image' of the BSC's original 'grand strategy' (Warren 1975), and its future fullscale implementation is very much in doubt. Without the investment and workforce reduction (by 50,000 workers, to 180,000 in the early 1980s) envisaged by the strategy, however, it is difficult to see how Britain's iron and steel industry can achieve the level of efficiency and low cost production enjoyed by foreign competitors and vital to a United Kingdom manufacturing economy dependent upon steel as the basic raw material for so many products.

7.3. Clothing

Despite its similar nineteenth-century origin, present-day employment and recent history of decline (table 7.1), the United Kingdom clothing industry exhibits many major differences from iron and steel manufacturing. For example, although some firms in certain clothing trades, notably men's tailoring, are quite large and employ mass-production methods on an extensive scale, the vast majority of clothing firms, typified by the highly fashion-conscious women's outerwear trade, are small single-plant enterprises employing only a few workers. As table 7.1 shows, average 1968 employment per establishment in the clothing industry was as low as fifty-two workers, while clothing production was carried on in no less than 6,700 separate workshops or factories. This compares with a mean plant size for iron and steel of no less than 398 workers, and for all manufacturing industry of eighty-five workers. A further very significant structural characteristic is that an extremely high proportion of clothing workers are women: the proportion in 1974 (table 7.1) was 81 per cent compared with 31 per cent for all United Kingdom industry and only 9 per cent for iron and steel. Yet another major difference is the very low value of net output per employee achieved by the clothing industry, and the relatively very high labour cost element in its production cost structure (table 7.1; see also Estall and Buchanan 1973, 94). Last, but by no means least, its inherited locational pattern and current rate of locational change (table 7.2) also differ substantially from those of iron and steel manufacturing. These last two characteristics will be considered in detail.

7.3.1. Locational development and pattern

Although employment in the clothing industry has been declining substantially ever since the beginning of this century (see section 7.1), its present-day distribution (fig. 7.2a) is still dominated by the three great nineteenth-century clothing industry centres of London, west Yorkshire and Manchester. In 1959, these centres together still accounted for no less than 51 per cent of total United Kingdom clothing employment, with London alone, by far the largest single centre, containing 129,000 or 28 per cent of all United Kingdom clothing workers. Outside these three conurbations, however, the industry was fairly widely scattered. The chief secondary centres were Clydeside and Northern Ireland (both 24,000 workers), the OMA, Nottingham/Derby and Tyneside (each with 15–20,000). But many other towns and areas also possessed a share of the industry, in broad relation to the distribution of population, with only thirteen of the country's sixty-two subregions recording a 1959 clothing employment of less than 500 workers. The chief single anomaly to this generalization was the West Midlands, especially the conurbation, which possessed a clothing industry far smaller than might be expected from its population or general scale of manufacturing activity.

Admittedly, this simple aggregate picture does conceal important differences in the spatial distribution of different clothing trades within the industry. The latter is divided by the official Standard Industrial Classification into no less than seven separate categories, ranging from 'hats, caps and millinery' (MLH 446) to 'dress industries not elsewhere specified' (MLH 449). Of these, the most important in employment terms are 'dresses, lingerie, infants wear, etc.' (102,000 United Kingdom workers, 1974) and 'men's and boys' tailored outerwear' (88,000 workers, 1974). Of secondary importance are 'women's and girl's tailored outerwear' (45,000 workers) and 'overalls and men's shirts, underwear, etc.' (48,000 workers). Locationally, the first of these, dresses, lingerie, etc., is relatively concentrated in Greater London (38 per cent of 1959 employment in this trade) and, to a much lesser extent, Manchester. The trade, and hence the capital's clothing sector, is associated with very small workshops and factories, average 1968 plant size nationally for this category being only forty employees. London's relative dominance of the similarly small-plant women's and girl's outerwear trade (average 1968 factory size thirty-nine employees) is even greater, with no less than 55 per cent of 1959 United Kingdom employment. On the other hand, the men's and boy's outerwear in-

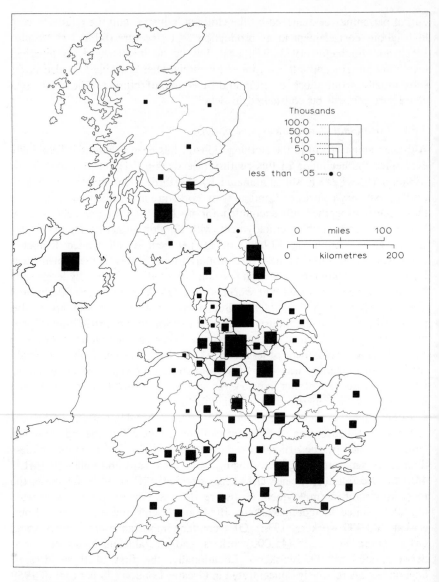

7.2a Subregional employment in clothing manufacturing, 1971
Source: unpublished Department of Employment statistics

dustry, which is carried on in fairly large factories (average 1968 plant size eighty-five employees), is in contrast relatively concentrated in west Yorkshire. The latter, centred on Leeds, accounted for 28 per cent of 1959 United Kingdom employment in this activity. Indeed, the men's outerwear trade

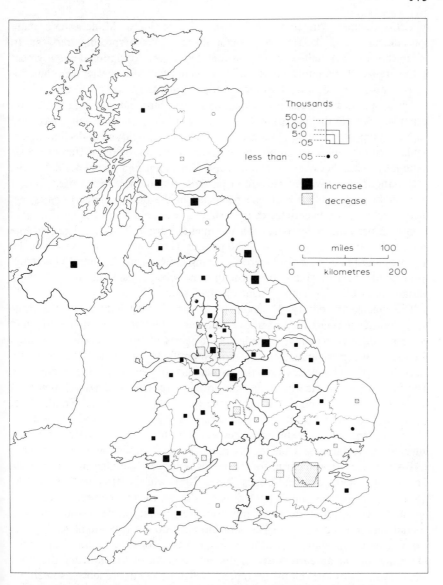

7.2b Subregional employment change in clothing manufacturing, 1959–71
Source: unpublished Department of Employment statistics

provided no less than 72 per cent of all west Yorkshire's clothing industry employment in that year, indicating the area's marked specialization within clothing on the manufacture of men's suits, jackets, trousers and so on. London was the second most important centre for this trade, with 18 per cent of 1959 United Kingdom employment. Interestingly, Manchester's main specialization is in the relatively minor trade of weatherproof outerwear. In 1959, this area accounted for no less than 59 per cent of national employment in this trade, which in turn provided 30 per cent of all Manchester's clothing industry jobs: a reflection of Manchester's traditionally notorious climate?

These spatial variations in the distribution of particular clothing trades are important both in themselves and, of course, in that they have had undoubted repercussions on the scale of recent overall clothing employment decline in particular centres, given variations in the rate of decline of the different trades nationally. Thus between 1959 and 1968 (Chisholm and Oeppen 1973, table 4.4), national employment change in particular clothing trades varied from a very slight increase (+0.7 of one per cent) in the dresses, lingerie category, theoretically to the benefit of centres such as London, to a decline of no less than 37.5 per cent in the hats, caps and millinery trade. The significant decline in men's outerwear employment (-13.6 per cent) has in turn inevitably produced a substantial fall in west Yorkshire's clothing industry employment. This structural factor must of course be borne in mind when considering recent spatial variations in clothing employment change (section 7.3.2).

The nineteenth-century development of the clothing industry in the three main industrial centres noted above, and the continuing dominance of these centres until very recently, is explicable in terms of four interrelated location factors – historical linkage with textile manufacturing, market accessibility, labour supply advantages and the availability of agglomeration economies. The first of these is clearly the primary original reason for the development of the west Yorkshire and Greater Manchester clothing industries (Smith 1953, ch. XI), which grew out of the much earlier established wool and worsted textile trades, and cotton textile trade respectively, for which these two areas are internationally famous. Thus locally-manufactured woollen and worsted cloth forms the basic raw material for the men's outerwear clothing industry of the Leeds area (Beresford and Jones 1967, 208), while cotton textiles are the traditional input, now supplemented by synthetics, for Manchester's dressmaking and weatherproof outwear industries. Of course, these traditional local spatial linkages between textiles and clothing do provide small savings on clothing input transport costs. But the main reason for their spatial coincidence is simply that at an early stage in the development of the industry the sheer local availiability of cloth prompted individual entrepreneurs, sometimes originating from the textile industry itself (Beresford and Jones 1967, 158), to establish clothing factories in the same general area as the textile mills. Once a concentration of such clothing firms had arisen, agglomeration and labour advantages accentuated the relative expansion of the industry in these two areas, at least up until the mid-twentieth century (Beresford and Jones 1967, 159).

On the other hand, the development of clothing manufacturing in Greater London was predominantly a response to the demand for clothing, as for example what used to be called 'retail bespoke' clothing, made to measure for particular customers, from London's enormous and relatively wealthy population. The nineteenth-century growth and twentieth-century persistence of the clothing industry in London is well documented (Hall 1962, ch. 4; Martin 1966, ch. 7). These studies stress the key importance in this development of rapid local access to customers, particularly for those types of clothing – dresses and women's outerwear in particular – the production of which cannot be standardized because of rapid fashion changes, and which as noted above have come to be concentrated in London. Access to wealthy customers, together with the prestige of a 'made-in-London' label, also explains the concentration in the West End of London of high-value bespoke men's tailoring, in contrast to the factory mass-production of ready-made men's outerwear which has developed in the Leeds area, more distant from the dominant South East clothing market. Indeed, this customer access factor even helps to explain the location of the clothing industry *within* London, with its marked emphasis on the capital's inner East End (wholesale ready-made clothing) and West End (retail bespoke and ready-made clothing), areas enjoying maximum access to Central London's wholesale and retail outlets (Hall 1962, 57–8).

London's traditional dominance, and the rise to significance of west Yorkshire and Manchester, also however reflect the labour and agglomeration economies afforded until the mid-twentieth century to clothing manufacturers by location in these large urban centres. Labour advantages stemmed from the geographical concentration in these areas of a very large supply of workers, men and women, willing to work at low wages because of the fear and all-too-high probability of unemployment before the post-war period. This was particularly true of London. As Hall (1962, 59) points out, 'today in the London clothing trades employers compete for supplies of scarce labour. But at least until the turn of the century many observers thought that London's critical advantage in clothing manufacture consisted in the exploitation of a great pool of cheap unskilled labour'. However, labour factors also aided the development of the industry in provincial centres such as Leeds, where at a critical early stage in the 1860s and 1870s, fortuitous decline in flax and other textile mill employment freed supplies of 'dexterous female labour' for employment in the new wholesale readymade clothing industry (Beresford and Jones 1967, 159). Moreover, and of great importance, in both London and west Yorkshire a vital role was played by immigrant Jews from Poland and Russia, who flooded into Britain especially after 1881, and provided both unskilled exploitable clothing labour and entrepreneurial talent in an industry to which entry was and is relatively easy (see section 6.2).

Agglomeration economies, at least in the London case, centre on the existence of a remarkable pattern of industrial linkages within what are known as the clothing 'quarters' of inner north London. These quarters, referred to in section 4.1.4, take the form of intensely-concentrated and often sharply-demarcated clusters of small clothing firms, many of which specialize in particular types of women's clothing production or process, but nonetheless enjoy external economies of scale because of linkage with other complementary local clothing firms. In a sense, the whole quarter acts as a single massive factory, with the street taking the place of the conveyor belt for movement of semi-finished clothes between specialist firms. The small size of workshops is of course a characteristic of the dress, lingerie and women's outerwear trades in which London specializes (see above), and in which fashion-conscious activities small plants have considerable advantages over larger concerns in terms of flexibility and rapid response to changes in demand. Although now undergoing rapid decline, the East and West End clothing quarters have existed for at least a century and bear remarkable witness to the agglomeration economies afforded to local clothing entrepreneurs by local industrial linkage, availability of numerous suitable cheap premises, maximum information-access in a fashion-conscious industry, and so on. Less pronounced agglomeration economies have also undoubtedly aided the past growth of the clothing industries of West Yorkshire and Manchester.

7.3.2. Current locational change

Sonce the second world war, however, the spatial distribution of clothing manufacture in the United Kingdom has altered considerably. As figure 7.2b shows, between 1959 and 1971 clothing employment in each of the three main traditional centres declined very substantially, with London alone recording a staggering loss of 49,000 workers, or 38 per cent of its 1959 workforce. This was of course despite some specialization in the very branch of the industry, dresses, lingerie, etc., which performed best of all the separate clothing trades in terms of national employment change (see above). By 1971, London, though still the country's single most important clothing centre (fig. 7.2a), accounted for only 20 per cent of national employment in the industry, while the share of the three leading conurbations together had fallen to only 39 per cent. On the other hand, no less than thirty-nine of the country's other subregions recorded an increase in clothing employment, despite of course substantial national-level decline in the industry over the period. Most of these were either assisted areas (twenty of the twenty-six peripheral subregions, for example), or traditionally rural areas such as East Anglia or rural Yorkshire not too far from the main centres of the industry. Entropy measurements of the resultant increased spatial dispersion of the clothing industry at both between-region and within-region scales have of course already been presented in section 7.1.

In terms of a components-of-change analysis, it is highly probable that these spatial shifts reflect two basic components. One is a significant rise in the death/closure rate of small clothing firms in the main clothing industry centres, with no compensating increase in the birth rate. The other is a much increased migration rate of existing medium or large firms from these centres to other, usually peripheral, areas, generally through branch plant establishment. In the latter context, it will be recalled that the clothing and footwear industry recorded the third highest industry movement rate 1966–71 (table 6.2), notably to the benefit of the peripheral assisted areas (table 6.5). Either way, however, the scale of spatial shift revealed by table 7.2 must involve large numbers of firms, given the very small average size of plant in the industry (table 7.1). The explanation for the shift is however fairly straightforward and attested by both micro-level survey evidence and, to a lesser extent, macro-level statistical analysis.

The chief source of survey evidence is the ILAG inquiry on 1964–7 manufacturing movement (Department of Trade and Industry 1973). From its many tables, three factors can be identified as explaining the movement of existing clothing firms. First and foremost was the acute shortage, and almost certainly associated relatively high labour costs, of *female* workers in the main traditional centres of the industry. Eighty per cent of the sixty or so clothing and footwear migrant firms surveyed reported this as a major reason for deciding to establish a plant away from their traditional location, while 55 per cent acknowledged it as the outstanding single reason (Department of Trade and Industry 1973, 548). No other industry approached anything like these proportions with regard to the labour supply question, viewed as a reason for movement *from* a particular origin. Correspondingly, virtually all (97 per cent) clothing and footwear firms surveyed reported that availability of labour, in practice female labour, was also a major influence upon choice of a new location. Again, no other industry recorded such a high percentage positive response to this location selection factor. The key importance of low-cost female labour availability in influencing clothing firm migration is also attested by other much earlier studies (Hague and Newman 1952, 44), and is of course fully consonant with the relatively very high labour cost ratio and female labour proportion characteristic of the industry (table 7.1). The establishment of small clothing plants in many rural and peripheral areas to tap local supplies of underemployed women workers is a primary reason for the recent dispersal of the industry.

Another, however, is government regional policy inducements. Again, the ILAG inquiry shows that a higher proportion (45 per cent) of clothing and footwear firms reported these as a major influence upon migration and location choice than did firms in any other industry except vehicles and textiles (the latter also recorded a 45 per cent response). It could well be that of the various post-1966 inducements provided for assisted-area development, the Regional Employment Premium subsidy has been particularly influential with regard to clothing firms, given their labour-intensive nature. But whether or not this is so, it is clear that migrant clothing firms have been powerfully attracted to peripheral locations by government policy inducements. The last general consideration behind locational shift, increasing agglomeration diseconomies in large urban centres, is almost certainly less significant a factor than the previous two discussed. But it is at least suggested by the importance mobile ILAG survey clothing and footwear firms apparently attached to the availability of suitable non-governmental premises in their new location (Department of Trade and Industry 1973, 586). Half the group of such firms reported this as an influence on choice. This could reflect the lower rents and rates of factories in non-industrialized areas, relative to the congested conurbations, although the ILAG survey did not really ask outright questions on factory cost differentials.

Table 7.3 *Regression result: percentage clothing employment change, 1959–71*

Percentage clothing employment change 1959–71 (log Y)

	b	SE_b	t-value
Clothing employment, 1959 (log)	−0.25982	0.03991	6.51
Assisted-area status	0.24430	0.15690	1.56

Constant $= 6.13972$ $SE_{est} = 0.5620$ $R^2 = 0.497$ $z = 0.0644$

The evidence thus clearly suggests that locational trends in the clothing industry conform closely to the periphery-centre model set out in section 4.2. This conclusion is to some extent at least reinforced by table 7.3, which records results of a stepwise multiple regression analysis of percentage change in clothing manufacturing employment 1959–71 by United Kingdom subregion, incorporating the set of independent variables discussed in section 5.3 (excluding industrial structure). This analysis is by no means as satisfactory as those presented earlier for total manufacturing activity, largely because of the much greater frequency of very 'small-sample' values in non-industrialized subregions. As a result, random fluctuations of only a few score employees may nonetheless yield high but basically meaningless *percentage* growth or decline values. This problem also bedevils the subsequent regression analyses for the motor vehicle and electronics industries. But even so, the clothing regression does identify two meaningful influences upon recent spatial change in the industry, and yields both a reasonable R^2 value and non-autocorrelated residuals. A very marked negative relationship with existing clothing employment supports the suggestion of agglomeration diseconomies in the major traditional centres of the industry, particularly if the latter are taken to include, as noted in section 4.2.2, labour shortages and relatively high wage costs. The inclusion of the assisted-areas status index corroborates the importance for this industry of government regional policy incentives.[11] The absence of more explicit identification of the labour variable almost certainly reflects inadequate experimental design, in that the unemployment-based labour availability measure included (but not selected as significant) related to total, not just female, workers, ignored activity rate variations, and was expressed as a percentage rate, rather than absolute total.

In general, then, micro- and macro-level evidence suggests that the apparently mobile clothing industry is rapidly altering its spatial distribution in Britain, with substantial decline in traditional centres and expansion in many peripheral and rural areas. These trends reflect differential labour advantages, government regional incentives and agglomeration diseconomies, and thus conform closely to the periphery-centre model set out in section 4.2.

7.4. Motor vehicles

The United Kingdom motor vehicle manufacturing industry is probably the country's single most important manufacturing activity. It directly employs over half a million workers (table 7.1), provides much indirect employment in supplier industries such as steel, and accounts for nearly 10 per cent (£1,200 million in 1973) by value of the country's total exports. It is of course a relatively capital-intensive, mass-production, assembly industry, a finished car or lorry being put together from thousands of parts and pieces: for example, the Vauxhall Motor Company buys in no fewer than 25,000 separate components and 1,700 different 'raw material' items, for its production of cars, vans, and truck and coach chassis. The industry is dominantly male-employing (table 7.1), and one in which substantial economies of scale can be achieved in large plants. In 1968, average plant size in the industry was three times that for all manufacturing activity (table 7.1), while 95 per cent of its vehicle output is accounted for by only four giant firms, British Leyland, Ford, Vauxhall and Chrysler UK. Until recently, motor vehicle manufacturing was one of the country's most rapidly growing activities.

7.4.1. Twentieth-century market concentration

As figure 7.3a indicates, by far the most important centres of the industry in Britain are the west Midlands conurbation, the Coventry area, Greater London and the OMA of South East England. In 1959, these four dominant areas accounted for no less than 65 per cent of total United Kingdom employment in the industry, a figure which rises to 72 per cent if the contiguous and intervening Oxfordshire subregion is included. This remarkable spatial concentration reflects the rapid rise to dominance of these areas during the very early years of motor vehicle manufacturing development in Britain (1890–1910), and the continuing agglomeration of the industry in these central locations until the 1960s. In turn, this suggests that the spatial development of the industry until 1960 conforms closely to the centre-periphery model set out in section 4.1.

In its very early stages, the industry was remarkably widely scattered, hand-built cars being produced by erstwhile small engineering, horse-drawn vehicle, or bicycle workshops as far afield as Glasgow, Southport, Cowes, Lowestoft and Bridgwater, as well as in London, Birmingham and Coventry (Riley 1973, 182). However, even by 1901, the West Midlands (eighteen firms) and London (fourteen) had moved into the lead amongst car producing centres, in terms of the fifty-five British firms which had by then actually produced a car. By 1913, of the eleven firms producing more than 1,000 cars a year, no less than eight were situated in Birmingham, Coventry and Wolverhampton, this area accounting for over half (53 per cent) of British car output (Riley 1973, 183). Interestingly, 28 per cent of output was at that time from Manchester, primarily from the Ford plant established at Trafford park in 1911, and only 4 per cent from London. Such was the growth of car manufacturing in South East England during the 1920s and 1930s, however, that by 1938 London (21 per cent), Luton (10 per cent) and Oxford (8 per cent) together accounted for 39 per cent of British car production (Riley 1973, 188), although the West Midlands had fully retained its leading position (60 per cent of car output). With the actual transfer of the Ford Company's production to Dagenham, east London, in 1931, car manufacturing in Manchester ceased completely.

The reasons for the early development and twentieth-century leadership of the West Midlands and South East are undoubtedly to be found in the closely related centre-periphery model components of market accessibility, innovation leadership, agglomeration economies and so on (section 4.1). In the West Midlands case, the region's existing engineering-dominated industrial complex provided an ideal environment for innovatory experimentation with the new, metal-based motor vehicle technology, in terms of suitable labour and entrepreneurial skills, the ready local availability of components or related products, and good proximity to potential customers. While the skilled labour/entrepreneurial factor was probably of key importance in development here until the 1920s, later massive consolidation of the industry in the West Midlands undoubtedly owed a very great deal to two factors – excellent market accessibility, reducing costs of shipping finished cars to customers, most of whom were in the South East and Midlands areas, and unrivalled local access to a vast range of component suppliers. There is little doubt that ever since the 1920s, the West Midlands has afforded vehicle assembly firms opportunities for more flexible, speedy and efficient industrial linkage with suppliers than any other region. Though not a dominant consideration in location, access to steel supplies, the largest single item (20–25 per cent on average) in the input purchase bill for most vehicle assemblers, is almost as good, given the proximity of the south Wales strip mills. The advantage conferred by proximity is not however a matter of minimized transport costs, which are in any case usually the responsibility of the supplier. Rather, it reduces the risk of costly delays and disruption of continuous flow-line assembly, for want of a single but essential component. Consolidation in the West Midlands during the 1920s and 1930s was of course set within the context of the advent of flow-line mass-production methods, and concentration of British vehicle output in a decreasing number of ever-larger assembly plants. These trends of course fit perfectly the Norcliffe argument (section 4.1.1) relating increasing average plant size to spatial concentration in central market locations.

In the London and South East case, the key initial advantages were innovatory leadership, in part linked to London's role as Britain's chief point of entry for entrepreneurs and innovations from Europe (Keeble 1972a, 113), the existence of an established substantial horse-drawn coach-building industry from which it was natural for car production to develop (Hall 1962, 154), and of course unrivalled market access. London's early innovatory role is well illustrated by the Vauxhall Motor Company, which grew out of an established inner London marine engineering firm, Vauxhall Ironworks, and actually produced its first cars (1903) in the capital. The move to Luton (1905) for reasons of space and expansion still provided a location closely accessible to the vital South East and Midlands markets (see table 4.1). Access to the latter has almost certainly been the predominant reason for the very rapid expansion of vehicle production in the South East since the 1920s, explaining for example the Ford Company's southward transfer from Manchester. As section 4.1.1 illustrates, in the motor vehicle industry transport cost penalties on shipments to customers from locations peripheral to major markets can be very considerable, even over the relatively short distances involved in Great Britain. Opportunities for industrial linkage in the South East are also very good, a factor of importance for firms such as Ford. The latter is traditionally the most self-contained United Kingdom vehicle manufacturer, yet still depends upon outside suppliers for inputs of components and materials costing exactly one-third of the value of its total gross vehicle output (£293 out of £890 million in 1973).

7.4.2. Recent locational change

Since about 1960, however, the relevance of the centre-periphery model as an explanation of locational change in the motor vehicle industry has weakened substantially. True, heavy continuing investment in the five traditional central subregions noted in 7.4.1 had boosted absolute motor vehicle manufacturing employment there by 1971 by nearly 30,000 extra workers (fig. 7.3b). And 72 per cent of British Leyland's (fig 7.5) 154,000 workforce was still in these areas in 1976. But, for other firms, growth elsewhere between 1959 and 1971 was far faster than in the five subregions, whose share of the total UK motor vehicle employment fell from 72 to only 58 per cent.

Of key importance in this dispersal of growth was the establishment of

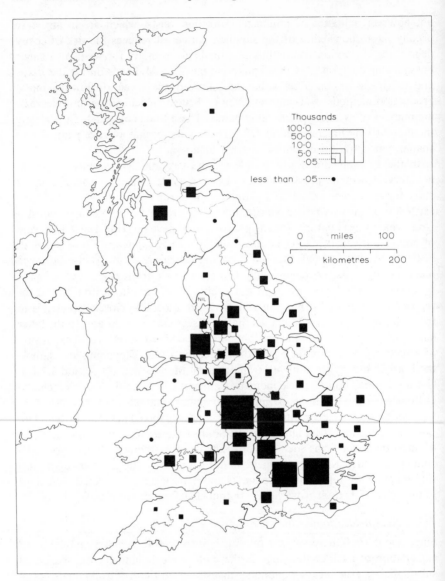

7.3a Subregional employment in motor vehicle manufacturing, 1971
Source: unpublished Department of Employment statistics

major car assembly plants on Merseyside (fig. 7.3b) in the early 1960s, which
expanded its motor vehicle employment from a mere 1,500 to 33,000 workers,
1959–71. Ford's massive Halewood car assembly plant alone now employs
14,000 workers, covers 346 acres and represents an investment of £97 million.

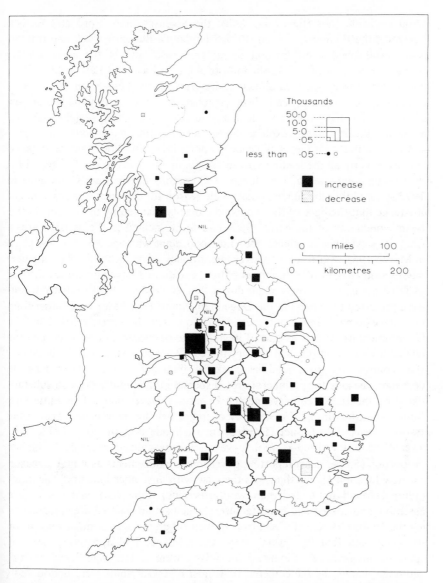

7.3b Subregional employment change in motor vehicle manufacturing, 1959–71
Source: unpublished Department of Employment statistics

Vauxhall's counterpart at Ellesmere Port cost £60 million, covers 397 acres, and provides 11,000 jobs.[12] British Leyland's Spare plant (fig. 7.5) employs 4,000.[12] Other growth areas have been Clydeside, most of whose new workers are employed in Chrysler's Linwood car plant, slimmed down 1975–6 from

7,000 to 5,000 jobs (figs 7.4a, 7.4b); the Swansea area (Ford and British Leyland); the Edinburgh region (British Leyland's Bathgate truck and tractor plant, established like Linwood on a 'greenfield' site in the early 1960s, employs over 5,000: fig. 7.5); the industrial North East, and East Anglia. That this dispersal thus operated almost entirely at the *between-region* rather than *within-region* level has already been established by the entropy index analysis of section 7.1. This points to the possible relevance of the periphery-centre model as at least a partial explanation of recent spatial change in the industry.

Considerable micro-level evidence supports this view. For example, detailed submissions by all the leading United Kingdom car firms to the Trade and Industry sub-committee of the House of Commons Expenditure Committee in 1972 stressed that the fundamental single reason for dispersal was government insistence that the bulk of the expanded capacity planned by these firms in the boom conditions of the early 1960s had to be located in the assisted areas. Chrysler's evidence is typical: 'our Linwood plant was opened as a new plant in March 1963 as a result of Government policy of not granting planning permission, other than of a minimum nature, except in a development area'.[13] Or as Ford pointed out, 'there is no doubt that in 1962–63 the Company would have preferred to expand in the Dagenham/South East Essex area rather than in a development area'; but such expansion 'was, however, refused by the Government of the day as part of its industrial development policy, despite the availability of a large unused acreage there'.[14] That government regional policy IDC controls and, to a much lesser extent, financial incentives have been the dominant reasons for peripheral area dispersal in the industry is also substantiated by the ILAG enquiry and the Economic Development Committee for Motor Manufacturing's 1969 survey of major new motor vehicle plants in the assisted areas. The former (Department of Trade and Industry 1973, 578) revealed that the 1964–7 mobile vehicle firms studied recorded a higher proportion (58 per cent) reporting government inducements as a major reason for new location choice than was the case with any other industry. The latter (1969, 4) found that no less than two-thirds (nine) of the fourteen major vehicle assembly and component manufacturers which set up assisted-area plants during the 1960s reported IDC controls in their origin areas as a major reason for so doing, and that 'in several cases the influence had apparently been of supreme importance'. Financial incentives were a less significant reason, although it must be remembered that most of these plants were undoubtedly set up during the early 1960s, when such incentives were very limited compared with later years.

Survey evidence also suggests that other components of the periphery-centre model are probably of some secondary relevance to this 1960s dispersal, although government policy is by far the most important. Thus ILAG shows (Department of Trade and Industry 1973, 600) that firms in the vehicle industry recorded the fifth highest response (out of thirteen industries), 74 per cent, on the major importance of labour availability in guiding new location choice. That the relatively greater availability of labour in peripheral areas has influenced motor vehicle dispersal is also attested by the EDC survey, which found that twelve of the fourteen firms studied reported this as an 'actually or potentially significant consideration in their location decisions'. So too are agglomeration diseconomies in traditional centres, in the shape of congested factory sites and high factory costs. The former, for example, was reported as a major reason for deciding to look for a new location by no less than 56 per cent of ILAG vehicle firms, far more than in any other industry. This of course reflects the markedly space-extensive nature of modern flow-line vehicle production.

Table 7.4 *Regression result: percentage motor vehicle employment change, 1959–71*

Percentage motor vehicle employment change, 1959–71

	b	SE_b	t-value
Assisted-area status	688.712	186.092	3.70
Market potential	21.545	8.369	2.57

Constant $= -1743.072$ $SE_{est} = 540.005$ $R^2 = 0.189$ $z = -1.0898$

These conclusions are to some extent further supported by regression analysis of 1959–71 subregional motor vehicle employment change (table 7.4). Although achieving only a low R^2 value, this nonetheless shows that the most significantly related independent variable was assisted-area status, exactly in accord with micro-level findings. On the other hand, and most interestingly, the analysis also pinpoints market potential as a secondary significant influence. This is of course one of the very few instances in the regression analyses presented in this study in which market accessibility is so identified, and provides striking evidence for the continuing though undoubtedly much weakened force of central location advantage in influencing investment and expansion in the motor vehicle industry, even in the face of very strong government policy pressures. The regression analysis thus illuminates in a most interesting way the undoubted locational compromise which has resulted in recent years in the motor vehicle case as a result of directly conflicting and very powerful central and peripheral locational forces.

7.4.3. Dispersal and cost minimization

In such an industrially-linked industry as motor vehicle manufacturing, peripheral dispersal has undoubtedly produced considerable 'stretching' of component and other linkages for most of the main vehicle producers. Thus Ford now operates no less than thirty exclusive liner trains a week between

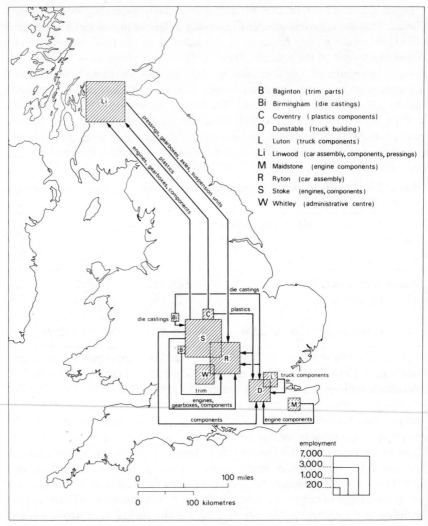

B   Baginton (trim parts)
Bi Birmingham (die castings)
C   Coventry (plastics components)
D   Dunstable (truck building)
L   Luton (truck components)
Li Linwood (car assembly, components, pressings)
M   Maidstone (engine components)
R   Ryton (car assembly)
S   Stoke (engines, components)
W   Whitley (administrative centre)

employment
7,000....
3,000....
1,000....
200....

0   100 miles

0   100 kilometres

7.4a Chrysler United Kingdom: inter-plant linkages, 1975
Source: Chrysler UK Ltd

Dagenham, Swansea, Halewood and Langley (Buckinghamshire), running virtually as an extension to the production lines (see also Goodwin 1965, 151).
The main flows are of engines from Dagenham to Halewood, Langley and
Southampton (the latter two plants, respectively, producing trucks and vans),
rear axles and truck gearboxes from Swansea to Halewood, Dagenham and
Langley, and gearboxes from Halewood to Dagenham. Ironically, Ford claims
that the company is now the biggest private user of British Rail services in

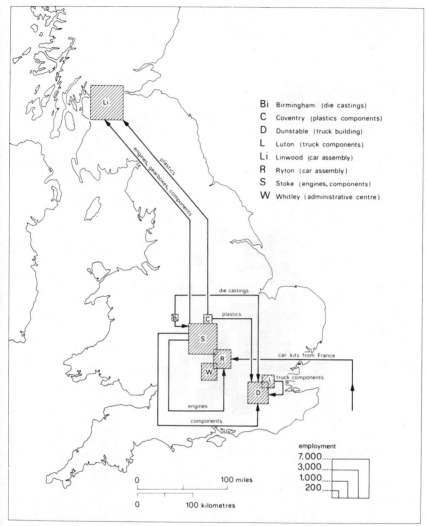

Bi   Birmingham (die castings)
C   Coventry (plastics components)
D   Dunstable (truck building)
L   Luton (truck components)
Li   Linwood (car assembly)
R   Ryton (car assembly)
S   Stoke (engines, components)
W   Whitley (administrative centre)

7.4b. Chrysler United Kingdom: inter-plant linkages, 1977.
Source: Press reports

Britain! An even more extreme case is afforded by Chrysler UK (fig. 7.4a), whose Linwood plant was until 1976 linked with the company's other major plants, Stoke and Ryton, both in Coventry, by a shuttle service of nine special container trains a week, carrying pressings, gearboxes, axles and suspension units southwards, and engines, gearboxes and other components northwards. The Linwood plant was also forced to purchase no less than 78 per cent of its total purchases of vendor (i.e. externally) supplied parts from firms located 400 or more kilometres (250 or more miles) away from Linwood. The overall

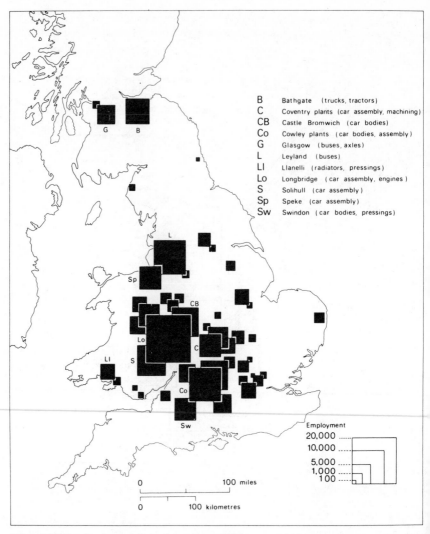

B   Bathgate   (trucks, tractors)
C   Coventry plants (car assembly, machining)
CB   Castle Bromwich (car bodies)
Co   Cowley plants (car bodies, assembly)
G   Glasgow (buses, axles)
L   Leyland (buses)
Ll   Llanelli (radiators, pressings)
Lo   Longbridge (car assembly, engines)
S   Solihull (car assembly)
Sp   Speke (car assembly)
Sw   Swindon (car bodies, pressings)

Employment
20,000
10,000
5,000
1,000
100

0   100 miles

0   100 kilometres

7.5 British Leyland manufacturing plants 1976
Source: British Leyland

transport bill incurred by the industry has thus undoubtedly been increased by peripheral dispersal. As a concrete example, Lord Stokes of British Leyland argued in his 1972 evidence that the cost of shipping English-produced components to Bathgate (fig. 7.5) added an extra £18 to the cost of an average 5-ton truck. Since 75 per cent of Bathgate's output is sold in the southern half of England, most trucks also incurred another £40 penalty on shipment south, making a total transport cost penalty of £58 per truck, or 3–4 per cent extra on top of the normal selling price. In 1972, Chrysler estimated its total *annual* additional transport cost on components and finished cars produced at Linwood, relative to a Coventry location, as being no less than £1.65 million, the bulk of these (£1.15 million) being incurred on components.

Particularly in the extreme Chrysler case, these are substantial sums. But they must of course be set in the context of a massive total industry monetary turnover, of over £4,000 million in 1972, of possible savings on other factors as a result of peripheral production, and of current government financial subsidies such as REP. In 1971, for example, Chrysler received £1.1 million in government grants, employment premium and loans for its activities at Linwood. And most other companies, especially those which dispersed to Merseyside or South Wales, have not incurred anything like these extreme extra transport costs. Indeed, Ford acknowledged that Halewood had *reduced* overall distribution costs from Ford plants in the United Kingdom by £100 thousand per annum, because of the plant's convenient location for Midland and Northern markets. In general, therefore, it seems probable that at least for peripheral plants in England and Wales, motor vehicle industry linkages have been reasonably easily and satisfactorily stretched to serve the new locations, and the EDC's conclusion (1969, 1) that there is 'little evidence that regional policy has proved disadvantageous to (motor vehicle) firms expanding into development areas' is correct. The extreme Chrysler case, with its loss-making Linwood plant, is probably an exception to this. At the same time, however, without Linwood, with its major political significance in the light of devolution and Scottish nationalism, Chrysler UK would almost certainly not have been granted the £163 million of government aid agreed in 1975 to maintain the company in existence. Significantly, the bulk of associated redundancies, 5,000 out of 8,000, have been in the Midlands, especially at Ryton: while assembly of Avenger cars has been transferred from Ryton to Linwood, with a consequent reduction in firm internal long-distance linkages (fig. 7.4b).

7.5. Electronic engineering

As table 3.1 shows, electronic engineering was the seventh fastest-growing manufacturing industry, out of 108 separate MLH-based categories, in Great Britain between 1959 and 1968, measured by employment. Indeed, in many ways this classic 'growth' industry is a creation only of the last thirty or forty years, being the product of extraordinarily rapid technological progress since

1940 which has rendered 'transistor', 'radar' and 'electronic computer' household words. As a rapidly developing activity, the exact scope of electronic engineering, covering as it does 'a very diverse range of products which is continuously changing and broadening' (Electronics Economic Development Committee 1974, 5), is not at all easy to define. But in broad terms, the industry manufactures products involving 'the conduction of electricity in a gas, vacuum, liquid or solid state material'. Many of these are components such as 'electron tubes (valves) and semi-conductors' which 'are combined with resistors, capacitors, transformers and similar components in equipments which detect, measure, record, compute and communicate information'. This official definition covers the great majority of products classified under the four 1968 SIC categories which together are here taken as 'electronic engineering'.[15] In aggregate (table 7.1), the industry employs significantly above-average numbers of women, is carried on in plants whose average size is twice that for all United Kingdom manufacturing industry, and manufactures products whose value reflects significantly higher-than-average labour cost, and lower-than-average material input cost elements than for all industry. Equally important, though not revealed by table 7.1, it is a markedly 'research-intensive' industry, employing and dependent upon an unusually high proportion of highly-qualified research scientists and engineers. In 1958, research expenditure as a proportion of net output in the United Kingdom electronics industry, at 12.8 per cent, was higher than in any other industry except aircraft manufacturing (Dunning and Thomas 1963, 131). While by 1965, the number of highly qualified scientists and technologists employed by British electronic engineering firms was almost certainly greater, at 15,000 (6.0 per cent of the total workforce), than that associated with any other single industry (Ministry of Labour 1967, table 3).

These aggregate indicators portray an industry geared to innovation and rapid technological change, in which access to information is likely to be of vital importance to firm growth; and yet whose cost structure and large plant size directs attention to labour costs and availability, both of women workers and highly qualified research personnel. This apparently complex picture is however simplified by disaggregation. For in fact electronics engineering may crudely be divided into at least two distinctive categories – professional electronics, including computers, aerospace and military electronics, and consumer/component electronics, including radio and television sets and the manufacture of components such as semiconductors, integrated circuits and cathode-ray tubes. The former are especially heavily research-oriented activities, producing unstandardized, often 'one-off', products with rapidly-changing technology, often for government or defence requirements. Many of their employees are therefore highly-skilled male research and development workers, the two MLH industries involved, electronic computers (MLH 366) and radio, radar and electronic capital goods (MLH 367), recording 1974 female employee percentages of only 27.3 and 27.9 respectively – *less* than the national average for all manufacturing industry (table 7.1). On the other hand, consumer and component electronic firms are more concerned with large-plant mass-production, as cheaply as possible, of standardized products in the development of which technological advance is not so rapid. It is these firms which are so heavily reliant upon dexterous but only semi-skilled female assembly workers, with MLHs 364, radio and electronic components, and 365, broadcast-receiving and sound-reproducing equipment, recording 1974 female employee proportions of no less than 56.0 and 56.2 per cent respectively, nearly double the average for all manufacturing. It must be stressed, however, that although oriented to different types of labour, both categories of electronic engineering conform to Estall's dictum (1966, 86) that 'the essential ingredients of a good location for most electronic product industries are human'. In cost terms, for example, both radio, radar and electronic capital goods, and radio and electronic components, each the bigger of the two MLHs in their respective categories, recorded unusually high 1968 labour cost ratios, of 0.33 and 0.26, respectively. The locational significance to both types of electronics activity of labour availability and cost is clearly illustrated by these figures, which in the former case are exceeded by no other industry studied in this chapter (table 7.1).

7.5.1. Twentieth-century growth and central concentration

Spatially, the electronic engineering industry as a whole is notable for its relatively high index of concentration (table 7.2). Moreover, this index, though declining, has fallen more slowly than might have been expected from the industry's very rapid recent growth. The reasons for initial clustering and current dispersion will be examined in the next two sections.

As figure 7.6a suggests, the industry's development over the last thirty or forty years has been extraordinarily concentrated upon South East England, and in particular the single subregion of Greater London. In 1959, the latter alone contained firms employing no less than 42 per cent of the industry's total United Kingdom workforce: while the South East as a whole accounted for 62 per cent. Were figures available for an earlier date still, the relative concentration on the South East would almost certainly be even greater, probably of the order of four-fifths in the late 1940s. Even by 1959, no other region of the country could boast even as many as 10 per cent of the national workforce, the nearest being the North West, with 8 per cent. This concentration bears striking witness to the strength of the locational forces encompassed within the centre-periphery model (section 4.1) upon the early spatial development of this very new manufacturing industry. Of particular significance, almost certainly, has been the South East's unique environmental advantages for innovative, information-hungry activities (section 4.1.2), its exceptional market accessibility (4.1.1), and the quality and skill of its resident labour force (4.1.5).

Historically, the South East's electronics industry developed almost inevitably out of the region's major inter-war radio and associated equipment industry, national leadership in which had stemmed equally naturally from London's total dominance of early BBC broadcasting and reception (Keeble 1972a, 112). But in this development, the unrivalled opportunities for innovation, acquisition and interchange of technological information provided by London in particular, with its unique international nodality and massive existing concentration of engineering firms and research scientists, undoubtedly played a major part. Vitally important too, however, was access to customers, whether government for specialized military and aerospace orders, or final consumers requiring mass-produced bulky, fragile and in some ways costly-to-transport, television sets (Estall 1966, 90). The development of the uniquely-high concentration of radio, radar and electronic capital goods manufacturing in South East England (72 per cent of total 1973 British employment, compared with only 49 per cent for the rest of the electronic engineering industry), for example, bears striking testimony to the necessity for close government contact in an activity whose 'sales are heavily influenced by public procurement policies for both civil and defence projects' (Electronics Economic Development Committee 1974, 27). The availability of skilled research engineers and scientists in a region long acknowledged as highly attractive, residentially, for this kind of worker is another major factor: in 1966, no less than 63 per cent of Britain's electronic engineers were resident in the South East (Buswell and Lewis 1970, 304). Large numbers of female production workers possessing industrial experience were also available in centres such as London, albeit at a cost. Until the 1950s and 1960s, all these factors worked to produce a remarkable concentration of *both* professional *and* consumer/component electronics firms in London and adjoining settlements. The north-west sector of outer London was particularly significant in this respect (Martin 1966, 102), as the 'seed-bed' origin or continuing base for such major electronics firms as GEC, Ultra, Honeywell, Erie and Racal.

7.5.2. Electronics: dispersal

Since the 1950s, however, this remarkable spatial concentration upon London has begun to decline, as indicated by table 7.2. As with motor vehicles, dispersion of electronic engineering firms is almost certainly a direct result of the industry's very rapid growth (section 7.1), which has stimulated much firm migration. However, it must be stressed that this dispersal is only *relative*, electronics employment in London, for example, still recording an absolute expansion of 12,000 workers, or 13 per cent, between 1959 and 1971 (fig. 7.6b), to a biggest-ever total of 102,000 employees. This of course occurred during a period in which London's manufacturing employment as a whole *declined* substantially, by no less than 370,000 workers, or 23 per cent (section 2.2.2). The continuing very powerful advantages of a central location are also strikingly

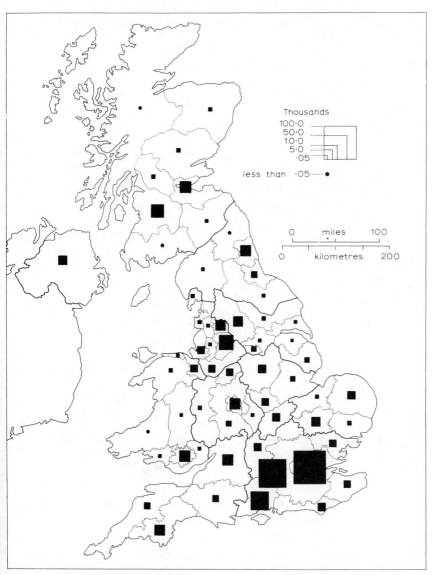

7.6a Subregional employment in electronic engineering, 1971
Source: unpublished Department of Employment statistics

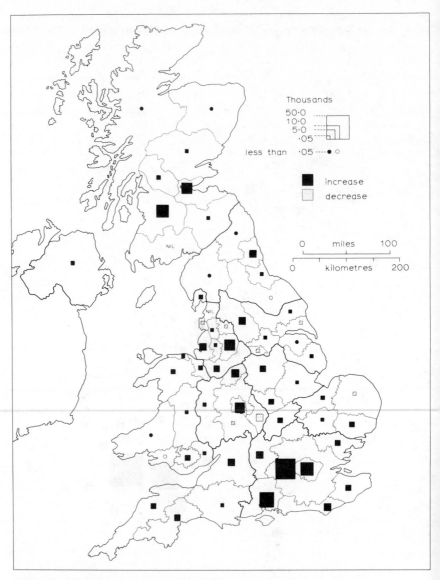

7.6b Subregional employment change in electronic engineering, 1959–71
Source: unpublished Department of Employment statistics

illustrated by the performance of the OMA and Solent subregions of the South East, electronic engineering employment in which expanded more considerably than in any other UK subregion (by no less than 39,000, 110 per cent, and 18,000, 250 per cent, respectively between 1959 and 1971 – see fig. 7.6b). This very rapid and substantial growth around London in fact ensured the preservation of the South East's total share of the much enlarged 1971 United Kingdom electronic engineering industry, at 61 per cent. London's individual share however inevitably fell, to only 29 per cent. These statistics clearly illustrate the significance of within-region dispersal in South East England as by far the most important component in the current spatial dispersion of the industry. The only significant between-region shift, in fact, was the growth of electronics employment in Scotland (fig. 7.6b), particularly in the Clydeside (+11,000 jobs, or 337 per cent) and Edinburgh subregions (+6,000 jobs, or 145 per cent). Scotland's overall share of the industry thus increased from 3.5 to 7.3 per cent, 1959–71, close to that of the North West, whose electronic employment growth (fig. 7.6b) was only sufficient to maintain the region's existing share (8 per cent). As will be illustrated below, American-owned companies, channelled to Scotland by government location of industry policy and pressures, have been the chief growth element in this region's recent electronic industry expansion. The longterm maintenance and scale of their Scottish electronic plants may however be more questionable.

These trends suggest that the basic centre-periphery model still holds as the predominant explanation for the recent locational development of the industry, albeit with substantial local dispersal within the central South East region, and some slight Scottish-specific between-region shift. This generalization, however, almost certainly conceals an interesting difference in the postwar dispersal behaviour of the two categories of electronics noted in section 7.5. As in North America (Estall 1966, 86–92), consumer goods, and especially component, electronics production has since 1945 become acutely sensitive to female labour availability and to a lesser degree costs, as increasing technological maturity, standardization of product and widening markets have encouraged large-plant mass-production. As a result, many London-based and incoming foreign electronics firms have set up branch component factories in peripheral areas and coastal settlements where female activity rates and labour costs are low. Between 1940 and 1964, for example, north-west London electronics firms set up eleven such plants, employing over 10,000 workers by the latter date, in peripheral areas such as central Scotland and Merseyside, and South East/East Anglia coastal towns such as Portsmouth and Great Yarmouth (Keeble 1968a, 16). That the dominant reason for this 'decentralization with maturity' has been the search for female labour is also strongly indicated by the ILAG survey, which showed (Department of Trade and Industry 1973, 600) that electrical engineering firms, half of the sample being electronics firms, recorded the third highest frequency response (79 per cent) of all thirteen industries on the major importance of labour availability in their choice of a new location. Detailed replies indicated that this reflected a need for female workers.

To a lesser degree, this trend has also affected some computer electronics firms, an excellent example being IBM (UK), which established a branch factory at Greenock in Scotland in 1952 to produce punch-card equipment. By 1971 this employed 2,000 workers, manufacturing a variety of computer data-entry, terminal and visual-display equipment on a mass-production basis. However, in this category, and that of other professional electronics, the more significant trend has been the development of dominantly male-employing, heavily research-based activity in attractive outlying residential areas of South East England, notably the OMA. Again, IBM provides a classic example, with the establishment in 1954 of its Hursley (near Alton, Hampshire) United Kingdom research laboratory. This not only now employs 1,750 highly qualified workers, chiefly males, on research and development of actual computers, but led directly to the 1967 establishment of a new computer-manufacturing plant at nearby Havant, outside Portsmouth, employing another 1,000 workers (1971). This neatly illustrates the way in which South East research 'spins off' adjacent production activity, given the rapidity of technological development in professional electronics and the need for constant liaison between research and production units. The advantages of the South East for research-based electronics have also been acknowledged by Honeywell, one of the largest Scottish electronics employers (4,600 workers in 1972 in factories centred on Newhouse, Lanarkshire), with its 1962 decision to establish a Hemel Hempstead research centre, now employing 500 workers. Choice of an OMA location was apparently a direct reflection of 'the need to attract an unusually large number of graduate engineers'.[16] These points are of course closely connected with the uniquely high labour cost element in this type of professional electronics manufacturing already noted in section 7.5.

The key locational influence upon this type of development, then, would

Table 7.5 *Regression result: percentage electronic engineering employment change, 1959–71*

Percentage electronic engineering employment change, 1959–71 (log *Y*)

	b	*SE_b*	*t*-value
Electronic engineering employment, 1959 (log)	−0.32063	0.05890	5.44
Residential space preference	0.01438	0.00674	2.13

Constant = 6.0908 SE_{est} = 1.1338 R^2 = 0.341 z = 1.2503

seem to be the availability of highly-qualified male workers. However, these are of course precisely the type of highly-mobile workers singled out in section 4.3 as most likely to be influenced in their choice of employer by the perceived quality of the local residential environment. In turn, then, it would seem logical to expect that this latter factor has influenced research-oriented professional electronics firms in their choice of locations for new laboratories and factories. This expectation is strikingly corroborated by the results of the stepwise multiple regression analysis of subregional 1959–71 electronic engineering employment change presented in table 7.5. For this analysis, though achieving only a moderate R^2 value, pinpointed the independent residential space preference measure as a positive and significant influence upon locational change in the industry, together with a negative relationship with existing scale of electronic manufacturing activity. The latter may well simply reflect the mathematics of percentage calculations (Keeble and Hauser 1971, 244), although some element of agglomeration diseconomies may perhaps be involved too. But selection of the space preference index undoubtedly supports the hypothesis that the largescale growth of electronics employment outside London in recent years has been significantly influenced by the perceived attractiveness of different locations, as a means of recruiting and holding the highly qualified staff so essential to large sections of this industry. Despite powerful government pressure and financial inducements to move to the assisted areas, most electronics firms thus appear to have insisted on maintaining and expanding their research-oriented South East activities, a fact again bearing witness to the continuing great importance of centre-periphery factors in this particular industry.

NOTES

1 Iron and steel manufacturing is here defined as the aggregate of Minimum List Headings 311 and 312, iron and steel (general) and steel tubes, of both the 1958 and 1968 Standard Industrial Classifications. Clothing is defined as the Clothing and Footwear Order of both SIC editions (Order XII 1958; Order XV 1968), *less* MLH 450, footwear.

2 I am greatly indebted to Mr A. Hives and Mr J. M. Lowell of the Department of Employment Statistics Division, and to Professor Michael Chisholm, for provision of the unpublished subregional MLH data for 1971 and 1959 respectively, on which much of the analysis of this chapter is based.

3 The motor vehicle industry is here defined as MLH 381, motor vehicle manufacturing, of the 1958 SIC, and the aggregate of MLHs 380 and 381, wheeled-tractor manufacturing, and motor vehicle manufacturing, of the 1968 SIC. Electronic engineering is defined as MLH 364, radio and other electronic apparatus, of the 1958 SIC, and the aggregate of MLHs 364, 365, 366 and 367, radio and electronic components, broadcast receiving

and sound-reproducing equipment, electronic computers, and radio, radar and electronic capital goods, of the 1968 SIC. These definitions are designed to ensure maximum possible comparability of the 1959 and 1971 statistics.

4 The Appleby-Frodingham and Normanby Park works at Scunthorpe were opened in 1890 and 1912 respectively, while the integrated Corby plant was set up in 1936 (Riley 1973, 98).

5 These were the four most important origins of imported United Kingdom ore in 1967 (Heal 1974, 128), accounting for 80 per cent of all ore imports.

6 The three established before 1958, with dates of commencement of plant construction, were Ebbw Vale (1935), Hawarden Bridge, Shotton (1937), and the Margam works, Port Talbot (1947, but production not until 1951).

7 Since 1974, ore has been imported through the Port Talbot terminal, then railed expensively the 40 miles to Llanwern (Warren 1969b, 9).

8 An attempt at multiple regression analysis of percentage subregional employment change in the iron and steel industry, 1959–71, utilizing the set of independent variables calculated for the total and migrant industrial employment change analyses of earlier chapters, proved abortive. The relationships identified as supposedly significant were largely meaningless, and the residuals were very significantly spatially autocorrelated.

9 This had risen through inflation to £6,000 million by 1976, with BSC anticipating an eventual cost by 1980 of £10,000 million.

10 'Scottish nationalism has undoubtedly been influential in securing expansion at Ravenscraig just as, 17 years ago, it succeeded in winning government approval for a strip mill for which, on commercial grounds, the location was quite unsuited'. See Warren 1975.

11 Although recording a t-value just short of the 10 per cent probability cut-off level, this variable was included because of its appearance as the only significant independent variable in the otherwise far less successful unlogged percentage change model, results of which are not presented here.

12 I am greatly indebted to the Ford Motor Company, Vauxhall Motors, Chrysler UK and British Leyland for many unpublished statistics used in this section.

13 House of Commons Expenditure Committee, Trade and Industry subcommittee, Session 1971–2, *Minutes of Evidence,* Wednesday 25 October 1972, London, HMSO, 508–ii.

14 House of Commons Expenditure Committee, Trade and Industry subcommittee, Session 1972–3, *Minutes of Evidence,* Tuesday 5 December 1972, London, HMSO, 42–i.

15 I am greatly indebted to Mr P. J. McDermott, of the Cambridge University Department of Geography, for helpful comments on this section.

16 House of Commons Expenditure Committee, Trade and Industry subcommittee, Session 1972–3, *Minutes of Evidence,* January 31 1973, London, HMSO.

8 Industrial location, regional policy and the assisted areas

8.1. Introduction

Various comments in the preceding chapters have drawn attention to the major importance for industrial location in the United Kingdom of recent government policy and planning. Conversely, the location of manufacturing industry has been viewed for many years by politicians and planners as of crucial significance in implementing spatial economic, social and land-use policies at both national and regional scales. The next two chapters thus single out the aims and impact of government manufacturing location policy and planning for detailed discussion and evaluation. The present chapter concentrates on regional policy, which operates at the national 'between-region' scale. Chapter 9 looks at so-called regional planning,[1] and government attempts to shape the 'within-region' distribution of manufacturing industry, notably in areas such as South East England. The opening sections of the present chapter examine the general importance of the location of manufacturing industry for both scale-differentiated types of government planning policy.

8.2. Manufacturing and services in regional policy and planning

The importance of manufacturing industry for regional policy and planning in Britain can scarcely be overestimated. From the earliest planning studies and legislation of the 1920s and 1930s, politicians and regional planners have viewed the location of manufacturing activity as the most important single variable controlling the country's economic and population geography, and thereby determining the success or failure of their policies. Virtually all the major regional planning statements and legislation of the last forty years – the 1934 Special Areas Act, the 1940 Barlow Commission Report, the 1945

Greater London Plan and Distribution of Industry Act, the 1960 Local Employment Act, the 1964 South East Study, the 1966 Industrial Development Act, the 1972 Industry Act, and so on — have assumed, implicitly or explicity, that the essential foundation for successful regional policy and planning is control over the location of new increments of manufacturing industry. Other types of economic activity, notably service industry, have generally attracted much less attention.

Perhaps not surprisingly, the validity of this assumption is now being questioned. As various commentators have recently pointed out (Hart 1972; Burrows 1973), service industries[2] provide a much greater share of total United Kingdom employment today (54.8 per cent, 1974) than do manufacturing plants (34.5 per cent, 1974) while, even more important, it is only in service trades that employment is now growing significantly. Thus between 1962 and 1971, only two of the fourteen manufacturing Orders distinguished by the 1958 Standard Industrial Classification expanded their Great Britain employment at all, whereas three of the six service industry Orders did so — and two of these, insurance, banking and finance, and professional and scientific services, grew by over 30 per cent (Treasury Information Division 1973, 4). Indeed, the employment losses recorded by the three manufacturing industries — textiles (−181,000), clothing and footwear (−99,000) and vehicles (−63,000) — which declined most substantially were far more than offset by the growth of over 750,000 employees in the professional and scientific services industry alone. The increasing relative importance of service employment is, of course, a phenomenon common to all developed countries. But in the British context, it has led to pleas for a reassessment of regional planning policies dominated by a concern for manufacturing industry (Rhodes and Kan 1971). These pleas have already produced one tangible result, with the introduction in 1973 of new government grants covering the cost of rent incurred in the assisted areas by service industry firms which possess a genuine choice of location between these areas and other parts of the country. These grants last for up to three years in Intermediate Areas, and up to five years in the Development Areas. Grants of £800 per head are also payable for each service industry employee moved to an assisted-area location, provided that the number of employees qualifying for the grant does not exceed 50 per cent of the additional jobs created in the assisted area.

The location of service industry is thus now rightly being recognized as of greater policy importance than hitherto. But concern over manufacturing industry remains a cornerstone of regional plans and policies, and for very good reasons. First, many consumer-oriented services have always been and remain closely tied to the local population which they exist to serve. Such activities are not therefore greatly amenable to direct locational control at the broader national or regional scales, and do not generate much external income for the locality they serve. They are often termed 'non-basic', as compared with 'basic' activities which are not controlled in location by access to local population, and which earn income from outside the areas concerned (Keeble 1967, 275–81). Most manufacturing firms can be considered 'basic' for planning purposes, and are important generators of exogenous income for their locality. This is well illustrated by Morrison's recent study of Peterborough, a town of about 80,000 population in north-west East Anglia. This study (Morrison 1972, 97–100) showed that in 1968 no less than 98.5 per cent (£123.6 million) of the output of the town's manufacturing industries was sold to customers outside Peterborough. In contrast, only 42.3 per cent (£21.8 million) of service industry output, excluding construction, represented sales outside the town. It is also interesting to note that although service industry accounted for 43 per cent of all Peterborough employment, it generated only 28 per cent of the total value of output of all economic activity in the town. The town's manufacturing firms, on the other hand, provided 52 per cent of employment, but 67 per cent of total output. The importance of manufacturing industry in many local economies in Britain today is well illustrated by these figures.

A second justification for the traditional policy preoccupation with manufacturing industry is partly connected with the first. Manufacturing industry is in practice far more mobile than service industry, in terms of the relative volume of movement of existing establishments, of the distances moved, and of the range of new locations selected. The remarkable scale of recent manufacturing movement within the United Kingdom, particularly over long distances to the peripheral areas, has already been discussed (section 6.6). In contrast, service firms have been relatively far less mobile and less willing to move any distance from their original location. Indeed, the only substantial flow of mobile service industry within Britain in recent years has been of office firms from Greater London. This movement has admittedly been fairly considerable; Hall's figures (Hall 1972) and official estimates of the total number of office establishments in London suggest, on the basis of a very crude calculation, a probable annual migration rate from Greater London of approximately 3.1 offices per 1,000 private office establishments between 1963 and 1969. However, as already noted (section 6.6.2), annual average *manufacturing* movement from Greater London totalled 4.0 moves per 1,000 London factories between 1960 and 1965, and no less than 4.7 moves per 1,000 factories between 1966 and 1971 (Keeble 1976). So even in the unique London case, the rate of manufacturing movement is significantly greater than that of offices.

Moreover, mobile London offices in any case move on average shorter distances than their manufacturing counterparts. Location of Offices Bureau figures show that only 26 per cent of all central London private office firms known to have moved out of London between 1963 and 1974 actually selected destinations beyond the boundaries of the South East (Location of Offices Bureau 1974, 36). In contrast, 52 per cent of manufacturing moves from the

GLC area during the 1966–71 period chose locations outside the South East, many of these involving long distance moves of two or three hundred miles to Development Areas such as Northern England, Scotland and Northern Ireland. The last point on the greater mobility of manufacturing firms is that, at the intra-regional scale, such firms seem willing to consider a much wider range of locations, including rural areas and small towns, than do service firms. While striking evidence on this point in relation to East Anglia is presented in section 9.4.2, it may be noted here that recent office movement into this particular region has been entirely confined to East Anglia's larger towns; whereas 30 per cent of all incoming manufacturing firms have located in rural areas, outside the region's major centres *and* expanded towns. Again, this significantly greater locational flexibility is an important justification for the regional planner's traditional concern for manufacturing rather than service industry.

A third important argument for this concern is that growth in manufacturing employment is likely to exert a greater multiplier effect upon a local or regional economy than is a comparable expansion in service industry, even when the latter is 'basic' in character. The main reason for this is that manufacturing employees are in general significantly better paid than workers in service industry. This is clearly illustrated by table 8.1, which shows the average gross weekly earnings of full-time adults in manufacturing and service industry in Great Britain during April 1970, based on large samples of workers. The earnings differential in favour of manufacturing is considerable for three of the four categories of workers defined by the statistics. In most cases, therefore, a unit increase in manufacturing employment will inject more wealth into a local or regional economy than a unit employment increase in 'basic' services.

A second reason for the potentially greater multiplier effect of manufacturing is that the latter is more often concerned with the purchase or sale of in-

Table 8.1 *Average earnings differentials between manufacturing and service industry in Great Britain*

	Average gross weekly earnings, full-time adults, April 1970		
	Manufacturing Industry [£]	Service industry (excl. construction) £	Percentage difference manuf. ÷ service
Manual males	28.5	24.8	+15
Non-manual males	36.7	34.5	+ 6
Manual females	14.0	12.6	+12
Non-manual females	15.8	18.4	−14

Source: Department of Employment Gazette 1971

termediate, semi-processed goods as part of an industrial linkage chain, than is service industry, which tends to cater more directly for the needs of final consumers. This point is stressed by Buck and Lowe (1972, 255), who calculate that in 1963, 40 per cent of total manufacturing output in the United Kingdom was sold as intermediate output rather than to the final demand sector. For service industry (construction, public utilities, distribution and miscellaneous services, but excluding public administration and defence) the proportion was only 28 per cent. Since industrial linkages may be stretched over considerable distances (see section 7.4.3), this fact provides no absolute guarantee of an increased local multiplier effect because of manufacturing rather than service growth. But there is at least a possibility of this, particularly at broader regional scales.

For all these reasons, therefore, it can be argued that the traditional preoccupation of British regional policy-makers and planners with manufacturing industry has considerable justification, although recent steps to extend locational controls and, in particular, incentives to service industry are to be welcomed. The history of British regional policy in particular is however largely one of the development and implementation of policies for restructuring the between-region spatial distribution of manufacturing industry. The changing scope of these policies, as they relate to manufacturing industry, must now be outlined.

8.3. Industrial location policy: departmental organization

One of the most striking aspects of spatial planning and industrial location policy in Britain is the way in which it operates at two distinct spatial scales, each of which tends to be the chief concern of a different government department using different policy instruments. At the national, inter-regional scale, regional policy is fundamentally concerned with the problem of the spatial imbalance in prosperity, industrial growth and unemployment between the peripheral and central regions of Britain. This policy, which is basically one of inter-regional resource allocation, has been the object of much legislation and extension since its effective inception in 1934, and has throughout been chiefly administered by the government department known at different times as the Board of Trade, the Department of Trade and Industry, and most recently, the Department of Industry. At the intra-regional scale, however, regional planning is traditionally concerned with the spatial restructuring of a region's population and economic geography towards some more desirable form. Most typical are the postwar attempts to disperse population and industry from central, 'congested' conurbations such as London, Birmingham, Glasgow and Belfast to outlying settlements and new towns. Regional plans of this type are the general responsibility of the Department of the Environment (formerly the Ministry of Housing and Local Government), operating in close relationship with local government planning departments.

This division of interests, though not of statutory responsibility (which rests squarely with the Department of Industry), in the location of industry has inevitably produced conflict at times between the departments involved. Mobile industry is always and inevitably in short supply, relative to the demands both from the Development Areas and from new or expanded towns in the more prosperous regions. For example, Moore and Rhodes (1974b, 227–8) have estimated that Scotland alone would have needed no less than four times as many new jobs (over 300,000) as were actually generated (70–80,000), largely as a result of manufacturing immigration (49–52,000 jobs), by regional policy measures during the 1960s, if Scotland's unemployment, activity and migration rates were to have been brought into line with those in the South East and Midlands. At the same time, however, the volume of mobile manufacturing employment envisaged for new town and growth zone development in South East England outside London under the original 1970 *Strategic Plan for the South East* was nearly twice as great (20,000 jobs per annum) as that which actually occurred (12,000 jobs per annum) during the 1950s and 1960s (Keeble 1971b, 72). True, the Department of Industry has undoubtedly done its utmost to reconcile and satisfy the demands of both types of area in exercising its statutory responsibility for industrial location control. New and expanded towns, for example, have been accorded a priority in IDC approvals second only to the assisted areas.[3] But departmental differences of view in this respect must nonetheless and inevitably have arisen at times, given the division of interest noted above. Indeed, such differences have probably even occurred within the single Department of Trade and Industry (or Board of Trade), charged as it has been for much of the post-war period with both location of industry policy and responsibility for the expansion of manufactured exports. Unfortunately, as already noted (section 6.6.1), exporting firms are often precisely those which are also expanding rapidly and hence potentially mobile; and the former Board of Trade was not infrequently unable to exert as much pressure, by Industrial Development Certificate refusal, on such firms to move to the Development Areas as it would have wished, because of the argument that this might damage exports.

8.4. The reasons for regional policy

Regional policy is concerned with the existence and amelioration of regional disparities in economic prosperity and growth, notably between the relatively prosperous South East and Midlands of Britain, and the economically-lagging peripheral regions of Wales, Northern England, Scotland and Northern Ireland. The economic disparities which have attracted most attention over the last forty years are those of unemployment rates, per capita income and employment growth, although reference is sometimes also made to labour activity rates and out-migration. Table 8.2 lists regional values for some of these

Table 8.2 *Regional economic indicators in the United Kingdom*

	Average unemployment rate,1973 [%]	Average per capita weekly income, 1972–3 [£]	Employment change, 1962–71 [%]	Average net annual migration, 1961–71, per 1,000 population 1971
South East	1.5	18.9	} −0.5	−0.2
East Anglia	1.9	15.1		+7.2
West Midlands	2.2	15.9	−1.9	−0.3
South West	2.4	15.7	+2.4	+5.9
East Midlands	2.1	15.2	} −3.8	+2.1
Yorkshire/ Humberside	2.9	14.2		−1.5
North West	3.6	15.4	−6.1	−1.7
Wales	3.5	14.4	−2.9	−0.1
North	4.7	14.5	−2.7	−3.3
Scotland	4.6	14.3	−5.4	−6.2
Northern Ireland	6.4	11.6	+7.3	−4.3
United Kingdom	2.7	16.1	−2.2	−0.6

Sources: Abstract of Regional Statistics, Central Statistical Office; Economic Progress Report No. 41, 1973, Information Division of the Treasury

economic indicators. Despite the great efforts made and expenditure incurred with regard to regional policy during the 1960s, it can be seen that in general, significant regional disparities persist. In 1973, unemployment rates ranged from a minimum of 1.5 per cent in the South East to over four times that value (6.4 per cent) in Northern Ireland. In terms of average per capita weekly income, Northern Ireland recorded a value in 1972–3 only 61 per cent (£11.6) of that enjoyed in the South East (£18.9). In the case of both these indicators, the four classic problem regions listed above were all significantly poorer off than the centrally-located prosperous regions of the South East and Midlands. A broadly similar picture is presented by the employment change and migration statistics, although anomalies here are Northern Ireland, which recorded the largest percentage employment growth, 1962 to 1971, of any United Kingdom region, and Wales, whose virtually zero net migration balance contrasts sharply with the large net migration losses of Northern England, Scotland and Northern Ireland.

8.4.1. The social equity argument

The existence for many years of disparities of this kind has given rise to various arguments justifying a regional policy of transferring demand for labour, which in practice has meant manufacturing industry, from the prosperous to the lagging regions. The earliest and most obvious of these arguments was and is that significant regional disparities are unacceptable on grounds of social equity in a democracy such as Britain. The onset of massive unemployment in the peripheral industrial regions during the 1920s and 1930s focused national attention on the social trauma resulting from the collapse of these region's staple industries – coal, steel, shipbuilding and textiles – and the dearth of newer activities which might take their place. By 1932, unemployment rates in the depressed areas were averaging 38 per cent of all insured employees. In west Cumberland and south Wales, no less than 46 and 41 per cent respectively of total employees were out of work. The contrast with the London and South East region, with its 15 per cent unemployment rate, was striking. It was thus the tragic social consequences of regional economic decline, manifested in lengthy dole queues, hunger marches and the flight south from depressed northern mill or mining towns of younger workers, which were the primary cause of the inauguration of regional location of industry policy in Britain.

Since 1945, of course, a recurrence of such acute regional social distress has been prevented by government demand management of the national economy so as to preserve full employment, and the introduction of national-scale social welfare policies which have reduced hardship through unemployment. But unemployment, income and other disparities have nonetheless persisted, albeit at a less dramatic level, despite wide acceptance of their social undesirability and an increasing unwillingness of the populations and political representatives of the regions involved to put up with their inferior economic and social status. The social equity argument has thus been crucially important as a justification for regional policy, particularly where this takes the form of moving work to the workers, in terms of mobile industry, rather than workers to the work.

8.4.2. The social capital argument

Other arguments for regional policy are however concerned with economic considerations. The earliest economic argument for government intervention to control and alter the regional distribution of industry also dates from the inter-war years, and has been termed the social capital argument. Social overhead capital refers to the stock of such fixed capital investment as housing, schools, hospitals, roads and similar, often publicly-financed, social facilities. In the 1930s, various commentators suggested that the acute economic distress and associated net out-migration of people from Britain's peripheral regions would lead to increasing under-utilization of these regions' social capital, while generating unnecessary extra demands for new investment in the growing regions. The result would be unnecessarily high social infrastructure investment and running costs generally, and a wasteful use of public funds.

It is now recognized, however, that this argument is largely invalid. New public infrastructure investment is often necessary for reasons of improved technology or sheer physical obsolescence, irrespective of population change, while the underutilization argument clearly implies a declining total population. In fact, however, birth rates in Britain's problem regions since the 1930s have been high enough fully to offset the loss of population through net out-migration, and population levels have thus risen, not fallen, in all these regions. While migration has resulted in a slower *rate* of increase in regions such as Northern England (+1.4 per cent, 1961–71) than in, for example, the South East (+5.8 per cent, 1961–71), the traditional argument concerning under-utilization of social overhead capital does not therefore apply at the regional level in post-war Britain. Moreover, while it is true that certain *parts* of the problem regions *have* suffered absolute population decline during this period, few if any have experienced a rate of decline greater than the average rate of replacement of social infrastructure (2 per cent per annum) necessitated by physical and technological obsolescence (Cameron 1974, 26). Only perhaps in the case of running, as opposed to capital investment, costs in declining sparsely-populated areas such as northern Scotland may the under-utilization argument have some relevance, in that decline must lead to higher operating and maintenance costs per head of the local population, given the need for some basic threshold provision of roads, schools, hospitals and other social in-frastructure (Keeble 1974b, 24–5).

8.4.3. The growth-region congestion argument

A second economic argument does however appear to have more validity. This has been termed the growth-region congestion argument. It centres on the fact that, almost by definition, growth regions such as South East England come over time to contain a greater density of urban development, population and economic activity than lagging regions. Thus South East England has steadily increased both its absolute population and relative share of the United Kingdom total, the latter from 27.5 per cent in 1901, to 29.4 per cent in 1931, 30.3 per cent in 1951, 30.9 per cent in 1961, and 31 per cent in 1971. By the last date, population density in this region, at 632 persons per square kilometre, was nearly ten times greater than in Scotland, the United Kingdom's least densely populated region, and was exceeded only by that in the North West (845 persons per sq. km.), with the West Midlands, the other traditionally most prosperous region of Britain, third (396 persons per sq. km.).

In a traditionally free-market economy such as Britain, growth-region con-gestion of course basically reflects the region's attractiveness, real and perceived, to private entrepreneurs and firms. However, this congestion often creates costs which have to be borne less by the firms themselves than by the rest of the community. Most notably, the high land costs associated with economic prosperity and growth in South East England (section 4.2.2) render public sector housing, schools, hospitals and roads more expensive, and sometimes substantially more expensive, than in most other regions. Thus for example the abortive 1969 GLC proposal for an urban motorway around inner London would have cost at 1971 prices over £12 million per kilometre (£19 million per mile), 30 per cent of which (nearly £4 million per kilometre) would have been expenditure on land and existing buildings. This compares with only £1 million per kilometre (£1.5 million per mile) at 1972 prices for the planned 23-kilometre (14-mile) M11 motorway extension around the western edge of Cambridge, East Anglia, where land costs are far lower.

Other growth region congestion costs which tend to fall more on the community than on the private firm include the often uneconomic costs of providing public transport facilities for peak-hour commuting flows (Keeble 1972a, 84), costs of air pollution, and intangible costs to individuals of loss of amenity, waste of time spent in travel to work (section 4.2.2), and so on. There thus seems to be general agreement that though self-evidently beneficial, in the short run at least, to the private firms involved, concentration of people and industry on the scale evident in the London city region results in substantial extra costs to the community. These costs are one important argument for regional policy (Brown 1972, 324–5; McCrone 1969, 46).

8.4.4. The labour reserve argument

This important argument centres on the existence, already documented in section 4.2.1, of substantial yet relatively immobile reserves of unemployed and underemployed workers in the peripheral lagging regions. It is thus often argued that the aggregate *national* economic growth rate might be accelerated by increasing the level of economic activity in these regions and hence making more effective use of their potentially productive labour resources. The gains in production which might thus be achieved are theoretically considerable, Brown's estimates (section 4.2.1) from 1966 figures being broadly supported by Ridley (1972). The latter suggests that equalization of unemployment rates in Scotland, Wales, Northern England, Yorkshire and Humberside, and the North West, Britain's five assisted-area regions, at the national full-employment level (taken as 1.5 per cent), would add 120,000 workers to Britain's employed workforce. An even larger increment (250,000 workers) would be added by raising these regions' female activity rates halfway towards the highest recorded regional activity rate. So economic expansion in these assisted-area regions could, on the basis of these 1972 estimates, bring into productive employment no less than 370,000 additional workers, increasing Britain's employed workforce by 1.7 per cent. Most commentators would thus seem to agree with Cameron (1974, 3) that 'the reserves of labour which exist in the peripheral regions represent a valuable resource which, if drawn into employment, could make a substantial contribution to national employment and national output'.

8.4.5. The wage inflation argument

The fourth and last economic argument for a regional location of industry policy also relates to the existence of underutilized peripheral region labour reserves. The latter reflect, of course, unequal regional demand for labour by industry. But this in turn is associated with the fact that in conditions of accelerating national economic expansion, labour demand tends to increase more rapidly in the prosperous than in the lagging regions. Unfortunately, such an increase in the prosperous regions cannot in the short-run be satisfied by increased immigration of workers from the lagging regions, because of the 'stickiness' of labour and inevitable time-lags in movement. The result therefore is an inflationary rise in wages and earnings in the prosperous regions, which is then transmitted by national-level trades union pressure to the rest of the country, aggravating the national inflation rate. This theoretical wage inflation argument is supported by empirical evidence. Thus a study of regional inequalities in unemployment rates by Thomas and Stoney (1971, 11) concluded that in the United Kingdom, 'unemployment dispersion (over the standard regions) exerted an upward pressure on aggregate rates of wage change of more than two percentage points in the postwar period'. Further work by Brown (1972, 331) and others at the National Institute of Economic and Social Research reached a similar conclusion:

> what also appears from our investigations . . . is that there is in addition a direct spread of wage inflation from the pace-making regions (the South East and perhaps the Midlands) to the others . . . there seems to be a reasonable presumption that a more even spreading of pressure of demand between regions would do something to reduce the speed of wage inflation.

These findings, and the wage inflation argument, thus provide further support for a government regional location of industry policy.

This is much less true, however, of an alternative wage inflation argument which focuses on the impact of net population transfers from the lagging to the growing regions. Some writers, such as Needleman (1965), have argued that in Britain such migration has also aggravated inflation by increasing the level of *demand* for housing and other social capital in the prosperous regions more than the level of supply of labour and hence productive capacity. The result, in their view, has been further wage inflation. This argument appears to be accepted by McCrone (1969, 39), who claims that:

> it is clear that social capital is already more or less fully utilized in the Midlands and South East of England, that further population inflow would therefore be likely to require heavy investment expenditure and that this might well, at least for a time, outweigh any increase in output which the inflowing labour could contribute. If this is so the effect would be inflationary.

However, McCrone does admit that the migration/inflation equation is a very complex one; while others, such as Manners (1972, 8) are very sceptical of its current relevance to Britain, particularly given the fact that the country's traditional growth regions, the South East and West Midlands, have been net *losers* of population by migration during the last decade (table 8.2). This alternative wage inflation argument is probably therefore not now, even if formerly, valid as a basis for government regional policy.

8.4.6. The political factor

At least since 1945, political considerations have substantially influenced the development of British regional location of industry policy. It is of course no accident that the two postwar periods – 1945–51 and 1964–70 – during which regional policy was operated most vigorously and markedly strengthened by new major policy instruments were both characterized by a Labour administration in Whitehall. For although in any case ideologically egalitarian, the Labour party has also always relied heavily upon the votes of electors in the peripheral regions for seats in the House of Commons. Indeed, as McCallum (1973, 271) points out, Labour's advent to power in 1964 largely reflected voting shifts in the poorer regions, the Conservatives losing 28 per cent of their previous seats in these regions, but only 12 per cent of their seats elsewhere in the country. The strengthening of regional policy which the Labour government then carried through was almost certainly in turn a major reason for the good showing of the Labour party in the subsequent 1970 election in the Development and Intermediate Areas, where it held on to 132 of the 188 seats involved. As McCallum stresses (1973, 283), it was only because of massive Conservative gains in the rest of the country (+64 seats) that the Labour government was forced out of office.

These straightforward political considerations help to explain the development of regional policy in Britain. But in a much wider sense, the 'political' concern of regional communities and the two peripheral nations of Scotland and Wales over the preservation of their cultural or social identity in the face of relative economic decline also represents a very important basis for such a policy. As Brown (1972, 51) points out, that certain United Kingdom regions 'do possess at least significantly widespread senses of their identity, history and culture as communities, of the value of their peculiar flavour of life, and of their claims as major components of the nation, is a fact to be reckoned with in considering regional policy. It is, indeed, one of the main reasons why one has to consider regional policy at all'. In turn, such broad political considerations may find direct expression in votes: the election to the House of Commons in February 1974 of no less than seven representatives of the Scottish National Party[4] clearly reflected in part mounting Scottish dissatisfaction with continuing relative economic decline (table 8.2), coupled with a desire for greater Scottish control over North Sea oil revenues. Political considerations have thus been an inevitable influence upon the development of regional industrial location policy.

8.5. The arguments against regional policy

In documenting the reasons for implementation of government regional policy, at least as these have been clarified in recent years, the preceding section has of course begged a very important question. Might this policy not be resulting in a net *loss* of national manufacturing output, including exports, for at least two reasons? Firstly, may not growth firms in the prosperous regions, faced with IDC expansion refusals, have preferred to abandon expansion plans altogether or invest abroad rather than establish peripheral area plants? And secondly, may not the assisted areas prove in the long run to be relatively uneconomic locations for modern industry, resulting in less efficient and hence reduced production and/or a long-term requirement for government operating cost subsidies? These arguments, emphasized strongly at times by the Confederation of British Industries, clearly demand careful attention.

The evidence with regard to the former is mixed, but generally opposed (Cameron 1974, 29). Department of Industry figures reveal (Moore and Rhodes 1976, table A2) that between 1950 and 1971 the annual proportion of total applications by manufacturing firms in South East England and the Midlands refused Industrial Development Certificates for expansion, measured by the expected employment involved, varied from a negligible 1.8 per cent (1956) to a high of only 29.9 per cent (1966). During the 1960s, the figure was usually between 20 and 30 per cent, but in any case it fell substantially after 1968. Moreover, most refused schemes apparently nonetheless go ahead, to some degree at least, in non-IDC controlled existing central region premises. So the absolute overall loss is unlikely to be greater than about 5 per cent of total employment in all IDC applications (Brown 1972, 303). On the other hand, industrialists frequently claim that many central region firms which would otherwise have expanded locally never even bother to apply for IDCs, in the belief that refusal is inevitable. But even here, CBI evidence (Brown 1972, 303) shows that between 1963 and 1968 only approximately 20 per cent of schemes which had been thought of by a large sample of South East firms for development in non-assisted areas were modified, deferred or abandoned because of the expectation of IDC restrictions; and this is no greater a mortality percentage than that common, for normal business reasons, for projects actually granted IDCs. So in general, Cameron's conclusion (1974, 29) that 'the loss of growth caused by IDC controls is not large' seems a reasonable one.

The validity of the long-term inefficiency argument is however much more difficult to assess. Specific criticism of peripheral regions as relatively uneconomic locations for manufacturing industry centre on the transport cost, and labour quality and relations, arguments. The fact that peripheral locations do result in higher transport costs for some firms, chiefly on finished goods to markets, has already been documented (sections 4.1.1 and 7.4.3). True, surveys of immigrant firms in peripheral areas have argued that the additional transport costs incurred are small, relative to other costs. Thus Luttrell (1962, 176) claimed from detailed study of ninety-eight immediately-postwar Development Area branch factories that such extra transport costs were 'quite unimportant in relation to the cost variations due to other factors'. While Begg's survey of Tayside (Scotland) manufacturing firms concluded (1972, 49) that 'the cost of delivering products to customers represented 4 per cent or less of total costs in 80 per cent of the firms responding'. However, the problem with such surveys is of course that they are by definition confined only to firms which *have* been willing to move to the periphery, and which may well therefore be self-selected in terms of proportionately low transport costs (Logan, referred to in Cameron 1974, 30).

More valid evidence against the anti-policy higher transport cost argument is provided by Woodward (1971), Chisholm (1971) and Edwards (1975). All of these are concerned with firms throughout Britain. The first points out that in 1963, and excluding certain unusual industries, only 4–5 per cent of all manufacturing costs incurred by United Kingdom firms were transport costs. 'In view of this, it seems unlikely that differences in the transport costs of alternative sites would generally have an effect on total costs of more than 1 to 2 per cent, less than the effects of regional variations in labour costs'. The latter variations of course work in favour of the assisted areas (section 4.2.1). Chisholm (1971, 239), concerned especially with larger manufacturing plants, comes to a similar conclusion. Census of Production cost data for such plants suggest that 'inter-regional location choices will make little difference to the nation's transport bill', although they 'may in some cases have an impact on the operating costs of the firm'. But 'overall, it seems most unlikely that there is any serious divergence between private and social considerations', with regard to peripheral region transport costs. Lastly, Edwards (1975, 125), after a most detailed analysis of 1963 regional variations in payments by British manufacturing firms for transport of goods, concludes that 'in very general terms, the indications are that the difference between the highest cost regions (Northern, Scotland and East Anglia) and the least cost (East and West Midlands and to some extent the South East) was (in 1963) relatively small, amounting to not more than 2 to 3 per cent of the value added by the manufacturing sector (and less than one per cent of its sales value)'. And of course even this small difference is likely to have declined still further since 1963, with motorway construction (Edwards 1975, 126). While it must be remembered that these transport cost findings reflect a distribution of firms between regions which could be deliberately designed to minimize such costs, it would seem nonetheless probable that the simple transport cost argument is not of major significance today for most British manufacturing firms. The relatively short distances separating the major peripheral and central industrial areas are one important consideration behind this conclusion.

The labour quality argument, that peripheral area workers are less productive for one reason or another than their central region counterparts, has also already been outlined in section 4.1.5. As noted there, assessment of this factor is made more difficult by the inevitable short-run problems and low productivity associated with the training of a new peripheral-area migrant factory workforce. Luttrell (1962, 122), for example, acknowledges that labour turnover in such plants is initially higher than in, for example, central region parent factories: but that this falls to become 'much the same (as in the parents) . . . by about the fourth year' after movement. A somewhat similar conclusion, of a subsequent fall in high initial labour turnover and low labour productivity, was reached by Morley and Townroe's survey (1974, 21–5) of factories immigrant to Northern England in the late 1960s. But as noted in section. 4.1.5, the ILAG survey's result, suggesting a significant regional difference in labour quality, does compare like with like in that both the central and peripheral firms surveyed were migrant, newly-established firms. Moreover, this survey also suggests a significant difference in the labour relations situation between centre and periphery, another important component in productivity and growth. In response to a direct question on labour relations in the new location (Department of Trade and Industry 1973, 635), the proportions of migrant firms settling in the South East and the Midlands reporting such relations to be worse than previously were only 11 per cent and 2 per cent, respectively. Whereas for Development Area migrants, the proportion was 20 per cent, with even higher percentages for movement to Scotland (23 per cent) and Merseyside (22 per cent). That peripheral industrial areas are characterized by more militant union attitudes and a greater frequency of strikes is also acknowledged by other commentators, such as Moore and Rhodes (1974a, 50). So although Morley and Townroe (1974, 25), for example, would argue that 'although labour factors were significant in contributing to high initial costs in the new plants, the companies moving to the Northern Region seem to have benefited from their new workforce rather than suffered', longterm and definitive conclusions on the question of labour quality and productivity are not easy to draw.

In addition to the transport and labour arguments, at least three other types of more general evidence have been cited by protagonists in this debate. One is the level of expressed general satisfaction with their new peripheral location on the part of migrant firms. For example, the ILAG survey showed (Department of Trade and Industry 1973, 667) that the great majority of Development Area immigrants were 'on balance . . . satisfied with the development' they had undertaken. In the case of moves to Northern England and Scotland, the percentage replying in the affirmative was as high as 80 per cent. On the face of it, this strongly supports the view that peripheral areas are suitable locations for modern manufacturing industry. But against this, it is also true that a considerably larger minority of Development Area movers were either dissatisfied with or uncertain about the outcome ('too early to say') than was the case with central area moves. In the Northern Ireland, Wales and Merseyside cases, this minority was as large as 39, 30 and 30 per cent respectively, compared with only 12 and 15 per cent respectively for movers to the South East and Midlands. A chi-square text, using of course actual numbers of firms involved, reveals that the overall two-sample Development Area/central region difference in this respect is statistically very significant, at the 0.0005 probability level. So this type of evidence can be used to support both pro- and anti-policy viewpoints, although it is of course again bedevilled by the shortness of the period since moving and hence only limited experience in their new locations of the firms involved.[5]

One way round this problem is to adopt the indirect approach of examining and comparing closure rates of previously mobile factories in peripheral and central locations. The hypothesis here, of course, is that if long-run operating conditions are poorer in the peripheral than the central regions, this will become apparent in higher long-term closure rates. Until recently, a marked dearth of reliable data prevented assessment of this hypothesis. But several recent studies do now permit certain conclusions to be drawn. The earliest, and the only one to use independent, non-government data, was that by the present author, of manufacturing migration from north-west London. This found (Keeble 1968a, 48) that for the 1940–64 period, so-called Provincial Zone migrants (moves more than 160 kilometres, or 100 miles, nearly all to Development Areas) appeared to be 'much more prone to subsequent closure (closure rate, 1 in 5.1 factories) than Metropolitan Zone plants (1 in 11.3 factories); and the difference in average factory age (in 1964) between the two groups (13.4 years and 9.3 years respectively) does not seem great enough wholly to account for this contrast'. Metropolitan Zone plants were those set up more than 16 but less than 160 kilometres from north-west London. Moreover, this conclusion is supported by Sant's analysis (1975b; 1975a, 101–9) of Board of Trade migrant factory closure data for 1945–60. These data must be treated with considerable caution, because of probable regional differences in accuracy and coverage of the closure records kept by regional Board of Trade offices during the period. The South East records, for example, are particularly suspect, because of difficulties with firm turnover in existing premises. But when adjusted for age differences, the crude data do reveal that during this period, the peripheral areas, defined as Northern Ireland, Scotland, Wales, Northern, North West and South West England, recorded a closure index of 117 compared with a United Kingdom average index of 100 and a value for the remainder of the country of only 83 (Sant 1975a, 106). This difference is almost certainly too great to be explained simply by data deficiencies.

These results strongly suggest that until the early 1960s, the peripheral areas did indeed record significantly higher migrant factory closure rates than more central regions, supporting the hypothesis of more difficult operating conditions, and higher operating costs or lower profitability, in peripheral areas. However, and of great importance, Sant's work, and that by Atkins (1973), reveal that since the early 1960s, this differential has markedly changed and now operates in *favour* of the periphery. Thus for migration between 1960 and 1965, age-adjusted closure indices fell in the periphery but rose in the rest of the United Kingdom, to a value of exactly 100 in each case; and this trend continued between 1966 and 1971, with a reversal of the differential to only 91 for peripheral moves but 107 for those to the remainder of the country (Sant 1975a, 106). Although dealing with the somewhat different case of long-established branches,[6] Atkins' study points to a somewhat similar conclusion, with mature branch closure rates between 1966 and 1971 in assisted and non-assisted areas being identical (2.1 per cent per annum, in both cases). The reason for this striking change is not difficult to find. Without much doubt, it is a direct reflection of the massive increase in regional policy financial assistance since the early 1960s, which now includes very large investment and operating cost subsidies. But this does of course leave unanswered the very important question as to whether such subsidies must be viewed as a long term if not permanent commitment, to offset intrinsic peripheral locational disadvantage; or whether the growth of more modern immigrant industry in the assisted areas will eventually become self-sustaining and subsidies can be removed without fear of a rise in these areas' closure rates.

The last general approach to the locational efficiency controversy is via shift-and-share analyses of manufacturing net output in differing areas. Census of Production figures reveal that throughout the postwar period, manufacturing industry in London and the South East has consistently produced a higher aggregate value of net output per employee than any other region. For example, table 8.3 shows that in 1968, the London and rest of South East values were no less than 11 and 10 per cent higher, respectively, than the national average. Wales also recorded a manufacturing net output value per employee significantly above the latter (+6 per cent), but Scotland and Northern Ireland were significantly below (−5 and −6 per cent respectively). By themselves, of course, these net output figures only hint at the possibility of more efficient manufacturing production in the South East, since they make no allowance for the very different industrial mix of the different regions. Thus the relatively high overall values recorded by Wales and the North are undoubtedly due in part, at least, to a bias in their industrial structures towards relatively capital-intensive industries, such as steel, oil-refining and chemicals, which by their nature record high net output values per worker employed. It is of course however possible to allow for this structural difference using shift-and-share analysis, as in a recent study carried out for the Greater London Development Plan (Greater London Council 1969, 73–5). This study, based on 1958 data, in fact concluded that 'London's high productivity was not due to structural factors', but to locational advantage. Indeed, only one-fifth (+£22)

Table 8.3 *Net manufacturing output per employee, by regions, in 1968*

	Net manufacturing output per employee [£]	*Percentage of UK value*
GLC area	2,166	110.8
Rest of South East	2,140	109.5
Wales	2,078	106.3
Northern	1,956	100.1
East Anglia	1,949	99.7
North West	1,938	99.2
South West	1,923	98.4
Scotland	1,861	95.2
East Midlands	1,849	94.6
West Midlands	1,841	94.2
Yorkshire and Humberside	1,791	91.7
Northern Ireland	1,651	84.5
United Kingdom	1,954	100.0

Source: Central Statistical Office (1973), *Abstract of Regional Statistics*, no. 9, table 45

of the overall difference (+£110) between the London (£1,111) and the British national (£1,001) values was ascribed to structural differences, four-fifths (+£88) apparently reflecting some sort of advantage specific to London. In contrast, the analysis also suggested that much of the high labour productivity of Wales and the North was simply a result of industrial structure, although there was also a substantial though smaller positive residual in each case which could not be explained in this way.

The implicit conclusion from this analysis is of course that many industries in London and the South East are more efficient than their counterparts in the lagging peripheral regions; and, perhaps, that greater efficiency is a reflection of a more suitable environment for manufacturing activity. However, several criticisms can be levied against the GLC analysis (Manners 1970). One is its dependence on aggregate Order-level statistics rather than detailed Minimum List Headings (see section 3.3). However, this criticism is countered by Brown's more recent study (1972, 153–5), which identified a very significant statistical association between presence in Greater London and 1954 above-average net output per head of manufacturing industries defined at this MLH level. Brown's analysis, which was deliberately aimed at testing whether or not high productivity across a wide range of industries was a characteristic of particular regions such as the South East, also revealed a significant association between high individual industry net output at this detailed level and location in the West Midlands conurbation, most of South East England outside London (the old Southern and Eastern standard regions), and the East Midlands (the old North Midlands region). This strongly suggests the general validity of the GLC shift-and-share analysis despite use of Order data.

On the other hand, Brown also draws attention in his study to the fact that net output per head is in many ways an arguable index of relative regional efficiency in manufacturing, because of the impact upon it of varying regional labour costs, in turn reflecting variations in the cost of living. Thus high net output values may in part mean that firms in the region concerned have to pay high wages, which are then passed on to customers in the form of higher prices and value of output. Put another way, Brown (1972, 158) thus suggests that to some degree the London and West Midlands conurbation high net output values are 'a matter more of necessity than of virtue'. This important criticism must to some extent reduce the significance of the GLC finding. The latter, as its authors fully acknowledge, may also be criticized for focusing solely on *labour* productivity, when the efficient use of *all* factors of production, including capital, should be the object of investigation. Moreover, for policy purposes, estimates of *marginal* rather than average productivity in different regions would be significantly more useful. The latter of course lump together the performance of old and new plants, and may therefore afford a misleading guide to the likely productivity of a new factory setting up in a particular region. But in the absence of either capital or marginal productivity data, there is force in the GLC study's claim that 'some analysis of the (available) data is a better basis for policy formulation than no analysis at all' (Greater London Council 1969, 73).

Though open to important criticisms, therefore, the GLC and Brown net output analyses nonetheless do provide some limited evidence for the view that central regions provide a better operating environment for many industries than most peripheral regions. So, too, looked at this time from the viewpoint of a classic peripheral area, does Cameron's recent net output study (1971, 330) of Scotland. In this, Cameron was concerned with precisely the question at issue: does location in certain regions – in this case Clydeside in particular and Scotland in general – reduce the efficiency and productivity of manufacturing industry? To answer this, Cameron carried out a series of analyses using various indices of Clydeside's recent economic performance, especially in manufacturing. One of these was a shift-and-share analysis of net output changes in Scotland's engineering industries between 1958 and 1963, at the

MLH level. The engineering trades were singled out because of their dominance in both Clydeside's and Scotland's manufacturing structure. Cameron's conclusion was that while important, 'the industry-mix factor explained only approximately half of the net relative shift' in Scottish engineering net output over this period. In other words, of equal importance was 'a deficient local growth' of industries which in Britain as a whole were expanding their output more rapidly. Cameron's net conclusion on this and other analyses was therefore that 'Clydeside's problems are not only structural but also consist of some very real, though undefined, local restraints on economic growth'.

The variety of often-conflicting evidence on the longterm implications of assisted-area manufacturing policy discrimination – evidence on transport costs, labour quality, migrant firm satisfaction and closure rates, and net output – is thus difficult to evaluate. But taken together, there do seem to be indications that certain peripheral areas, notably the more distant ones of Scotland and Northern Ireland, do not afford all sectors of modern manufacturing industry with as efficient an operating environment as the central regions of the South East and Midlands. Achievement of regional policy's prime goal, 'a better economic balance between the different parts of the country' (Department of Trade and Industry 1971, 8), for the social and wider economic reasons set out in section 8.4, may well therefore involve a certain loss of national manufacturing output through less efficient production, and may hence require some longterm operating subsidies.

8.6. The history of regional industrial location policy

The development of regional industrial location policy in the United Kingdom is a major topic in its own right, and only a brief synopsis can be attempted here.[7] This synopsis is the more difficult because policy development has not really been a continuous process, but subject to rapid fluctuations in intensity of controls, scale of financial inducements, extent of areas affected, and range of policy instruments, consequent primarily on changes in national and regional economic fortunes and in government administrations. But it is true that by the 1970s, the magnitude of this policy, measured in almost any of these ways, was very markedly greater than during earlier periods. It must also be stressed that the following discussion concentrates on spatially-discriminatory measures aimed directly at private manufacturing industry. Indirect effects, notably those resulting from recent preferential road investment in the assisted areas, have already been touched on elsewhere (section 4.2.4); while space prevents any detailed consideration of government industry-based assistance or intervention, even though much of this, notably in regard to steel (section 7.2) and shipbuilding, has of course helped to maintain jobs and economic activity in the peripheral regions (Manners 1972, 47–8). Direct support for the shipbuilding industry, for example, cost the taxpayer no less than £156 million between 1965 and 1974, in loans, grants and the value of shares in such firms as Harland and Wolff, which employs 10,000 Belfast workers, Govan Shipbuilders, with 5,300 jobs on Clydeside, and Cammell Laird, Merseyside. Further expenditure of £60 million to meet lossses by Harland and Wolff and £17 million for Govan Shipbuilders was announced in 1975. Until recently, industry-based assistance has thus tended to reinforce general spatially-discriminatory policies in promoting manufacturing activity in peripheral rather than central regions.

8.6.1. Policy before 1945

The earliest regional location of industry legislation was the 1934 Special Areas (Development and Improvement) Act. Prompted by massive peripheral unemployment (section 8.4.1), this designated four Special Areas with acute unemployment problems, namely south Wales, north-east England, west Cumberland and Clydeside, but excluding their regional urban centres (fig. 8.1a), for certain financial assistance. This help was to be disbursed by government Commissioners, one each for England and Wales, and for Scotland. In practice, however, the Commissioners' powers were extremely limited, since they were not allowed to advance funds to private industry or carry out major public works. Some loan finance for industrial development did become available after 1936 through the government-backed Special Areas Reconstruction Association (for small firms only), the Nuffield Trust, and after the Special Areas Amendment Act of 1937, directly from the Treasury. The latter legislation also made available certain tax incentives to new Special Area firms. In all, loans of nearly £5 million were advanced to Special Area industrialists between 1934 and 1939. But the Commissioners' most successful activity was the establishment of several important industrial, or as they were then called, trading estates, notably at Team Valley south of Newcastle, at Treforest in South Wales, and at Hillington south-west of Glasgow. By 1938, the relatively cheap rented factories thus provided had helped to increase the Special Areas' share of national new factory construction to 17 per cent, compared with only 3 per cent in 1936; and many of the new firms were from outside the peripheral areas, some being refugee concerns from the continent, others dispersed 'shadow' factories for wartime production. By 1944–5 many of these had grown substantially.

8.6.2. Policy between 1945 and 1960

The background to postwar industrial location policy was of course the so-called Barlow Report of 1940. This report was produced by the Royal Commission on the Distribution of the Industrial Population, set up in 1937 under the chairmanship of Sir Montague Barlow 'to inquire into the causes which have influenced the present distribution of industrial population . . . to consider what social, economic or strategical disadvantages arise from the concentration of industries . . . and to report what remedial measures if any should be taken in the national interest' (Royal Commission 1940, 1). On the basis of a vast mass of evidence, the Commission concluded that 'the continued drift of the industrial population to London and the Home Counties constitutes a social, economic and strategical problem which demands immediate attention' (Royal Commission 1940, 202), and recommended that the government take powers to achieve a better regional balance of manufacturing industry. In particular, it advocated the imposition of controls on new factory construction in the South East, preferably through a Central Authority with regulatory, advisory and research powers. Although only partially implemented, these recommendations and the report as a whole were of great importance in crystallizing informed public opinion on the need for a government industrial location policy. Also of considerable significance in this respect was the 1944 White Paper on Employment Policy, which explicitly accepted the need to encourage industrial growth in the peripheral regions as an integral part of a postwar full employment policy.

These documents led directly to the 1945 Distribution of Industry Act. This act, 'the foundation of British regional policy from 1945 to 1960' (McCrone 1969, 107), replaced the Special Areas by four significantly larger Development Areas which included the major regional centres of Glasgow, Cardiff, Swansea and Newcastle (fig. 8.1b). Also included for the first time was Teesside, western south Wales, and the Dundee area. In 1946, two small additional Development Areas were scheduled – Wrexham and south Lancashire – while 1949 saw the addition of Merseyside and the Scottish Highlands around Inverness, and 1953 the addition of north-east Lancashire (fig. 8.1b). Within these areas, the 1945 Distribution of Industry Act empowered the Board of Trade to engage widely in industrial development promotion. In particular, the Board was enabled to purchase land and build factories, to make loans to industrial estate companies, to reclaim derelict land and to provide basic public services – transport, power, lighting – for industry. At the same time, the Treasury, guided by the advice of the Development Areas Treasury Advisory Committee (DATAC), was empowered under certain conditions to make grants or loans to specific Development Area manufacturing firms. Although undoubtedly the worst problem region of the United Kingdom, Northern Ireland, with its own provincial government, was not included under this legislation but took its own action to provide generous grants to new industry and establish industrial estates operated by the Northern Ireland Ministry of Commerce.

The opposite side of the coin to Development Area manufacturing promotion, industrial controls in the prosperous regions, were not in fact

8.1a The Special Areas, 1934–45

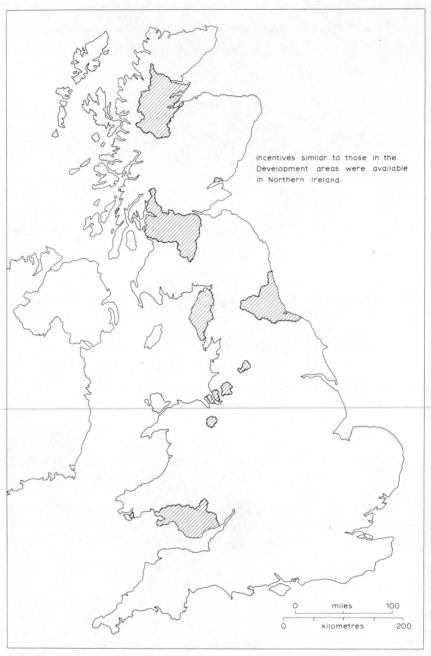

Incentives similar to those in the Development areas were available in Northern Ireland.

8.1b The Development Areas, 1945–60

covered by the Distribution of Industry Act. Instead, the government, through the Board of Trade, elected to use the existing building licence system introduced during the war, and its control of allocations of constructional steel. This method, though very effective in drastically restricting factory construction in the London area for example, was replaced as from 1 July 1948 by the Industrial Development Certificate system. The latter was established by the 1947 Town and Country Planning Act, which made it compulsory for any industrial building scheme of more than 465 square metres (5,000 sq. ft) to have an Industrial Development Certificate issued by the Board of Trade, as a token of the fact that 'the development in question can be carried out consistently with the proper distribution of industry'. This system has been a fundamental basis for regional industrial location policy ever since, although operated with very different degrees of rigour at different periods.

The postwar Labour administration utilized these powers of manufacturing location control and promotion with great force. Between 1945 and 1947, for example, a period of rapid industrial expansion to satisfy pent-up wartime consumer demands, the Development Areas received 51 per cent of all new factory building in Britain, although they contained only 20 per cent of the insured population (McCrone 1969, 112). Between 1945 and 1951, the peripheral areas as a whole also received exactly 50 per cent (463 out of 933) of all inter-subregion United Kingdom manufacturing moves recorded by the Board of Trade and surviving to 1966, and no less than 64 per cent (237,000 jobs) of the manufacturing employment created (by 1966) in such moves (Howard 1968, 23). By 1956, the Board of Trade was operating Development Area factories totalling 3.86 million square metres (42 million sq. ft) of floorspace and employing 186,000 workers. These statistics bear witness to the considerable short-term success of location policy at that time, despite only very limited actual government expenditure, and that primarily on constructing factories and industrial estates (see table 8.4).

However, by the later 1950s, after a period of Conservative government and very passive regional policy, unemployment began to rise steeply in a number of peripheral locations. This trend, the result both of national recession and the return of the long-term trend of decline in the periphery's staple industries, forced new government action. The immediate result was the Distribution of Industry (Industrial Finance) Act of 1958, which extended the Treasury's Development Area powers to make loans or grants on DATAC advice to cover a wide range of new smaller localities suffering from particularly acute and persistent unemployment. The first list of such areas included such new localities as Cornwall, north-east Suffolk, and coastal parts of Devon, Kent, Norfolk, Lincolnshire and Yorkshire – a striking tribute to the centre-periphery spatial structure of unemployment and economic prosperity in Britain (fig. 8.2a: Caesar 1964, 236). This interim measure was however soon superseded by the plethora of legislation which characterized the 1960s.

8.6.3. Policy during the 1960s

Since 1960, a much steeper economic decline in the peripheral region's traditional industries – coal, steel, shipbuilding and textiles – has resulted in a massive intensification of regional policy, particularly after 1963. However, the 1960 Local Employment Act was nonetheless of considerable significance, in that by repealing the earlier Distribution of Industry Acts it acknowledged the need for a new approach to the problem. One of its main provisions was the replacement of the old Development Areas by new, smaller Development Districts, defined as 'localities in which, in the opinion of the Board, a high rate of unemployment exists or is imminent or is likely to persist' (McCrone 1969, 122). The areas thus scheduled, nearly all on the basis of an unemployment rate greater than 4.5 per cent, are shown in figure 8.2a. Equally important, however, the 1960 Act strengthened somewhat the financial incentives available in these Districts to new manufacturing firms. Transferred to come under the Board of Trade, the advisory committee was given greater freedom to make loans and grants for the purchase of plant and machinery, while modest but completely new building grants were introduced for immigrant Development District manufacturers preferring to construct their own factories rather than to rent from the government. From this point on, government regional policy expenditure on manufacturing industry began to climb substantially, while IDC controls were applied increasingly strictly, percentage refusals in the South East and Midlands measured by expected employment rising from 13.7 per cent in 1959 to 24.2 per cent in 1962, and to a peak of 29.9 per cent in 1966 (Moore and Rhodes 1976, table A2). Government expenditure on factory building, loans and grants, which had averaged £5 million a year over the eight years before 1960–61, rose to an average £37 million during the following three years.

A further marked strengthening of location policy took place in 1963, a year which also saw the publication of two White Papers on central Scotland and north-east England which advocated the establishment of selected growth centres for manufacturing development in these areas. Thus the Local Employment Act of 1963 replaced the confusing 1960 building grant provisions, which had in practice met about 17 per cent of building costs, by a standard 25 per cent grant towards Development District factory construction. It also empowered the Board of Trade, for the first time, to make cash grants of up to 10 per cent of the cost of new plant and machinery. At the same time, the 1963 Finance Act included a provision for the granting of so-called 'free depreciation' for tax purposes of the cost of new plant and machinery installed by manufacturing firms in the Development Districts. Allowed by this provision to write off their expenses on such equipment against taxable profits at whatever rate they wished, industrialists were thus able to reduce their tax liability to zero until they had recovered the full cost of the new equipment. While eventual total taxation was not reduced, this did in effect provide an

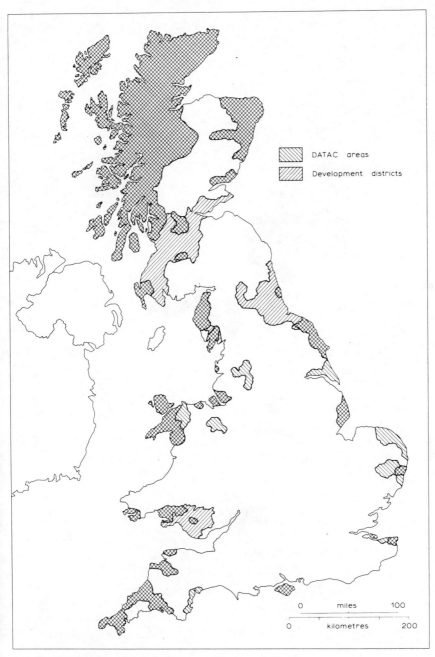

DATAC areas

Development districts

8.2a DATAC areas and Development Districts, 1958–66

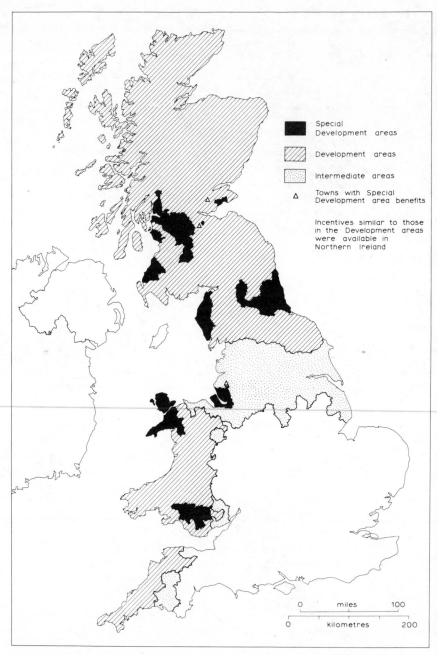

Special
Development areas

Development areas

Intermediate areas

△ Towns with Special
Development area benefits

Incentives similar to those
in the Development areas
were available in
Northern Ireland

0 miles 100

0 kilometres 200

8.2b The Special Development, Development and Intermediate Areas, 1966–75

interest-free loan from the Inland Revenue for a certain period (McCrone 1969, 135), and proved a popular measure.

The advent of the Labour administration in 1964 was followed by a series of even more radical changes. Of minor importance was the immediate lowering of the IDC threshold (in 1965) for development in the South East, East Anglia and the Midlands, to only 93 square metres (1,000 sq. ft). It was almost as immediately raised again (in 1966), to 279 square metres (3,000 sq. ft), given an extension of the definition of industrial building in these regions to include storage and ancillary space. Much more important were the provisions of the 1966 Industrial Development Act, which abolished the Development Districts in force since 1960, replacing them by new and much enlarged Development Areas (fig. 8.2b). It also drastically altered the method and scale of aiding investment in new plant and machinery in these areas, by abolishing the existing 10 per cent grants and free depreciation system in favour of standard and substantial investment grants. The latter, available outside the Development Areas at a rate of 20 per cent, were payable within them at the rate of no less than 40 per cent of incurred equipment costs. For 1967–8 only, both these rates were temporarily increased by 5 per cent, to 25 per cent and 45 per cent respectively. The 1966 Act also retained the existing 25 per cent development location building grant, but empowered this to be increased to 35 per cent in special cases.

The following year, 1967, witnessed the introduction of the Regional Employment Premium and the Special Development Area programme. The former was a direct reply to critics who had argued (see section 8.8.1) that the investment grant system was likely to encourage an over-concentration in manufacturing development in the peripheral areas upon capital-intensive industry, providing relatively few jobs. It took the form of a direct payroll subsidy to all existing manufacturing employees in the Development Areas, whether immigrant or not, of 30s. 0d. a week for men, 15s. 0d. for women and boys, and 9s. 6d. for girls. When introduced, its value was approximately 7 per cent of average earnings of male manual workers. This radical innovation in policy instruments has been the target of much criticism (MacKay 1972; 1974), but is now a major plank in government regional policy. The creation of Special Development Areas *within* the main Development regions (fig. 8.2b) was a simple welfare response to acute unemployment problems in certain former coalmining localities, industrialists moving to these areas being accorded a 35 per cent factory building grant or a five-year period of rent-free occupancy of a government factory, together with the possibility of special short-term 'operational' grants. Yet another category of assisted area, the Intermediate Area, was the chief recommendation of the 1969 Hunt Committee report (Department of Economic Affairs 1969), dealing with the so-called 'grey' areas, notably of North West England, Yorkshire and Humberside, in which reasonably low unemployment rates concealed major structural economic problems, high net outmigration, low activity rates and poor physical infrastructure. However, in the short-term these recommendations were largely ignored by the government, probably for financial reasons and for fear of spreading the jam of mobile industry too thinly over too wide an area (McCallum 1973, 280). The ensuing 1970 Local Employment Act thus designated only a small number of Intermediate Areas covering a minor part of the North West and Yorkshire/Humberside. Within these, industrialists were eligible for a 25 per cent building grant, but no assistance with equipment costs, while the Board of Trade was empowered to construct government factories.

The 1960s thus witnessed a massive increase in regional policy assistance to both immigrant and existing manufacturing firms within the peripheral areas, themselves defined far more widely by 1970 than ever before. The scale of this increase and the widened range of policy instruments aimed specifically at manufacturing industry is illustrated in table 8.4. By 1970–71, special regional assistance was costing the Exchequer no less than £270 million a year, representing a fivefold increase in simple monetary terms since 1960–61; and most of this increase involved non-recoverable cash grants and subsidies of one form or another. As Brown (1972, 290) wryly comments, expenditure on regional policy had indeed reached a 'range of magnitudes where it might be expected to have an appreciable impact on regional economies'.

8.6.4. Policy since 1970

The return to power of a Conservative government in 1970 produced what McCallum (1973, 283) for one has termed 'a brief interlude of anti-policy'. This was characterized by an immediate and substantial relaxation of IDC controls, the abolition of investment grants on plant and machinery, and their replacement by tax allowance incentives. A regional differential was incorporated by granting free depreciation on plant and machinery expenditure in the Development Areas, compared with only a 60 per cent initial allowance in the rest of the country. The former were also allowed a higher initial depreciation allowance (40 per cent as opposed to 30 per cent elsewhere) on the cost of new factories. Factory building grants were however retained and indeed raised, from 25 to 35 per cent (Development Areas) and 35 to 45 per cent (Special Development Areas). The basis for SDA operational grants was also changed, to 20 per cent of wage and salary costs of the new project during its first three years.

The realities of power, and in particular the economic recession of 1971–2, however, soon forced a rapid reappraisal of these measures. In February 1971, Special Development Area status was extended for the first time to several major peripheral industrial areas, notably Clydeside, Tyneside and Wearside (fig. 8.2b), while the SDA operational grant was increased to 30 per cent. In March 1971, Intermediate Area status was granted to certain other areas,

Table 8.4 *Regional policy payments to manufacturing industry in Britain, 1947–74*

	Special regional assistance to manufacturing industry in the assisted areas, Great Britain, £ million					
	1947–8	1954–5	1960–1	1965–6	1970–1	1973–4
Recoverable or mainly recoverable aid						
Government factory building	12.5	4.5	21.0	12.4	7.9	11.9
Loans	0.3	1.7	23.5	9.6	28.0	1.1
Total recoverable aid	12.8	6.2	44.5	22.0	35.9	13.0
Non-recoverable aid						
Under Local Employment Acts:						
building grants			3.3	13.8	30.1	23.5
plant and machinery grants				6.1	0.2	
other grants			2.7	0.5	4.0	1.3
Investment grants					90.0	29.5
Free depreciation				45.0		
Regional Employment Premium					110.0	115.0
Regional development grants						107.2
Selective regional assistance (loans and grants)						24.9
Total non-recoverable aid			6.0	65.4	234.3	301.4
Grand total, all aid	12.8	6.2	50.5	87.4	270.2	314.4

Sources: Moore and Rhodes 1974a, 61–62; Secretary of State for Industry 1974, *Industry Act 1972, Annual Report for the year ended 31 March 1974;* Chancellor of the Exchequer 1975, *Public Expenditure to 1978–79*, Cmnd 5879

notably Edinburgh. However, the major and radical change took the form of a White Paper on Industrial and Regional Development, published a year later in March 1972 (Keeble 1972d). In a complete about-turn forced by the evident failure of its earlier policy, the Conservative government announced its intention of abandoning the tax incentive approach and reverting to the payment of grants. Since the 1972 Industry Act, therefore, regional development grants, at a rate of 20 per cent in the Development Areas and 22 per cent in the Special Development Areas, have been payable for new investment in both plant and machinery and factory-building. Wilson (1973, 168) estimates that these grants alone represent a saving of between 1 and 2.5 per cent of total costs to manufacturing industry investing in the Development Areas, depending on the industry, or 2 to 5.5 per cent of net value added. In the Intermediate Areas, 20 per cent regional development grants are available for factory building only. Moreover, the Act granted the Secretary of State for Industry radical new powers of selective regional assistance, in practice so far chiefly in the form of loans, interest-relief and removal grants, replacing most of the aid formerly available under the Local Employment Acts. This selective assistance was not to be tied to job creation, being available for both employment-creating and modernization schemes in the assisted areas, and was to be disbursed through a new, regionally-based, Industrial Development Executive,[8] advised by regional Industrial Development Boards with considerable local autonomy in allocation of assistance.[9] Other significant 1972 measures were the extension of Intermediate Area status to the entire remainder of the North West, Yorkshire and Humberside, and Wales, the abolition of IDCs altogether in the Development and Special Development Areas, and the raising of the IDC threshold to 1,395 square metres (15,000 sq. ft) elsewhere except in the South East, where it was increased to 930 square metres (10,000 sq. ft).

The acceptability of this policy package to the incoming 1974 Labour administration has ensured its general continuation, at least for the time being. The only important changes to 1976 were the August 1974 decisions to double the value of the Regional Employment Premium instead of phasing it out, as intended by the Conservatives; to reduce IDC thresholds, yet again, to 465 square metres (5,000 sq. ft) in the South East and 930 square metres (10,000 sq. ft) in the rest of England outside the assisted areas (while retaining it at 1,395 square metres, or 15,000 square feet, in the Intermediate Areas); and to extend Development Area status to Edinburgh and Cardiff, and Special Development Area status to Merseyside and parts of north-west Wales (fig. 8.2b). By 1976, the assisted areas thus contained no less than 43 per cent of all Britain's employed population and covered a wider area than ever before. Moreover an actual 1973–4 regional policy cost of over £310 million (table 8.4) was expected, on official government estimates,[10] to rise to no less than £575 million by 1976–7, and £603 million by 1979–80. These very large totals primarily reflected massive regional development grant (£243 million, 1976–7) and Regional Employment Premium (£213 million, 1976–7) payments. In fact, however, expenditure on both these incentives will be less than this, possibly by some £40 million per annum, following the July 1976 public expenditure cuts. These included decisions to pay a single lower rate of REP (£2 for *both* men and women, and to delay grant payments by three months. Nevertheless, the impact of regional policy upon manufacturing industry would seem certain to remain substantial, if not increase still further with the creation and investment activities of the controversial National Enterprise Board, and more important, the setting up in 1976 of entirely new Welsh and Scottish Development Agencies operating under regional control to restructure the economies of these areas, as it were, from within. The Scottish Agency is empowered to spend £200 million, the Welsh Agency £100 million, over the five years to 1980, primarily upon improving infrastructure, derelict land clearance, and the promotion of indigenous manufacturing growth by small Scottish or Welsh companies. It is however to assess the magnitude of recent regional policy impacts upon manufacturing activity that we must now turn.

8.7. The impact of inter-regional industrial location policy

In their 1973 report on Regional Development Incentives, the House of Commons Expenditure Committee were severely critical of the lack of objective evaluation of the impact of inter-regional location policy. Indeed, in emphasizing 'the obscurity surrounding the effects of regional policy', the Committee (1973, 72) in a memorable phrase described regional policy as 'empiricism run mad, a game of hit-and-miss, played with more enthusiasm than success'. This judgement is however becoming rapidly less valid, in the face of recent research aimed at quantifying the impact of recent regional policy, notably upon manufacturing employment in different regions.

That regional policy in aggregate has significantly influenced the national spatial pattern of both manufacturing employment and floorspace changes, and of manufacturing migration, since the mid-1960s was of course one of the main conclusions of the regression analyses of chapter 5 and section 6.6.4. To this important finding, however, can be added those by Brown (1972) and Moore and Rhodes (1973; 1974b; 1976). The first of these, after careful examination of trends in industrial movement and factory-building approvals, the latter between 1956 and 1970, concluded (Brown 1972, 301) that between the later 1950s and later 1960s, there occurred a very significant increase in manufacturing job creation in the Development Areas relative both to the earlier period and to the rest of the country; that this increase 'may be put, very broadly, at 30,000 jobs a year or more'; and that 'most of the change of pattern in moves and approvals was due to the strengthening of policy' (Brown 1972, 318), as described in preceding sections.

The more fully-documented Moore and Rhodes' analyses looked separately at total manufacturing employment and manufacturing movement to the Development Areas. In the former case (Moore and Rhodes 1973), their approach was to subject regional manufacturing employment data for 1963 to a form of shift-and-share analysis, utilizing national annual growth rates by industry to estimate expected annual levels of total manufacturing employment *allowing* for structural differences over the 1951–70 period. Shipbuilding and metal manufacturing were however excluded, on the grounds that special industry-based government assistance rendered assessment of broad regional policy effects in these cases difficult (see section 8.6). The calculation was performed for both the Development Area set of regions (Scotland, Wales, Northern England and Northern Ireland) and the Midlands/South East. The year 1963 was selected as the most reasonable date for dividing previous 'passive' and subsequent 'active' policy periods. The study found that for the period up to 1963, the estimates of 'expected' manufacturing employment in the Development Area regions, on the basis of national industry growth rates and regional industrial structure, yielded a very good fit with actual recorded manufacturing employment levels; but that after 1963, actual and expected values diverged substantially, the former rising fairly steeply to 1971, relative to the latter. Conversely, a reasonable pre–1963 fit in the Midlands/South East case gave way after 1963 to increasing divergence, with actual manufacturing employment declining substantially relative to expected levels. In quantitative terms, Moore and Rhodes thus estimate that intensified regional policy after 1963 resulted in an increase of approximately 12 per cent (150,000 jobs) by 1970 in manufacturing employment in the four Development Area regions studied, relative to what it would have been without any strengthening of regional policy. Inclusion of a crude estimate for the Merseyside and South West Development Areas (33,000 jobs) and for the effect of government assistance to the shipbuilding and metal-manufacturing industries (10,000 jobs) raises this total to 193,000 manufacturing jobs by 1970. With great caution, the authors also estimate that somewhere between 20,000 and 50,000 of these jobs may have been due specifically to the controversial Regional Employment Premium.

Moore and Rhodes' 1976 movement of industry paper adopts the different approach of constructing multiple regression models to assess the relative contribution of different regional policy instruments to increasing annual rates of manufacturing movement to the Development Areas as a whole between 1950 and 1971. Their models thus incorporate four main independent variables, measured for each year over the period – the Great Britain male unemployment rate, included as an index of the pressure of demand on firm expansion and hence movement, an index of the intensity of IDC controls in the South East and Midlands, current values of regional investment incentives, and a measure of the real value of REP. The last two variables record zero values before 1963 and 1967 respectively. Allowing for serial autocorrelation, their basic model explained 95 per cent of the statistical variation in annual movement, with each of the three policy variables yielding significant regression coefficients. Moreover, allowing for the effects of such additional changes as the Special Development Area programme and extension in geographical extent of the assisted areas did not fundamentally change this result, except that the estimated REP impact was reduced in favour of the SDA programme impact. Their equations thus suggest that, allowing for a maximum and almost certainly unrealistic SDA effect, the relative contributions of the different policy instruments were as recorded in table 8.5.

Table 8.5 *The impact of different policy instruments on manufacturing movement to the Development Areas, 1960–71*

Policy instrument and years in force, 1960–71	Manufacturing movement to the Development Areas, 1960–71	
	Annual average number of moves	Total jobs created by movement 1960–71
Stronger IDC policy, as compared with 1950s (12 years)	46	100,000
Investment incentives (8 years)	36	47,000
Regional Employment Premium (4 years)	26	14,000
Special Development Areas (4 years)	20	10,000
Total	128	171,000

Source: Moore and Rhodes 1976, tables 1 and 3

While Moore and Rhodes conclude that average natural demand pressures during the 1960s would have generated some 10–15 moves per annum to the Development Areas even without policy, their analysis clearly suggests that by far the most important reason for such movement is regional policy controls and incentives. This is of course exactly the conclusion drawn earlier (sections 4.2.4 and 6.6.2) on more general evidence. Of the different policy measures, and in contrast to the pessimistic views of some commentators (Moxon 1972), they identify stronger IDC controls as the most important, followed in turn by investment incentives and REP. They also note that while the total policy-induced movement job creation estimate, of over 160,000 jobs, cannot directly be compared with the figures from their earlier 1973 analysis, 'it is clear that this mechanism of regional policy (i.e. manufacturing movement) accounts for a high proportion of all manufacturing jobs generated by regional policy'. This very interesting study, and the results discussed above, clearly indicate, and provide some quantitative estimate of, the dominant importance of regional location of industry policy in recent relative and absolute manufacturing growth in the peripheral assisted regions of the United Kingdom.

8.8. Industrial promotion in the assisted areas: selected issues

The final sections of this chapter deal, very briefly, with three controversial issues concerning government industrial promotion in the assisted areas – the effect of investment grants, the dominance of movement by branch factories, and the question of industrially-linked growth centres or 'industrial complexes'.

8.8.1. Investment grants and capital-intensive industry

The Labour government's reliance before 1967 upon investment grants prompted some contemporary commentators to argue that such an approach both encouraged the development in the assisted areas of capital-intensive industry providing relatively few jobs, and resulted in massive government payments to firms which, for basic locational reasons such as deep-water access (see section 4.2.3), would have selected locations in these areas anyway. Thus Warren (1971, 206–7) concludes that in heavy chemical manufacturing, concentrated as it is in the assisted areas of North West England and Teesside, 'big Development Area grants have assisted the progress to giant plants but with little new employment', resulting in terms of jobs in 'scant return for large government financial help'. Moreover, Brown (Department of Economic Affairs, 1969, 237–8), utilizing plant and machinery investment grant data for 1966–7, has demonstrated from regression analysis that the proportion of investment in different industries going to the Development Areas during this period was significantly and positively related to the capital-intensiveness of the industry and the proportion of its existing employment already situated in the assisted areas. In other words, as the Hunt Committee accepted, while the development of capital-intensive industry in these areas is a natural result of the existing spatial distribution and location requirements of such industry in Britain, 'there seems in addition a clear tendency for investment grants to segregate capital-intensive industry into development areas' (Department of Economic Affairs 1969, 44).

This conclusion has admittedly been challenged by Chisholm (1970b) on the grounds that Brown's data were somewhat suspect, omitting in particular measures of investment in factory *building* in addition to plant and machinery. But Chisholm's view that 'the case is not proven either way' does not appear to have been accepted by subsequent commentators, such as Moore and Rhodes (1974a, 51), or indeed Brown himself (1972, 313). However, even if as seems most probable Brown's findings are generally correct, it is perhaps too extreme to claim, as he does, that 'no obvious benefit to the assisted areas or the economy as a whole stems from the very expensive gearing of incentives predominantly or exclusively to capital cost'. For as Wilson (1973, 166) points out, capital-intensive projects may on occasion be key elements in larger industrial complexes of considerable value to an assisted area, as perhaps with the proposed Lackenby-Redcar steel complex on Teesside (section 7.2.3). They are also usually dominantly male-employing as opposed to much migrant industry which tends to be biased, relative to the national average, towards female workers (Howard 1968, 33). For these reasons, in Wilson's view, 'a general condemnation of capital-intensive development in labour surplus areas cannot be sustained', although it would now seem generally accepted that greater selectivity in grants to capital-intensive projects *and* parallel labour-oriented policy assistance, such as REP, are desirable (House of Commons Expenditure Committee 1973, 75).

8.8.2. Assisted-area branch migration and indigenous industry

Despite the very substantial success of regional policy in channelling mobile industry to the assisted areas, important criticisms have been levied at the *type* of mobile plants thus attracted. These criticisms centre on the dominance of peripheral area movement by branch plants, documented in section 6.6.3. This dominance is viewed by many regional commentators as undesirable, on at least four grounds. First, it is seen as transferring effective control of the regional or, in the case of Wales and Scotland, national economy to boards of directors outside the area, notably in South East England and the Midlands, who are regarded as possessing little or no longterm allegiance to the region involved. Certainly the scale of 'outside' control over manufacturing in particular peripheral regions is very considerable. Thus for example Tomkins and Lovering (1973, 31) have estimated that in 1969, no less than 61 per cent (713) of all privately owned manufacturing and primarily industrial establishments[11] in Wales employing more than twenty-five workers were owned or operated by firms with headquarters outside the principality. Of these, 327 (28 per cent of the total) were direct branches of companies with headquarters elsewhere in the United Kingdom, while 312 (27 per cent) were subsidiaries of such companies. Some seventy-four establishments (6 per cent) were directly or indirectly owned by non-United Kingdom companies. In Northern Ireland, 45 per cent of the very largest industrial firms, employing 500 workers or more in the province, are reportedly controlled from headquarters in Britain, with another 20 per cent being controlled from the USA and 10 per cent from other EEC countries.[12] In west-central Scotland, 58 per cent of total manufacturing employment in 1968 'was in plants where the ultimate control lay outside Scotland' (Firn 1975, 397), with 27 per cent of total employment in actual branch factories.

Socio-political concern with this situation, linked as it often is with a strong regional consciousness and concern over a relatively lagging regional economy, is entirely to be expected. But in economic terms, the three further criticisms of branch or subsidiary domination, discussed in detail in an important recent paper by Townroe (1975), are more important. One is that such branch plants are significantly more likely to close down, particularly in recession, than either transfers to these regions or the parent factories involved. This oft-quoted view is not however supported by the available data. Thus for example, the present author discovered (Keeble 1968a, 48) that admittedly high closure rates in peripheral area north-west London migrant plants were similar for *both* branches *and* complete transfers. More significantly, Atkins' study (1973) discussed earlier (section 8.5) reported identical mature branch closure rates, 1966–71, in both the assisted and non-assisted areas. Moreover, although the assisted-area branches exhibited a slightly greater closure rate (2.1 per cent per annum) than their non-assisted-area parent factories (1.6 per cent per annum), the employment provided by the former declined over the 1966–71 period by very much less (14,600 jobs, or 8.1 per cent) than that in the parent plants (54,100 or 13.7 per cent). Specific and similar findings for manufacturing migration to Devon and Cornwall between 1939 and 1967 are reported by Spooner (1974, 79). There is thus now general agreement with Townroe's recent conclusion (1975, 57) that 'in aggregate, fears of the propensity-to-close of branch plants seem to have little justification'.

A second economic criticism argues that assisted-area branch plants often exert a smaller local or regional multiplier effect than do transfers or indigenous firms, in that purchases of components or materials are more likely to be drawn from suppliers outside the assisted area which already serve the parent factory involved. This view is apparently supported by such linkage evidence as that discussed in section 7.4.3 for the motor vehicle industry, and provided by Lever (1974a, 120). The latter's detailed 1970/71 survey of twelve Clydeside immigrant branch plants revealed, for example, that only 18.5 per cent of total inputs by value were purchased from other firms in the whole of Scotland. However, as Townroe (1975, 58–9) shows from a 1972 survey of manufacturing firms settling in East Anglia and Northern England, this pattern is just as true for transfers as for branches. Even more strikingly, Lever's study reveals that a sample of twelve *indigenous* Clydeside manufacturing plants from the same industries as the branches he studied recorded an almost equally low Scottish input proportion (23.7 per cent), the difference in his view being 'scarcely significant'. So this local linkage argument does not seem to be particularly valid either.

The remaining criticism concerns the arguably low proportion of high-level, managerial and research-type jobs offered by branch plants as opposed to transfers or indigenous industry, and the former's greater bias towards female as opposed to male labour. While Townroe (1975, 53) shows that there is no difference in female/male proportions as between branches and transfers moving to the assisted areas since 1945, there has in the past been a tendency for migrant plants to offer proportionately slightly fewer jobs to men than do indigenous manufacturing firms (Howard 1968, 33–4). This is one argument for greater concern with promoting indigenous manufacturing growth in the periphery. So too is Townroe's finding (1975, 49–52) that assisted-area branch plants do tend to function primarily as production units, with only relatively limited purchasing, marketing and research functions, powers of autonomous investment decision, and hence availability of 'high-level' jobs. These arguments are supported by Firn (1975, 410–12).

These last two points together with the socio-political concern noted earlier help to explain recent demands for a reorientation of regional industrial location policy towards greater emphasis on indigenous peripheral manufacturing industry. Thus Cameron (1974, 38) has urged that 'the whole question of how to stimulate new growth from within the problem economies and especially of how to encourage small new enterprises should be given high priority'; while Gaskin (1974, 213) advocates the use of selective regional assistance under the 1972 Industry Act for 'the stimulation of local industrial initiative and on measures to improve the efficiency and accelerate the adaptation of firms already established' in the assisted regions. This view, undoubtedly partly embodied in the 1972 Act, has already found expression in Department of Industry activities in areas such as Yorkshire and Humberside (Sant 1974, 256–9), and has substantially influenced the announced aims of the Welsh and Scottish Development Agencies (see section 8.6.4). While a welcome extension of location policy concern, this development should not however distract attention from the continuing importance to the assisted areas of attracting mobile industry. For not only as noted above are certain traditional criticisms of such industry unjustified, but immigrant industry possesses significant attributes which sometimes arguably render it of greater value to assisted areas than the indigenous component. As section 6.6.1 shows, migrant industry is more growth-oriented, more outward-looking in relation to marketing and sales, and involves industries of precisely the kind needed for wider and less vulnerable structural diversification in peripheral regions. For example, immigrant United States-owned manufacturing branches in Scotland (Forsyth 1972, 55–80) have grown more rapidly, recorded higher rates of investment, and have been more productive on all counts than their indigenous Scottish counterparts, even allowing for differences in industrial structure. Similarly, Spooner (1974, 81) concludes that the significant qualitative differences between incoming and indigenous manufacturing plants in Devon and Cornwall render the former, on balance, the more valuable component for future industrial progress: 'self-help is unlikely to be sufficient'.

8.8.3. Industrial complex planning and the assisted areas

The last special issue in industrial location policy for the assisted areas concerns the desirability and feasibility of so-called industrial complex planning. In recent years, certain commentators have argued that one desirable, if not optimal, approach to the problem of generating self-sustaining industrial growth in lagging regions is the planned creation of geographically-restricted linked industrial complexes. This idea owes much to the so-called growth pole theory of the French economist Perroux (1955) and his followers, although it also has independent origins in American work, notably by Isard (Isard and Vietorisz 1955). However, the specific application of Perroux' ideas to an actual region in the shape of a planned industrial complex was first recommended and worked out in detail by Tosco, in the EEC-sponsored Italconsult plan for an industrial growth centre in the Bari-Taranto zone of southern Italy (Newcombe 1969; Allen and MacLennan 1970, 318–27). More recently, the concept has formed the basis of proposals by Economic Consultants Ltd at the request of the former Department of Economic Affairs for the industrial development of the central Lancashire new town (Economic Consultants 1969; Livesey 1972) and for an industrial growth centre in the New Brunswick province of eastern Canada.

These proposals are based on the view that one of the major problems of lagging regions, both in stimulating self-sustaining industrial growth and in attracting mobile industry, is the relative dearth of related supporting industries upon which key growth industries may depend for inputs and specialized services. Attempts to attract the latter, it is argued, will thus either be unsuccessful or, if successful, will have little multiplier effect upon the region in that most inputs will still be purchased by the incoming industry from elsewhere. Moreover, in the longer term, the extra transfer and other costs incurred as a result of these enforced long-distance linkages may render the activities of the new industry uneconomic. Protagonists of the industrial complex approach thus argue that the best policy for mobile industry attraction and the generation of self-sustaining growth is a selective one, involving identification of a suitable expanding and interlinked industry or set of industries. This is then followed by the simultaneous establishment within part of the lagging region of a carefully structured group of principal and subsidiary manufacturing units in this industry, such that the principal units benefit from the local availability of specialized and related inputs, while the subsidiary units are assured of major local outlets for their components or services. The central Lancashire plan, for example, envisaged the establishment of some 16–24 principal units, chosen from such activities as power tools, brewing machinery and optical instruments, between 1971 and 1981, together with some 19–24 smaller intermediate units. Together, these units were to provide 17,000 jobs by the end of the decade. However, scale factors are likely to be important here, since only a fairly substantial complex might be expected to generate adequate demand for the services of subsidiary or specialized producers (Allen and Stevenson 1974, 205); unless, as in the central Lancashire case, existing major engineering firms in the general region can be expected to provide such demand in addition to the complex's own principal units. In general, however, the attractive apparent logic of this type of approach has certainly led such economists as Thirlwall to assert, specifically in the British assisted-area context, that 'the largescale development of growth centres containing industries which purchase from each other still offers the best solution for achieving regional balance' (quoted in Keeble 1972d, 136).

In fact, however, the central Lancashire industrial complex proposals were in effect rejected by the government, while the southern Italy plan has almost entirely failed (Allen and Stevenson 1974, 206). The former decision almost certainly reflects at least three major defects in this approach. First, in a country as small as Britain, most firms appear able to 'stretch' their linkages over reasonable distances without incurring substantial problems in component and material supplies (Moseley and Townroe, 1973). This is documented for the motor vehicle industry, an activity peculiarly dependent upon a host of input linkages, in section 7.4.3. So close complex proximity, the key theoretical advantage of this approach, does not appear in practice to be a significant attraction or requirement for mobile firms (Keeble 1976). Secondly, the only apparent way of establishing a planned complex in a democracy such as Britain is by providing as 'bait' a level of preferential financial assistance which is politically unacceptable to other areas. Thus the fact that Economic Consultants were forced to propose special additional financial incentives for their central Lancashire complex, *vis-à-vis* the remaining Development Area regions of Britain, in order to ensure the availability of appropriate industry, was almost certainly a major reason for government rejection.

Thirdly, industrial complex planning is of course basically a selective approach to industrial development, aiming at *specialization* upon a particular sector rather than diversification, the traditional British assisted-area policy aim. The problem with specialization, however, is that as Perroux (1955) himself acknowledges, it is all too easy in the long run for growth to be replaced by decline. 'The concentrations of men and of fixed and definite capital accompanied by the inflexibility of the installations and of the structures which accompanied the initial development of the pole all make their consequences felt once decline begins: the pole which used to be an area of prosperity and growth becomes a centre of stagnation'. That this applies even at the local level has been established by recent statistical analysis of spatial variations in manufacturing change within outer South East England (Keeble and Hauser 1971, 246; 1972, 29), probably the chief single conclusion of which was that manufacturing specialization was significantly associated with below-average industrial growth or decline. The long term vulnerability of an intrinsically-specialized industrial complex thus represents another argument against this approach.

NOTES

1 The difference between regional policy and planning is considered in Alden and Morgan 1974, 84–5.

2 Defined as Orders XXII to XXVII of the 1968 SIC, inclusive. These comprise transport and communication; distributive trades; insurance, banking, finance and business services; professional and scientific services; miscellaneous services; and public administration and defence.

3 'Subject to this overriding requirement – the need for providing appropriate employment in development areas – special consideration is also given to the employment needs of intermediate areas. In considering applications the industrial needs of the new and expanding towns are also borne in mind' (Department of Trade and Industry 1971, 8).

4 Increased to ten in the October 1974 election, together with three Plaid Cymru (Welsh National Party) members.

5 The ILAG survey was carried out in late 1968 and 1969, and covered all moves taking place between 1964 and 1967 inclusive.

6 This study examined the closure and employment change performance, 1966–71, of migrant branches established between 1945 and 1961.

7 For fuller accounts, see Dowie 1968; McCrone 1969; and McCallum 1973.

8 The functions of this body were absorbed by the newly-formed Department of Industry in 1974.

9 Department of Industry offices in the assisted regions were given discretion to provide selective assistance loans of up to £1 million in 1974, and £2 million in 1976, without recourse to headquarters in London.

10 Chancellor of the Exchequer (1976), *Public Expenditure to 1979–80*, Cmnd 6393, HMSO, London, 149 pp.

11 Primary industry, comprising agriculture, forestry, fishing and mining and quarrying, accounted for a maximum of eighty-four establishments, out of a total of 1,160.

12 R. W. Shakespeare, Ulster will need more help for a long time to come, *The Times*, 10 March 1975.

9 Industrial location, regional planning and South East England/East Anglia

9.1. Introduction

As in part noted in section 8.3, government intervention in the location of manufacturing industry at the within-region, or regional planning, scale in the United Kingdom has been the prime responsibility of the Department of Environment (formerly the Ministry of Housing and Local Government) and local planning authorities, not the Department of Industry. It has also involved different and far less powerful policy instruments than interregional policy, and has in fact proved successful only because it has, perhaps unwittingly, generally coincided with and reinforced very powerful existing natural trends. Regional planning is a term used in a variety of confusing ways. But in practice it usually relates to the spatial planning of areas larger than cities or towns but smaller than countries (Alden and Morgan 1974, 2). Although currently fashionable to play down the spatial component, proposals for future spatial structuring of population and economic activity nonetheless remain central to such recent regional plans as those for North West England (North West Joint Planning Team 1974) and East Anglia (East Anglia Regional Strategy Team 1974). The location of manufacturing industry in particular is thus of crucial importance to regional planning, given for example the necessity of matching local population growth and employment availability, and the significantly greater spatial flexibility and mobility of manufacturing compared with service industry documented in section 8.2.

Until recently, nearly all British regional plans accepted as a fundamental starting point the need to disperse population and industry within the region involved, away from such central congested conurbations as London, Birmingham or Glasgow to outlying settlements. This dispersal policy was of course a direct product of the Barlow Report's recommendations, and the influence these had on the great immediately-postwar plans for South East

England, Clydeside and other areas. Indeed, both the former, Abercrombie's *Greater London Plan 1944* and *Clyde Valley Regional Plan*, were actually drawn up by a member of the Barlow Commission itself. The arguments for such dispersal were concerned with the extreme 'congestion' of people and buildings in large conurbations and the perceived need for and advantages of urban renewal at lower densities in improving the residential environment and general quality of life in these areas. More recent decentralization arguments include the very high cost of land and buildings in such centres, with its impact upon public sector costs, and uneconomic provision of public transport services (Keeble 1972a, 79–86; 1974b, 9–11). Decentralization was also seen as providing a better operating environment for industrial firms and their employees, although this was very much a minor argument for such policy. Indeed, manufacturing firms were generally implicitly expected to be reluctant to accept 'decanting' from central conurbations, and to require persuasion and pressure in order to move.

However, the rapid recent industrial decline of such central conurbations as London and the West Midlands documented in chapter 2 is now producing a growing reaction against traditional decentralization policy, specifically as it applies to manufacturing and other industry, for various reasons. Thus the Greater London Council's 1969 Development Plan expressed great concern with recent decline because of London's vital economic contribution to national output and efficiency (Keeble 1972a, 94–7). Other arguments concern maintenance of household incomes in the capital, the rise in metropolitan local authority running costs, and the serious implications for local authority income of static or declining industrial rateable values. As Lever (1974b, 201) points out with regard to Glasgow, the 'increasing suburbanisation of manufacturing' there is likely to result in a tendency for rateable income to 'fall in the central city and rise in surrounding areas. This tendency will be intensified if central manufacturing industry is replaced by such land uses as roads or public recreational space which are not directly rateable'. Again, Hollocks (1975) has recently claimed that 'the income of the poorest 25 per cent of London's households *dropped* by 12 per cent (1965–73) compared with a 12 per cent *increase* for the same group in the rest of England and Wales'. The latter's concern is shared by Eversley (1975, 208–9), who argues that recent official earnings data 'have shown the deterioration of urban incomes ... and that if household incomes were maintained at all in London it was because there were more homes with two wage-earners', this being an enforced response to very high living costs. In Eversley's judgement, therefore, 'the employment problem of the inner city is now that of the maintenance of all incomes, private and public', a problem which, he argues, 'has become critical'.

Admittedly, this viewpoint was not shared by the Layfield Panel of inquiry into the Greater London Development Plan, nor by Foster and Richardson (1973). The latter, after detailed study of London unemployment and, to a lesser extent, household income and earnings data for the 1960s and early 1970s, concluded that 'from the inadequate information available, it is not easy to discern extensive hardship in London arising from declining city size'. Thus, for example, between 1965 and 1969, real household income in Greater London actually increased by a faster rate than in the rest of Great Britain. This was true not only for median income but for lower and higher income groups, too. So while stressing that, for example, 'such hardship may appear in the future', they concluded that 'there is not visible to us a strong empirical case which would justify as yet a dramatic change in policy designed to alter the nature of existing emigration forces' (Foster and Richardson 1973, 118).

Clearly, Hollocks' and Eversley's claims, based on more recent data, suggest that the London income situation may have worsened since 1969. Certainly, continuing pressure from a Labour-controlled GLC deeply concerned about current trends has recently (March 1975) achieved reluctant central government acknowledgment of some case for slight moderation of IDC controls on small metropolitan manufacturing firms. Since that date, manufacturing schemes in Greater London of between 465 square metres (5,000 sq. ft) and 930 square metres (10,000 sq. ft) which are supported by the local planning authority have not normally been refused IDC permission except on the personal decision of the Secretary of State for Industry. While unlikely to have any measurable impact in halting manufacturing decline and emigration, this first-ever concession could be very significant in the future longer term context of central government policy towards manufacturing industry in London. As yet, however, decentralization planning policies still remain the currently-accepted framework for spatial change in manufacturing and population location within most large city-regions.

9.2. Regional planning policy instruments

The methods available in Britain for shaping the within-region spatial arrangement of manufacturing industry in accordance with regional plans are far more limited than those used at the between-region level. True, the Board of Trade/Department of Industry's IDC and other powers are available and undoubtedly used at the within-region scale to some extent. Thus for example, relatively rapid growth of manufacturing industry in East Kent and the Portsmouth area during the early 1960s (Keeble and Hauser 1971, figs 4–8) was primarily due to the Board of Trade's concern with localized high unemployment rates in these localities (see fig. 8.2a), and its channelling of mobile London firms to them via IDC policy (Twyman 1967). While in East Anglia, 'special consideration is also given to the employment needs of North Norfolk and other rural areas of East Anglia where agricultural employment is declining' (Department of Trade and Industry 1971, 10–11). Without doubt, too, the Board's full co-operation, subject to the over-riding priority in allocation of mobile employment of the Development Areas (see section 8.3), in new and expanded town development in the South East Anglia and the Midlands, has been of crucial importance in attracting manufacturing firms to these centres.

However, it is also true that the preoccupation of the Board with inter-regional and unemployment disparities has at times led it to act independently of, and indeed even in opposition to, regional planning considerations. Thus, for example, it is interesting to note that east Kent does not in fact figure as a preferred location for industrial or population growth on regional planning grounds in either the 1964 *South East Study* (Ministry of Housing and Local Government 1964) or the 1970 *Strategic Plan for the South East* (South East Joint Planning Team 1970). More striking still, natural Board of Trade concern with high unemployment in the Greater Glasgow area, including north Lanarkshire, led to a very marked 1945–59 concentration of Scottish factory building by the Board's agent, the Scottish Industrial Estates Corporation, in that area. The latter thus received no less than 62 per cent of all Scottish immigrant manufacturing plants during this period (Welch 1970, 144). While it is true that most of these firms settled outside the City of Glasgow itself, such general concentration was undoubtedly opposed to the spirit if not the letter of Abercrombie's 1946 Clyde Valley plan, with its proposed dispersal of industry and population from the Glasgow area. Not surprisingly, therefore, as Welch (1970, 143) notes, 'the results of this concentration were not wholly good', since it only aggravated existing local planning problems of land, labour and transport availability. Subsequent SIEC factory construction has thus favoured areas elsewhere in Scotland.

The main direct policy instruments thus available during the postwar period for implementing regional planning industrial location policies have been local authority planning powers, and the designation of new and expanded towns. The former stem from the apparatus of development plans, and more recently structure and local plans, and of development control, established by successive Town and Country Planning Acts, beginning with that of 1947. Thus local authority development plans, in force from the late 1940s to the early 1970s, were required to specify the area and location of land to be allocated for industrial use: while the legal requirement of local authority planning permission established by the 1947 act forced industrialists or developers contemplating factory or industrial estate construction generally to conform to the spatial pattern laid down in the development plan (Cullingworth 1974, 80–81). In England and Wales, development plans are now giving way to structure plans introduced by the 1968 Town and Country Planning Act, which are essentially statements 'of general policy designed to channel major forces in socially and economically desirable directions' (Cullingworth 1974, 100). These are being prepared for fairly large areas – the post-1974 counties – and are explicitly required to reflect wider regional planning considerations by having 'regard to current policies with respect to the economic planning and development of the region as a whole'. The nine new Scottish regional councils have similar statutory responsibilities for the preparation of 'regional reports'.

Theoretically, local authority planning powers over manufacturing development and siting have thus been considerable. At the regional scale, however, the problems of achieving uniform inter-authority acceptance of a region-wide planning policy, the frequent absence of any detailed specification of the precise local implications of such policies (Jay 1974, 173–80), and normal local community pressures for additional jobs, rate income and hence factory expansion, have until recently at least ruled out effective and co-ordinated regional as opposed to local planning action. Local authority planners in South East England and the Midlands have thus played little positive part in shaping the postwar spatial distribution of industry in these regions compared with very powerful 'natural' forces on the one hand and central government, through IDC control, on the other. Of course, there are exceptions to this. The City of Cambridge, for example, has been the object of a restrictive local planning policy with respect to factory construction ever since the recommendation to that effect of the 1950 Holford and Wright report on the future planning of Cambridge. Admittedly powerfully reinforced by the Board of Trade,[1] this policy succeeded in restricting manufacturing employment growth in the Cambridge employment exchange area between 1951 and 1971 to only 5,200 jobs or 30 per cent of 1951 manufacturing employment, during a period in which manufacturing activity in the rest of the Cambridge subregion was expanding its workforce by no less than 15,300 workers or 192 per cent (Lewis 1974, 118). At the same time, however, this control has enabled the County planning authority positively to channel small expanding Cambridge manufacturing firms to outlying villages in need of employment and population growth.

A far more important case is that of London, where Abercrombie's original 1945 recommendation, that 'the Greater London area . . . normally be banned to new industry and to any but minor extensions of existing enterprises' (Abercrombie 1945, 38), has formed the background to a generally restrictive planning policy for manufacturing industry. This, coupled with the existence of unusually large numbers of 'non-conforming'[2] manufacturing firms in the older inner areas of the conurbation, many of which such as the South Acton Comprehensive Development Area have been subject to planned redevelopment (Keeble 1969a, 178-9), has played some part in restricting the capital's industrial expansion and displacing growing firms to other, usually surrounding, locations. Thus the ILAG survey, for example, found that 'town planning difficulties', including both planned area redevelopment and refusal of planning permission for factory extension to nonconforming firms, was reported as a major reason for movement out of Greater London between 1964 and 1967 more frequently (18 per cent of firms) than for moves from any other single origin area in Britain (Department of Trade and Industry 1973, 558–9).

But even this example of course indicates that direct local authority planning action has had only a minor impact on manufacturing location trends: over 75 per cent of London origin movers emigrate for reasons, major or minor, other than planning. The absence of any major region-wide influence is also clear from much other evidence. For example, Camina's recent survey of local authority efforts to attract mobile manufacturing firms concluded that, particularly as far as lower-tier authorities were concerned (municipal boroughs, urban and rural districts), such action was the exception rather than the rule in areas such as the South East. Only 27 per cent of lower-tier authorities in England and Wales outside the assisted areas and East Anglia had appointed a specific industrial development officer, for example, on either a part-time or full-time basis (Camina 1974, 555); and few were spending more than token sums on advertising, publicity or financial assistance to firms. Even more relevant evidence is provided by the Keeble and Hauser study; for this contained a direct test of the hypothesized impact of local planning on manufacturing change in outer South East England during the early 1960s. In this test (Keeble and Hauser 1971, 255–6, 1972, 26–7), detailed estimates of the area of vacant land zoned by planning authorities for industrial development in about 1960 in twenty-seven local areas of Hampshire and Essex were included in a stepwise multiple regression analysis of both manufacturing employment and floorspace change, measured in various ways. This land availability variable thus included the designation by local planners or other bodies of industrial estates, a method recently singled out by Lever (1974b, 202) as one of the most effective approaches to positive location planning at the city-region scale. In the event, however, in all but one of several separate dependent variable tests, the zoned land measure was not selected as associated either positively or negatively with manufacturing change. The one exception almost certainly chiefly reflected the inclusion of two new and two expanded towns, where large land allocations were naturally associated with unusually rapid manufacturing growth. More 'ordinary' local planning action, through land allocation, does not seem to have been a significant influence.

On the other hand, the impact of new and expanded towns, particularly upon manufacturing location change in the South East and East Anglia, has been considerable. In accord with Abercrombie's *Greater London Plan 1944*, and under the 1946 New Towns Act, eight New Towns were officially established in South East England between 1946 and 1949 (fig. 9.1) as reception centres for population and manufacturing industry from congested London. The need for such dispersal, even in the face of an anticipated static London population, arose of course from Abercrombie's recommendation of extensive redevelopment at lower densities in the inner areas of the conurbation, which incidentally also contained the bulk of London's manufacturing industry (Hall 1962, 30–31). A further three, much larger London-oriented new towns –

Milton Keynes, Peterborough and Northampton – were designated in 1967–8. By January 1975, these eleven London new towns had constructed no less than 1,130 factories, in which over 120,000 workers were employed,[3] largely in firms from London. At the same time, the twenty-four smaller towns which had by January 1974 signed agreements with the Greater London Council under the Town Development Act of 1952 for smaller-scale dispersal of both

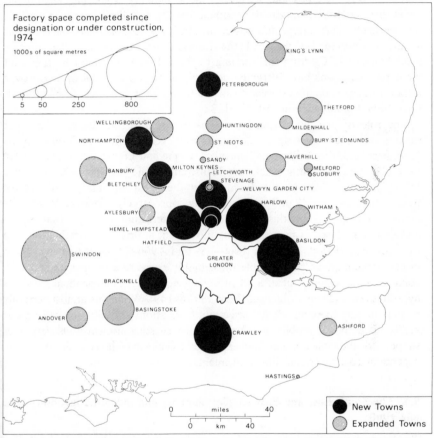

9.1 Manufacturing floorspace in new and expanded towns in the South East and East Anglia, 1975
Source: Town and Country Planning 1975, 9, 1

population and industry from the capital (fig. 9.1) had constructed 1,021 factories, covering nearly 3 million square metres (31 million sq. ft), in which were employed at least a further 80,000 workers. As already noted in section 4.4, this rapid manufacturing growth is undoubtedly partly a reflection of the general dispersal of industry in the region, and the natural attractiveness of the locations selected for designation in terms of residential environment, proximity to London, excellent road and rail access and so on. But it is also clear that new or expanded town status itself, given associated publicity and the unique opportunity afforded by these towns of transferring a complete workforce with the firm, has prompted a higher volume of movement from London than even otherwise would have occurred (Keeble 1968a, 44). Complete workforce transfer is of course possible because of the availability of specially-built housing in these centres set apart for occupancy by the families of workers with incoming firms. This unique and powerful advantage, coupled with the excellent locations selected for most of the London new towns and the greater availability of IDCs for firms moving to them, help to explain why they and the expanded towns have attracted probably about 40 per cent of all postwar London migrant plants established in the South East and East Anglia (South East Joint Planning Team 1971a, 133).

The role of new and expanded towns in within-region dispersal in other regions has been much less significant. But even so, Scotland's new towns (Cumbernauld, East Kilbride, Glenrothes, Irvine and Livingston) had attracted over 600 immigrant manufacturing firms, employing nearly 50,000 workers, by 1975; while Telford and Redditch in the West Midlands had received over 350 firms and 27,000 manufacturing jobs, largely from the West Midlands conurbation. In this context, it is interesting to note that Sant's correlation analyses of manufacturing movement in Britain by destination area for the three periods 1952–9, 1960–65, and 1966–71 identified new town target population as the variable most highly correlated in each period with volume of movement, out of a set of seventeen different independent variables hypothesized as likely influences (Sant 1975a, 149). While this almost certainly reflects in part the coincidental selection as locations for such towns of areas highly attractive to mobile industry for other reasons, it clearly also provides support for the view that new and expanded towns have played a significant independent role in channelling movement.

9.3. The South East and East Anglia: planning and industrial location to the mid-1960s

The South East is not only the single most important manufacturing region of the United Kingdom, but has also been the object of more regional planning proposals since 1945 than any other area. The remainder of this chapter will therefore concentrate on the postwar history of regional planning in the South East and adjoining East Anglia, as a case study of the influence of planning and other locational considerations on the changing within-region spatial distribution of industry. In the South East case, the post–1945 regional planning context has been provided until recently by Abercrombie's famous *Greater London Plan 1944*. The fundamental recommendation of this plan was that 'working within the Barlow contention that London is too large, or at any rate large enough, some detailed attempt must be made to redistribute the population and industry within the region' (Abercrombie 1945, 12). This redistribution was envisaged as taking place in the context of a virtually static total regional stock of manufacturing activity, given the assumed ban by central government on any significant industrial expansion in the Greater London area (see section 9.2). In detail, therefore, Abercrombie (1945, 50) estimated that given a population decentralization target of just over one million people, postwar regional planning should aim at a parallel manufacturing dispersal from Greater London to the rest of the South East of 'sufficient factories to give direct employment to approximately 258,000 persons (2,580 factories if a figure of 100 persons per factory is assumed)'. Within the conurbation, no new industrial development should be allowed, except in a very few outer suburban areas such as Barking/Dagenham and Mitcham/Croydon where a dearth of local industry forced the occupants of large prewar housing estates to travel considerable distances to work. Outside the conurbation, decentralized industry, moving voluntarily from London because of 'the need for more spacious sites with their opportunities for expansion', should be accommodated almost entirely within certain specified 'new satellite towns and existing towns planned for industrial expansion' (Abercrombie 1945, 58), rather than allowed to settle anywhere. Wholesale industrial development in towns and villages around London was to be avoided at all costs: 'if industry ... is allowed to settle in almost any village or town in the Region ... then the whole fabric of the industrial proposals ... will fall to the ground' (Abercrombie 1945, 58).

The Abercrombie plan thus defined a number of clear and carefully-coordinated aims for manufacturing location planning within postwar South East England. Indeed, such planning was clearly regarded by Abercrombie (1945, 48) as the key to his whole strategy: 'there can be no effective planning in the Greater London Region without control over the size of its towns; there can be no control over town size without control of industry and over its subsequent expansion'. Of crucial importance, clearly, in this connection was Abercrombie's vision of no fewer than ten new towns, including such centres as White Waltham, Berkshire, Chipping Ongar, Essex, and Crowhurst, Surrey, which were to accommodate about half the total decentralized population and industry. But decentralization on a substantial scale was also to be permitted to specified existing centres both inside and outside Abercrombie's proposed 'Green Belt', such as Slough, High Wycombe, East Tilbury, Letchworth, Hatfield, St Albans and Welwyn.

9.3.1. The new towns

In the event, only two — Harlow and Stevenage — of the eight first-generation London new towns were actually established on sites suggested by Abercrombie. But two others — Hatfield and Welwyn — were in his list of proposed existing centre expansions, while the general locations chosen were very much along Abercrombie lines. All eight, for example, were sited within about 50 kilometres (30 miles) of central London, such close proximity being regarded both by Abercrombie and industrialists eventually moving to these towns (Brown 1966, 241) as essential for the successful attraction of London manufacturing firms. That large numbers of such firms have so been attracted, after an admittedly slow start during the late 1940s, is clear from the figures given in section 9.2 and Brown's 1963 survey (Brown 1966, 240). The latter revealed that no fewer than eighty five – 71 per cent – of the total sample of 120 London new town manufacturing firms investigated had moved from the capital. Twelve others were local moves, and sixteen moves were from other parts of the South East. Only one originated elsewhere in the United Kingdom outside the South East. Moreover, Brown demonstrates that most of the towns have attracted a radial flow of manufacturing industry, drawing largely from that sector of Greater London closest to the town. Hemel Hempstead, for example, has drawn many firms from outer north-west London (Keeble 1968a, 47), while Basildon's migrant firm catchment area is dominated by the Lea Valley industrial zone of north-east London. South London firms have tended to move to Crawley rather than to new towns north of the river. This fascinating radial migration tendency is partly to be explained by deliberate early Ministry of Town and Country Planning attempts to link exporting suburbs and particular new towns on a radial/sectoral basis, presumably on grounds of maximum proximity and hence feasibility of persuading firms and workers to move. But it must be stressed that radial movement is in fact typical of total within-region manufacturing migration from central conurbations in Britain, whether or not new towns are involved (Keeble 1968a, 46–7; 1974a, 26–7). This pattern, common to movement in the South East, West Midlands and Clydeside for example, is a clear reflection of the dominantly radial road and rail communications network which fans out in all directions from such central conurbations. Firms migrating radially can thus ensure maximum continuing access to former customers, suppliers and services in their original location, as well as, often, to the homes of directors, managers and workers who have earlier chosen residencies in cheaper or more attractive outlying areas of the same sector. Radially-based information availability on vacant factories or industrial land, randomly acquired by industrialists in the course of radially-structured journeys within the region, may well be another factor in radial movement preference.

Successful attraction of mobile London manufacturing firms has had important consequences for new town economic expansion, particularly given the atypical nature of mobile firms documented in section 6.6.1. First, the new towns are predominantly manufacturing towns. In 1971, for example, when manufacturing industry accounted for only 36.4 and 30 per cent respectively of total employment in the United Kingdom and South East England, its share of the workforce in the Harlow, Basildon, Stevenage and Crawley employment exchange areas was no less than 58.5, 58.1, 58 and 42.8 per cent respectively. All else being equal, this means that new town workers have enjoyed higher average wages than those in other towns of similar size but higher service employment proportion (see section 8.2). Second, within the new towns, manufacturing is dominated by modern growth industries, notably electrical engineering (especially electronics and computers), mechanical engineering and vehicles (Trimble 1973, 220). Thus in 1966, the three engineering industries listed in table 9.1 accounted for over 38 per cent of total manufacturing employment in each of the four new towns concerned, and as much as 55 and 61 per cent respectively in Harlow and

Table 9.1 *Manufacturing structure of selected London new towns, 1966*

SIC Order	Manufacturing employees, employed and unemployed, 1966 Employment exchange area			
	Stevenage	Harlow	Hemel Hempstead	Crawley
III Food, drink and tobacco	55	1,219	132	638
IV Chemicals and allied industries	—	877	1,511	740
V Metal manufacture	336	725	306	1,532
VI (331–49) Mechanical engineering	2,070	2,467	3,278	5,740
VI (351–2) Instrument engineering	2,844	482	545	1,119
VI (361–9) Electrical engineering	3,909	6,961	3,726	5,465
VII/VIII Vehicles	5,867	62	1,278	680
IX Other metal goods	196	586	1,066	1,031
X Textiles	41	34	47	9
XI Leather and fur	29	—	41	4
XII Clothing and footwear	136	325	472	159
XIII Bricks, pottery, etc.	177	1,463	386	360
XIV Timber, furniture	804	940	517	709
XV Paper, printing, etc.	866	1,478	5,719	763
XVI Other manufacturing	2,008	472	432	1,165
All manufacturing	19,338	18,091	19,456	20,114

Source: unpublished employment records

Crawley. Electrical engineering figured as one of the two most important single industries in each of the four towns, the other leading industry being vehicles (i.e. aircraft) in Stevenage, mechanical engineering in Harlow and Crawley, and paper, printing and publishing in Hemel Hempstead. In both Basildon and Bracknell, electrical engineering also shared the leadership, with motor vehicles in the former and mechanical engineering in the latter. Admittedly, some of these industries, notably motor vehicles and aircraft, have shed labour in recent years because of altered national demand conditions. This helps to explain the actual manufacturing employment decline, 1966–71 (figs. 9.4 and 9.5), of three of the London new towns, Stevenage (−12.6 per cent), Welwyn (−5.5 per cent) and Crawley (−1.8 per cent). At the same time, however, the fairly wide range of industries attracted (table 9.1) has helped to cushion the impact of such redundancies. Thus in 1960, five of the London new towns recorded manufacturing industry specialization indices, measured by the Britton statistic, *lower* than the median (40.3) for all 112 outer South East local areas, with Hemel Hempstead as low as 28.4. Only Hatfield, dominated by aircraft manufacturing, recorded a value (73.8) greater than the highest sextile (Keeble and Hauser 1971, 247). A diversified manufacturing structure thus represents another important economic advantage conferred on these towns by immigrant London industry.

A third, perhaps less welcome, consequence of the dominance of manufacturing in these new towns by immigrant London firms is a larger than average firm size. Thus, for example, no less than 87, 85 and 82 per cent respectively of total manufacturing employment in Stevenage, Welwyn and Hatfield was provided in 1963 by large firms (employing over 200 workers); such firms also accounted for 60 per cent or more of manufacturing employment in Crawley, Harlow and Hemel Hempstead. These compare with a median value of only 48 per cent for all 112 local areas of South East England outside Greater London (Keeble and Hauser 1971, 248). As Trimble (1973, 220) also acknowledges, this means that while the London new towns do contain many smaller firms, 'most towns have a few very large establishments which employ a majority of their labour forces.' This undoubtedly poses a potential threat in terms of the vulnerability of local employment and prosperity to changes in the fortunes of these firms, and is probably another factor helping to explain recent manufacturing employment decline in Stevenage and Welwyn.

  The last important consequence of mobile firm dominance is a marked bi-modal bias in new town employment structure towards *both* skilled male workers *and* female employees. On the basis of 1961 census evidence (Keeble and Hauser 1971, 255), no less than five of the London new towns – Basildon (406), Crawley (401), Harlow (380), Hemel Hempstead (361) and Stevenage (353) – were amongst the top twenty-one out of 112 local areas in outer South East England in terms of the ratio of skilled male workers per 1,000 economically active resident males. Welwyn and Hatfield also recorded above-average though lower values. Interestingly, regression analysis revealed that variations in this ratio within the set of fourteen London new and expanded towns considered by the Keeble and Hauser study were significantly and positively associated with variations in the percentage rate of manufacturing employment growth, 1960–66. So the greater the dominance of local industry by firms employing skilled males, the faster the town's manufacturing growth, at least during the early 1960s. The less significant female worker bias is noted by Trimble (1973, 220), who observes that in 1971 the London new towns recorded a female manufacturing employee proportion of 31–2 per cent, as compared with a South East region value of only 28 per cent. This bias simply reflects the even greater female employee proportion amongst all within-region migrant South East firms, 36 per cent of all end–1966 jobs in such moves being held by women (Howard 1968, 34). All these statistics indicate, however, that the dominance of South East new town manufacturing activity by immigrant London firms has produced an unusual local manufacturing structure in these centres, geared to expansion, special types of industry and labour, and relatively high wages and prosperity.

9.3.2. General location factors

Substantial manufacturing expansion in the eight original London New Towns at first sight suggests that Abercrombie's 1945 plan has been implemented, with respect to manufacturing industry at least, with considerable success. So too does the massive decline of manufacturing employment in Greater London since 1961, of the order of 570,000 jobs or over 40 per cent to 1975. Moreover, this is of course partly due to actual emigration of manufacturing firms to surrounding areas, of exactly the type envisaged by Abercrombie. Between 1945 and 1965, no less than 875 London firms, employing by 1966 196,000 workers in their new locations, had established branches in or transferred production completely to outer areas of the South East and East Anglia; while 1966–71 witnessed the dispersal to these locations of a further 312 factories established by London firms, involving 28,000 jobs by 1971.[4] Though not entirely comparable, these employment figures are of course of similar magnitude to those envisaged by Abercrombie, as future regional planning targets.

In fact, however, this apparent evidence for the success of the 1945 regional plan is largely spurious. For it is clear, as noted earlier, that new town manufacturing growth, the decline of industry in London, and substantial within-region dispersal of metropolitan firms, owe much less to direct local or regional planning action than to natural decentralization forces, coupled with central government pressures and controls. The general ineffectiveness of implementation of the Abercrombie Plan is most strikingly illustrated by the wide dispersal within the South East and East Anglia *outside* the new or expanded towns of both manufacturing movement from London and general manufacturing growth. In complete contrast to Abercrombie's express and, in his view, crucial recommendation (see section 9.3), industry has since about 1950 indeed settled and expanded in almost every village and town in these two regions. This remarkable within-region dispersal is clearly evident, for example, from figures 9.2 and 9.3, which map manufacturing employment change between 1960 and 1966 in South East England, and reveal that no less than 90 per cent (101) of the 112 local areas distinguished outside the Greater London conurbation recorded manufacturing growth during this period. True, figure 9.3 indicates that the volume of manufacturing growth in the new towns was especially considerable. Thus five of the ten local areas which expanded their manufacturing workforce by more than 4,000 employees over this period were new towns – Basildon, Crawley, Harlow, Stevenage and Hemel Hempstead – while two more, Basingstoke and Aylesbury, were expanded towns. But in terms of *rate* of manufacturing growth (fig. 9.2), the picture is very different, with only three new or expanded towns (Basildon, Bletchley and Basingstoke) figuring among the nineteen fastest growing areas. The remainder were scattered widely around the region, including both London fringe settlements (Sevenoaks and Brentwood), traditionally rural areas and small market towns (East Grinstead, Haywards Heath, Leighton Buzzard, Wantage and Winchester), and in particular, coastal settlements and resorts (Herne Bay, Ramsgate, Sandwich, Eastbourne, Newhaven, Littlehampton, Bognor, Havant and Fareham). The last peripherally-located category thus accounted for nearly half of this group of fastest-growing areas. While in many cases rapid growth admittedly reflected an initially small manufacturing base, the predominance in this group of attractive small coastal or traditionally rural settlements clearly supports the argument that much manufacturing dispersal reflects the increasing significance of residential space preferences in industrial location decisions. So too does the fact that no less than fourteen of these nineteen areas lie to the south of the Thames, in that part of the South East identified in the Gould and White study (section 5.3.6; fig. 5.4) as the most desirable residential zone not just of the region but of the country as a whole, and this despite the fact that most existing manufacturing industry in London and its immediately surrounding settlements, the chief origins of actual manufacturing movement, is located to the north of the Thames.

Admittedly, this residential space preference factor was not identified as an influence in two recent statistical studies of industrial location change and movement in outer South East England carried out by the present author. The first of these, with Dr Hauser, yielded the stepwise multiple regression equation recorded in table 9.2 for spatial variation in percentage manufacturing employment change in the 112 local areas outside London mapped in figure 9.2. As the table shows, the analysis suggested that the most important single positive influence on variations in rate of manufacturing change were labour availability variables – unemployment rate and population growth during the *previous* decade. This is in full accordance with the ILAG survey, which

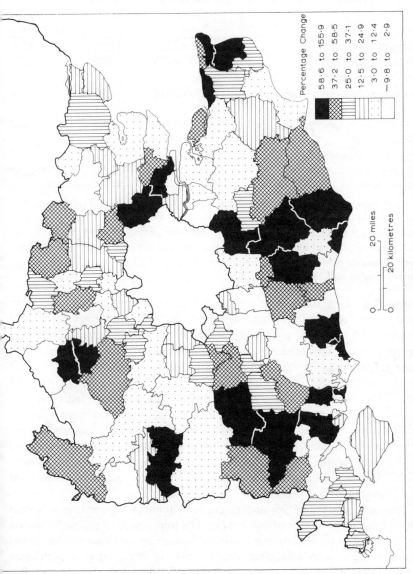

9.2 Percentage manufacturing employment change in South East England, 1960–66
Source: unpublished Department of Employment statistics

Percentage Change

58·6 to 155·9
37·2 to 58·5
25·0 to 37·1
12·5 to 24·9
3·0 to 12·4
−9·8 to 2·9

0   20 miles
0   20 kilometres

Table 9.2 *Regression result: percentage manufacturing employment change, 1960–66, in outer South East England*

Percentage manufacturing employment change, 1960–66 [Y]			
	b	SE_b	partial correlation
Unemployment rate, 1960	21.641	3.398	0.53
Total manufacturing employment 1960	−0.00139	0.00031	−0.40
Absolute population change, 1951–61	0.00088	0.00023	0.35
Manufacturing specialization index, 1960	−0.4598	0.185	−0.24
Population density, 1961	−0.0118	0.00492	−0.23
Market potential, 1960	0.773*	0.379	0.20*

Constant $= 48.39$ $SE_{est} = 23.84$ $R^2 = 0.480$ $z =$ not sig. at 0.05 level

*In the original study, a negative coefficient for this variable reflected the, confusing, inverse measurement of local market potential values as deviations from 100, the maximum (London) value.
Source: Keeble and Hauser 1972, 20

showed that as elsewhere in Britain, a much higher proportion (63 per cent) of mobile firms, chiefly from London, settling in South East England between 1964 and 1967 reported availability of labour as a major locational influence than so reported any other single factor. Inclusion of firms reporting it as a minor influence raises this proportion still further, to 86 per cent. In East Anglia, corresponding proportions were even higher (69 and 93 per cent respectively). Moreover, the second statistical analysis mentioned above, involving stepwise regression of volume of manufacturing movement 1945–65 from London, measured by employment created, to fourteen destination zones of the South East and East Anglia, also singled out a weighted unemployed workers index as the key statistically significant independent variable (Keeble 1972c). Together with movement distance, this variable 'explained' 73 per cent of movement volume variation.

These independent micro- and macro-level findings support the view that labour availability, not planning, is of crucial importance in explaining the recent dispersal of manufacturing within the South East and East Anglia. But of course it must be remembered that, at least in terms of past population growth, labour availability itself is probably influenced today by the very factor of environmental and residential space preferences (section 4.3). In addition, and perhaps fortuitously, unemployment rates and patterns in the South East happen to exhibit a strikingly regular coastal periphery/central location

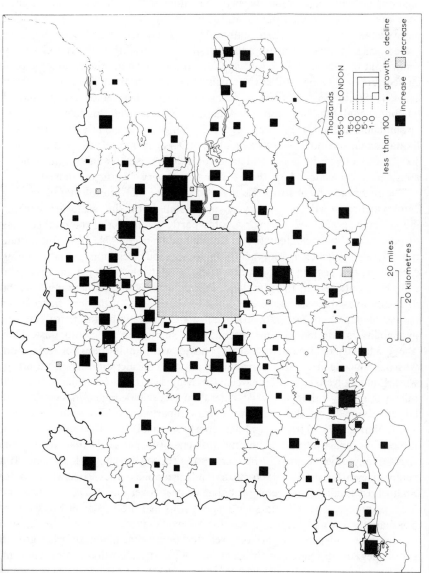

9.3 Manufacturing employment change in South East England, 1960–66
Source: unpublished Department of Employment statistics

spatial pattern (Keeble and Hauser 1971, 236) which coincides in many ways with the residential space preference surface identified by Gould and White (fig. 5.4). Moreover, the regression results of table 9.2 also include a negative relationship with population density, indicating that — all else being equal — rural areas have attracted significantly more rapid manufacturing growth than more densely-populated urban centres. This also clearly accords with the space preference hypothesis. Lastly, and perhaps most strikingly, the ILAG survey found that taking all reported influences, both major and minor, on locational choice, 'good amenities and environment' was reported more frequently (79 per cent) by South East destination firms than any other factor except that of labour availability (see above). Amongst East Anglian mobile firms, environmental attractiveness was reported even more frequently (81 per cent), though again second to labour availability (Department of Trade and Industry, 1973, 600). Given the noted reluctance of industrialists to admit to this kind of consideration (section 4.3), these findings are very significant indeed.

The regression results of table 9.2 also indicate that rate of manufacturing employment growth is negatively associated with the scale of existing manufacturing activity. This is probably partly a function of the mathematics of percentage change calculations (Keeble and Hauser 1971, 244). But it quite possibly also indicates the impact of agglomeration diseconomies and planning constraints (see section 5.3.3) even within the relatively small leading industrial centres of outer South East England. Particularly significant here may well be a greater availability, relative of course to centre size, of modern factories or industrial land in less industrialized areas. The importance of factory availability is attested by most mobile firm surveys in the South East. Thus 'the availability of a modern factory, or site, with ample room for expansion' was acknowledged as an important locational consideration by more north-west London transfers (72 per cent) moving less than 160 kilometres (100 miles) than і іy other single consideration (Keeble 1968a, 36). Similarly, a larger proporцon of ILAG survey firms (Department of Trade and Industry 1973, 586) settling in the South East reported 'availability of a non-government factory' as an important locational influence (46 per cent) than did mobile firms in any other region (32 per cent in the rest of the United Kingdom). If a centre-size differential in factory or land availability does exist within outer South East England, as seems probable, central government IDC controls and local planning constraints in such larger towns as Luton, Watford, Oxford or Southampton would be the most obvious explanation.

The other independent variables selected reveal that manufacturing growth rate is negatively related to the degree of local specialization in particular industries, but positively associated with market accessibility. The former variable was measured by Britton's I index calculated for employment over twenty-two manufacturing industries (Keeble and Hauser 1971, 246). Its inclusion reflects the sluggish growth or decline experienced by such highly specialized manufacturing centres as Stanford-le-Hope (specialization index, 96.1: 1960–66 employment change, −7.2 per cent) and Hythe in Hampshire (64.7: −6.6 per cent), both dominated by oil-refining and associated chemical industries; Hatfield (73.8: −8.9 per cent) with its aircraft manufacturing; and Oxford (75.6: +5.5 per cent) and Luton (56.1: −4.8 per cent), dependent largely upon motor vehicles. The latter variable clearly suggests that reasonable proximity to London, with its peak market potential value, together perhaps with location along the London–Southampton ridge of higher market potential (Keeble and Hauser 1971, 251) resulting from both the concentration of people and purchasing power in South Hampshire and access to the port of Southampton for exports (see section 4.1.1), is of importance for manufacturing industry. This is certainly also suggested by mobile firm surveys. Indeed, the north-west London study (Keeble 1968a, 37) found that the locational consideration most frequently cited by firms moving less than 160 kilometres (100 miles) was 'proximity to London'; and that for over half the transfers investigated this reflected a perceived need to maintain the closest possible contact with customers. The ILAG survey also noted (Department of Trade and Industry 1973, 584) that 'access to markets' was reported significantly more frequently as a major or minor locational choice influence by firms settling in the South East (41 and 16 per cent respectively) than by firms in the rest of the country (on the ILAG figures, only 28 and 14 per cent respectively). At the same time, it should be noted that this factor is almost certainly decreasing in significance for manufacturing location at this within-region South East scale, at least in terms of encouraging manufacturing growth close to rather than away from London. The reason for this view is of course the very substantial improvement in radial motorways and electrified rail facilities within South East England which has taken place since about 1960, involving for example the construction outwards from London of such wholly new high-speed radial roads as the M1, M40, M4, M3, M23, M20 and M11 (fig. 4.2). Rapid access to and from London customers is thus now possible for firms in many outlying areas of the region, a factor undoubtedly encouraging still further the very powerful dispersal tendency noted above.

9.4. The South East and East Anglia: planning and industrial location since the mid-1960s

The period since about the mid-1960s has witnessed the publication of several important regional planning reports relating to the South East and East Anglia. Although all are based squarely on the Abercrombie thesis, that the basic aim of regional planning in the South East is to promote and accommodate substantial manufacturing and population decentralization from London, their relevance for recent and future spatial trends in manufacturing activity varies considerably. However, the establishment in 1962 and gradual strengthening since of a joint local planning authority coordinating body, the Standing

Conference on London and South East Regional Planning, and the acceptance by the government in 1971 of the basic proposals of the 1970 *Strategic Plan for the South East*, do suggest the likelihood of greater regional planning impact in the future than in the past.

The first of these reports, *The South East Study 1961–1981*, was published in 1964 by Ministry of Housing and Local Government. This central government plan was concerned with the whole of the South East and East Anglia, and placed great emphasis upon the powerful forces making for continuing regional growth of employment, including that provided by manufacturing firms especially in and around London. The latter 'naturally dominates the whole area and is a tremendous magnet' (Ministry of Housing and Local Government 1964, 14). Indeed, of the two 'special problems' singled out by the study with respect to employment growth and regional planning in the South East, one was 'the rapid rate of industrial growth in the outer metropolitan region' (Ministry of Housing and Local Government 1964, 19), where manufacturing was expanding its workforce three times faster than in the country as a whole. The other problem was of office employment growth in central London. The study also drew attention to the substantial future population growth forecast for the region at that time, of the order of 3.5 million extra inhabitants, 1961–1981. It therefore recommended the designation of a series of large urban growth centres, or 'counter-magnets' to London, based on existing often substantial settlements located at the edges of the area. The most important of these, involving big new cities, were to be between Southampton and Portsmouth, around Bletchley, and around Newbury. These three were clearly chosen in large part because of their probable locational attractiveness to manufacturing industry,[5] as also were the 'big new expansions' of existing towns proposed for Stansted, Ashford, Ipswich, Northampton, Peterborough and Swindon.

In the event, however, subsequent downward revision of population forecasts, and factors such as strong local opposition, led to the abandoning of most of these schemes, with the very important exceptions of Milton Keynes (i.e. the Bletchley area), Peterborough and Northampton. These three were designated in 1967–8 as new towns for the receipt of industry and population from London. Despite very difficult economic conditions nationally and hence an inevitably slow start, each had by 1975 expanded its manufacturing employment by 5,000 workers or more.

These three towns, and the other counter-magnets proposed by *The South East Study*, also figured in a second and stimulating South East regional planning report, *A Strategy for the South East*, produced in 1967 by the South East Economic Planning Council. In practice this report, lacking the executive force of either central or local government comitment, has had little identifiable effect on subsequent planning decisions, although its ideas were taken into account by the later South East Joint Planning Team. But in strongly supporting *The South East Study*'s emphasis on the value of large urban developments in the outer parts of South East England, and in stressing the advantages to firms, people and transport services of locating some development along the major radial communications *between* London and these outlying centres, the *Strategy* report did draw further attention to planning concepts of considerable interest. In the latter connection, it is interesting to note that the *Strategy*'s contention (South East Economic Planning Council 1967, 7) that access to good communications has been an important local influence on postwar industrial location in the region, is to some small degree supported by the Keeble and Hauser study. The latter (1972, 20–25) did identify local area distance from one or other of sixteen key radial trunk roads as significantly and negatively related both to percentage manufacturing employment change, and floorspace growth per unit urban area, within the set of new and expanded towns investigated. It also found a significant relationship with manufacturing employment change per unit urban area, for the whole study region *and* the region excluding the new and expanded towns. So there does exist some, though very limited, empirical evidence for the *Strategy*'s argument.

The most important regional planning study produced since Abercrombie, however, is the *Strategic Plan for the South East,* published in 1970 and prepared by a special joint team of planners drawn from both central and local government. The decision to produce such a major new regional plan reflected in part the need to reconcile important differences of view on future patterns of development between the central government-appointed South East Economic Planning Council and the local authority-based Standing Conference. But it also reflected important changes in forecast regional population levels, the need for a regional plan which could operate beyond 1981, the supposed terminal date of *The South East Study,* and the realization that the latter had left largely unanswered the question of future planning strategy for the area *between* its proposed 'counter-magnets' and London – i.e. the Outer Metropolitan Area, which had borne the brunt of massive population and industrial growth during the 1950s and early 1960s. In its work, the team had time for the construction and critical comparison of only two alternative 1991 planning 'scenarios'. One of these, 1991A, was based on SEEPC concepts and emphasized 'accommodation of as much population and employment as possible in new cities and other large counter-magnet developments 40 to 80 miles away from London', together with 'accommodation of the rest of the region's population and employment growth, so far as possible, in sectors along the main radial communication routes between London and the more distance developments' (South East Joint Planning Team 1970, 56). The other, 1991B, placed 'greater emphasis on development closer in to London', largely, be it noted, for industrial location reasons, the outer metropolitan region being an area 'where it appeared additional employment might become more readily available than in some of the more remote growth points envisaged in 1991A' (South East Joint Planning Team 1970, 60).

The eventual proposed strategy, perhaps inevitably, turned out to be a compromise between the two scenarios (Keeble 1971b; 1972a, 150–51). Its key features were the recommended designatioñ of five major growth areas – Milton Keynes, South Hampshire, Reading/Basingstoke, South Essex and Crawley – together with eight medium-growth centres, Maidstone/Medway, Ashford, Eastbourne/Hastings, Bournemouth/Poole, Aylesbury, Bishops Stortford/Harlow and Chelmsford. As this list indicates, development areas were deliberately selected 'at varying distances from London', including for the first time such major OMA locations as Reading and South Essex. The latter is only approximately 50 kilometres (30 miles), the former only 60–70 kilometres (40 or so miles) from central London. The plan also recommended continued dispersal of population and industry from London, to enable redevelopment and rehabilitation of the capital, particularly for the benefit of 'the less privileged who live in Inner London' (South East Joint Planning Team 1970, 80). Countryside conservation measures were to be encouraged, the Green Belt maintained, and road and rail links between the main South East centres improved.

In the present context, one of the most interesting aspects of these proposals is that they were heavily influenced by industrial migration research within the region. Three findings of firm surveys especially conducted by Economic Consultants Ltd appear to have been particularly important in this respect. First, most recorded moves by these surveyed South East manufacturing firms, all of which employed 100 workers or more in 1968, were over short distances. In particular (South East Joint Planning Team 1971b, 3), no less than 68 per cent were of less than 50 km (30 miles). Moreover, the surveys also indicated that distance was differentially associated with the proportion of different types of workers moving with the firm. While quite long distance moves nonetheless did their utmost to retain existing 'high level' qualified, skilled and specialist staff, the proportion of 'low level' semi-skilled, clerical and unskilled workers transferring with the firm fell very much more sharply and regularly with distance. Thus moves of only 8–16 kilometres (5–10 miles) retained on average fairly high percentages of both high level (88 per cent) and low level (61 per cent) existing workers. But moves of more than 100 kilometres (60 miles), while still retaining a majority (64 per cent) of the former, took with them only a bare 8 per cent of the latter (South East Joint Planning Team 1970, 17). These findings were clearly of key importance in influencing the team's recommendation on the South Essex major growth area, and to a lesser extent, Reading-Basingstoke. Thus as a direct consequence of the fact that 'the movement of many factories and offices both within and out of London has, in the past, been over short distances' and that 'least skilled workers appear not to have shared proportionately in recent population movement out of London but have remained concentrated around Central London, especially to the north and east', 'South Essex appeared to be a most suitable area for development closely linked with London' (South East Joint Planning Team 1970, 60).

The latter conclusion also however reflected Economic Consultants' second significant finding, namely the dominance of radial migration from the conurbation. This phenomenon, already known from earlier research (section 9.3.1), has meant that since 1945 more manufacturing movement from London has settled to the north and west of the capital than has gone to the south and east (Keeble 1971a, 63). While the consultants were careful to point out that there did not appear to be any intrinsic locational variation outside London in local industrial environment with regard to efficient manufacturing production, this radial finding does seem to have encouraged the team to recommend substantially greater future population and industrial development to the north and west, including south-west, than to the south and east. The north-west and south-west quadrants of the region, defined by north-south/east-west axes through central London, are thus recommended for 61 per cent of envisaged growth area population expansion, 1981–2001, compared with only 39 per cent in the north-east and south-east quadrants (Keeble 1971b, 73). The third major Economic Consultants' finding, of the arguably greater advantages to manufacturing firms of large as opposed to small urban centres, is discussed in detail in section 9.5. But again, this particular finding largely explains the fundamental *Strategic Plan* recommendation of concentrating population and industrial development into a few relatively large growth areas.

The *Strategic Plan* can be criticized on various grounds. Certain doubts about the key growth area concept, for example, are expressed later. Equally significant is the drastic downward revision of regional population forecasts because of a steeply falling birth rate. Thus the latest (1975) and somewhat optimistic Office of Population Censuses and Surveys projection implies a 1973–91 South East population increase of only 341,000, compared with the *Strategic Plan*'s 1966–91 forecast growth of over 3 *million*. This revision, together with changed national economic conditions, and problems of relating the *Strategic Plan*'s recommendations to the new post-1974 counties and county structure plans, prompted the inauguration in 1975 of a *Strategic Plan* development and updating exercise, to be carried out jointly by the Department of the Environment and the Standing Conference. The latter would seem to support earlier doubts (Keeble 1971b, 73) over the long term viability of all the growth centres proposed, in terms particularly of available mobile employment. Thus the authors of the *Strategic Plan*, while deliberately designating areas likely to enjoy above-average spontaneous industrial growth so as to minimize employment generation problems, nonetheless estimated its implementation to require perhaps 15–20,000 mobile manufacturing jobs a year (South East Joint Planning Team 1970, 81). In querying the feasibility of this, the present author pointed out that earlier 1945–65 movement, to all locations throughout the region outside London, had been of the order of only 11–12,000 jobs a year (Keeble 1971b, 72). More strikingly still, the most recent unpublished Department of Industry figures show that for 1966–71, annual mobile manufacturing employment, measured by mid-1971 jobs created in the South East outside London by inter-subregional moves, fell to only 5,100 jobs. So doubts on the feasibility of post-1981 implementation of the Plan, at least in its entirety, would seem justified, as also is the joint team's own plea for careful future monitoring and adjustment of the plan's recommendations 'as a result of changing demographic, economic and social conditions'. Nonetheless, the pragmatism and general acceptability of its proposals resulted in its approval, with the exception of the Bishops Stortford/Harlow development, as the official regional strategy for future South East planning by the Secretary of State for the Environment in 1971.

The last, and most recent, regional planning study concerns East Anglia, defined as the three new counties of Cambridgeshire, Norfolk and Suffolk. Although included in the *South East Study 1961–1981,* East Anglia was designated a separate official planning region in 1966 and hence excluded from the *South East Strategy* and *Strategic Plan* studies. An initial and largely fact-finding planning report on the region was published by the East Anglia Economic Planning Council in 1968, entitled *East Anglia: a study.* This suggested that the best framework for future planning in the region was that provided by the four city-regions focused upon Norwich, Ipswich, Cambridge and Peterborough, although attention also needed to be paid to the problems of small declining market towns (Keeble 1972a, 144–5). However, as with South East England, it was decided that a fullscale regional planning study, jointly commissioned and prepared by central and local government planners, was needed. This study, *Strategic Choice for East Anglia,* was published in 1974. While breaking new ground in devoting greater attention than most previous regional planning documents to non-spatial issues, such as local and central government financing and provision of services to the region's inhabitants, the report nonetheless recommends a specific locational strategy for future industrial and population development. In broad terms, this involves a shift in emphasis of anticipated very substantial growth away from the southern and western sectors of the region, which have borne the brunt of considerable manufacturing and population immigration from London and the South East since 1960 (fig. 9.1), to the more central, northern and eastern areas of East Anglia. Within this broad strategy, the report also suggests the development of a set of 'secondary centres' outside the four main city regions, notably in the King's Lynn, Thetford, Bury St Edmunds and (possibly) Diss-Eye areas. In accord with the proposals of an earlier East Anglian *Small Towns Study* (1972), it also advocates 'the selection of a number of small towns to act as growth points' (East Anglia Regional Strategy Team 1974, 66). These recommendations, especially those on secondary centres and small town growth points, do owe something to recent research on industrial location, migration and local manufacturing impact in the region, notably that carried out at the University of East Anglia, Norwich (Sant 1970; Moseley 1973a, 1973b; Moseley and Townroe 1973; Lemon 1975; Sant and Moseley 1976). Some of this research is discussed further in section 9.4.3.

9.4.1. The expanded towns

The impact of all these recent plans upon manufacturing location change in the South East and East Anglia has as yet been fairly small, with certain local exceptions such as the Milton Keynes and Peterborough new towns. At the same time, most of the early London new towns had, by about the mid-1960s, attained an approximate equilibrium level of manufacturing activity, or at least have not since been accepting new immigrant firms from London. The most significant, but nonetheless generally limited, positive planning impact upon manufacturing location in these regions since 1966 has therefore come from the expanded town programme. Early progress, following the Town Development Act of 1952, was very slow, significant expanded town development having only occurred since the early- or mid-1960s. But between 1966 and 1971, expanded towns (Witham, Andover and Bletchley) accounted for three of the five fastest-growing manufacturing centres in South East England, as well as three (Bletchley, Ashford and Basingstoke) of the seven areas recording the greatest volumes of manufacturing employment expansion (figs 9.4 and 9.5). Expanded town growth in East Anglia has been relatively more important, such centres as Thetford, Haverhill, Bury St Edmunds and King's Lynn (fig. 9.1) dominating the spatial pattern of manufacturing growth in the region during the later 1960s and early 1970s. In particular, these centres received no less than two-thirds (6,300) of all jobs (9,500) generated by 1972 in manufacturing firms immigrant to East Anglia between 1966 and 1970, with only 11 per cent of such inward movement (1,000 jobs) going to the region's major towns (Norwich, Cambridge, Ipswich, Peterborough, Great Yarmouth and Lowestoft). Some 23 per cent (2,200 jobs) went to remaining rural areas and small market towns (East Anglia Regional Strategy Team 1974, 34).

Largely as a result of such immigration, most of it (65 per cent of all immigrant firms) of course from London, East Anglia's expanded towns increased their aggregate manufacturing employment, 1960–9, by no less than 96 per cent or 18,000 workers. This may be compared with a net manufacturing employment growth of 17 per cent or 18,700 workers in the region's six largest industrial centres, and of 56 per cent or 13,000 workers in the rest of East Anglia. But while important, the expanded towns still only accounted for just over one-third (36 per cent) of total regional manufacturing employment growth (49,700 jobs) during this period. Moreover, in general it can be argued that the expanded town programme has only reinforced recent powerful natural tendencies towards above-average manufacturing growth rates in smaller, less industrialized areas and settlements located towards the periphery of the South East and in more distant East Anglia. On the other

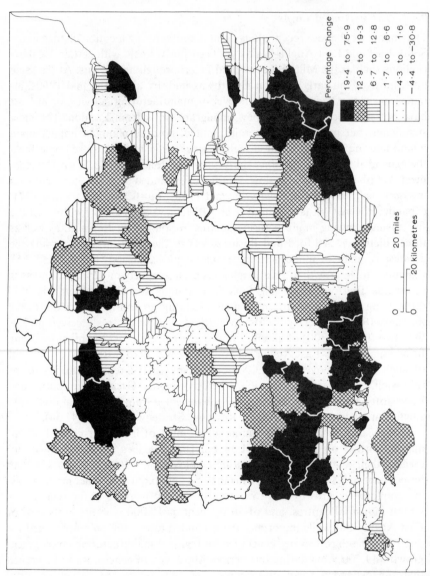

Percentage Change

	19·4 to 75·9
	12·9 to 19·3
	6·7 to 12·8
	1·7 to 6·6
	−4·3 to 1·6
	−4·4 to −30·8

20 miles

20 kilometres

hand, as with the new towns, the industrial structures of the expanded towns have become unusually strongly oriented to expanding industries, while nonetheless attracting a wide and probably more diversified range of manufacturing firms (Seeley 1968, 73). Thus in 1971, the two chief manufacturing industries in Bury St Edmunds were food and drink (33 per cent local manufacturing employment) and mechanical engineering (26 per cent); in Thetford, chemicals and allied industries (23 per cent) and mechanical engineering (18 per cent); and in Andover, mechanical engineering (24 per cent) and paper, printing and publishing (17 per cent). Industrial diversity probably also reflects the below-average size of migrant factories established in these towns, average 1972 employment in the 181 surviving moves to East Anglia's expanded towns, 1955–71, being only eighty-three workers. This may be compared with, for example, a mean 1966 migrant factory size for all moves over a roughly similar length of time, 1952–65, to locations throughout the South East and East Anglia, of 202 workers (Howard 1968).

9.4.2. Recent industrial location trends

The relatively limited impact of the expanded and new town programmes since the mid-1960s, both spatially and in terms of volume of growth, means that other factors must be of greater significance in influencing recent industrial location trends in the South East and East Anglia. These trends are illustrated for the South East by figures 9.4 and 9.5, and may be described in one word – *dispersion*. Dispersion of manufacturing activity is occurring in at least two senses of the word. First, as figure 9.4 most strikingly reveals, the geographical centre of the region, notably London but including a ring of adjacent industrial satellites, is losing manufacturing activity at a considerable rate. In contrast, the most rapidly growing industrial areas are all grouped around the South East's periphery, notably in south Hampshire and west Sussex, and the Kent/Sussex border, but also scattered around the north of the region. In general, however, as in the early 1960s, it is the southern periphery of the region which has attracted the higher rates of manufacturing expansion, rather than its northern counterpart. Thus no less than two-thirds (twenty-four) of the thirty-seven fastest-growing South East local areas 1966–71 were situated south of the Thames, although this zone only contained 53 per cent (fifty-seven) of the 108 areas distinguished outside London.

The second, non-spatial, dispersion trend is occurring through the decline of manufacturing employment in a majority of the region's largest industrial centres, wherever these are located, coupled with manufacturing growth in almost all rural and less-industrialized areas. Thus between 1966 and 1971, two-thirds (thirteen) of those twenty South East centres including London which employed over 20,000 manufacturing workers at the beginning of this period recorded net manufacturing *decline*. This list included such outlying centres as Portsmouth, Brighton, Oxford and Bedford, as well as Slough, Wat-

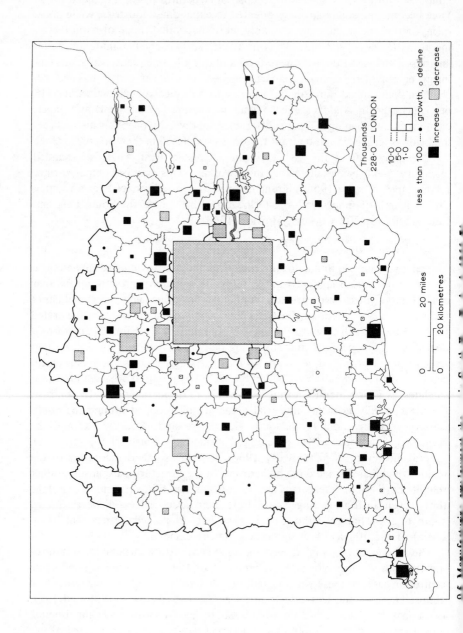

ford, Weybridge and Grays/Tilbury close to London. In striking contrast, no less than 89 per cent (thirty-nine) of the forty-four areas employing less than 5,000 manufacturing workers in 1966 experienced manufacturing employment *growth* during the ensuing five-year period. As a result, the latter group of rural areas and small towns expanded its aggregate manufacturing employment by no less than 22,000 workers, despite the very limited existing industrial activity in most of these areas; whereas the nineteen major centres, even excluding the abnormal case of London, recorded a *decline* in aggregate manufacturing employment of approximately the same amount (19,750 workers). In other words, exactly the same striking trend towards significantly greater dispersion of manufacturing activity from larger to smaller centres as has been documented earlier at the national, inter-subregional, level (section 2.3) is operating at the within-region, inter-urban, scale in South East England. That this powerful dispersion trend is scale-independent is a very significant finding, with considerable implications for planning policy at all levels.

Moreover, lest it be thought that the South East case might be atypical, an independent recent study by Martin (1972) reveals that manufacturing dispersion also characterizes the traditionally unindustrialized region of East Anglia. Thus the value of the entropy index calculated by him for the distribution of manufacturing employment between the thirty-five employment exchange areas in East Anglia declined steadily and regularly each year, 1960–69, from a value of 1.273 in 1960 to one of only 0.752 in 1969, a fall of just over 40 per cent. This compares with an equally steady and striking *increase* in spatial concentration of service industry employment[6] over the same period. Moreover, Martin's analysis demonstrates that virtually all the manufacturing index decline is due to dispersion at the *within*-subregion level, rather than between the four subregions into which he divides East Anglia, with relatively much more rapid manufacturing growth in smaller settlements and expanded towns than in the region's four main traditional industrial centres.

Clearly, one important mechanism behind dispersion is manufacturing migration, from larger to smaller centres, and from the more central parts of the South East, notably London, to its periphery. For example, on Department of Industry estimates, manufacturing migration to East Anglia from the South East between 1966 and 1970 accounted for about 40 per cent of East Anglia's manufacturing employment growth during this period: and this ignores additional growth by South East firms which had moved into East Anglia before 1966. Moreover, as already noted, this movement has largely benefited the region's expanded towns and rural areas, rather than the six biggest urban centres; while what limited movement has occurred *within* East Anglia has been almost entirely dispersal from the latter centres to remaining rural areas (600 jobs by 1972, from migration 1966–70) and expanded towns (200 jobs).

Even more striking dispersion trends characterize movement within the South East. Thus no less than 96 per cent of the 42,000 manufacturing jobs

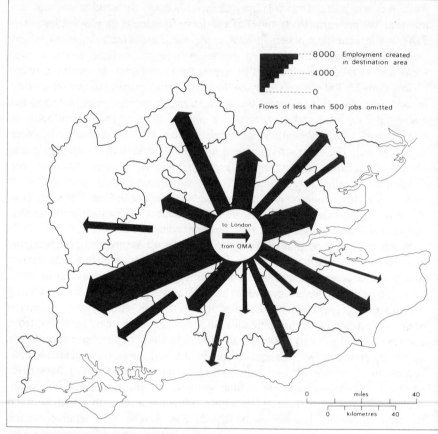

9.6 Manufacturing movement within South East England, 1966–74
Source: unpublished Department of Industry statistics

created by movement between 1966 and 1974 across the internal regional
boundaries shown in figure 9.6 resulted from *outward* flows from central to
more peripheral South East locations, as opposed to inward or orbital flows.[7]
No less than 82 per cent originated in Greater London alone. Moreover, as
figure 9.6 indicates, this outward dispersal benefited outlying less-industrialized
areas significantly more than settlements immediately around London. Thus
while the OMA gained 17,500 jobs, all but a handful from London, the OSE
received 23,200 jobs from the rest of the region, with 6,100 coming from the
OMA. The equal share of total London-origin movement received by the
OMA and OSE (17,100 jobs in each case) is in contrast with earlier periods
such as 1945–65 when 60 per cent of all South East destination moves from
London, measured by employment, settled within about 50 kilometres (30
miles) of the metropolis.[8] Interestingly, figure 9.6 also reveals a major
difference in movement patterns north and south of London, with a preference

in the south for long distance coastal area movement, but in the north for shorter distance OMA destination moves. The residential attractiveness of the south coast, especially Solent, the region's most important destination area, could be an important factor in this.

The general reasons for widespread manufacturing dispersion and migration within the South East and East Anglia have of course already been considered in section 9.3.2. It seems probable that residential space preferences, a search for available workers, agglomeration diseconomies and planning constraints in larger centres, and the rapid improvement of intra-regional radial communications with London, are all significant factors. The new and expanded town programmes have also played an important part. But of all these, it could well be that residential preference and the 'image' of an area as an attractive place in which to live and work is becoming of key importance, influencing at a basic psychological level a host of individual decisions by industrialists, managers, workers and factory developers. Whatever the cause, manufacturing dispersion to outlying areas and smaller less-industrialized settlements within South East England and East Anglia is clearly the dominant industrial location trend of the 1970s.

9.5 Growth centres, industry and regional planning

The final topic to be considered in this chapter is that of growth centre planning for manufacturing industry. In its most general form, this refers simply to deliberate government-inspired concentration of development, especially of manufacturing industry, in a relatively restricted geographical area which forms part of a wider region. In practice, growth centre proposals in Britain thus range from the wide 'growth zone', covering most of North East England, proposed by the 1963 White Paper on that region (Board of Trade, 1963), through the *South East Strategic Plan's* 'growth areas', to the small town 'growth points' recommended by the East Anglia Regional Strategy Team. As these proposals indicate, such spatial concentration has been and is favoured by many regional planners and commentators. While the specific industrial complex form of growth proposal has been heavily criticized, in the British context, in section 8.8.3, a number of arguments do seem to support general growth centre planning.

One of the most obvious of these – the *location suitability* argument – is that within a region, certain areas may possess intrinsic locational or other advantages for industrial growth, relative to remaining areas. When, therefore, the region concerned is a lagging region in special need of mobile growth industry, *or* when decentralization proposals for a prosperous region require a high rate of manufacturing job generation in outlying areas, concentration of planning effort upon such locationally more attractive areas would seem a fairly obvious strategy. Thus in the Scottish case, for example, rugged topography, a very sparse population, limited communications and relative isolation rule out most of the Scottish Highlands for significant industrial growth. As a result, the Highlands and Islands Development Board has been forced to concentrate its recent industrial development efforts upon such intrinsically more suitable areas as the lowlands around the Moray Firth. By 1971, this area had accounted for half of all industrial sites selected for assistance by the Board, as well as of factories and workshops constructed or paid for by it (Moseley 1974, 30). Similarly, the *Strategic Plan for the South East* quite deliberately selected the five major growth areas noted in section 9.4 because they were all 'existing major centres which were considered to have good prospects for further growth' (South East Joint Planning Team 1970, 76) on locational and other grounds, thus minimizing the need for attracting scarce mobile industry.

A second, and indeed secondary, argument for growth centre planning is that geographical concentration of development is necessary to preserve elsewhere attractive areas of countryside and high quality farmland. Again, this *countryside conservation* argument was one, minor, reason for the growth area proposals of the *Strategic Plan for the South East*. Thus, as the team pointed out, one of the advantages of their approach was that 'concentrated development, by restricting the impact of urban intrusion to a limited number of districts, allows for the preservation of extensive areas of open countryside' (South East Joint Planning Team 1970, 31). A similar claim was made for the 1967 *South East Strategy*'s 'growth sector' plan, 'which concentrates the largest possible share of the population growth in a relatively few sectors', in that this concentration pattern 'offers the best chances of preserving large-scale areas of rural countryside from the pressures of urban and industrial expansion' (South East Economic Planning Council 1967, 8–9).

However, the major arguments for this type of regional planning approach are the *public expenditure* and *agglomeration economies* arguments. In the past, the public expenditure argument has tended to focus on the assertion that the development of large concentrations of population and industry involves lower per unit costs of public infrastructure and service provision and maintenance than if the same population were spread in a more diffuse fashion over a number of smaller settlements. This economies of scale argument is accepted, for example, by McCrone (1969, 213), who claims that a population size of 150–500,000 is increasingly being accepted as 'optimal' from the viewpoint of minimizing per unit infrastructure costs. However, as Moseley (1974, ch. 4) in a detailed evaluation of this argument shows, what empirical evidence exists seems to point if anything in the opposite direction, at least above a certain threshold size. Work by P. A. Stone, for example, suggests that per capita road construction costs *rise*, not fall, with increasing urban population, for settlements larger than 50,000 people; while in any case, cost analyses ignore the very important question of *benefits*. Thus possibly increasing per unit costs with increasing settlement size may well be offset by a greater than proportional increase in benefits enjoyed by the inhabitants of the area. Measurement of benefits is however extremely difficult (Richardson 1973, 87). So in

Moseley's view (1974, 74–5), all that can be concluded on this traditional argument is that there is probably 'a minimum size, around 30,000–50,000 perhaps, which is necessary if economies of scale are to be reaped in the provision of certain basic public services'; but that above this, 'it is impossible to define a "best size" towards which public policy should strive'.

On the other hand, larger concentrated development may offer significant public infrastructure advantages in at least two ways not explicitly encompassed in the questionable unit cost argument. First, because of undoubted *thresholds* in public infrastructure investment, larger developments can offer their residents certain *types* of public services which are wholly uneconomic to provide for smaller projects. An excellent example in many rural areas is hospital facilities. In East Anglia, for example, limited and scattered population has meant that it has been economic to develop fully-equipped district hospitals in only six centres: Cambridge, Norwich, Ipswich, Peterborough, King's Lynn and Bury St Edmunds (East Anglia Regional Strategy Team 1974, 86). As a result, the inhabitants of small centres such as Thetford with under 20,000 population are forced to travel considerable distances to such facilities. Not surprisingly, a 1971 survey of Thetford residents (Moseley 1973a, 276) found that 'access to hospital facilities' was the single most widely-felt problem of small town life. A similar point is made by McCrone (1969, 214), who points out that 'small units of 30,000 or so can scarcely justify frequent rail services or technical colleges, let alone airports or universities'. Yet the latter facilities may be of considerable importance, not only to the quality of life expected by many people today, but also as 'bait' to attract immigrant industrialists. This general public service threshold argument is also stressed in the *Strategic Plan for the South East,* in justification for its growth area policy: 'socially, large centres are likely to offer a wider range of services than small towns' (South East Joint Planning Team 1970, 31).

The second valid public infrastructure argument for growth concentration concerns the provision of *public transport*. It is an acknowledged fact that road- and rail-based public transport systems operate most efficiently and economically when demand for their services, in the form of population and industry, is spatially concentrated, preferably along lines. As pointed out in the *Strategic Plan for the South East,* 'in transport terms, concentrated development facilitates provision of effective public transport systems' (South East Joint Planning Team 1970, 31); while the *Strategic Choice for East Anglia* report singles out 'the encouragement of more concentrated forms of development to reduce the dependence of the region on the private car, (and) to give more support to public transport' (East Anglia Regional Strategy Team 1974, 62) as one of its key locational principles for future population development. In regional planning terms, therefore, growth centres of one sort or another are probably essential for the future maintenance, let alone expansion, of public transport facilities.

The *agglomeration economies* argument for growth-centre planning is explicitly concerned with the postulated cost savings to industry, especially manufacturing industry, arising from location in large urban industrial centres. Such economies have of course already been discussed in the broad centre-periphery context in section 4.1.4. Certain points must however be stressed here. First, growth-centre commentators, influenced by Perroux' growth pole theory and industrial complex analysis, have often argued that such centres engender above-average industrial growth and are attractive to manufacturing industry because of 'specific' economies resulting from local industrial linkage. However, as noted in section 4.1.4, empirical research indicates that *local* as opposed to region-wide linkages are of relatively little significance for most firms even in large urban industrial centres. Thus recent detailed analysis of migrant firms settling in East Anglia and Northern England (Moseley and Townroe 1973) revealed that very few of these felt any great need to develop local linkages after movement, most being apparently quite content to stretch their existing linkages with suppliers etc. over the sometimes considerable extra distance resulting from movement. These authors (1973, 143–4) therefore conclude, explicitly with regard to growth centre planning, that 'local linkages are not a necessary condition for operation for all but a small group of companies' and that 'less attention should be paid to industrial linkage ... in planning thinking than to other and more important attributes of the space economy'. Moseley's similar conclusion (1973a, 266) explicitly on the post-move *subcontracting* linkage experience of migrants to Thetford and Haverhill, that 'very few firms appeared in serious difficulties in this respect', also lends weight to this view, in contrast perhaps to the *Strategic Plan for the South East*'s claim that 'for some industries a large industrial base is necessary for the development and survival of specialist subcontracting and service activities' (South East Joint Planning Team 1970, 31). On the other hand, 'general' agglomeration economies for manufacturing industry in large centres (section 4.1.4) may well be more significant and a valid argument for growth-centre planning, though their extent is very difficult to quantify.

The third major aspect of the agglomeration economies argument concerns the labour-supply advantages of larger centres. It is here that the Economic Consultants' research referred to in section 9.4 is of particular interest. Part of this research was concerned with the labour recruitment experience of eighty-nine mobile larger South East manufacturing firms following migration. This investigation (South East Joint Planning Team 1971b, 76) found that whereas 65 per cent of the twenty-three sample firms moving to large towns (more than 50,000 population) or within London reported minimal or 'little' subsequent labour recruitment difficulty, this was true of only 45 per cent of moves to smaller, new or expanded towns. Conversely, only 35 per cent of large town moves reported 'moderate' difficulty, and none 'severe' difficulty, compared with 42 and 12 per cent respectively of the smaller town sample. In other words, with regard to 'problems of recruitment', 'firms in large established centres experience comparatively less difficulty than firms in small centres' (South East Joint Planning Team 1971b, 7). Moreover this finding, which is admittedly based on a fairly small sample of only large firms (100 employees or more), is independently supported by Moseley's East Anglian research (1973a, 269). Thus his surveys discovered that nearly three-quarters of the migrant firms established in Thetford and Haverhill favoured further local urban industrial growth; and by far the most frequently listed single reason for so doing (57 per cent of firms) was 'to enlarge the pool of labour', especially skilled labour. These findings lend some support to Moseley's assertion (1974, 112) that 'the most important single element of the agglomeration economies which derive from urban scale relates to labour availability'. This view and Economic Consultants' specific research findings, together of course with the benefits to workers themselves of 'large labour markets . . . which offer a wide variety of job opportunities' (South East Joint Planning Team 1970, 31), were clearly of considerable importance in prompting the *Strategic Plan for the South East*'s growth centre approach.

Most of the various arguments for growth-centre planning at the within-region scale thus appear to have considerable force. However, certain criticisms, specifically in relation to manufacturing location, must also be noted. One concerns the spatial impact of growth centres upon other areas. Such centres have been advocated as planning instruments for backward regions partly on the basis of an hypothesized ensuing spread of prosperity and improved living standards to surrounding areas (Keeble 1967, 283–6). Two of the mechanisms adduced for such 'spread' or 'trickling-down' effects are what have been termed 'indirect' and 'induced' job creation through inter-firm purchases and service multiplier effects respectively. However, in his Thetford and Haverhill work, Moseley (1973b) discovered that indirect job creation within East Anglia through changed material purchasing patterns of immigrant firms, far from benefiting surrounding areas or other needy small towns, in fact tended to expand employment in the region's existing major urban in-dustrial centres such as Cambridge and Norwich. Similarly, the increased purchasing power wielded by the growing industrial population of the two ex-panded towns benefited most, after the towns themselves, the same larger higher-order regional service centres. So although surrounding rural areas and small towns gained by increasing commuting, there was a marked tendency for other growth impulses to 'trickle-up', not 'trickle-down', the settlement hierarchy, benefiting the region's largest and most prosperous centres rather than rural communities.

A much more significant criticism however relates to actual real-world loca-tion trends. For despite the theoretical and empirically-verified advantages for manufacturing activity of larger urban industrial centres, all the evidence dis-cussed earlier (sections 9.3.2 and 9.4.2) indicates that manufacturing disper-sion, not concentration, is in practice the dominant current trend within regions such as the South East and East Anglia. Moreover, manufacturing decline applies not only to larger conurbations, from London downwards, but also to most towns of over 150,000 population. Conversely, it is the small centres, of up to perhaps 30,000 inhabitants, which are exhibiting the most widespread manufacturing growth, measured by rate *and* volume. While, as noted above, planning controls in larger centres may be playing some part in this remarkable dispersion, it must primarily reflect very powerful natural forces. Put another way, many firms appear in practice to be more strongly influenced by the attractions of a non-industrialized rural or small town location than by those advantages, such as an easier labour market, noted earlier for large centres. Bearing in mind the relative weakness of regional planning policy instruments (section 9.2), this suggests that planning proposals, as in the South East, to concentrate most industrial growth into a relatively few geographically-restricted substantial growth areas, ranging in eventual population size from a minimum of 500,000 to a maximum of 1.4 million, may well prove unrealistic. On the other hand, the manufacturing development of much smaller-scale growth centres, such as those envisaged as secondary settlements and growth points by the *Strategic Choice for East Anglia* report, and for which the planning case is stronger, would seem eminently feasible in the light of these current trends. Despite the attractiveness in certain respects of larger scale growth-centre planning proposals, therefore, the powerful trend towards manufacturing dispersion which characterizes regions throughout Britain (see section 2.3) must cast doubt on the feasibility, and possibly even desirability, of their full implementation.

NOTES

1 'In ... areas such as Cambridge ... IDCs are likely to be issued only for rebuilding schemes' and locally-tied projects with low labour demands (Department of Trade and Industry 1971, 10).
2 'Nonconforming' industry is that located in areas zoned by the local development plan for other land uses, usually residential.
3 *Town and Country Planning*, February 1975.
4 Statistics from published and unpublished Department of Industry records.
5 Thus Bletchley was recommended largely because 'it would be difficult to find an area which would be more attractive to industrialists' (Ministry of Housing and Local Government 1964, 73).
6 Defined as Orders XIX to XXIV inclusive of the 1958 SIC.
7 It should be noted that the flowlines between OMA and OSE subregions relate to plants with origins *throughout* the whole OMA, not just in the particular OMA subregion from which the flowline is drawn. I am greatly indebted to Mrs C. M. E. Hunter of the Department of Industry for access to these unpublished figures.
8 Source: unpublished Board of Trade statistics (Keeble 1972c).

10 Conclusions

This final chapter attempts to draw together the key conclusions of earlier analysis, as well as considering two questions concerning future manufacturing location trends in Britain which have not already been discussed. The latter are the longer term impact on industrial location of the United Kingdom's 1973 entry into the European Economic Community and of the discovery and landing of North Sea oil and gas.

10.1. Manufacturing location and the EEC

In recent years, various commentators have argued that the United Kingdom's membership of the European Economic Community since 1973 is likely to accentuate the longterm manufacturing advantages and growth of mainland Europe relative to Britain, and of the South East corner of England relative to the rest of the country, especially the peripheral assisted areas. Thus, as the Royal Town Planning Institute's working party (1973, 2) on EEC entry pointed out, 'there is ... a lurking fear that international companies may transfer the emphasis of their undertakings to plants and cities which appear to be more centrally located in relation to markets within the Community', thus benefiting both the South East and more central areas of mainland Europe. Again, Brown (1972, 337) concludes that 'entry into the EEC would seem likely to increase the differences' in regional economic disparities within the United Kingdom: 'when the central growth area is one stretching from Lombardy to Paris and Hamburg, Scotland, Wales and Northern Ireland will presumably suffer more from positions peripheral to their market area than they do now'. In this context, Stewart (1971) is amongst various writers who have referred to the 'golden triangle' defined by the three base points of Birmingham, Paris and the Ruhr, and to 'fears in Britain's regions that entry into the Common Market will lead to a concentration of industry in the "golden triangle" to the detriment of more peripheral areas'. This possibility is also noted by McCrone (1969, 269).

The logic behind it, of course, is that a central market location within a free trade area such as the EEC confers significant advantages upon manufacturing firms, in terms of reduced transfer costs to customers, increased sales through closer contact and speedier service, lower per unit costs because of larger output and hence economies of scale, higher rates of innovation, more substantial agglomeration economies, and so on – in short, the national centre/periphery model outlined in chapter 4, operating over the wider western European scale because of the removal of national tariff barriers, freer trade, and greater capital mobility. This view is generally supported by such desk studies as that of Clark, Wilson and Bradley (1969), which suggests that maximum market potential within an enlarged Community,[1] measured by income, is enjoyed by the Antwerp-Cologne area. South East England as a whole records potential values 16–19 per cent lower than this more central zone, on a par with those for southern France, Denmark and northern Italy. The fact that this study used 1962 income data, and that in real terms growth of income per head in Britain has fallen substantially behind that in the other EEC countries since that date, clearly suggests that a similar calculation for the mid-1970s would yield an even greater differential in favour of mainland Europe. On the other hand, the study also suggests that market potential differences *within* Britain have not in fact been increased by entry, and indeed in certain cases (e.g. Wales versus the South East) may have fallen.

The view that the longterm implications for manufacturing location of EEC entry are to the relative detriment of the United Kingdom in general and the peripheral regions of the country in particular appears also to be supported by some empirical, though fragmentary, evidence. For example, certain multinational firms are known to have transferred production from Britain to mainland continental plants, or preferred to locate new investment in the latter rather than former area. An example is the Kiwi shoe polish company, of New Zealand origin, whose Ealing, London, factory was closed in 1975 in order to concentrate production and achieve economies of scale at its Paris factory. The latter is now supplying both the French and British markets. More generally, a 1973 report prepared for the European Community Commission apparently revealed that at that date by far the largest share of foreign manufacturing investment in particular EEC countries was enjoyed by Belgium (33 per cent of the total), West Germany (18 per cent) and Holland (15 per cent), with Britain coming sixth (9 per cent) after Italy and France.[2] The close correlation between these national percentage shares and the general market potential pattern suggested by Clark, Wilson and Bradley is most striking. On the other hand, it must be stressed that these figures obviously reflect investment patterns during the 1960s and early 1970s, when Britain was outside the EEC and hence by definition unattractive to non-European investors, notably from the United States, establishing European plants to serve the Common Market. So they are in fact probably of limited value as a guide to the longterm implications for foreign manufacturing investment of Britain's EEC membership.

Moreover, other factors and arguments can be adduced against the view that membership *per se* will result in a relative shift of manufacturing to mainland Europe, or at the within-Britain scale to balance the claim that entry 'has reinforced the attractions of eastern and southern locations within the United Kingdom at the expense of the west and north' (House 1973, 357). First, there are certain what might be called 'no change' arguments. For example, it is surely more logical to expect substantial factory development by British manufacturing firms in mainland Europe were Britain to have remained *outside* the Community, in order to jump over the external tariff wall, than under present conditions in which no such tariff barrier exists, or at least is being dismantled. So membership of the EEC does to that degree encourage British firms to invest in Britain rather than on the mainland. Second, as noted earlier, transport cost variations, which are often adduced as a reason for the hypothesized future locational advantage of mainland Europe, do not seem to be of more than minor significance for most manufacturing industries today even at the wider EEC scale. As Chisholm (1974, 244) has stressed, 'there is a good deal of evidence to show that for intra-Community trade the costs of transport, and hence the effect of location, is not all that important'. And after all, the overland distance from London to Paris or Brussels is only of the order of 400 kilometres (250 miles), or the same distance as London-Newcastle. Third, there is the argument that in a world in which, since 1973, the Arab oil-producing countries have joined North America and western Europe as the three great world markets for manufactured goods, Britain and its peripheral regions are no less well placed in locational terms for export-led manufacturing growth than the rest of the Community. Again in Chisholm's words (1974, 244), 'foreign (i.e. extra-Community) trade is a major consideration and in this context the peripheral regions are not necessarily at a disadvantage' compared with central areas of the EEC.

To these 'no-change' arguments may however be added more positive ones. For example, it can be argued that within the enlarged EEC tariff wall, Britain in general and its peripheral regions in particular offer an especially attractive location for future EEC-directed manufacturing investment from North America and to a lesser extent Japan, for several reasons. One, with regard to North America, is the advantage of a common language minimizing difficulties in plant establishment and operation by North American management personnel (Royal Town Planning Institute Professional Activities Committee 1973). Second, and more generally, is the factor of available labour, notably in the peripheral assisted areas, relative to the acute labour shortages common until the post-1973 world recession in the leading German and French industrial core areas. Thus in terms of average unemployment rates over the three-year period 1970–73, Wales, Scotland and Northern England ranked 38th, 39th and 40th (with respective rates of 4.3, 5.1 and 5.2 per cent) out of the forty-eight official 'community regions' into which the EEC as a whole can be divided. Even the favoured South East ranked only 11th (1.8 per cent), the leading Community labour-shortage areas on this basis being Baden-Wurtemburg (0.6 per cent), Hamburg (0.8 per cent) and regions such as Est-France, Hessen, Westphalia, Rhineland and the Paris Basin (Department of the Environment 1975, table 14).

Third, the presence of a powerful British regional policy provides of course significant financial advantages to foreign manufacturing companies investing in Britain's assisted areas, relative to most of the rest of the Community and the South East. Moreover, these incentives could be enhanced by the recently-created European Regional Development Fund, set up technically at least from 1 January 1975. This fund, established only after considerable argument between the nine Community countries, will make available £542 million for regional development purposes in the lagging regions of the Community during its first three years, with Britain receiving £151 million of this, or 28 per cent. By the end of 1975 grants to British projects totalled £36 million. Admittedly, uncertainty exists over whether the British government will, as some observers suggest, simply use such grants to offset part of the existing substantial cost of regional policy assistance or, as intended by the European Commission, regard them as additional aid on top of existing payments. It is also true that the longterm rules under which such EEC regional aid will be disbursed have not yet been agreed, although the 1973 interim EEC classification of the Development and Special Development Areas as 'peripheral' rather than 'central' areas of the Community was, in one observer's opinion at least, 'highly satisfactory from the British point of view' (Dashwood 1974). The latter decision means that no EEC-imposed limit exists to the amount of state aid to industry within these assisted areas, although within the rest of the country, including the Intermediate Areas, 'central' EEC status implies a maximum of 20 per cent of state aid for any particular industrial investment (Chisholm 1974, 220). In answer to commentators who have claimed that EEC aid regulations will shackle British government regional policy action, therefore, Dashwood concludes that 'EEC control of state aids does not put governments in a strait-jacket. They retain a large measure of unfettered discretion'. The latter is in fact neatly illustrated by the Labour Government's 1974 decision, accepted by the EEC Commissioners, to double the value of the Regional Employment Premium, a regional policy instrument viewed by some earlier observers as an obvious target for EEC concern (Stewart 1971, 37; Wilson 1973, 169). So while uncertainties exist, notably over whether other EEC countries will eventually agree to adopt IDC-type controls to prevent investment refused permission in South East England from going to other central industrial areas of mainland Europe, the specific regional policy aspects of EEC membership would seem unlikely to diminish Britain's future advantages for manufacturing investment, and could possibly enhance them.

The last and longterm positive point concerning EEC membership relates to the question of economic growth. It has frequently been argued that membership could in the long term help to induce a rate of national economic growth greater than that achieved in recent decades, when the United Kingdom has lagged substantially behind most of the rest of Europe. If this is so, and the post-1973 world recession alone makes any judgement on this exceedingly speculative, it could prove of great significance for Britain's peripheral assisted areas. The logic here is simply that, as documented in section 6.6.1, one important direct by-product of economic growth is an enhanced rate of manufacturing movement. Given the continuation of strong regional policy, such movement could be channelled to the peripheral regions. Theoretically at least, this could be a key longterm mechanism through which EEC membership benefits the latter. But even without this, there do seem to be sufficient grounds for concluding, not that membership is likely to aggravate centre-periphery economic disparities, but with the Royal Town Planning Institute working party (1973, 3) 'that United Kingdom regions outside the south east of England will retain, and probably gain, strength from EEC entry' in relation specifically to manufacturing investment and activity.

10.2. Manufacturing location and North Sea oil and gas

The discovery during the past decade of substantial reserves of natural gas and oil in the southern and northern North Sea, respectively, has attracted considerable attention from geographers and others in relation to its likely impact upon other activities. The scale of these reserves has indeed proved larger than many earlier commentators envisaged. Thus by 1975, known oil and gas reserves in the United Kingdom sector of the North Sea totalled 1,800 million tons (2 per cent of world reserves) and $47.5 \ 10^{12}$ cubic feet, respectively, while possible eventual total reserves could be of the order of 4,200 million tons of oil and $85 \ 10^{12}$ cubic feet of gas (Mackay and Mackay 1975, 63–5). By 1975, North Sea gas production from fields such as Leman Bank and West Sole had reached 4,000 million cubic feet per day, while that year also saw the landing of the first North Sea oil from the small Argyll field. It is anticipated that by 1980, the North Sea fields will be producing 150 million tons of crude oil a year, relative to a United Kingdom anticipated consumption of 127 million tons.

The early finds of North Sea natural gas, and expectation of oil, were greeted by some observers as heralding the possibility of major shifts in the location of manufacturing activity within Britain, towards the east coast. One such commentator was Odell (1966), who in discussing the mid-1960 gas discoveries envisaged the development of 'a major new zone of industrialisation along the east coast of England from the Humber to Lowestoft'. Manufacturing growth in this zone would be based on 'the petro-chemical industry and . . . energy-intensive industrial processes such as those found in the production of iron and steel, in metal refining and in cement manufacture'. Also 'the production of basic chemicals will then provide the raw materials for industries concerned with plastics and artificial fibres and so on, which in turn will encourage the local development of industries producing consumer goods using such products'. A similar chain reaction based on iron and steel would 'lead to the establishment of metal fabricating plants'. This development scenario was envisaged on the basis of a marked spatial variation in natural gas costs because 'the onward transportation of the gas to our existing inland industrial areas will add significantly to the price', increasing it from about 2d. to 5d. per therm.

In practice, however, no such dramatic shift has occurred, nor indeed was ever really likely. One simple reason for this was the decision by the Gas Council (now the British Gas Corporation) to charge relatively uniform prices throughout the country, rather than cost gas to customers simply on the basis of distance from the North Sea fields. But even more important is the fact that such modern energy sources and raw materials as oil and gas are both eminently easy to transport and locationally significant, in terms for example of proportion of total costs, only for a very few industries, notably actual oil refining and dependent petro-chemicals. Thus natural gas is now distributed throughout Britain from the three North Sea field terminals at Easington (Yorkshire), Bacton (Norfolk) and Theddlethorpe (Lincolnshire) via a 3,600-kilometre (2,300-mile) pipeline network, with a further 1,400 or more kilometres (900 miles) under construction from St Fergus near Peterhead, the terminal for the Frigg gas field off Shetland. Moreover, as previous chapters have shown, consumer goods industries and even activities such as iron and steel have been primarily influenced in their recent locational development by factors other than local availability of energy sources such as oil and gas. On the other hand, it might be argued that oil at least is only now beginning to come ashore in quantity, and that east coast oil-based manufacturing development may therefore occur in the future. Moreover, what of the manufacturing activity directly generated by the development of the oilfields themselves, with their demand for drilling rigs, production platforms and so on?

These last questions are examined in detail in a recent study by Mackay and Mackay (1975). On both counts of manufacturing for the North Sea oil firms and of the development of oil-using industry they conclude that relatively little manufacturing expansion has occurred or can be expected at east coast locations. Thus they estimate that the manufacture of production platforms, rigs and drilling ships for the North Sea oil industry had generated by the end of 1974 a total of only 5,000 to 6,000 jobs in North East England, and only

8,700 jobs in Scotland, the two United Kingdom regions in which such activities have been established (Mackay and Mackay 1975, 117–18). Moreover,
they also calculate that in both areas, only limited future growth of these
manufacturing activities is likely, reaching for example a maximum of 10,000
jobs in 1976 in Scotland, with a fall thereafter to only 8,000 workers by 1980.
The relatively limited response by British manufacturing firms to the opportunities provided by North Sea oil development is indicated by these authors'
estimate that such firms had attracted orders representing only a third (£525
million) of the £1,600 million of development expenditure by North Sea oil
companies to the end of 1974. Admittedly, the *local* impact of such manufacturing activity may be considerable. Most striking here is the Moray Firth area
of the Scottish Highlands, where the establishment since 1972 of three large
manufacturing firms had created no less than 4,000 jobs by 1974, chiefly in
the £20-million Highland Fabricators steel production platform works at Nigg
Bay. Other platform production sites have been established at Loch Kishorn
on the west coast opposite Skye, in Argyll, on the Firth of Forth, and on
Teesside. Interestingly, the Mackays show that the oft-quoted economic expansion of the Aberdeen area is in contrast almost entirely due to the establishment of over 200 oil company administrative and related service firms, not to
oil-geared manufacturing expansion. But in total, the manufacturing jobs
created and manufacturing investment committed within the United Kingdom
to service the North Sea development have really been very small.

So too is the likely impact of North Sea oil on the location of the refining
and petro-chemical industries, let alone any other oil-using manufacturing activity. As the Mackays point out (1975, 115), the British oil refining industry
already possesses substantial *surplus* refining capacity (see section 4.2.3), while
in any case, 'on the basis of the plans that have been made to date, it appears
that only 30 to 40 per cent of North Sea oil will be refined in the United
Kingdom'. This is because the relatively light nature of North Sea crude is
more suited to refinery products in greatest demand in North America and
mainland Europe, and it is therefore more economic for the international oil
companies involved to ship it to and refine it in these areas. Government
pressure may of course intervene here to increase the domestic refining proportion. But while some North Sea oriented petro-chemical development at British
Petroleum's Grangemouth refinery and on Teesside is likely, the former being
linked directly by pipeline to the Forties field via Cruden Bay near Peterhead,
only one new major installation geared to North Sea oil seems probable, in the
shape of a new Scottish oil refinery, possibly located at Nigg Bay.[3] There is
also a strong possibility of the development of an ammonia and feedstock
plant at the St Fergus natural gas terminal. In general, however, refining of
North Sea crude at existing Scottish, Teesside and Thameside refineries seems
unlikely to have any substantial impact upon the location even of the British
oil-refining and petro-chemicals industries. So while of great importance for

Britain's balance of payments position, government revenues, and general national economic growth, the North Sea oil and gas 'bonanza' is unlikely to have more than a minimal and local impact upon the geographical distribution of manufacturing industry within the United Kingdom.

10.3. Manufacturing location: key conclusions

The evidence and analyses presented in previous chapters have suggested many conclusions on recent and current trends in manufacturing location within the United Kingdom. Of these, however, several are of such importance as to justify concluding re-emphasis. First and foremost, it has been shown that such trends can simply but strikingly be characterized by the single word *dispersion*. Whether at the inter-regional, inter-subregional, or inter-urban scales, by the late 1960s and early 1970s, manufacturing industry in Britain was rapidly declining in most larger existing industrial centres while growing, equally rapidly, in most smaller traditionally non-industrial locations. Moreover, dispersion in this sense also characterizes a wide range of different industries (section 7.1), although rates of dispersion vary significantly between industries. This non-spatial dispersion tendency, the speed of which has been measured by entropy index values such as those presented in chapter 2, has moreover been accompanied by a rapid *spatial* shift in the distribution of manufacturing industry away from traditional 'central' industrial conurbations towards peripheral areas. Again, this is true not only at the national scale (chapter 2), but equally at the within-region scale, as exemplified by the South East England case (section 9.4.2; fig. 9.4). In both cases, an important component in dispersion has been the actual physical migration of existing manufacturing firms (section 6.6). But the strength of the locational forces at work is indicated by the fact that dispersion is clearly even more a product of differential rates of *in situ* contraction and expansion, and closure, of existing manufacturing firms (sections 6.3–5). While many of these have deliberately and consciously 'adapted' to these forces, others, with less locational precipience, have or have not been 'adopted' by them, with consequent enforced changes in their manufacturing production because of declining or expanding orders, production constraints or opportunities, and so on.

Clearly, one major corollary of dispersion is that at the national scale, the classic centre-periphery model described in section 4.1 no longer obtains as either an overall description or explanation of current manufacturing location trends. This is a very important finding indeed, given the enormous literature devoted to this topic and the deeply-engrained impression in many minds of an inexorable and continuing concentration of industry in the central prosperous regions of the country. The strength of this impression is neatly illustrated by such recent confident but erroneous assertions as 'by the early 1970s the main trends in the changing distribution of economic activity within the UK space through to the end of the next decade have already been firmly established', with a variety of centre-periphery mechanisms tending 'to increase the attractions of market locations at the national and regional levels, modified only marginally at present by government action influencing some of the more flexible manufacturing and service activities'; 'the regions benefiting . . . most will be the South East and the Midlands' (House 1973, 356–7). These judgements would probably have been valid as an appraisal of manufacturing trends during the 1950s: as an accurate verdict on the 1960s, let alone a forecast for the 1970s, they are gravely misleading.[4] Since the early 1960s, the balance of manufacturing locational advantage has swung in favour of the periphery. It is the periphery-centre model as set out in section 4.2 which therefore now best describes and explains national-scale trends in the distribution of manufacturing activity.

This conclusion leads naturally to another. At the broad interregional scale, the evidence presented earlier indicates that the most important single influence upon current manufacturing location trends is government industrial location policy. Thus it will be recalled that assisted-area status was pinpointed as being of key significance since the mid-1960s in subregional manufacturing employment and floorspace change, *and* in net manufacturing migration trends, by the regression analyses of chapters 5 and 6. Moreover, section 8.7 drew attention to other independent regional-scale studies, again of manufacturing employment and migration, which conclude that no other satisfactory explanation can be advanced for the established and marked improvement in the peripheral regions' manufacturing growth performance over the past decade or so. Admittedly, these conclusions are not accepted by all commentators. Chisholm (1974, 218) for one claims that 'the construction of models showing what the state of the regions would have been in the absence of specific pieces of legislation' is 'impossible', because of the complexities involved; while the House of Commons Expenditure Committee's subcommittee (1973, 51) on regional development incentives expressed 'some reservations' on the Moore and Rhodes' analysis, for example.

However, Chisholm's view is in turn not shared by others, Cameron (1974, 24) for example referring to the Brown and Moore/Rhodes analyses as being 'skilful', 'careful' and 'valuable'; while even the House of Commons subcommittee were forced to acknowledge that despite their reservations on the Moore/Rhodes study, the basis for which the subcommittee fail to make clear, they nonetheless 'did not receive any alternative analysis which seemed to contradict' the findings of the two authors in question. Although it might be possible to question the precise magnitudes of policy-induced employment or manufacturing movement arrived at by these investigations, the existence of a substantial policy effect is fully supported by the present study. Thus, for example, an exceedingly crude and simple calculation reveals that whereas, on the average national United Kingdom trend (−6.4 per cent), manufacturing employment in the twenty-six assisted-area subregions of the country would have been expected to decline, 1966–71, by no less than 134,000 jobs, the actual fall was of only 37,000, indicating a relative *gain* of no less than 97,000 manufacturing jobs. This of course makes no allowance for the relatively adverse manufacturing structures of the majority (fourteen) of these subregions (fig. 5.3), which should have resulted in a *greater* rather than smaller rate of decline, relative to the country as a whole. Most important of all, the extensive discussion presented earlier did not throw up any really significant alternative explanation, operating only since about the mid-1960s, which might account for this greatly improved performance relative to earlier years. So on all the evidence, to which the present study contributes significantly, government IDC policy and assisted-area incentives must be accepted as the dominant reason for the recent shift in balance of manufacturing locational advantage in favour of the periphery.

The last main conclusion qualifies that just presented. For at the national but inter-subregional scale, which therefore incorporates within-region as well as between-region manufacturing shifts, the present study can claim a striking original finding in its identification by statistical analysis of residential space preference as probably a major current locational influence on manufacturing industry. True, the regression analyses and survey evidence of chapters 5, 6, 7 and 9 suggest that a variety of other factors have also to lesser or greater degree influenced recent changes in the spatial distribution of industry in the United Kingdom, these including agglomeration diseconomies and factory congestion in larger centres, labour availability, existing manufacturing structure or level of industrial specialization, and even market accessibility and distance constraints (for mobile industry). The first three of these are clearly of considerable importance, although market access and distance appear to be of declining significance, presumably partly in response to the rapid recent improvement of motorway and other communications within and between different regions. But the statistical analyses of chapter 5 and section 9.3.2 do clearly also support the hypothesis that the 'image' of particular localities as attractive residential environments is now, in the 1970s, a factor of major importance in manufacturing growth, strongly influencing the locational decisions of both workers and industrialists. The implications of this for both regional policy and regional planning, in terms of the need to rehabilitate the urban and industrial environments of the older peripheral manufacturing areas, the problems posed for decaying inner city areas of London or Birmingham, and the growing pressures on attractive rural, coastal or small town locations, are going to require very close attention during the remaining decades of the twentieth century.

NOTES

1. Including Norway, although this is unlikely to affect the results significantly.
2. See Judging giants, *The Times*, 14 July 1973.
3. R. Vielvoye, Oil refiners assess their priorities, *The Times,* 21 March 1975.
4 This is equally true for *total* economic activity, including service industry: thus the South East and West Midlands shares of UK *total* employment fell from 33.2 and 10.0 per cent in 1971, to 32.7 and 9.9 per cent in 1974 respectively. The 1974 South East figure is adjusted for boundary changes.

References

ABERCROMBIE, P. (1945) *Greater London Plan 1944.* London, HMSO, 221 pp.

ALCHIAN, A. (1950) Uncertainty, evolution and economic theory. *Journal of Political Economy,* 58, 2, 211–21.

ALDEN, J. and MORGAN, R. (1974) *Regional Planning: a Comprehensive View.* Leighton Buzzard, Leonard Hill, 364 pp.

ALLEN, K. J. and MACLENNAN, M. C. (1970) *Regional Problems and Policies in Italy and France.* London, Allen and Unwin, 352 pp.

ALLEN, K. J. and STEVENSON, A. A. (1974) *An Introduction to the Italian Economy.* London, Martin Robertson, 300 pp.

ALLEN, K. J. and YUILL, D. (1976) *The Accuracy of Pre-1971 Employment Data.* University of Glasgow, Department of Social and Economic Research.

ATKINS, D. H. W. (1973) Employment change in branch and parent manufacturing plants in the U.K.: 1966–71. *Trade and Industry,* 30 August, 437–9.

BAKER, J. N. L. and GILBERT, E. W. (1944) The doctrine of an axial belt of industry in England. *Geographical Journal,* 103, 49–72.

BEESLEY, M. (1955) The birth and death of industrial establishments: experience in the West Midlands Conurbation. *Journal of Industrial Economics,* 4, 1, 45–61.

BEGG, H. M. (1972) Remoteness and the location of the firm. *Scottish Geographical Magazine,* 88, 1, 48–52.

BERESFORD, M. W. and JONES, G. R. J., eds (1967) *Leeds and its region.* Leeds, British Association for the Advancement of Science, 298 pp.

BISHOP, K. C. and SIMPSON, C. E. (1972) Components of change analysis:

problems of alternative approaches to industrial structure. *Regional Studies*, 6, 1, 59–68.

BOARD OF TRADE (1963) *The North East: a Programme for Development and Growth.* Cmnd 2206, London, HMSO.

BRONOWSKI, J. (1960) *The Common Sense of Science.* London, Heinemann.

BROWN, A. J. (1969) Surveys of applied economics: regional economics, with special reference to the United Kingdom. *Economic Journal*, 79, 316, 759–96.

BROWN, A. J. (1972) *The framework of regional economics in the United Kingdom.* Cambridge University Press, 352 pp.

BROWN, C. M. (1966) The industry of the new towns of the London region. In J. E. Martin, *Greater London: An Industrial Geography*, London, Bell, 292 pp.

BUCK, T. W. (1970) Shift and share analysis: a guide to regional policy? *Regional Studies*, 4, 4, 445–50.

BUCK, T. W. and LOWE, J. F. (1972) Regional policy and the distribution of investment. *Scottish Journal of Political Economy*, 19, 3, 252–71.

BURROWS, E. M. (1973) Office employment and the regional problem. *Regional Studies*, 7, 1, 17–31.

BUSWELL, R. J. and LEWIS, E. W. (1970) The geographical distribution of industrial research activity in the United Kingdom. *Regional Studies*, 4, 3, 297–306.

CAESAR, A. A. L. (1964) Planning and the geography of Great Britain. *Advancement of Science*, 21, 230–40.

CAMERON, G. C. (1971) Economic analysis for a declining urban economy. *Scottish Journal of Political Economy*, 18, 3, 315–45.

CAMERON, G. C. (1974) Regional economic policy in the United Kingdom. In M. Sant (ed.) *Regional Policy and Planning for Europe*, Farnborough, Saxon House, 268 pp.

CAMERON, G. C. and CLARK, B. D. (1966) Industrial movement and the regional problem. *University of Glasgow, Social and Economic Studies, Occasional Papers*, no. 5, 220 pp.

CAMERON, G. C. and REID, G. L. (1966) Scottish economic planning and the attraction of industry. *University of Glasgow, Social and Economic Studies, Occasional Papers*, no. 6, 72 pp.

CAMERON, J. E. (1965) Research and industry in and around Cambridge. In J. A. Steers (ed.) *The Cambridge Region 1965*, Cambridge, British Association for the Advancement of Science, 249 pp.

CAMINA, M. M. (1974) Local authorities and the attraction of new employment. *The Planner*, 60, 2, 553–8.

CANNING TOWN COMMUNITY DEVELOPMENT PROJECT (1975) *Canning Town to North Woolwich: the aims of industry?* mimeo, 75 pp.

CHAPMAN, K. (1973) Agglomeration and linkage in the United Kingdom petrochemical industry. *Transactions of the Institute of British Geographers*, 60, 33–68.

CHINITZ, B. (1961) Contrasts in agglomeration: New York and Pittsburgh. *American Economic Review*, 51, 2, 279–89.

CHISHOLM, M. (1964) Must we all live in southeast England? *Geography*, 49, 1–14.

CHISHOLM, M. (1970a) *Geography and economics*. London, Bell, 219 pp.

CHISHOLM, M. (1970b) On the making of a myth? How capital intensive is industry investing in the Development Areas? *Urban Studies*, 7, 3, 289–93.

CHISHOLM, M. (1971) Freight transport costs, industrial location and regional development. In M. Chisholm and G. Manners (eds), *Spatial policy problems of the British economy*, Cambridge University Press, 248 pp.

CHISHOLM, M (1975) Regional policies for the 1970s. *Geographical Journal*, 140, 2, 215–44.

CHISHOLM, M. and OEPPEN, J. (1973) *The Changing Pattern of Employment: regional specialisation and industrial localisation in Britain*. London, Croom Helm, 127 pp.

CLARK, A. (1976) *Government policy and the spatial distribution of investment in Great Britain, 1964–1969*. Unpubl. dissertation, Department of Geography, University of Cambridge.

CLARK, C. (1966) Industrial location and economic potential. *Lloyds Bank Review*, 82, 1–17.

CLARK, C., WILSON, F. and BRADLEY, J. (1969) Industrial location and economic potential in Western Europe. *Regional Studies*, 3, 2, 197–212.

CLIFF, A. and ORD, K. (1972) Testing for spatial autocorrelation among regression residuals. *Geographical Analysis*, 4, 3, 267–84.

CLIFF, A. D. and ORD, J. K. (1973) *Spatial autocorrelation*. London, Pion, 178 pp.

COATES, B. E. and RAWSTRON, E. M. (1971) *Regional Variations in Britain: studies in economic and social geography*. London, Batsford, 304 pp.

COLLINS, L. (1975) A procedure for forecasting changes in manufacturing activity. In L. Collins and D. F. Walker (eds), *Locational Dynamics of Manufacturing Activity*. London, Wiley, 402 pp.

COLLINS, L. and WALKER, D. F., eds. (1975) *Locational Dynamics of Manufacturing Activity*. London, Wiley, 402 pp.

CULLINGWORTH, J. B. (1974) *Town and Country Planning in Britain*. London, Allen and Unwin, 356 pp.

DASHWOOD, A. (1974) Freedoms and restraints in EEC policy on regional and industrial aid, *The Times*, 2 October 1974, 21.

DENNISON, S. R. (1937) State control of industrial location. *Manchester School of Economic and Social Studies*, 8, 2, 147–69.

DEPARTMENT OF ECONOMIC AFFAIRS (1969) *The Intermediate Areas: report of a committee under the chairmanship of Sir Joseph Hunt.* Cmnd 3998, London, HMSO, 256 pp.

DEPARTMENT OF THE ENVIRONMENT (1975) The South East region in a European context. *Strategic Plan for the South East, Development and Up-Dating Working Paper*, 21 pp.

DEPARTMENT OF TRADE AND INDUSTRY (1971) Industrial Development Certificate control – a guide for industry. *Trade and Industry*, 4, 8–11.

DEPARTMENT OF TRADE AND INDUSTRY (1973) Memorandum on the inquiry into location attitudes and experience. *Minutes of Evidence*, Trade and Industry sub-committee of the House of Commons Expenditure Committee, Wednesday, July 4th, Session 1972–3, London, HMSO, 525–668.

DOWIE, R. (1968) Government assistance to industry: a review of the legislation of the 1960s. *Centre for Research in the Social Sciences, University of Kent, Ashford Study Paper*, II, 24 pp.

DUNNING, J. H. and THOMAS, C. J. (1963) *British Industry: change and development in the twentieth century.* London, Hutchinson, 242 pp.

EAST ANGLIA ECONOMIC PLANNING COUNCIL (1968) *East Anglia: a study.* London, HMSO, 152 pp.

EAST ANGLIA REGIONAL STRATEGY TEAM (1974) *Strategic Choice for East Anglia.* London, HMSO, 168 pp.

ECONOMIC CONSULTANTS LTD (1969) *Study for an industrial complex in central Lancashire.* Unpubl. study for the Department of Economic Affairs.

ECONOMIC DEVELOPMENT COMMITTEE FOR MOTOR MANUFACTURING (1969) *Regional Policy and the Motor Industry.* National Economic Development Office, 7 pp.

EDWARDS, R. S. and TOWNSEND, H. (1958) *Business Enterprise: its growth and organisation.* London, Macmillan, 607 pp.

EDWARDS, S. L. (1975) Regional variations in freight cost. *Journal of Transport Economics and Policy*, 9, 2, 115–26.

ELECTRONICS ECONOMIC DEVELOPMENT COMMITTEE (1974) *Annual Statistical Survey of the Electronics Industry.* National Economic Development Office, 59 pp.

ESTALL, R. C. (1966) *New England: a study in industrial adjustment.* London, Bell, 296 pp.

ESTALL, R. C. and BUCHANAN, R. O. (1973) *Industrial Activity and Economic Geography.* London, Hutchinson, 252 pp.

EVERSLEY, D. E. C. (1965), Social and psychological factors in the determination of industrial location. In T. Wilson (ed.), *Papers on Regional Development*, Oxford, Blackwell, 130 pp.

EVERSLEY, D. (1975) Employment planning and income maintenance. *Town and Country Planning*, 43, 7, 206–9.

FIRN, J. R. (1975) External control and regional development: the case of Scotland. *Environment and Planning*, 7, 4, 393–414.

FORSYTH, D. J. C. (1972) *U.S. Investment in Scotland*. New York, Praeger, 320 pp.

FOSTER, C. D. and RICHARDSON, R. (1973) Employment trends in London in the 1960s and their relevance for the future. In D. Donnison and D. Eversley (eds.), *London: urban patterns, problems and policies*, London, Heinemann, 452 pp.

FUCHS, V. R. (1959) Changes in the location of U.S. manufacturing since 1929. *Journal of Regional Science*, 1, 2, 1–17.

GARRISON, C. B. and PAULSON, A. S. (1973) An entropy measure of the geographic concentration of economic activity. *Economic Geography*, 49, 4, 319–24.

GASKIN, M. (1974) Centre and region in regional policy. In M. Sant (ed.) *Regional Policy and Planning for Europe*. Farnborough, Saxon House, 268 pp.

GODDARD, J. B. (1974) The national system of cities as a framework for urban and regional policy. In M. Sant (ed.) *Regional Policy and Planning for Europe*. Farnborough, Saxon House, 268 pp.

GOODWIN, W. (1965) The structure and position of the British motor vehicle industry. *Tijdschrift voor Economische en Sociale Geografie*, 56, 4, 145–56.

GOULD, P. R. and WHITE, R. R. (1968) The mental maps of British school leavers. *Regional Studies*, 2, 2, 161–82.

GREATER LONDON COUNCIL (1969) *Greater London Development Plan: report of studies*. London, Greater London Council, 327 pp.

GREEN, D. H. (1974) *Information, perception and decision-making in the industrial relocation decision*. Unpubl. Ph.D. thesis, University of Reading, 414 pp.

HAGGETT, P. (1965) *Locational analysis in human geography*. London, Edward Arnold, 339 pp.

HAGUE, D. C. and NEWMAN, P. K. (1952) Costs in alternative locations: the clothing industry. *National Institute of Economic and Social Research, Occasional Papers* 15, Cambridge University Press, 73 pp.

HALL, M. (1970) Industry grows where the grass is greener. *Area*, 3, 40–6.

HALL, P. G. (1962) *The Industries of London Since 1861*. London, Hutchinson, 192 pp.

HALL, P. (1969) *London 2000*. London, Faber and Faber, 287 pp.

HALL, P. (1975) Migration. *New Society*, 6 February 1975.

HALL, R. K. (1972) The movement of offices from central London. *Regional Studies*, 6, 4, 385–92.

HAMILTON, F. E. I. (1967) Models of industrial location. In R. J. Chorley and P. Haggett (eds) *Models in Geography*, London, Methuen, 816 pp.

HAMILTON, F. E. I., ed. (1974) *Spatial Perspectives on Industrial Organisation and Decision-Making*. London, Wiley, 533 pp.

HAMMOND, E. (1964) Improving the machinery. *Town and Country Planning*, 32, 3, 138–41.

HARRIS, C. D. (1954) The market as a factor in the localization of industry in the United States. *Annals of the Association of American Geographers*, 44, 3, 315–48.

HART, R. A. (1971) The distribution of new industrial building in the 1960s. *Scottish Journal of Political Economy*, 18, 2, 181–97.

HART, R. A. (1972) The regional growth in employment in the manufacturing and service sectors, 1960–1975: the United Kingdom experience and expectation. *Tijdschrift voor Economische en Sociale Geografie*, 63, 2, 88–93.

HAUSER, D. P. (1974) Some problems in the use of stepwise regression techniques in geographical research. *Canadian Geographer*, 18, 2, 148–58.

HEAL, D. W. (1974) *The Steel Industry in Postwar Britain*. Newton Abbot, David and Charles, 224 pp.

HEPPLE, L. W. (1974) The impact of stochastic process theory upon spatial analysis in human geography. In C. Board *et al., Progress in Geography*, No. 6.

HOARE, A. G. (1974) International airports as growth poles: a case study of Heathrow Airport. *Transactions of the Institute of British Geographers*, 63, 75–96.

HOARE, A. G. (1975) Linkage flows, locational evaluation and industrial geography: a case study of Greater London. *Environment and Planning*, 7, 41–58.

HOLLOCKS, F. T. (1975) London's problems and the GLC. *The Times*, 5 September 1975, 15.

HOTELLING, H. (1929) Stability in competition. *Economic Journal*, 39, 153, 41–57.

HOUSE OF COMMONS EXPENDITURE COMMITTEE (1973) *Regional development incentives*. Second Report, Session 1973–74, London, HMSO, 78 pp.

HOUSE, J. W., ed. (1973) *The UK Space: resources, environment and the future*. London, Weidenfeld and Nicolson, 371 pp.

HOUSTON, C. (1969), Market potential and potential transport costs: an evaluation of the concepts and their surface patterns in the USSR. *Canadian Geographer*, 13, 3, 216–36.

HOWARD, R. S. (1968) *The Movement of Manufacturing Industry in the United Kingdom 1945–65*. London, HMSO for the Board of Trade, 54 pp.

ISARD, W. and VIETORISZ, T. (1955) Industrial complex analysis and regional development. *Papers and Proceedings of the Regional Science Association*, 1, 227–47.

JAY, L. S. (1974) Regional policy and sub-regional planning: the confused state. In M. Sant (ed.), *Regional Policy and Planning for Europe*, Farnborough, Saxon House, 268 pp.

JOHNSTON, J. (1972) *Econometric Methods*. New York, McGraw Hill, 437 pp.

KEEBLE, D. E. (1966) *Industrial growth in north-west London: a geographical analysis*. Unpubl. Ph.D. thesis, University of Cambridge, 433 pp.

KEEBLE, D. E. (1967) Models of economic development. In R. J. Chorley and P. Haggett (eds) *Models in Geography*, London, Methuen, 816 pp.

KEEBLE, D. E. (1968a) Industrial decentralization and the metropolis: the North-West London case. *Transactions of the Institute of British Geographers*, 44, 1–54.

KEEBLE, D. E. (1968b) Regional representation at a 'national' university. *Universities Quarterly*, 23, 1, 66–73.

KEEBLE, D. E. (1968c) Airport location, exporting and industrial growth. *Town and Country Planning*, 36, 4, 209–14.

KEEBLE, D. E. (1969a) Local industrial linkage and manufacturing growth in outer London. *Town Planning Review*, 40, 2, 163–88.

KEEBLE, D. (1969b) The proper place for industry. *Geographical Magazine*, 41, 844–55.

KEEBLE, D. (1971a) Employment mobility in Britain. In M. Chisholm and G. Manners (eds) *Spatial Policy Problems of the British Economy*, Cambridge University Press, 248 pp.

KEEBLE, D. E. (1971b) Planning and South East England. *Area*, 3, 69–74.

KEEBLE, D. (1972a) The South East and East Anglia. In G. Manners, D. Keeble, B. Rodgers and K. Warren, *Regional Development in Britain*, London, Wiley, 448 pp.

KEEBLE, D. E. (1972b) Industrial movement and regional development in the United Kingdom. *Town Planning Review*, 43, 1, 3–25.

KEEBLE, D. E. (1972c) Modelling industrial movement: the southeast England case. In W. P. Adams and F. M. Helleiner (eds), *International Geography 1972*, vol. 1, University of Toronto Press, 694 pp.

KEEBLE, D. (1972d) Regional policy after Davies. *Area*, 4, 2, 132–6.

KEEBLE, D. (1974a) The movement of firms. Unit 8, Course D342, *Regional Analysis and Development*, Milton Keynes, The Open University, 42 pp.

KEEBLE, D. (1974b) Reasons for government intervention. Unit 12, Course D342, *Regional Analysis and Development*, Milton Keynes, The Open University, 33 pp.

KEEBLE, D. E. (1975) Industrial mobility: in which industries has plant location changed most? – a comment. *Regional Studies*, 9, 3, 297–99.

KEEBLE, D. E. (1976) Regional development and the attraction of industry. In P. Drury (ed.), *Regional and Rural Development: essays in theory and practice*, Chalfont St Giles, Alpha Academic Books.

KEEBLE, D. E. and HAUSER, D. P. (1971) Spatial analysis of manufacturing growth in outer south-east England 1960–67: 1. Hypotheses and variables. *Regional Studies*, 5, 4, 229–61.

KEEBLE, D. E. and HAUSER, D. P. (1972) Spatial analysis of manufacturing growth in outer south-east England 1960–67: 2. Method and results. *Regional Studies*, 6, 1, 11–36.

KUKLINSKI, A. R. (1967) *Criteria for Location of Industrial Plants*. Economic Commission for Europe, United Nations, New York, 117 pp.

LEMON, A. (1975) Postwar industrial growth in East Anglian small towns: a study of migrant firms 1945–1970. *Oxford University Geography Research Paper*, 12, 40 pp.

LESZCZYCKI, S. (1972) Perspective on development of geographical sciences. *IGU Bulletin*, 23, 2, 1–10.

LEVER, W. F. (1972a) The intra-urban movement of manufacturing: a Markov approach. *Transactions of the Institute of British Geographers*, 56, 21–38.

LEVER, W. F. (1972b) Industrial movement, spatial association and functional linkages. *Regional Studies*, 6, 4, 371–84.

LEVER, W. F. (1974a) Regional multipliers and demand leakages at establishment level. *Scottish Journal of Political Economy*, 21, 2, 111–22.

LEVER, W. F. (1974b) Planning and manufacturing industry. In J. Forbes (ed.), *Studies in social science and planning*, Edinburgh, Scottish Academic Press, 321 pp.

LEVER, W. F. (1974c) Manufacturing linkages and the search for suppliers and markets. In F. E. I. Hamilton (ed.), *Spatial Perspectives on Industrial Organisation and Decision-Making*, London, Wiley, 533 pp.

LEWIS, E. W. (1971) *The location of manufacturing industry in the western home counties*. Unpubl. M.Phil. thesis, University of London, 362 pp.

LEWIS, J. PARRY (1974) *A Study of the Cambridge Sub-Region*, Pt 2. London, HMSO, 386 pp.

LIVESEY, F. (1972) Industrial complexity and regional economic development. *Town Planning Review*, 43, 3, 225–42.

LLOYD, P. E. and DICKEN, P. (1972) *Location in Space: a theoretical approach to economic geography*. New York, Harper and Row, 292 pp.

LOASBY, B. J. (1961) The experience of West Midlands industrial dispersal projects. *Town and Country Planning*, 29, 8, 309–13.

LOCATION OF OFFICES BUREAU (1974) *Annual report 1973–74*. 39 pp.

LÖSCH, A. (1954) *The Economics of Location*. Yale University Press, New Haven, 520 pp. Translated by W. H. Woglom from *Die räumliche Ordnung der Wirtschaft* (first edition, Jena, 1940).

LUTTRELL, W. F. (1962) *Factory Location and Industrial Movement: a study of recent experience in Great Britain.* National Institute of Economic and Social Research, London, vol. 1, 422 pp.

MACKAY, D. I. (1968) Industrial structure and regional growth: a methodological problem. *Scottish Journal of Political Economy,* 15, 2, 129–43.

MACKAY, D. I. and MACKAY, G. A. (1975) *The Political Economy of North Sea Oil.* London, Martin Robertson, 193 pp.

MACKAY, R. R. (1972) Employment creation in the Development Areas. *Scottish Journal of Political Economy,* 19, 287–96.

MACKAY, R. R. (1974) Evaluating the effects of British regional economic policy – a comment. *Economic Journal,* 84, 367–72.

MANNERS, G. (1962) Regional protection: a factor in economic geography. *Economic Geography,* 38, 2, 122–9.

MANNERS, G. (1970) Greater London Development Plan: location policy for manufacturing industry. *Area,* 3, 54–6.

MANNERS, G. (1972) National perspectives. In G. Manners, D. Keeble, B. Rodgers and K. Warren, *Regional Development in Britain,* London, Wiley, 448 pp.

MARCH, L. (1969) The spatial organisation of hyperurban societies. *Town and Country Planning Summer School, 1969, Report of Proceedings,* 4–12.

MARTIN, J. E. (1961) *The location of industry in inner north-east London: a study in industrial geography.* Unpubl. Ph.D. thesis, University of London, 436 pp.

MARTIN, J. E. (1966) *Greater London: an industrial geography.* London, Bell 292 pp.

MARTIN, J. E. and SEAMAN, J. M. (1975) The fate of the London factory: twenty years of change. *Town and Country Planning,* 43, 11, 492–5.

MARTIN, R. L. (1972) *Information theory and employment location trends in East Anglia.* Department of Geography, University of Cambridge, mimeo, 14 pp.

MARTIN, R. L. (1974) On spatial dependence, bias and the use of first spatial differences in regression analysis. *Area,* 6, 3, 185–94.

MCCALLUM, J. D. (1973) U.K. regional policy 1964–72. In G. C. Cameron and L. Wingo (eds), *Cities, Regions and Public Policy,* Edinburgh, Oliver and Boyd, 337 pp.

MCCRONE, G. (1969) *Regional policy in Britain.* London, Allen and Unwin, 280 pp.

MCDERMOTT, P. J. (1973) Spatial margins and industrial location in New Zealand. *New Zealand Geographer,* 29, 1, 64–74

MCDERMOTT, P. J. (1975) *External constraints and the industrial location decision.* Department of Geography, University of Cambridge, mimeo, 18 pp.

MINISTRY OF HOUSING AND LOCAL GOVERNMENT (1964) *The South East Study 1961–1981.* London, HMSO, 145 pp.

MINISTRY OF HOUSING AND LOCAL GOVERNMENT (1969) Floorspace in industrial, shopping and office use: changes April 1964 to March 1967. *Statistics for Town and Country Planning, Series II, Floorspace,* No. 1, 32 pp.

MINISTRY OF LABOUR (1967) *Manpower studies no. 5: Electronics.* London, HMSO, 72 pp.

MOORE, B. and RHODES, J. (1973) Evaluating the effects of British regional economic policy. *Economic Journal,* 83, 87–110.

MOORE, B. and RHODES, J. (1974a) The effects of regional economic policy in the United Kingdom. In M. Sant (ed.), *Regional Policy and Planning for Europe,* Farnborough, Saxon House, 268 pp.

MOORE, B. and RHODES, J. (1974b) Regional policy and the Scottish economy. *Scottish Journal of Political Economy,* 21, 3, 215–35.

MOORE, B. and RHODES, J. (1976) Regional economic policy and the movement of manufacturing firms to Development Areas. *Economica,* 43, 1, 17–31.

MORLEY, R. and TOWNROE, P. M. (1974) The experience of migrant industrial plants in the Northern Region. *Planning Outlook,* 15, 18–34.

MORRISON, W. I. (1972) *Urban interindustry analysis: an input-output study of the Peterborough economy.* Unpubl. Ph.D. thesis, University of London, 267 pp.

MORTLOCK, D. (1972) Employment changes in Greater London. *Greater London Council Intelligence Unit Quarterly Bulletin,* 20, 16–26.

MOSELEY, M. J. (1973a) Some problems of small expanding towns. *Town Planning Review,* 44, 3, 263–78.

MOSELEY, M. J. (1973b) The impact of growth centres in rural regions – II: an analysis of spatial 'flows' in East Anglia. *Regional Studies,* 7, 1, 77–94.

MOSELEY, M. J. (1974) *Growth centres in spatial planning.* Oxford, Pergamon, 192 pp.

MOSELEY, M. J. and TOWNROE, P. M. (1973) Linkage adjustment following industrial movement. *Tijdschrift voor Economische en Sociale Geografie,* 64, 3, 137–44.

MOXON, J. W. J. (1972) The industrial development certificate system and employment creation. *Urban Studies,* 9, 229–33.

MURIE, A. S., BIRRELL, W. D., HILLYARD, P. A. R. and ROCHE, D. J. D. (1973) A survey of industrial movement in Northern Ireland between 1965 and 1969. *Economic and Social Review,* 4, 2, 231–44.

MYRDAL, G. (1957) *Economic theory and underdeveloped regions.* London, Duckworth, 168 pp.

NEEDLEMAN, L. (1965) What are we to do about the Regional Problem? *Lloyds Bank Review,* 75, 45–58.

NEWCOMBE, V. Z. (1969) Creating an industrial development pole in southern Italy. *Journal of the Town Planning Institute*, 55, 4, 157–61.

NORCLIFFE, G. B. (1970) *Industrial location dynamics: a positive theory, measurement, and a case study of changing patterns of manufacturing plant location*. Unpubl. Ph.D. thesis, University of Bristol.

NORTH, D. J. (1974) The process of locational change in different manufacturing organisations. In F. E. I. Hamilton (ed.), *Spatial Perspectives on Industrial Organisation and Decision-Making*, London, Wiley, 533 pp.

NORTH, D. (1975) Acquisition and spatial change. *Middlesex Polytechnic Industrial Location Research Project Working Paper*, 8, 25 pp.

NORTH WEST JOINT PLANNING TEAM (1974) *Strategic Plan for the North West*, London, HMSO, 283 pp.

ODELL, P. R. (1966) What will gas do to the east coast? *New Society*, 188, 5 May, 8–9.

OLSSON, G. (1965) *Distance and human interaction*. Regional Science Research Institute, Philadelphia, 112 pp.

PERROUX, F. (1955) Note on the concept of 'growth poles'. translated into English as chapter 7 in D. L. McKee, R. D. Dean and W. H. Leahy (eds), *Regional Economics: theory and practice*, 1970, New York. The Free Press, 264 pp.

POLITICAL AND ECONOMIC PLANNING (1939) *Report on the Location of Industry in Great Britain*. London, 314 pp.

POOLE, M. A. and O'FARRELL, P. N. (1971) The assumptions of the linear regression model. *Transactions of the Institute of British Geographers*, 52, 145–58.

PRED, A. (1967) Behaviour and location: foundations for a geographic and dynamic location theory, Part I. *Lund Studies in Geography, Series B, Human Geography*, 27, 128 pp.

PRED, A. R. (1974) Industry, information and city-system interdependencies. In F. E. I. Hamilton (ed.), *Spatial Perspectives on Industrial Organisation and Decision-Making*, London, Wiley, 533 pp.

RAKE, D. J. (1972) *The economic geography of the multilocational industrial firm with special reference to the East Midlands*. Unpubl. Ph.D. thesis, University of Nottingham, 975 pp.

RANDALL, J. N. (1973) Shift-share analysis as a guide to the employment performance of West Central Scotland. *Scottish Journal of Political Economy*, 20, 1, 1–26.

RHODES, J. and KAN, A. (1971) Office dispersal and regional policy. *University of Cambridge Department of Applied Economics Occasional Papers*, No. 30, 132 pp.

RICHARDSON, H. W. (1969) *Regional Economics: location theory, urban structure and regional change*. London, Weidenfeld and Nicolson, 457 pp.

RICHARDSON, H. W. (1973) *The Economics of Urban Size*, Farnborough, Saxon House, 243 pp.

RIDLEY, A. (1972) *Regional policy: theory and practice*. Unpubl. paper to Urban Studies Association Conference, Oxford.

RILEY, R. C. (1973) *Industrial Geography*. London, Chatto and Windus, 240 pp.

ROBSON, B. T. (1973) *Urban Growth: an approach*. London, Methuen, 268 pp.

ROYAL COMMISSION (1940) *Report of the Royal Commission on the Distribution of the Industrial Population*. Cmnd 6153, London, HMSO, 320 pp.

ROYAL TOWN PLANNING INSTITUTE PROFESSIONAL ACTIVITIES COMMITTEE (1973) Report of the subcommittee on the effect of EEC entry on British planning. *Royal Town Planning Institute Planning Papers*, No. 2, 12 pp.

SANT, M. E. C. (1970) Age and area in industrial location: a study of manufacturing establishments in East Anglia. *Regional Studies*, 4, 3, 349–58.

SANT, M., ed. (1974) *Regional Policy and Planning for Europe*. Farnborough, Saxon House, 268 pp.

SANT, M. (1975a) *Industrial Movement and Regional Development: the British case*. Oxford, Pergamon, 253 pp.

SANT, M. E. C. (1975b), Interregional industrial movement: the case of the non-survivors. In A. D. M. Phillips and B. J. Turton (eds), *Environment, Man and Economic Change*, London, Longman, 501 pp.

SANT, M. E. C. and MOSELEY, M. J. (1976) *Industrial Britain: East Anglia*. Newton Abbot, David and Charles.

SEAMAN, J. M. (1970) *The location of manufacturing in south-east London: an industrial geography*. Unpubl. M.Sc.(Econ.) thesis, University of London, 331 pp.

SEELEY, I. H. (1968) *Planned Expansion of Country Towns*. London, George Godwin, 270 pp.

SEMPLE, R. K. (1973) Recent trends in the spatial concentration of corporate headquarters. *Economic Geography*, 49, 4, 309–18.

SLEEMAN, J. F. (1969) A new look at the distribution of private cars in Britain. *Scottish Journal of Political Economy*, 16, 306–18.

SMALL TOWNS STUDY (1972) Report to the East Anglia Economic Planning Council and East Anglia Consultative Committee, 94 pp.

SMITH, B. M. D. (1975) Industrial mobility: in which industries has plant location changed most? *Regional Studies*, 9, 1, 27–38.

SMITH, D. H. (1933) *The Industries of Greater London*, London, P. S. King and Son, 188 pp.

SMITH, D. M. (1969) Industrial location and regional development – some recent trends in north-west England. *Environment and Planning*, 1, 2, 173–91.

SMITH, D. M. (1971) *Industrial Location: an economic geographical analysis.* New York, Wiley, 553 pp.

SMITH, T. R. (1954) Locational analysis of new manufacturing plants in the United States. *Tijdschrift voor Economische en Sociale Geografie,* 45, 2, 46–50.

SMITH, W. (1953) *An Economic Geography of Great Britain.* London, Methuen, 756 pp.

SOUTH EAST ECONOMIC PLANNING COUNCIL (1967) *A Strategy for the South East.* London, HMSO, 100 pp.

SOUTH EAST JOINT PLANNING TEAM (1970) *Strategic Plan for the South East.* London, HMSO, 110 pp.

SOUTH EAST JOINT PLANNING TEAM (1971b) *Strategic Plan for the South East: Studies volume 1: population and employment.* London, HMSO, 265 pp.

SOUTH EAST JOINT PLANNING TEAM (1971b) *Strategic Plan for the South East: Studies volume 5: report of Economic Consultants Ltd.* London, HMSO, 102 pp.

SPOONER, D. J. (1972) Industrial movement and the rural periphery: the case of Devon and Cornwall. *Regional Studies,* 6, 2, 197–215.

SPOONER, D. J. (1974) Some qualitative aspects of industrial movement in a problem region in the United Kingdom. *Town Planning Review,* 45, 1, 63–83.

STAFFORD, H. A. (1972) The geography of manufacturers. In C. Board *et al., Progress in Geography,* No. 4.

STAFFORD, H. A. (1974) The anatomy of the location decision: content analysis of case studies. In F. E. I. Hamilton (ed.), *Spatial Perspectives on Industrial Organisation and Decision-Making,* London, Wiley, 533 pp.

STEED, G. P. F. (1967) Locational changes: a 'shift-and-share' analysis of Northern Ireland's manufacturing mix, 1950–1964. *Tijdschrift voor Economische en Sociale Geografie,* 58, 5, 265–70.

STEED, G. P. F. and THOMAS, M. D. (1971) Regional industrial change: Northern Ireland. *Annals of the Association of American Geographers,* 61, 2, 344–60.

STEWART, J. A. (1971) Industrial location: Great Britain and Europe. *Town and Country Planning Summer School 1971, Report of Proceedings,* 33–7.

STEWART, J. M. W. (1972) Mobility of employment in Greater London. *Greater London Development Plan Inquiry Paper,* B629, 24 pp.

STILWELL, F. J. B. (1968) Location of industry and business efficiency. *Business Ratios,* Winter, 1–15.

STILWELL, F. J. B. (1969) Regional growth and structural adaptation. *Urban Studies,* 6, 2, 162–78.

STILWELL, F. J. B. (1970) Further thoughts on the shift and share approach. *Regional Studies*, 4, 4, 451–8.

TANNER, M. F. and WILLIAMS, A. F. (1967) Port development and national planning strategy: the implications of the Portbury decision. *Journal of Transport Economics and Policy*, 1, 3, 1–10.

TAYLOR, E. G. R. (1938) Discussion on the geographical distribution of industry. *Geographical Journal*, 92, 1, 22–39.

TAYLOR, M. J. (1970) Location decisions of small firms. *Area*, 2, 51–4.

TAYLOR, M. J. (1973) Local linkage, external economies and the ironfoundry industry of the West Midlands and East Lancashire conurbations. *Regional Studies*, 7, 4, 387–400.

THEIL, H. (1967) *Economics and information theory.* Amsterdam, North-Holland, 488 pp.

THIRLWALL, A. P. (1967) A measure of the 'proper distribution of industry'. *Oxford Economic Papers*, 19, 46–58.

THOMAS, R. L. and STONEY, P. J. M. (1971) Unemployment dispersion as a determinant of wage inflation in the U.K. 1925–66. *Manchester School of Economic and Social Studies*, 39, 2, 83–116.

THOMPSON, W. R. (1968) Internal and external factors in the development of urban economies. In H. S. Perloff and L. Wingo (eds), *Issues in Urban Economics*, Baltimore, John Hopkins Press, 668 pp.

TIEBOUT, C. M. (1957) Location theory, empirical evidence and economic evolution. *Papers and Proceedings of the Regional Science Association*, 3, 74–86.

TOMKINS, C. and LOVERING, J. (1973) *Location, Size, Ownership and Control Tables for Welsh Industry*, The Welsh Council, 39 pp.

TOWNROE, P. M. (1969) Industrial structure and regional economic growth – a comment. *Scottish Journal of Political Economy*, 16, 95–8.

TOWNROE, P. M. (1970) Industrial linkage, agglomeration and external economies. *Journal of the Town Planning Institute*, 56, 1, 18–20.

TOWNROE, P. M. (1972) Some behavioural considerations in the industrial location decision. *Regional Studies*, 6, 3, 261–72.

TOWNROE, P. M. (1973) The supply of mobile industry: a cross sectional analysis. *Regional and Urban Economics*, 2, 4, 371–86.

TOWNROE, P. M. (1974) Post-move stability and the location decision. In F. E. I. Hamilton (ed.), *Spatial Perspectives on Industrial Organisation and Decision-Making*, London, Wiley, 533 pp.

TOWNROE, P. M. (1975) Branch plants and regional development. *Town Planning Review*, 46, 1, 47–62.

TOWNSEND, A. R. and GAULT, F. D. (1972) A national model of factory movement and resulting employment. *Area*, 4, 2, 92–8.

TREASURY INFORMATION DIVISION (1973) Changing patterns of employment – 2. *Economic Progress Report*, 42, 4.

TRIMBLE, N. (1973) Industry in the new towns of Great Britain. *Town and Country Planning*, 41, 4, 219–22.

TURNER, G. (1964) *The Car Makers*. Harmondsworth, Penguin Books, 270 pp.

TWYMAN, P. H. (1967) *Industrial location in East Kent, with special reference to factory relocation and branch plant establishment.* Unpubl. M.Sc. thesis, University of London, 240 pp.

UNWIN, D. J. and HEPPLE, L. W. (1975) The statistical analysis of spatial series. *The Statistician*, 23, 3/4, 211–27.

WALKER, D. F. (1975) A behavioural approach to industrial location. In L. Collins and D. F. Walker (eds.) *Locational Dynamics of Manufacturing Activity*, London, Wiley, 402 pp.

WARREN, K. (1969a), Recent changes in the geographical location of the British steel industry. *Geographical Journal*, 135, 3, 343–64.

WARREN, K. (1969b) Coastal steelworks: a case for argument? *Three Banks Review*, 82, 25–38.

WARREN, K. (1970) *The British iron and sheet steel industry since 1840.* London, Bell, 313 pp.

WARREN, K. (1971) Growth, technical change and planning problems in heavy industry with special reference to the chemical industry. In M. Chisholm and G. Manners (eds), *Spatial Policy Problems of the British Economy*, Cambridge University Press, 248 pp.

WARREN, K. (1975) Rationalizing steel: saga of lost chances. *The Times*, 17 April.

WATTS, H. D. (1972) Further observations on regional growth and large corporations. *Area*, 4, 4, 269–73.

WATTS, H. D. (1974) Spatial rationalization in multi-plant enterprises. *Geoforum*, 17, 69–76.

WEBBER, M. J. (1972) *Impact of uncertainty on location.* Cambridge: Mass., M.I.T. Press, 310 pp.

WEBER, A. (1929) *Alfred Weber's Theory of the Location of Industries.* translated by C. J. Friedrich, from *Über den standort der industrien* 1909, University of Chicago Press, 256 pp.

WELCH, R. V. (1970) Immigrant manufacturing industry established in Scotland between 1945 and 1968: some structural and locational characteristics. *Scottish Geographical Magazine*, 86, 2, 134–48.

WESTAWAY, J. (1974) Contact potential and the occupational structure of the British urban system 1961–1966: an empirical study. *Regional Studies*, 8, 1, 57–73.

WHEAT, L. F. (1973) *Regional Growth and Industrial Location: an empirical viewpoint.* Lexington, D. C. Heath, 223 pp.

WILSON, T. (1973) British regional policy in the European context. *The Banker*, 123, 164–9.

WISE, M. J. (1951) On the evolution of the jewellery and gun quarters in Bir-mingham. *Transactions and Papers of the Institute of British Geographers, 1949*, No. 15, 59–72.

WOODWARD, V. H. (1971) Review of 'Optimal patterns of location' by J. Serck-Hanssen. *Economic Journal*, 81, 395–7.

WRAY, M., MARKHAM, R. and WATTS, D. R. (1974) *Location of Industry in Hertfordshire: planning and industry in the post-war period*. Hatfield Polytechnic, 312 pp.

Author Index

Subject Index